PREHISTORIC AND ROMAN LANDSCAPES

Prehistoric and Roman Landscapes

Edited by Andrew Fleming and Richard Hingley

Landscape History after Hoskins

Volume 1

Series Editor: Christopher Dyer

WINDgather
PRESS

Prehistoric and Roman Landscapes: Landscape History after Hoskins, Volume 1

Published by: Windgather Press Ltd, 29 Bishop Road, Bollington, Macclesfield, Cheshire SK10 5NX

Distributed by: Oxbow Books, 10 Hythe Bridge Street, Oxford, OX1 2EW

British Library Cataloguing-in-Publication Data

A catalogue record for this book is available from the British Library

ISBN 978-1-905119-17-2

Designed, typeset and originated by Carnegie Book Production, Lancaster
Printed and bound by Cambridge Printing, Cambridge

Contents

List of Figures vii
Acknowledgements xi

Series Foreword: Landscape History after Hoskins xiii
Christopher Dyer

Preface xv
Andrew Fleming and Richard Hingley

1 1955 and All That: Prehistoric Landscapes in *The Making* 1
Andrew Fleming

2 A New Downland Prehistory: Long-term Environmental Change on the Southern English Chalklands 16
Michael J. Allen and Rob Scaife

3 Making Strange: Monuments and the Creation of the Earlier Prehistoric Landscape 33
Richard Bradley

4 Geophysical Survey and the Emergence of Underground Archaeological Landscapes: The Heart of Neolithic Orkney World Heritage Site 43
Nick Card, John Gater, Chris Gaffney and Emma Wood

5 Bronze Age Field Systems and the English Channel–North Sea Cultural Region 57
David Yates

6 Claylands Revisited: The Prehistory of W. G. Hoskins's Midlands Plain 70
Patrick Clay

7 Hillforts and Human Movement: Unlocking the Iron Age Landscapes of Mid Wales 83
Toby Driver

8 The Roman Landscape of Britain: From Hoskins to Today 101
Richard Hingley

9 Beyond the Economic in the Roman Fenland: Reconsidering Land, Water, Hoards and Religion 113
Adam Rogers

10 What Did the Romans Ever Do For Us? Roman Iron Production in the East Midlands and the Forest of Dean 131
Irene Schrüfer-Kolb

11 Roman Towns, Roman Landscapes: The Cultural Terrain of Town and Country in the Roman Period 143
Steven Willis

Contributors 165
Bibliography 167
Index 189

List of Figures

1. Location of some of the key sites of the chalk downland of southern England 18
2. Diagram of the Mesolithic open pine and hazel woodland at Stonehenge 24
3. Pollen diagram of the early post-glacial and Holocene sequence in the Allen valley 25
4. Land snail diagram from Strawberry Hill, Wiltshire 26
5. Pollen diagram from the Avon floodplain near Durrington Walls, Wiltshire 26
6. Interpretation of Windmill Hill early Neolithic causewayed enclosure 27
7. Land snail diagram from Southerham, Grey Pit, near Lewes, East Sussex 28
8a. Plan and section of a chalk fan excavated at Strawberry Hill, Wiltshire 30
8b. Chalk fan as a result of rill erosion from an arable field 30
9a. A view of the excavation at Ashcombe Bottom, East Sussex 31
9b. The same view showing a fan of mud concealing a gravel fan 31
10. Summary section and plan of the excavated hillwash at Ashcombe Bottom 32
11. Bank barrows at Cleaven Dyke and Auchenlaich and rectangular enclosure at Douglasmuir 34
12. Outline plans of the Rudston and the Dorset cursuses 36
13. Cursus and two Neolithic mortuary monuments at Eynesbury 37
14. Outline plans of three cursus monuments and associated enclosures 39
15. The relationship between cursuses, causewayed enclosures and bank barrows 40
16. The Orkney World Heritage Site 48
17. The Wasbister Area 49
18. The Ring of Brodgar 50
19. The Ness of Brodgar 51

20. Stenness 53
21. Around the Barnhouse Stone 54
22. Maes Howe 55
23. South Hornchurch Late Bronze Age ringwork and field system 58
24. Later Bronze Age fields and enclosures along the Thames Valley 61
25. Sussex and the Hampshire Basin 62
26. The Fens and feeder rivers 63
27. Late prehistoric linear field systems in the English Channel–North Sea Region 65
28. Area of regional survey, showing the present counties, major towns and survey areas 73
29. The study area, showing Earlier Neolithic core areas, ritual areas and findspots 75
30. The Medbourne area survey 76
31. The Swift valley survey 77
32. The study area, showing Later Neolithic–Earlier Bronze Age core areas, ritual areas and findspots 78
33. Fragment of a stone plaque with incised decoration 81
34. North Ceredigion 84
35. Pen y Bannau hillfort, near Strata Florida 85
36. Conspicuous use of a massive quartz block at a gateway terminal 88
37. Caer Lletty Llwyd 89
38. Map showing the relationship between Caer Lletty Llwyd (left) & Pen Dinas, Elerch (right) 90
39. Interpretative sketch of the western face of Pen Dinas, Elerch 90
40. Aerial view of Castell Grogwynion 91
41. Close view from the west-northwest of Castell Grogwynion 92
42. Interpretative sketch of Castell Grogwynion 93
43. Aerial view of Gaer Fawr 93
44. The Cors Caron façade scheme 94
45. The Central Wales Zone of Cultural Contact 96
46. The proportion of Roman sites excavated in four periods in the twentieth century 103
47. Map of the Fenland 114
48. The dates of hoard discovery in the Fenland 115
49. The types of material deposited in the Fenland 116
50. The contexts in which hoards have been found in the Fenland 120
51. The major bronzework hoards found within the Fenland 123

52. Roman iron mining regions in Britain 133
53. Distribution of Roman iron production sites on the Jurassic Ridge 135
54. Opencast mining pits in Wakerley Wood, Northants 136
55. Roman iron production sites in the east midlands 137
56. Roman mining and iron production sites in the Forest of Dean and Severn Estuary 138
57. Sites mentioned in the text 144
58. Tongeren, Belgium. A view of the Plinius site in 2006 148
59. Canterbury, Kent. A view looking south-east 155
60. Canterbury, Kent. A map from the Canterbury Urban Archaeology Database showing Roman Canterbury 156
61. Caistor St Edmund, Norfolk 158

Acknowledgements

The conference on which this book is based was organised by a committee drawn from the School of Archaeology and Ancient History and the Centre for English Local History in the University of Leicester, with David Palliser as a representative of the Royal Historical Society, and Tony Brown for the Society for Landscape Studies. It attracted support and sponsorship from English Heritage, the British Academy, the Friends of the Centre for English Local History, the Historical Geography Research Group, the Medieval Settlement Research Group, Oadby and Wigston Borough Council, Oxbow Books, the Royal Historical Society, the Society for Landscape Studies and Windgather Press. The excursions were led by the late Harold Fox, Graham Jones and Charles Phythian-Adams. Impeccable organisation was provided by Barbara Johnson, with help from David Johnson and Mike Thompson. Publication of the papers in a series of three volumes has depended on the services of the editors: P. S. Barnwell, Andrew Fleming, Mark Gardiner, Richard Hingley, Marilyn Palmer and Stephen Rippon. An anonymous referee gave valuable service. All of the editors and contributors are indebted to Richard Purslow of Windgather Press for his help and support in producing this series, and to Sarah Harrison, who prepared the index for each volume. Financial help for the costs of publication from the Aurelius Trust is gratefully acknowledged.

Christopher Dyer

Landscape History after Hoskins,
Series Editor, Christopher Dyer

Volume 1
Prehistoric and Roman Landscapes
edited by Andrew Fleming and Richard Hingley

Volume 2
Medieval Landscapes
edited by Mark Gardiner and Stephen Rippon

Volume 3
Post-Medieval Landscapes
edited by P. S. Barnwell and Marilyn Palmer

SERIES FOREWORD

Landscape History after Hoskins

Christopher Dyer

This book celebrates a great scholar; it emerged from an inspiring occasion; and it reflects the vigour of an enthralling subject, the history of the landscape. It contains a selection of the papers presented to a conference called *W. G. Hoskins and the Making of the British Landscape*, held at the University of Leicester on 7–10 July 2005 to mark the fiftieth anniversary of the publication of *The Making of the English Landscape* by W.G. Hoskins. A Devon man, Hoskins spent the early part of his life as a student in that county, and returned to it in retirement. He held the post of Reader in Economic History at Oxford in 1951–65, and he lived in London when he held a wartime post in the civil service. Leicester was the appropriate place for a conference to honour his work in landscape history, as he had developed his approach to local history and topography in his time on the staff of the University College in the 1930s and late 1940s (he briefly returned as Professor in 1965–8). He was active in the Leicestershire Archaeological Society, and contributed some notable articles to that Society's *Transactions*. He attracted an enthusiastic following to his adult education lectures at Vaughan College. His books on Leicestershire included *The Midland Peasant* and, for a wider readership, the Shell Guide. While at Leicester he founded the University's Department (later Centre) of English Local History.

The Making of the English Landscape appeared in 1955 and had a major impact on the reading public, as it was well written, accessible, and revealed a new way of looking at the past. Hoskins showed that our everyday surroundings – roads, hedges, trees, buildings – had an historical significance, and he was tapping a new source of evidence. The Ordnance Survey map became in his hands a vital document, and he asserted that the landscape was 'the richest historical record we possess'. *The Making* was admired by academics as well as a wider readership, and went through a number of versions, including a Penguin paperback and a Folio Society edition. It was followed by a series of studies of individual counties, which made good progress but was not completed. The book produced a rather delayed response in academia, in the sense that the discipline of Landscape History did not grow rapidly until the 1970s and 1980s, when it was widely practised by archaeologists and geographers, rather than historians. It gained a society and journal with the foundation of the Society for Landscape Studies in 1979, which has published *Landscape*

History ever since. So much research and writing was being done on the subject, and it attracted so much interest from the public as well as professional scholars, that a second journal, *Landscapes*, was launched in 2000.

At the 2005 Leicester conference sixty papers were given in two parallel sessions under ten themes: prehistoric/Roman landscapes; rural settlement; towns; industry; buildings; designed landscapes; environments; ritual; perceptions; and techniques of mapping. The conference was attended by 250 people, and indeed the need to limit the numbers in each lecture room meant that latecomers had to be turned away. Plenary talks were given at the beginning by Christopher Taylor (a landscape archaeologist who knew Hoskins well), Elisabeth Zadora Rio (who provided a continental European perspective), and Fiona Reynolds of the National Trust, who had been influenced by *The Making* when she read it as a student. Three receptions were held, and excursions on three alternative routes occupied one afternoon. The beginning of the conference on 7 July was overshadowed by the London bombings but, in spite of this setback, a cheerful and positive atmosphere prevailed, helped by the sunny weather, good hospitality and attractive surroundings.

Those who gave papers at the conference were encouraged from the beginning not to think of the event as a memorial or a retrospective. W. G. Hoskins was the starting point, and almost every speaker made some reference to the pioneer, but they were focused on recent research and future developments. A number of themes covered subjects which Hoskins himself did not consider in much detail and used techniques that have emerged since 1955. The organisers had hoped that the conference would attract representatives of different disciplines, and would promote interdisciplinary contacts, and this was achieved. Younger scholars were encouraged to attend and to contribute, and a good number responded. The papers in this book, only a selection of those presented at the conference, reflect the progress in landscape history after Hoskins, and readers will gain an impression of the liveliness of the discipline, the new thinking, and the wide range of subject matter.

Christopher Dyer
Professor of Regional and Local History and Director of the Centre for English Local History
Chair of the Conference Organising Committee

Preface

For W. G. Hoskins, the most important thing about the landscapes of England was their Englishness. The history of the English landscape encapsulated deep, enduring truths about the history and character of the English people – truths all the more powerful and evocative for never being made fully explicit. Measured against this grand narrative, the history of ancient Britons, Celts and Romans seemed of questionable significance. Thus in *The Making of the English Landscape* Hoskins famously devoted only twenty-odd pages to the predecessors of the English. He would not get away with this today; his publisher, knowing how much has been unearthed (literally) by archaeologists and palaeo-environmentalists, and how much has been written by prehistorians, would surely have insisted on a companion volume.

The author of such a volume would have to deal with an intimidating range of topics. The list would include, at the very least, landscapes of post-glacial hunter-gatherers, of early farmers, and of ceremonial monuments; landscapes of later farmers (involving field systems, land boundaries, etc.); landscapes of settlement, enclosure and fortification in the well-peopled countryside of the Iron Age; and for the Roman period, military and civilian landscapes, the organisation of agriculture, urbanisation, industry, religion, markets and so on. Our author would also have to be familiar with the work done by palaeo environmentalists – their ecological models and insights, as well as the evidence of pollen, land-snails, soils, buried charcoals, relevant classical texts and so on. And there are impassioned debates to take into account. Should the study of 'landscape' in prehistory and Roman times be mostly about the material conditions of existence, the logistics of making a living? Does landscape tell us anything about past socio-political organisation, or the exercise of 'power in the land'? Should we forgo 'materialist' interpretations, in a quest for the meaning (or meanings) of past landscapes? Should we attempt to re-create the sensory experience of living in them? And if so, should we invent new ways of doing fieldwork, approaches which might have left 'WG' spluttering into his picnic hamper?

Working on the landscape history of prehistoric and Roman times is very different in 'feel' from the study of later, 'text-aided' periods. For prehistoric periods and for much of our knowledge of Roman Britain we depend almost entirely on archaeological evidence (including palaeo environmental data) in one form or another. Often, our discourse is strongly affected by the fact that we are still working on the development and refinement of field methodologies.

By definition, we are not given the opportunity of fitting the implications of our evidence into a document-based historian's model; if we have coherent models (and often we do not) they tend to owe quite a lot to the insights of anthropologists. For us, envisaging and conceptualising the Strangeness or Otherness of the people of prehistory is a major area of concern, as Richard Bradley points out here. For later periods much use has been made of the limited classical texts, mostly written for the entertainment of the landed elite of imperial Rome; but since the 1970s many landscape archaeologists have come to work in a way that marginalises these. Initially landscape approaches stressed economic and political issues, but we shall see that Romanists too have recently begun to address the otherness of the landscapes with which they work.

Prehistory does not yet possess the mature sub-disciplines familiar to the historian (though we may be moving in that direction); among the community of prehistorians, the economic prehistorian, the social prehistorian, the expert on the prehistory of thought and ideas, even the specialist in prehistoric technology, are barely identifiable; the same is true, in general, for Romanists. Some colleagues do not regard such specialisms simply as components of a wider, more holistic field of enquiry, or as contributions to narratives of the past. Rather, they see these fields in the context of passionate, often politicised debate about the nature of human culture, and how it should be studied – the materialist/mentalist debate of the 1980s and 1990s. Areas of study which seem absolutely basic to one sector of opinion seem mundane or pretentious (but not both!) to the other. Furthermore, some archaeological theorists have discovered that 'landscape' is a concept open to elaboration, nuance and studied vagueness to an almost infinite degree – and thus very tempting ground to choose for the fighting of this particular intellectual battle. 'Landscape' has thus been treated not only as a kind of proxy for human culture – perhaps the most convenient shorthand expression of the core of what some prehistorians and Romanists think we should be writing about – but also as an area where ideas may be worked out in the field, where rhetoric tries to justify and illustrate itself by new modes of fieldwork. In consequence, even those of us who look askance at the more extreme claims of post-modernists have come to recognise that 'what would the countryside have looked like in those days?' is not necessarily the most interesting or even the most basic question to ask. We cannot jettison empiricism, but we should beware of becoming over-dependent upon it.

This, then, is the theatre within which prehistorians and Roman specialists who are also landscape archaeologists must operate. It is, therefore, unsurprising that not many of us regard ourselves as part of the landscape history community, or publish regularly in landscape history journals. In a nutshell, the reason why the links between Hoskins's first chapter, 'The landscape before the English settlement' and the contributions to this volume seem tenuous is that they are tenuous. We cannot now write landscape prehistory as Hoskins did, as a simple if evocative overture, the introduction of a slightly mystical Celtic theme as a prelude to the main work, the Requiem for the English Yeoman. The multiple and sometimes discordant themes of contemporary studies of landscape prior to the medieval period mark it as very definitely a work in progress, a symphony in itself which is attempting to exploit the potential of the full orchestra.

That said, we believe that the essays in this book present a stimulating if necessarily selective survey of our field, demonstrating how far prehistoric and Romano-British landscape studies in Britain have moved since 1955, providing some sense of the research frontier, and setting contemporary studies of prehistoric and Roman landscapes in their intellectual and historical context. The integration of prehistorians' and historians' narratives of British landscape – something which should certainly be attempted – is surely a project for the next fifty years.

Andrew Fleming and Richard Hingley
January 2007

CHAPTER ONE

1955 and All That: Prehistoric Landscapes in *The Making*

Andrew Fleming

'The direct prehistoric contribution to the landscape is small', wrote W.G. Hoskins in *The Making of the English Landscape* (Hoskins 1955, 19) (hereinafter referred to as *The Making*). And the contribution of the prehistoric landscape to his text was correspondingly modest – barely ten pages, or 4 per cent of the book. Later, Hoskins was to admit that his treatment of the prehistoric and Roman periods had been too brief; their contribution to the English landscape 'was not obvious at first sight' (Hoskins 1973a, 6). But, nevertheless, this statement seems disingenuous. He could, after all, have started with the Anglo-Saxons, as he did at Wigston Magna (Hoskins 1957a) – a permissible course of action, one might think, given the book's title. But having chosen to include the prehistoric and Roman periods, he did not make very much of them. It seems to me that we need to explain not only his cursory treatment of prehistory, but also how he arrived at the version which he wrote; it may then be possible to develop some understanding of why prehistory has tended to play such a peripheral role in mainstream landscape history. As will become evident, Hoskins actually had two narratives of prehistory from which to choose, one more 'scientific' and archaeology-based, the other biased towards ethnology. There was a fair degree of overlap between these two traditions; nevertheless, the divergence which they represented had existed since the 1860s.

Hoskins's choice

Hoskins might have paraphrased the work of mainstream prehistorians. There were very few professional prehistorians in Britain in the early 1950s; but they were prolific writers, and had produced several general accounts of British prehistory. There was Gordon Childe's *Prehistoric Communities of the British Isles* (3 editions, 1940–9) and Grahame Clark's *Prehistoric England* (also 1940, with a fourth edition published in 1948), not to mention Christopher and Jacquetta Hawkes' *Prehistoric Britain* (1943, hardback 1947). At this time it was conventional to write prehistory as a march-past of 'cultures', groups of artefacts recurrently found together, the cultural sequence being more important as a basic chronological framework in the days before radiocarbon dating. Nevertheless, these texts were quite landscape-oriented; the photogenic earthworks of the southern English chalklands had long played a pivotal role in accounts of British prehistory. *Prehistoric England*, in particular, reached the standard of landscape photography that readers of Batsford books had come to expect. Hoskins liked high-quality, evocative photographs, and indeed used them in *The Making*; but only one real 'prehistoric landscape', the Fyfield Down fields, is featured among the eight illustrations in his prehistory chapter. He must have known the Crawford and Keiller classic, *Wessex from the Air* (1928), which had been in circulation for over a quarter of a century, yet curiously cites Crawford's older and much less relevant work, *Man and his Past*. In any case, Hoskins evidently chose not to try to write landscape prehistory as Clark or Crawford might have done.

There was, of course, another tradition of writing about prehistory, which owed rather more to the expansive reach of geography. After all, no university-based training in prehistoric archaeology was available in the first two decades of the twentieth century. O. G. S. Crawford, for instance, had managed to obtain the partial training in geography offered at Oxford (Crawford 1955, 42–61). Sir Cyril Fox had been involved in field- and laboratory-based work in veterinary science before proceeding almost directly, as a mature student, to a Cambridge doctorate (Scott-Fox 2002). Fox's geographical insights pervaded his *The Personality of Britain*, which was evidently much in demand (it was first published in 1932, with its last reissue in 1952). In the first half of the twentieth century, several scholars now considered to have been essentially historical geographers or folklife experts were archaeologists in all but name. As we shall see, the Welsh geographer H. J. Fleure, a zoologist by training, frequently wrote about prehistory in considerable detail, and did some excavation (Hawkes 1982, 80). Daryll Forde's work at Pen Dinas, Aberystwyth (1933–7) still represents the most comprehensive excavation of a Ceredigion hillfort (Forde *et al.* 1963) (see Driver, this volume). Iorwerth Peate, the Welsh rural ethnographer, could turn his hand to conventional prehistory (Peate 1926). One of the best-known products of British historical geography was H. J. Fleure's *A Natural History of Man in Britain*, first published in 1951. This *tour de force* uses a good deal of archaeological evidence, in the broadest sense, and it is hard to believe that Fleure's highly effective use of photographs of buildings and landscapes had no influence on *The Making*. Like Hoskins, Fleure liked to write about continuity as well as change, and about specific places; like Hoskins, he could turn an evocative phrase. 'Villages in southern and eastern England', he wrote, were 'too often desperately poor, with dwellings all roses outside, all thorns within' (Fleure 1951, 239). Though contemporary prehistorians would probably have found some of his subject matter problematic, in the *Natural History* Fleure managed to produce nearly 100 well-illustrated pages on British prehistory. But this, too, was not a lead which Hoskins chose to follow.

Prehistoric Landscapes in The Making

At first sight it seems that the author of *The Making* might not have been *au fait* with the recent achievements of British prehistoric studies – that Hoskins was not prepared to paraphrase general works on prehistory, or have his attention caught by specific archaeological projects. He was left cold, apparently, by the discovery of the big Iron Age round house at Little Woodbury (Bersu 1940), despite the tremendous publicity achieved by its reconstruction for the Festival of Britain in 1951. He borrowed little, it seems, from a paper recently published by Ralegh Radford (1952), which offered a synthesis of the settlement archaeology of Dartmoor, in the heart of his beloved Devon, though he knew Radford's work and had received help from him (Hoskins 1954, xvii). And despite the splash made by the excavations at Maiden Castle in the 1930s (Wheeler 1943), hillforts get just one passing mention, on page 19. But they fare better than ceremonial monuments. The reader of *The Making* encounters no long barrows or megalithic tombs, a synthesis of which had recently been published (Daniel 1950). Despite their prominence in the upland landscapes of Devon and Cornwall which appear most prominently in *The Making*, there is no mention of burial mounds, although a good general account of them had been published by Leslie Grinsell (1936). Nor does Stonehenge feature, despite the publicity which attended the recent discovery of axe and possible dagger carvings on the stones, leading to the postulation of a Mycenaean architect by one of the discoverers (Atkinson 1952).

But ignorance was not the problem. Hoskins had already done a good deal of basic research on British prehistory for his *Devon*, published the year before *The Making*. He knew about Windmill Hill, 'causewayed camps', beakers, the Wessex culture, the ABC of the Iron Age (Hawkes 1931; 1959), and hillforts; he managed to produce a competent, up-to-date summary of Dartmoor prehistory (Hoskins 1954, Chapter II). Thus it is not hindsight which makes Hoskins's approach to the prehistoric landscape seem perfunctory; his course of action must have been quite deliberate. The notion that it was evidently his intention to write about prehistory's *contribution to present landscapes*, rather than landscapes *in* prehistory, does not entirely carry conviction. His research for *Devon*, for instance, had included reading Tansley's *Britain's Green Mantle* (Tansley 1949) and noting the results of pollen analysis reported therein (Hoskins 1954, 537). This was definitely a flirtation with environmental reconstruction rather than a quest for what might have survived into the present-day landscape. Hoskins needed to believe in a wilderness (Hoskins 1955, 35) for his pioneering Anglo-Saxons to clear, and although he sustained his view largely through place-names, he must have been aware that the nascent science of pollen analysis had the potential to make its own direct contribution to knowledge in this area.

So what choice *did* Hoskins make? After a brief encounter with the Iron Age 'village' at Chysauster and the 'Celtic' fields on Fyfield Down, the rest of the prehistoric section is devoted to the quest for 'Celtic continuity' in the south-west. Hoskins felt that it should be possible to bring together 'Celtic' place-names – including those incorporating personal names – patterns of primitive-looking fields, and perhaps lengths of boundary ditch, to pick up fossilised 'survivals' of a 'Celtic' culture whose roots lay in the Iron Age or beyond. (This, by the way, is our only encounter with prehistoric linear earthworks or 'ranch boundaries' in *The Making*, despite the existence of fifty-year-old literature on the abundant examples from the Yorkshire Wolds (Mortimer 1905, folding map) and fairly recent discussions about such features in Wessex – Piggott 1944).

For Hoskins, as for many of his contemporaries, the narrative only really got going with the arrival of colonists from across the North Sea, the Anglo-Saxons or 'Old English', who undertook the first serious woodland clearance, the installation of open-field systems and the founding of many villages. Hoskins described the pre-existing inhabitants of England as 'Celts' and sought continuity and survival in the far south-west – the sole English region which could lay claim to an enduring Celtic presence. Here there are echoes of Cyril Fox's dissertation on the long-term influence of Britain's geography upon its history; his Lowland Zone was characterised by cultures which were *imposed* and possessed of more unity than those of the Highland Zone, which tended to be *absorbed* and to display greater continuity (Fox 1932, 77–8). In *The Making*, Hoskins dutifully mentions the Bronze Age – Early, Middle and Late – and the Early Iron Age, but otherwise he displays no interest in 'scientific' prehistory, which resolutely used the Three Age system (Stone, Bronze and Iron) as classificatory structure and chronological framework, and frequently as narrative line too. During the 1940s Glyn Daniel was emphasising the importance of the Three Age system in the growth of archaeology as a discipline (Daniel 1943). In the Anglophone world, as Daniel acknowledged, this tradition owed much to John Lubbock's *Pre-historic times* (1865), a book which committed itself both to Science with a capital S and to the Three Age system within its first three pages.

Ethnic narratives, Anglo-Saxon attitudes

For many archaeologists of Hoskins's era, it was scientifically imperative for prehistory to base itself on *archaeological* methodologies and to develop classificatory frameworks deriving mostly from the character of the archaeological record. As Morse's recent work has ably demonstrated (Morse 2005, Chapter V), the Three Age system, far from being interpreted as a declaration of independence for a prehistory based mostly on the archaeological record, was initially seen as providing a chronological check for a prehistory in which a robust model of the 'peopling' of Europe was the central objective. During the mid-nineteenth century, the use of studies of the origins of languages to pursue this objective was joined and to some extent superseded by ethnology and the study of skull forms (craniology); eventually racial and indeed racist perspectives became part of the mix, for some writers at least (Morse 2005). A century later it was both politically and methodologically essential for prehistory to free itself from this tradition.

In these terms, Hoskins's preference for the characterisation of long-term British history in ethnological terms was backward-looking. Ethnic and racial narratives involving British prehistory and archaeological evidence had a long history, going back to Beddoe's *The Races of Britain* (1971; first published 1885) and Davis and Thurnam's *Crania Britannica* (1865). Matthew Arnold, writing in 1867, was convinced that the British national destiny would be irrevocably implicated in the hybridisation of Germanic, Celtic and Norman stereotypes (Arnold 1976). Davis and Thurnam (1865, 238) were able to quote recent research which purported to show that the English ranked highest in 'the Teutonic family', in terms of cranial capacity. Lubbock, publishing in the same year, tended to confine his stereotyping to the differences between 'savages' and civilised humanity, in the context of a broadly Darwinian view of evolution and progress. Such narratives were at their most ambitious in Wales, where remarkably determined efforts were made to create links between language, physical anthropology, distributions of artefacts, tribal groups named by Roman writers, and even hypothetical vegetation and settlement history. Boyd Dawkins, for example, linked the archaeological record with tales of 'the Iberic Silures' (or aborigines), the Goidels and the Brythons, not to mention 'the small dark Welshmen of today' who, he claimed, are descended from pre-Aryan Neolithic tribes (Dawkins 1912, 73, 106). From the perspective of cultural nationalism, the desired emphasis was on ethnic *continuity*; intrusive prehistoric peoples were portrayed as immigrant aristocracies, contributing to 'Celtic' cultural history in ways unachieved by English 'invaders' or Scandinavian 'freebooters' (Dawkins 1912, 106). In the years leading up to the First World War, H.J. Fleure and T.C. James continued to promote this line of research, undertaking physical anthropological fieldwork in Wales and publishing major articles on the subject (Fleure and James 1916; Fleure, 1917). In 1923, Fleure's stated agenda for a distinctive Welsh archaeology involved forging 'somehow a link between archaeology, tradition, history and linguistics' (Fleure 1923, 242). Further physical anthropological fieldwork carried out in Wales in the 1930s was eventually published by Fleure and Davies in 1958. At this time E.G. Bowen, who had taken up the Aberystwyth School baton, still found space for such matters – with the addition of blood groups (Bowen 1957) – although he omitted them in his later historical writings.

So ethnological and racial narratives survived the Second World War. In *A Natural History of Britain*, Fleure reproduced the Three Age narratives of more conventional contemporary prehistorians, but he was evidently reluctant to abandon other ways of telling. He was interested in the idea that late Palaeolithic skull forms might still be seen in parts of Wales, publishing a photograph of a named man from the Plynlymon district (wearing a collar and tie) to illustrate the point (Fleure 1951, 37, plate VIII). Even more arresting, perhaps, were his portraits of Darwin, showing 'features similar to those of the beaker-making immigrants of 1900–1800 B.C.', and of Robert Burns, 'showing features of the dark-haired longheads' (Fleure 1951, plates IX, X). As far as the Neolithic was concerned, Fleure felt that the old generalisation about long barrows/long heads: round barrows/round heads was still of historical significance. He mentioned the 'considerable beauty' of the women ('and a few of the youths') of 'Mediterranean' (long-headed) type whose descendants could still be seen in parts of Britain; and the 'little nests of people with broad heads and faces and moderate to dark colouring' which were to be found in Cornwall and north-west Wales (Fleure 1951, 66–7). And then in the late Iron Age, sexual relations between Belgic immigrants (many of them 'vigorous young warriors' and 'big, fair-haired men') and 'virgin women of the country' did much to improve the 'quality' of a much-inbred people (Fleure 1951, 95–6). Linguistic history also helped to maintain the ethnic side of Fleure's narrative, though he acknowledged differences of opinion concerning the chronology of the origins of Celtic languages in Britain (Fleure 1951, 92–3). Fleure's chapter on the implications of physical anthropology, 'The People', attempted to link aspects of the archaeological record with cephalic indices, measurements of height and (briefly) blood groups. Apparently in recent times the 'smaller, darker people' in the towns had been multiplying faster than the 'taller, fairer' element, the latter's preference for 'rural life and adventure' leading them to emigrate in greater numbers (Fleure 1951, 196). Paradoxically perhaps, 'the old Neolithic type' could apparently 'best withstand the great city and town aggregations' (Fleure and Whitehouse 1916, 126).

In Jacquetta Hawkes' *A Land*, published in the same year as the *Natural History* and reissued as late as 1978, we are told that the inhabitants of Mesolithic Britain are likely to have been 'a fairish people, early members of the Nordic race'. They contrasted with the Neolithic folk, immigrants who 'would not look out of place in a Sicilian olive grove'; in modern Wales, apparently, one could sometimes come across a whole family of them (Hawkes 1951, 160–1). Then came further invaders, with their 'stronger bodies' and regrettably masculinist attitudes, an 'Indo-European aristocracy' which 'made its last stand with the guards regiments that were cut to pieces at Calais in 1940' (Hawkes 1951, 161–2). Hawkes put the supposed invasions of the Celts 'before the end of the Bronze Age'. 'Celtic fields' (first named as such in 1923 – Crawford 1953, 87) were exactly what their name implies; the Celts introduced settled farming. However, 'in part' they must have been like the type of Highlander spotted by Daniel Defoe in Edinburgh in the eighteenth century, heavily armed and quick to avenge any slur on his honour, yet often seen driving a cow down the street (Hawkes 1951, 168–9, 172).

In *The Making*, Hoskins kept it simple; the early part of his story embraced Celts, Romans and Saxons, the ethnological framework long familiar from treatments of protohistory. One can hardly blame him for colouring late prehistory Celtic. As we have seen, ethnic models of prehistory featured in the contemporary writings of respected scholars. And, indeed, the European Iron Age continued to be written as the story of the Celts, and of a widespread Celtic 'civilisation', most notably in Terence Powell's authoritative and widely read book *The Celts* (first published in 1958). And it has always been tempting, not least from a sales point of view, to insert the words 'Celts' or 'Celtic' into a book title, whatever the author's particular angle on later prehistory. Only in the last couple of decades of the twentieth century have prehistorians started to point out the problematic nature of a Celtic stereotype created by melding the scanty, problematic accounts of classical authors with texts produced by medieval monks, and the difficulty of demonstrating that those who spoke 'Celtic' languages shared a widely distributed, long-enduring set of archaeologically recognisable lifeways. We have had to be reminded that there is no documentary evidence that people in Britain called themselves Celts, even if they did speak languages later christened 'Celtic' (Collis 2003, 27). Furthermore, the 'Celtic' stereotype has made Iron Age studies 'boring'; prehistorians rightly now insist on treating the Iron Age as just as culturally 'strange' as the Neolithic, and to reclaim the period for archaeology (Hill 1989). The concept of 'Celtic landscapes' has never really taken root among prehistorians; for the most part we no longer write about 'Celtic' fields, preferring to refer to Bronze Age landscapes, Iron Age landscapes, and so on. But the situation can be confusing for new readers. For instance, Barry Cunliffe, one of our leading experts and our most prolific writer on the British Iron Age, had tended to talk mostly about the 'Iron Age' when he is writing for the archaeological constituency (e.g. Cunliffe 1991). For a wider audience, he has made much more of the Celts (see, for example, Cunliffe 1997). Most recently, in *Facing the Ocean* (2001), Cunliffe has reduced the issue to that of the origins of 'Celtic' languages. Interestingly, Wheeler was an early sceptic, noting 'the many hazardous approximations between archaeological and philological theory which have clouded the Celtic Question' and 'the scarcity of any definitely "Celtic" culture in Wales during prehistoric times' (Wheeler 1925, 6–7).

Given the background sketched above, it is entirely understandable that Hoskins was relaxed about writing in 'ethnic' terms. But there was more to it than that. Hoskins was proud to be descended from Devon yeomen (Hoskins 1949, 80), and ultimately from the 'Old English'. And, of course, back in the 1950s the English village and open-field systems were still thought to have been introduced by Teutonic colonists; Fleure's *Natural History* (1951, fig. 66), for instance, included a map of a German *Haufendorf* showing one individual's dispersed strip-holdings. The Anglo-Saxons, Hoskins wrote, 'covered the whole of England with their villages' (1955, 42). In the 1950s, pollen analysis was still in very sporadic use, so Hoskins, unrestrained by the complex and variegated vegetation history which was to emerge later, was able to make much of the idea that the Anglo-Saxons spent their time energetically 'reclaiming' land 'from the natural wilderness' (Hoskins 1955, 46). Before the revolutionary redating of planned villages and open fields (Thirsk 1964; Sheppard 1966; Allerston 1970) the uncertainties which confront the student of the early post-Roman period today, especially at local level, were still to come. Hoskins's Chapter II, then, could be rich in its archaeological content, highlighting the critical breakthrough in the formation of the English landscape (including more dispersed landscapes of hamlets and single farms, as in parts of Devon). And it could craft an English origin myth which found its most evocative expression in landscapes which Hoskins loved, in places which evoked the hard work and creativity of his own ancestors.

The Celtic version

Hoskins's sturdy Anglo-Saxon attitudes did not go unchallenged. Soon Glanville Jones started to develop his 'multiple estate' model (e.g. Jones 1961). Seeking to 'undermine the claim that permanent settlement in the lowlands of Britain was essentially *an Anglo-Saxon achievement*' (my italics), he aimed to demonstrate that 'the basic patterns of settlement distribution in the English lowlands date from at least Celtic times'; he saw 'the Celts' as an intrusive, probably Bronze Age, ruling caste (Jones 1961, 231, 221), like the Angles and Saxons. He argued that the dispersed hamlets grouped under a *maenor*, a *caput* or a *villa regalis* in the Middle Ages must have corresponded, in terms of scale, to the large territory which would have to be controlled by a hillfort if its builders were to obtain the resources they required. 'For the large multiple estate with its caput near an iron-age fort or a Roman settlement a considerable antiquity can be inferred', he later asserted (Jones 1976, 40). From the early 1970s he used the term 'multiple estate' to define a characteristic territorial and fiscal entity, reconstructing multiple estates in various localities. He never published the definitive book on this topic; as far as I know, the most explicit presentation of his general model was published in a relatively obscure volume of conference papers (Jones 1971), although it will probably have got through to most readers through his 1976 paper in Peter Sawyer's edited volume *Medieval Settlement*. Landscape historians have varying views on the value of the multiple estate concept, and what kind of historical reality it might represent (see, e.g. Gregson 1985). Jones's hypothesis that multiple estates had originated as Iron Age hillfort territories (1961) – published in *Antiquity* by Glyn Daniel, a fellow Celt – was swiftly and effectively dismissed by the archaeologist Leslie Alcock (1962), though in my opinion this rebuttal by no means settled the questions raised in Jones's paper.

As a Welshman based in England, Glanville Jones probably derived a certain satisfaction from his recognition of multiple estates in Saxon heartlands – for example at Malling in Sussex, a territory which includes the quintessentially English establishment watering-hole of Glyndebourne (Jones 1976, 26–35). Although this Anglo-Welsh argument is muted in the literature, it had a certain edge. Jones wished to refute characterisations of medieval Wales as 'a late surviving Wild-West inhabited by footloose Celtic cowboys' (Jones 1961, 222). This was a direct reference to a phrase used by Piggott (1958, 25) with reference to the Roman Iron Age in Scotland and Wales; it obviously irritated Jones, who could no doubt imagine Piggott delivering it in his memorably patrician tones (there is a further, later allusion to the phrase in Jones 1976, 15). As we have seen, previous work had created a recognisable crossover between physical anthropology and class politics – with the Celts portrayed as small, dark-haired, perhaps dusky people, natural cattle herders who were tough enough to make the transition to working in mines and factories. Taller, blonder types did best in their natural habitat, the countryside and the officers' mess (or writing *The Origin of Species*). In the 1950s it was perhaps preferable to make oneself responsive to the idea that the antecedents of these blonde types were Aryans, Indo-Europeans or 'Beaker folk', rather than Teutons.

Some English scholars had an annoying habit of regarding the rural ethnography and cultural traditions of the 'Celtic' countries not so much as the heritage of emergent nations, but rather as 'survivals' from prehistory, or more neutrally as 'ethnographic parallels'. British archaeologists in those days had a great respect for the work of Estyn Evans, who wrote about 'exploring the living past' and of 'the marginal survival of archaic elements of the Indo-European world'; for Evans the Irish famine 'marked the end of an era that might well be termed prehistoric' (Evans 1957, xiii, xiv). (In more recent times this approach has been the subject of a persuasive critique; it has been argued that the 'primitive' characteristics of rural culture in the west of Ireland reflected 'grotesque, unbelievable, bizarre and unprecedented demographic circumstances' (Whelan 1994 and references).) In fact, the argument between 'scientific' archaeology and the study of cultural and ethnic traditions had already been fought out within Wales and in the context of Welsh rural history. When Sir Cyril Fox was director of the fledgling National Museum of Wales, from 1926 to 1948, his relationship with his colleague Iorwerth Peate was frosty at times (Scott-Fox 2002, 92, 143, 160, 195). Aileen Fox (2000, 78) saw Peate as 'an arrogant Welsh-speaking Welshman'. Both men worked on Welsh vernacular architecture, and both were deeply involved in the genesis of the Museum of Welsh Life at St Fagans. But they took rather different views of the significance of this material. Peate had something of a struggle to win acceptance for the use of the term 'folk culture' over Fox's preference for 'bygones' (Scott-Fox 2002, 143). For Fox, the questions posed by 'vernacular building' involved the challenge of using archaeological methods and studying ground plans and building techniques to understand the development and time-range of each 'style' and to define gaps in 'the evolutionary record' (Fox and Raglan 1951–4, vol. 1, 10). For Peate, however, his own book *The Welsh House* was 'a study in Folk Culture, not in architecture *per se*' (Peate 1940, xi). He deplored the study of 'bygones' used in 'elucidating the study of prehistoric archaeology' or 'displayed as appendages to archaeological research' to the 'complete neglect of Folk Culture' (Peate 1940, 1). For 'a nation bereft of its sovereignty' the Welsh house, he wrote, 'is an expression of Welsh life' (Peate 1940, 3, 4). The Welsh croft system had not 'broken down', as Fox suggested; in fact 'a large part of the social system traditional to the Welsh countryside was deliberately destroyed' (Peate 1940, 86). Furthermore, on the first page of his preface Peate pointedly drew attention to his deliberate omission of distribution maps; 'some critics', he wrote, 'feel that the value of distribution-maps in archaeological work is grossly over-estimated' (Peate 1940, vii). There are no prizes for guessing which contributor to *The Personality of Britain* was in the firing-line here. Even Peate's orthography came into the fight, with the use of his preferred spelling 'Keltic'. Unsurprisingly, perhaps, *The Welsh House* was reviewed 'quite unfavourably' by Cyril Fox (Scott-Fox 2002, 160).

Alternative prehistories

Despite the large gap left in the landscape history of the post-Roman period caused by the redating of the 'Old English' village and its open fields, as far as I am aware Hoskins did not critically engage with the multiple estate hypothesis, though he *was* interested in large Saxon 'estates' (Hoskins 1952, 301–8). In Glanville Jones's hands, the multiple estate presented an expansive vision of the 'Celtic' – that is, late prehistoric – mode of land control and management. In the 1950s, this perspective did not prevail. In his discussion of prehistory, Hoskins highlighted the pattern of 'small, irregular' fields characteristic of parts of Penwith, in Cornwall (Hoskins 1955, 25) – though nowadays it is believed that more regular patterns, coaxial and 'brick-shaped' fields, were just as prevalent, arguably forming the earlier signature (Peter Herring, forthcoming and pers. comm.), as at Chysauster itself (Smith 1996). And among archaeologists the considerable interest aroused – with good reason – by the excavation of tiny 'fields' at Gwithian during the 1950s (Fowler and Thomas 1962) was complemented by their perverse refusal to recognise the prehistoric date of the very large parallel reave systems of Dartmoor, despite the implications of the field evidence (see Fleming 1988, 21). The general expectation was that prehistoric land division and management would have involved small plots of land. In *The Making* (1955, 24) Hoskins suggested that the field pattern at Babeny Farm, Dartmoor, implied the existence of 'Celtic' farmers. Ironically, the Babeny fields *do* lie within one of the largest known prehistoric field systems in Britain – the Dartmeet parallel reave system – but the long axis of the Babeny boundaries runs at right angles to the axis of the Dartmeet system. Hoskins would have done better to identify the fields at Rogue's Roost, just across the Walla Brook, as perpetuating a prehistoric pattern.

In the 1950s, then, there was a choice. One might adopt a 'scientific' prehistory which relied on relatively free-standing archaeological evidence deployed by mainstream prehistorians (who had not, however, entirely stopped using the term 'Celtic'). In this world, the word 'culture' was used in an archaeological sense, to signify ' a recurring assemblage of archaeological types', as Gordon Childe famously defined it (1956). But there was another prehistory which tried to forge links between the archaeological record and racial origins and ethnic traditions, not least the genesis, flowering and 'survival' of Celtic culture; here, of course, the word 'culture' was used much more holistically, and could flow into cultural and political nationalism. In this context Hoskins could certainly get away with treating prehistory as a brief 'Celtic' overture to the making of the English landscape.

Hoskins and the Celts

So what was Hoskins's attitude to the 'Celtic' past? The 'Old English' obviously had a deep hold over his affections. He liked to refer to them occasionally as 'the good old Anglo-Saxons'; we also read of 'good old Scandinavian [personal] names' and the Midlands as a bastion of 'solid "Englishness"' (Hoskins 1949, 20, v). In *Devon*, he picked up on Beddoe's 1885 attribution of the blonds (not to mention the 'singularly beautiful' blonds of the Taw and Torridge estuaries) to Frisian or Danish ancestry (Beddoe 1971, 285), and promptly reclaimed them for the Saxon settlers. By contrast, on the Devon coasts, as in 'nearly all the Cornish fishing harbours', there were 'dark and broad-headed, stalwart men', 'coastal types', descendants of the Iberian immigrants who brought the megalithic culture (in the Neolithic). 'Pre-Saxon types' apparently abound on the fringes of Dartmoor. These people had hung on endogamously in 'formerly isolated clefts in the south-western coast' (Hoskins 1954, 47–8).

It seems to me that it is only at first sight, and then with hindsight, that Hoskins's interest in these matters appears politically suspect. In fact, of course, he had merely followed the line taken by the well-respected H.J. Fleure, and by Jacquetta Hawkes, a writer with good credentials as a prehistorian, whose political views were not easily pigeon-holed (she was soon to become a founder member of the Campaign for Nuclear Disarmament). In Britain, at any rate after the Second World War, believing in the objective existence of 'race' did not imply a consequential political agenda; the 'scientific' study of race was part of the curriculum of physical anthropology (and thus part of my own undergraduate education in the mid 1960s). Acceptance of the 'findings' of science did not necessarily imply racist attitudes or political innocence. Nevertheless, in the works of these three authors, the contrast made between tall, blond, Teutonic invaders and short, dark indigenes, whether Celtic or pre-Celtic, looks unfortunate, to say the least. The contrast is heightened when one recalls how energetic and successful the Old English were in Hoskins's narratives. They were the ones who cut down the trees and founded the villages, claiming and naming the land. Effectively, Hoskins was developing a landscape version of the 'Saxonist' perspective on English history, which went back ultimately to the era of Shakespeare (Pittock 1999, 55). In this account the Celts had mostly fled, surviving in small enclaves – the Waltons, Brettons and Combertons, still to be found on the map. They were more passive, mysterious folk, and their role in landscape history was much more elusive. The Celts, characterised in the late nineteenth century as 'shy, sensitive and imaginative', evidently had comparable landscapes. It is not hard to recognise here the antithesis, made familiar by the work of cultural geographers and other commentators on colonial and imperial history, between 'male' conquerors and 'female' natives. Pittock quotes D.H. Lawrence, whose portrait of a young Irishman identified something characteristic of 'negroes' – 'aeons of acquiescence in race destiny' (see, e.g. Pittock 1999, chapter 1 and 70–1).

One might perhaps characterise Hoskins not so much as a conscious propagator of crypto-racist historical narratives, but rather as an innocent or intellectually lazy carrier of the world-view of a substantial proportion of the pre-war cultural establishment, and a younger generation born in the Edwardian age. But this would not really be fair. In the space between *Devon* and *The Making*, Hoskins had jettisoned racial and ethnic baggage, except for the Celts. Perhaps contact with Cyril Fox (his 'old friend' – Hoskins 1957a, xi) in Exeter had been influential here; he was certainly stimulated by the Foxes' arrival in Devon (Hoskins 1954, xvii). But other considerations come into play. Hoskins had waxed lyrical about the landscapes of the south-east Midlands (e.g. Hoskins 1949). On moving to Oxfordshire in the early 1950s, the house he chose at Steeple Barton lay in an area which looks like one of the best bits of Leicestershire. But his boyhood affection for his native county had never gone away; he was already working on Devon, and was soon living in Exeter, not least to get away from the appalling aircraft noise from the local American air base at Upper Heyford. And the Devon landscape was already giving his work a dimension unavailable or much less obvious in Leicestershire – the quest for Celtic survival, and for 'continuity', potentially from pre-Roman times (Hoskins 1952, 300). Perhaps, like many English writers before and since, Hoskins was fascinated by the Otherness of the Celts. It is also possible that where landscape history was concerned, he came to feel that it was only fair to try to put the Celts back into the picture. Hoskins's interest in 'continuity' became something of an obsession. This reveals itself strikingly in the text of his *English Landscapes*, most notably where he suspects that 'some of our villages stand upon sites first chosen by Bronze Age farmers – perhaps even neolithic' (Hoskins 1973a, 10). Here Hoskins seems to be striving for dramatic effect (understandably, perhaps, in the context of a television series). But what kind of 'continuity' is implied? A prehistorian might well ask: should the quest for chronological depth in one location take precedence over the need to phase the site and contextualise each phase? The search for continuity for its own sake seems to me an unhelpful elaboration of the principle that the prehistoric past should be presented mostly as a mysterious prelude to the Middle Ages.

It is clear from his writings that Hoskins tried to empathise with people from the past, and to explore his own feelings about the lived experience of humanity through contemplating the past lives of others. Perhaps most evocative is his account of how the peasant in the Wigston Magna of Henry VIII's day, if he had been able to visit his great-grandson, would have 'felt at home, back in a timeless world in which all the fields had their familiar names ... the smells alone would have told him that nothing had really changed: the sweet mild scent of the great field of flowering beans, the astringent dry smell of straw in barns and yards, the heavy summer scent of the hawthorns ... the ancient sounds of timber being sawn, of iron being hammered, of the creak of laden carts. In the fields the wind still seethed through the wheat and shook the barley. This was the ancient, unchanging life of the village, whatever else had happened in the meantime' (Hoskins 1957a, 190). In the early 1950s, as we have seen, Hoskins was confronted by alternative visions of British prehistory. There was the increasingly self-confident 'scientific' version, which dealt in terms of the Three Age system, and successions of classificatory entities, 'cultures', which could be constructed from the archaeological record; in 1954, for instance, Stuart Piggott published his *Neolithic* Cultures *of the British Isles* (my emphasis). Prehistory as cultural succession could be extremely dry; one wonders, for instance, how far human geographers like Fleure or Bowen enjoyed Grimes's summary of Welsh prehistory (1946), with its mind-numbing succession of intricately shaded distribution maps. Authors such as Jacquetta Hawkes or Fleure tried to demonstrate their knowledge and understanding of the work of 'scientific' archaeologists and prehistorians, *and* to communicate a warmer-hearted, less bloodless version of British prehistory. In writing about Celts, or even about olive-skinned 'Mediterranean' Neolithic types, they could still write about *people*, not pottery. When Hoskins wrote his *Devon*, he was still very much in the Fleure/Hawkes camp, attempting to mix archaeological understanding with the more people-centred narratives which came with the ethnological perspective.

In *The Making*, each half of this equation is treated in a much more perfunctory, indeed unsatisfactory, fashion. We are presented with a version of prehistory which Hoskins would certainly have acknowledged as inadequate by the standards of contemporary prehistorians; continuity and the Celts supplied the human interest. (Although in the famous example of 'continuity' cited in *The Making*, Hoskins apparently got the place-name derivation wrong. Treable in Devon does not get its name from the name of a tenth-century 'Celtic' landowner called Ebell; it is more likely to come from a British river name – see Coates and Breeze 2000, 138–9). It seems that where prehistory was concerned Hoskins was now less interested in merely purveying the conventional narratives of the day. He was becoming much more concerned to write about the challenge of the research frontier at the threshold of protohistory – the quest for Celts and continuity, involving maps, muddy boots, sunken lanes and so on. In the opening pages of *The Making*, Hoskins writes evocatively about the music of landscape, the 'programme of symphonies that the English landscape provides' (1955, 19). I find it ironic that his evocation of the excitement of landscape archaeology on the research frontier comes so near the beginning of the book. For it was Hoskins's sketchy overture which arguably became the most influential part of the work as a whole. This was where he seriously entered his proselytising phase, making his greatest breakthrough as a communicator of the idea of landscape history.

Aftermath

To this day there is something of a gulf between landscape historians and landscape-focused prehistorians, as the contents pages of *Landscapes* or *Landscape History* will readily reveal. Prehistorians have had to concern themselves with the creation of robust, structured ways of approaching a time period where the only direct evidence comes in archaeological forms. They have not been attracted by the notion of 'Celtic' landscapes in the form of multiple estates. As archaeologists, they have preferred to pursue 'scientific' approaches, concentrating to a large extent on prospection and recording. Some have espoused locational analysis, creating hypothetical territories by drawing Thiessen polygons around megalithic tombs, hillforts and other sites which might be supposed to have acted as 'central places' (see, for example, Cunliffe 1991, figs. 14.26, 14.28). At Danebury, straight lines at right angles to watercourses demarcated the theoretical boundaries of no less than eighteen farms within the catchment area of the hillfort (e.g. Cunliffe 1993, illus. 60). Cunliffe, in particular, has tended to treat these patterns on the map as proxy representations of Iron Age socio-political structures. For the south-west of England and of Wales, he has suggested that the absence of large hillforts and the apparent prevalence of pastoralism indicated 'a lack of centralized government' in comparison with south-east England (Cunliffe 1991, 260, 269); for Devon and Cornwall he proposed 'a three-tier [social] structure' with the livestock-loving elite living in major enclosures, their cereal-growing 'vassals' in the minor enclosures and the unfree living in unenclosed settlements (Cunliffe 1991, 259–60 and fig. 20.5). South-west Wales was comparable (Cunliffe 1991, 269). Taking his comparison with Wessex into account, Cunliffe's 'minor dispersed aristocracy' (Cunliffe 1991, 539) of south-west Britain is somewhat reminiscent of Piggott's 'footloose Celtic cowboys'. Nowadays, prehistorians are trying to find new ways of thinking about Iron Age society (e.g. Hill 1995a; 2006).

Return to the 1950s?

In the early 1950s, while *The Making* was in preparation, Crick, Watson and their colleagues were cracking the genetic code, laying the foundations for a renewed and better-founded study of the peopling of Britain than had previously been possible. And as this essay goes to press, prehistorians are wondering how best to react to Bryan Sykes's *Blood of the Isles* and Stephen Oppenheimer's *The Origins of the British* (both 2006). Oppenheimer's thesis is that 'three quarters of British ancestors arrived long before the first farmers' (2006, 406) – more apparently coming from south-west Europe than from other parts of the continent. The rate of Neolithic intrusion was low – varying effectively from 2 per cent in Cornwall to 8–11 per cent in what is now southern England, where more immigrants apparently came from north-west Germany and Scandinavia than from the near Continent. Following Renfrew (1987) and various others, Oppenheimer suggests that insular Celtic languages probably came in from the south-west, introduced by a small number of people in the Neolithic, perhaps 'an invading cultural elite with no stronger claims to aboriginal status than the Anglo-Saxons'. If, he writes, the '2–10% of immigrating southern Neolithic, Bronze or Iron Age genes are taken as identifying people rather than language, they would be even less "aboriginal" in Ireland and Wales than in the rest of the British Isles' (Oppenheimer 2006, 410). He argues that a Germanic language, an early form of English, may have been widely spoken in the south-east of Britain long before the days of Hengist and Horsa. He suggests a figure of 4 per cent Anglo-Saxon male immigration for Britain as a whole, perhaps reaching 9–15 per cent in certain areas. Such an intrusion, he writes, was more numerically significant than comparable processes in the Neolithic and Bronze Age – not a minor event, but certainly far from a 'wipeout' (Oppenheimer 2006, 379).

In the face of this 'deep chronology' for the peopling and languages of Britain, both Hoskins's Celts and his Anglo-Saxons look more than ever like projections of the ethnic preoccupations of the nineteenth and early twentieth centuries. If these 'peoples' were originally intrusive elites (incidentally, in Oppenheimer's view the Saxons have very different origins from the Anglians), Hoskins's attempt to write 'history on the ground' by tying local settlement types, field systems and farming practices to named peoples now seems ironic as well as misguided, in hindsight.

On the other hand, his interest in 'continuity' now looks worth reviving or recalibrating, from different perspectives. Some of the more ethnologically focused writings of the 1950s now look strangely prescient. I don't believe that we should return to ethnic stereotyping, or do more than simply note Tacitus' remarks (quoted in Oppenheimer 2006, 269) about the red-headed Caledonians and their German ancestry, or the dark-complexioned, curly-haired Silures and their Iberian roots. Trying to work out what our ancestors looked like is not a major preoccupation for prehistorians; appraising a bloke in a pub of his 'Mesolithic' genes is something best left to television presenters.

It is widely accepted, of course, that genetic inheritance, language, ethnicity and material culture are 'diffused' and 'inherited' in different ways. Nevertheless, we may well have to revisit the notion of 'continuity', not least in relation to landscape history. We may need to find more time (and patience) for Glanville Jones's multiple estate hypothesis – or at least for his kind of approach, and the intuition which informed it. We may have to read some of the ideas in Sir Cyril Fox's *Personality of Britain* in a different way, replacing his 'geographical determinism' with a more nuanced antithesis between long-term continuity and externally driven change, between *la longue durée* and *les événements*. Hoskins's interests in the ethnicity of peoples of the past, in continuity, in the Celt behind the Saxon, did not take him very far, in *The Making* or afterwards. But the 1950s have come back to haunt us; the issues which he confronted then, consciously or unconsciously, remain very much with us to this day.

CHAPTER TWO

A New Downland Prehistory: Long-term Environmental Change on the Southern English Chalklands

Michael J. Allen and Rob Scaife

In memory of John Evans and Geoff Dimbleby

As other authors in this volume have pointed out, Hoskins dealt only cursorily with the prehistoric landscape; his account took up less than 4 per cent of *The Making of the English Landscape*. When he was writing, knowledge of both the physical environment and the impact of human societies on the land was limited. One of our most recognisable rural landscapes is the chalk downland of southern England, an area that has received a wealth of archaeological attention in the past two centuries; over the past forty years it has seen significant attempts to understand the nature of the physical landscape in which prehistoric communities operated.

When Hoskins, an economic historian aiming at a wider readership, was writing *The Making of the English Landscape* (1955), the chalk downland was commonly seen as a beautiful natural landscape, upon which the 'impression' of ancient fields and farmsteads was left as a faint, but sometimes extensive, reminder of prehistoric communities. The chalklands of southern England were perceived by some in terms of a quintessential rural idyll, with rolling green downland pasture gradually being turned brown under the ever-expanding ploughscape. At the same time, palaeogeographers considered the development of these landscapes in terms of a simple, single and more or less uniform history, from a cold and open landscape in the wake of the withdrawal of the ice-sheets, through mixed oak forest, followed by the clearance of the woods to create the present open downland. That sequence has been well rehearsed in vegetation (or climatic) terms (for example, Table 1), and has been used as a model against which we can examine the modification of that countryside by prehistoric communities at different locations and times.

Work by environmental archaeologists over the past twenty-five years has radically altered this perception. This essay provides a new narrative for the downland. It includes evidence for pine as a former constituent of the post-glacial vegetation. We now know that post-glacial forest did not form a uniform blanket, and we understand better the consequences of the varied tree cover for prehistoric societies. Here, we attempt to summarise the model developed by John Evans for chalklands (Evans and Jones 1979) subsequent to the writings of W. G. Hoskins, and present some new thoughts on both the natural changes and the impressive consequence of human activities which, by the Roman period, had 'made' the chalkland landscape we recognise today.

Understanding the chalkland landscape

Archaeologists often use the term 'landscape' for the arena within which human activity took place. Here, however, we take this word to encompass the *nature* of the countryside – its soils, trees, vegetation and animals, among which modern humans became the pre-eminent force. The archaeology of the chalklands has been well documented. The countryside is embellished with archaeological monuments dating from Neolithic times to the present day, and strewn with artefacts from the even earlier Mesolithic period (for example, Cranborne Chase – Arnold *et al.* 1988; Gardiner 1985). There is a mass of monumental, artefactual, and other site data with which archaeologists can wrestle and formulate hypotheses and opinions. Constructs of material culture, origins and relationships have been proposed (e.g. Piggott 1954). However, as these prehistoric communities were initially composed of hunters and gatherers experimenting with farming, and then more fully committed farmers, an understanding of the nature of the landscape and countryside around them is fundamental to any comprehension of their activity and lifestyle.

Despite the long and distinguished history of archaeological research, understanding of the Holocene chalkland landscape environment by geographers or environmental archaeologists was thwarted in its initial stages by the lack of wetland mires preserving pollen sequences (Scaife 1987a; in prep.). Much of the vegetation history of the British Isles was slowly mapped from, and recorded by, a series of pollen records; a general chronological climatic scheme was developed, which was comparable with that for north-western Europe. The chalklands, although devoid of their own data, were presumed to fit into that generalised history. The paucity of peat accumulations on the downland of southern England, and poor or absent pollen preservation where such deposits do exist, has meant that the past vegetation of and developments on the chalklands have remained largely enigmatic (Turner 1970). Indeed, Judith Turner even lamented that 'It is rather unfortunate that the South-East chalk lands, long regarded on archaeological grounds as an area densely settled by Neolithic man, should be so poor in plant preserving deposits' (Turner 1970, 98–9).

The 'problem' of the south English chalk downland

A lack of long pollen sequences encouraged many prehistorians, geographers and naturalists to assume the downland landscapes to have been essentially unchanging. When Gordon Childe was writing *The Dawn of European Civilisation* (1925; with revised editions to 1957) he discussed the Neolithic of the Wessex and Sussex Downs; throughout his text there was an unwritten assumption that the downs were open grassland. Cecil Curwen, the doyen of Sussex archaeologists, wrote in the first (1937) edition of his classic *Archaeology of Sussex*: 'in prehistoric times both the western and eastern [South] downs were in all probability open grassland with a variable amount of scrub' (Curwen 1937, 13) – clearly a case of projecting then current perceptions of landscape into the past. This view remained unchanged in the 1954 edition.

By the time Stuart Piggott wrote *The Neolithic Cultures of the British Isles* (1954), there was a growing realisation among archaeologists that the chalk may have been wooded. It was the absence of peat and pollen data that led Piggott to believe that chalklands constituted a 'special problem' (Piggott 1954, 5). This led to uncertainty. Controversy reigned, against the background of a rather poor and questionable chronological framework. Salisbury and Jane (1940) contended from charcoal evidence (from Maiden Castle) that in Neolithic times the chalk was clothed with closed woodland but, surprisingly, Godwin and Tansley (1941) considered that 'no sound evidence is presented for any such belief'. They too suggested that much of the Wessex downland was bare of trees in the Neolithic, just as Curwen had proposed in 1937. Early land snail studies, largely by A. S. Kennard (e.g. 1933; 1935; 1936; 1943), provided an independent and unquestionably local interpretation (although the discipline was clearly in its infancy). Kennard suggested that the snail evidence indicated climatic and vegetation associations local to the sampling sites, providing evidence of woodland despite the absence of corroborative botanical evidence.

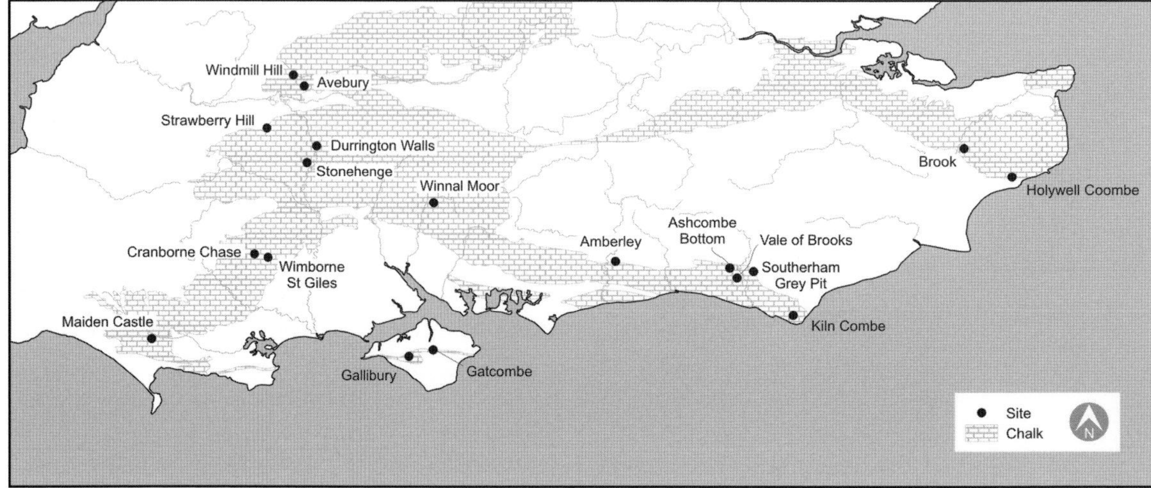

FIGURE 1.
Location of some of the key sites of the chalk downland of southern England. (Allen 2005b)

This debate, and our understanding of the chalk landscape, was tardy in comparison with what took place in many other areas of Britain (Figure 1). This delay was principally due to the paucity of peat accumulations and mires, and the relatively late onset of soil pollen studies (Dimbleby 1957; 1961; 1985). Nevertheless, views slowly changed as a result of two developments. The first was the increasingly pervasive and persuasive influence of palaeoecologists such as Godwin (1940; *et seq.* see Godwin 1975), who promoted the climatic vegetation sequence developed in northern Europe by the Scandinavian botanists Blytt and Sernander (Lowe and Walker 1984, 132–3). Even Kennard's snail data were seen to be not incompatible with Blytt and Sernander's climatic phases: Atlantic, Sub-Boreal and Sub-Atlantic. The second development was the physical change resulting from the outbreak of myxomatosis in 1953–4. This epidemic culled rabbit populations that had been maintaining the close-cropped downland sward; their absence led to rapid scrub and open woodland regeneration (Thomas 1960; 1963), indicating that the chalkland could support a woodland ecosystem (Sumption and Flowerdew 1985). The idea that the downland might once have been wooded was reinforced by pollen analysis by Godwin (1940 *et seq.*) and others, who suggested that after the last glaciation much of Britain became heavily wooded; this was the environment in which early communities existed, hewed openings and clear-felled forest to till the soil beneath.

Pioneering work by Godwin (1962) on peat adjacent to the downs at Wingham and Frogholt in Kent indicated the existence of woodland and its subsequent deforestation by human agencies, rather than natural causes. Important studies of peat in river valleys by Anne Thorley at Amberley Wild Brooks, Arundel and Vale of Brooks, Lewes (Thorley 1971; 1981) and, latterly, by Waller (Waller and Hamilton 2000), and also by Waton at Winnal Moor, Winchester (Waton 1982; 1986), demonstrated the presence of post-glacial woodland on the downs, and confirmed that the vegetation history followed the general pattern seen elsewhere in Britain (Table 1). This was supported by Dimbleby's analysis of soil pollen in conjunction with Evans's land snail analyses in their seminal paper (Dimbleby and Evans 1979). This showed that pollen may be preserved in buried soils under archaeological monuments, allowing some limited confirmatory pollen data to be obtained from the chalk itself. At the same time John Evans obtained land snail evidence, sampling widely from archaeological monuments in Wessex. It was not until Evans had demonstrated the presence, and then clearance, of woodland across the downlands (Evans 1971; Evans and Jones 1979, 209) that a comprehensive, concise and convincing understanding of the prehistoric chalkland countryside was presented (see Allen 2006). Thus, in the 1970s, Evans and Dimbleby rewrote the understanding of the downland landscape and providing basic models for the vegetation history of the chalk which differed radically from those available to Hoskins (Table 2).

This contrasted significantly with the previously long-held view that the downlands were a natural phenomenon, utilised by prehistoric communities because of their openness and ease of access. The hypothesis of extensive

Climatic zone	Pollen zone Godwin/West	Archaeological period	Climate and vegetation	approx. date calibrated BC/(*BP*)
FLANDRIAN				
Sub-Atlantic	VIII	Roman period Iron Age Late Bronze Age	*Deterioration* Cold and wet, general deterioration. High rainfall. Decline of lime. Increase of ash, birch and beech.	
	Fl. III			1250 cal BC
		Middle Bronze Age Early Bronze Age Final Neolithic	*Stable* Warm and dry, low rainfall, wind-blown deposits. Woodland regeneration in southern England.	(*c.2900 BP*)
Sub-Boreal	VIIb			3200 cal BC
		Late Neolithic Middle Neolithic Early Neolithic	Declining warmth. Landnam and first agriculture. Elm decline: 3800 BC/(*5050 BP*).	(*4500 BP*)
	Fl. II			4000 cal BC
Atlantic	VIIa	Later Mesolithic	*Optimum* Climatic optimum, warm and wet. Increase of 2°C, poly-climax forest. Increase of alder, some clearances.	(*5200 BP*)
	VI			6300 cal BC
Boreal	V	Mesolithic	*Ameliorating* Continental climate, warm and dry. Assynchronous expansions of mixed oak forest with hazel and successional from pine.	(*7500 BP*)
	Fl. I			8900 cal BC
Pre-Boreal	IV	Early Mesolithic	*Rapid Amelioration* Sharp increase in warmth at 10,000 BP. Birch, juniper and pine woodland.	(*9500 BP*)
				10,000 cal BC

TABLE 1. Outline of climatic zonation, basic vegetational change and archaeological events for southern England. This enables pollen zones quoted in many specialist pollen and quaternary geography reports to be equated to the archaeological chronology and activity (Allen 2000b).

post-glacial woodland on the chalk was challenged in its turn by pollen analysis from mires on the chalk of the Yorkshire Wolds (Bush 1988; 1989; Bush and Flenley 1986); but the application of this model to the southern chalk downlands was vigorously refuted on the basis of evidence from southern England (Thomas 1989). So the 'problem of the south English chalk downland' (Piggott 1954, 5) continues to intrigue. However, thirty years after the pioneering work of John Evans and Geoff Dimbleby, and following in their footsteps,

Toadeshole, E. Sx	Subsoil hollow	2140–1680 cal BC	3350±90 BP, OxA–3079
Toadeshole, E. Sx	Subsoil hollow	2140–1680 cal BC	3380±90 BP, OxA–3078
Grey Pit, E. Sx	Colluvium	Pre *c.*2000 BC	—
Thickthorn Dwn, Dorset	Pits under long barrow	Pre 4220–3800 cal BC	5160±45 BP, BM–2355
Ashcombe, E. Sx	Subsoil hollow	Post *c.*6000 BC	—
Itford Bottom, E. Sx	Subsoil hollow	8200–7650 cal BC	8770±85 BP, BM–1544
Hambledon Hill, Dorset	Posthole	7580–7350 cal BC	8400±60 BP, OxA–7845
Hambledon Hill, Dorset	Posthole	7600–7340 cal BC	8480±55 BP, OxA–7846
Hambledon Hill, Dorset	Posthole	7970–7590 cal BC	8725±55 BP, OxA–7816
Stonehenge, Wilts.	Postpit	7350–6650 cal BC	8090±140 BP, HAR–456
Stonehenge, Wilts.	Postpit	7600–7160 cal BC	8400±100 BP, OxA–4920
Stonehenge, Wilts.	Postpit	7750–7350 cal BC	8520±80 BP, OxA–4919
Stonehenge, Wilts.	Postpit	8300–7600 cal BC	8880±120 BP, GU–5109
Stonehenge, Wilts.	Postpit	8800–7700 cal BC	9130±180 BP, HAR–455
Strawberry Hill, Wilts.	Ditch under colluvium	9150–8250cal BC	9350±120 BP, OxA–3040

TABLE 2. List of dated pine charcoal on the chalk in Southern Britain (see Allen and Gardiner 2002; Allen 2005a, 28).

we may now use a much larger database of extensive studies of land snails, hillwash, soil pollen and chalkland mires in order to modify the history of the downland, providing better resolution in both space and time.

A new prehistoric chalkland landscape

In the past twenty-five years work largely by Rob Scaife has provided a series of key pollen sequences from, for example, Mesolithic contexts at Stonehenge (Scaife 1995), Neolithic deposits at Gatcombe Withy Beds, Isle of Wight (Scaife 1980; Tomalin and Scaife 1979), Bronze Age buried soil at Gallibury Down, Isle of Wight (Scaife 1984) and alluvial sequences at Durrington (Scaife 2004) and Cranborne Chase (Scaife in French *et al.* 2003; 2007). The amount of land snail analysis has increased significantly, and we have now started to look at spatial resolution and mapping of past environments *within* landscapes rather than considering single sites or sample points to be wholly representative of their landscapes. This has been facilitated by commercial archaeology (for example, on the Dorchester bypass) and personal research, involving very detailed molluscan analysis. Studies of defined chalkland research areas have thus enabled us to move from a two-dimensional history to the point where we may map the history of vegetation and land-use in three dimensions (Allen 2000a), as at Dorchester (Allen 1997a), Stonehenge (Allen *et al.* 1990; Allen 1997b) and Cranborne Chase (Allen 2000b; 2002; Allen in French *et al.* 2003; French *et al.* 2007).

Period	*Environment*
Medieval/Romano–British/ Iron Age	Intermittent cultivation and grassland. Formation of ploughwash deposits.
Bronze Age	Open environment of grassland or arable. Cultivation/ grazing intermittent. Formation of wind-lain material.
Late Neolithic	Woodland regeneration. Not at Woodhenge.
Late Neolithic	Construction of henge monuments.
Neolithic	Long period of grassland, probably maintained by grazing.
Neolithic	Woodland clearance. Ploughing and possibly other forms of tillage. Ploughmarks at Avebury.
(Mesolithic) Atlantic (?)	Dense woodland. Recorded only at Avebury, but probably at most sites.
Mesolithic Boreal (?)	Open woodland. Evidence of fire and possible influence of Mesolithic man (Evans 1972, 219, 256).
(Upper Palaeolithic) Late glacial	Subarctic environment, probably tundra. Formation of periglacial structures and wind-lain material.

TABLE 3. Main environmental events on the chalk of Wiltshire and Dorset in the late-glacial and post-glacial periods, from Evans and Jones (1979, 209) also reworked and republished by Entwistle and Bowden (1991, table 2).

Nature of the post-glacial woodland

According to the Blytt and Serander scheme, which can be modified for southern England (Table 1), pine was a significant constituent of the birch, juniper and pine Pre-Boreal woodland (*c.*10,000–8900 BC), and of the pine and hazel to mixed oak woodland of the Boreal phase (8900–6300 BC). The presence of pine across most of Britain is not an issue; it is demonstrated in pollen spectra (Godwin 1940; 1975). It has, however, been argued that pine cannot survive on the thin chalkland soils as it tends to suffer from chlorosis, a condition arising from its inability to obtain sufficient magnesium in the presence of calcium carbonate (Wood and Nimmo 1962). Its presence on the chalk itself cannot be confirmed by pollen. Nevertheless, pollen in the Ouse valley near Lewes indicated that pine was a significant woodland constituent before 5680–5080 cal BC (6290±180 BP, Birm–168), surviving well into the Middle Bronze Age at *c.*1450 cal BC (Thorley 1971; 1981). It was also a significant component of the calcareous fen at Winnal Moor near Winchester prior to about 6000 cal BC (Waton 1982) and of the chalk edge mire at Gatcombe Withy Beds, Isle of Wight, in the period from 9950–9250 cal BC (9970±50 BP; SRR–1433) to about 5480–5290 cal BC (6385±50 BP; SRR–1339; Scaife 1980; 1982; 1987b). These occurrences can, however, be argued to represent local pine, growing off the chalk, or long-distance pollen transport. Such arguments cannot be applied where pine charcoals occur in chalkland contexts. These have been found from a number of dated contexts on archaeological sites (Allen 1988; 1995a; 2005a). There is increasing evidence from charcoal for Mesolithic pine woodland in locations distributed from Dorset to Sussex (Table 2), a finding which has been taken to indicate that thicker loessic soils existed on the chalk. Recently, pine charcoal dating from as late as 2140–1600 cal BC has been recovered from the Sussex Downs, apparently indicating that pine survived locally well into the Bronze Age, accompanied by thicker, fertile loessic soils which were attractive for cultivation (Allen 1988; Holleyman 1935).

Despite its limited volume, this evidence allows us to suggest that in some areas pine was a significant component of the early post-glacial woodland on the chalk; that the soils supporting it may have been thicker and less calcareous (brown earths or argillic brown earths) than they are now; and that in some areas pine persisted well into the Bronze Age (Sub-Boreal). We may argue that the chalklands followed, in general terms, the basic vegetation patterns described for Britain during the early post-glacial epochs (Table 1). Thus the accepted model of post-glacial vegetation history now follows Tansley's ecological developmental progression (1939) through vegetation seres to climax woodland (though this has been recently challenged (Bush 1988; 1989; Bush and Flenley 1986) and defended (Thomas 1989; Evans 2006, 75)). That post-glacial woodland did occur on the chalk is not in question; this is adequately demonstrated by evidence from across southern England (Evans 1971; 1972).

Extent and cover of the post-glacial woodland

This model, however, has led archaeologists and palaeogeographers to assume total woodland cover across the southern English chalk, and relatively uniform changes in vegetation history, punctuated only by the 'interference' of prehistoric communities. It also led to the assumption of the blanket presence of closed woodland prior to human activity; evidence of open countryside in Neolithic and Early Bronze Age (4000–2000 BC) was assumed to demonstrate woodland clearance. We confidently assume evidence for a more open downland to be evidence for anthropogenic deforestation. This assumption strongly influences archaeologists' interpretations of the roles of individual sites and their perceptions of human/landscape interactions, as well as the 'mapping' of vegetation and land-use development in our study areas (e.g. Smith 1984; Allen 1997a; 2000a).

Evans's general land-use scheme (Table 2) is undoubtedly applicable at the landscape or regional scale, as he intended. But our unquestioning assumption that woodland existed, and was cleared, tends to inhibit us from challenging or modifying this model on a local, site-by-site basis. It is perhaps necessary to *prove* the existence of closed woodland, rather than assume it; prehistoric populations may have deliberately exploited niche habitats. Most of Evans's work, which produced his evidence for land use, was necessarily from a small and specific topographic zone containing upland hilltop sites such as Neolithic long barrows of the thirty-seventh century BC and causewayed enclosures of the thirty-sixth century BC.

If we approach chalkland landscapes by attempting to *prove* the existence of woodland, rather than assuming it, then the examination of selected, well-studied areas is informative. In the Dorchester landscape to the north of Maiden Castle, analysis of over 260 snail samples from nine prehistoric sites (Allen 1997a) with over 75,000 snail identifications failed to prove conclusively the existence of prehistoric closed woodland. Perhaps the sampling was biased in favour of archaeological sites where woodland was cleared. But it is also possible that a full post-glacial woodland maximum did not exist. Yet at Maiden Castle itself John Evans (Evans and Rouse 1991) clearly demonstrated the presence of an ancient woodland. So – contrary to Evans's suggestion that this was representative of the landscape – perhaps Maiden Castle survived as a wooded hilltop on open downland, as Danebury does today? Two hundred and fifty metres north-west of Stonehenge, Mesolithic posts (around 7000 cal BC) were erected in a 'clearing' in an open pine and hazel woodland (Figure 2); the first, earthen, monument at Stonehenge itself (2950 cal BC) was constructed on long-established and expansive open downland. On Cranborne Chase, an even more extensive land snail programme of over 400 samples from twenty-two sites and over 175,000 snail identifications in an area smaller than that studied at Dorchester, has also failed to produce evidence for extensive closed post-glacial woodland, a finding confirmed by pollen analysis from peats in the chalkland valley at Wimborne St Giles (Figure 3).

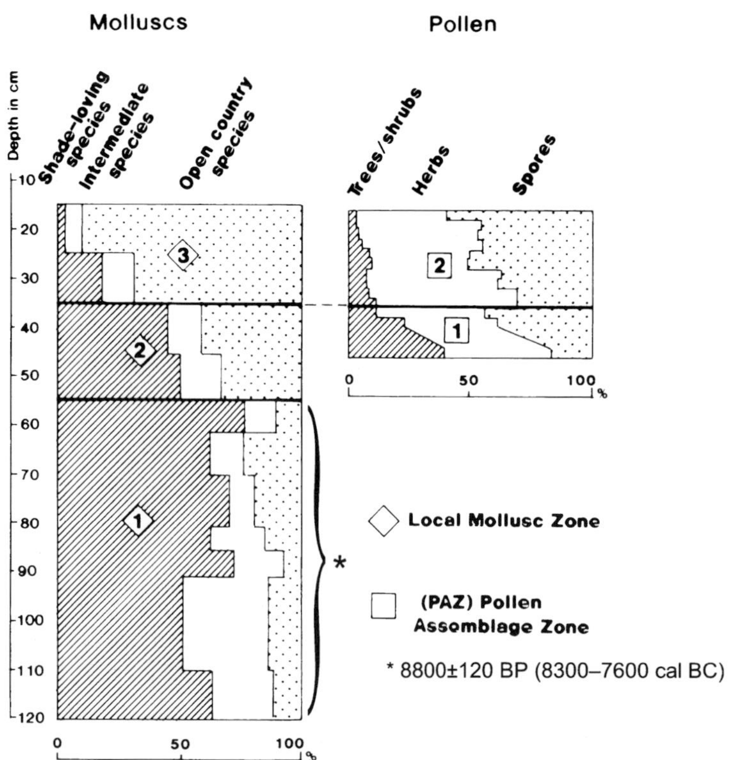

FIGURE 2.
Summary diagram of the Mesolithic (Boreal) open pine and hazel woodland depicted in pollen and mollusc data from Mesolithic pit 9580 in the Stonehenge carpark. (Allen 1995b)

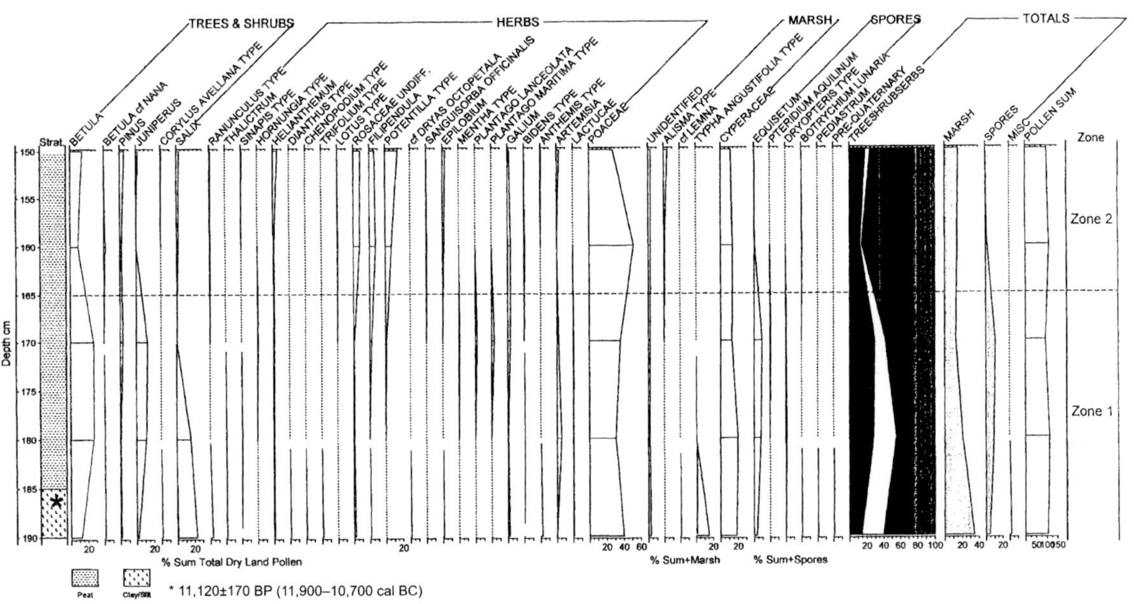

FIGURE 3.
Pollen diagram of the early post-glacial and Holocene sequence in the Allen valley, Cranborne Chase, at Wimborne St Giles, Dorset.

Evidently woodland development was retarded in some locations. It seems increasingly likely that natural clearings or glades comprising grassland, scrub and some trees were part of the natural ecological variation and patchiness in a large and extensive forest. Some of these relatively open areas may have been as large as an English parish. They would have invited vegetational diversity, the woodland fringes providing a niche for soft fruiting trees and berries. These fruits would have encouraged a range of herbivores to feed and browse and thus maintain the glades. Such locations would also have drawn Mesolithic communities attracted by opportunities for hunting and gathering; they may even have maintained and perpetuated these glades artificially. It is perhaps not too far-fetched to suggest that these areas attracted some of the first large human populations and that in consequence they survive today as zones of more concentrated monuments and sites. It may be no coincidence that three of the apparently most densely populated parts of the prehistoric downland, all containing major earlier Neolithic monuments, have significant evidence of Mesolithic activity, and that these areas (Dorchester, Cranborne and Stonehenge) all seem to have been open downland. This concept has been explored further for the southern chalkland (Allen 2000a; French *et al.* 2003), and is being discussed in more detail elsewhere (see below).

Ironically, these ideas of open park woodland propagated initially by Bush (1988) and Bush and Flenley (1986) for the Yorkshire Wolds were independently postulated for areas of the Dorset Downs from 1988 to 1997 (see Allen 1997a, 278). Reassuringly, these ideas conform with ecological models developed by Vera (2000), featuring landscape mosaics which included 'half-open' and park-like landscapes in lowland areas, maintained by wild herbivores. We postulate that it was precisely these areas which were exploited by Mesolithic

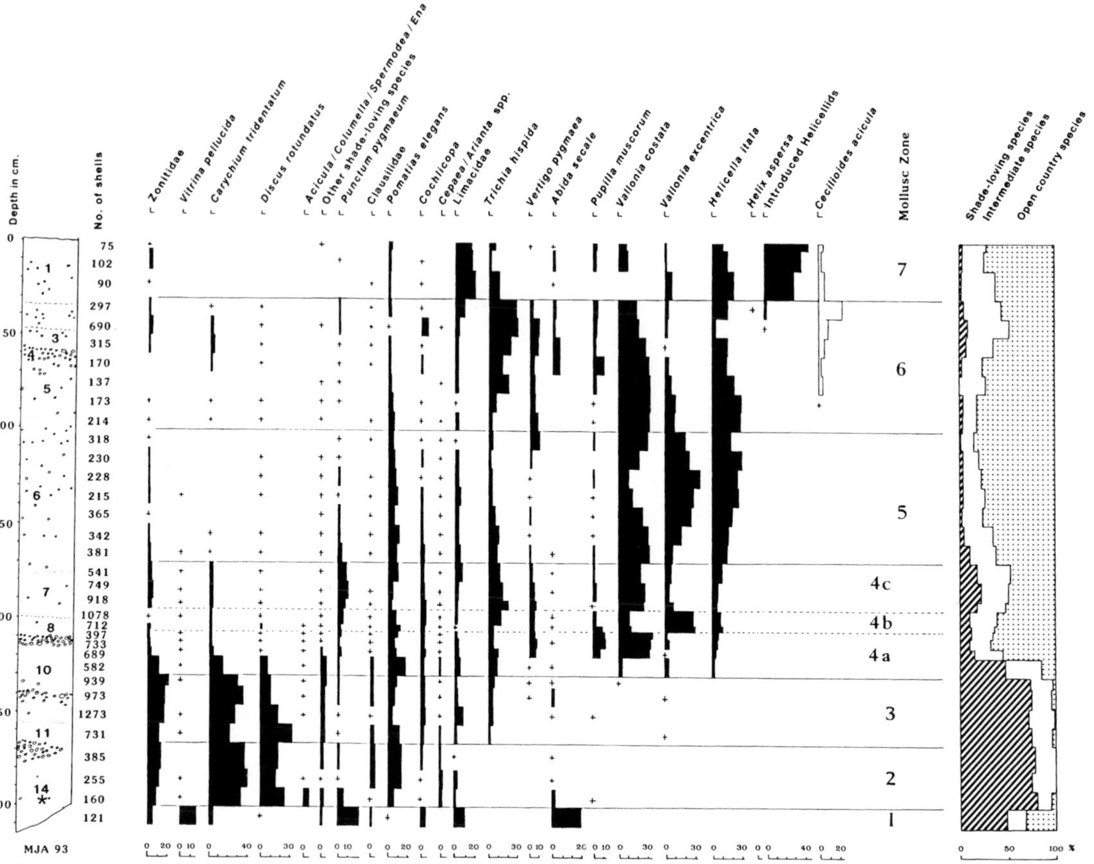

Depth in cm.
No. of shells
Zonitidae
Vitrina pellucida
Carychium tridentatum
Discus rotundatus
Acicula / Columella / Spermodea / Ena
Other shade-loving species
Punctum pygmaeum
Clausiliidae
Pomatias elegans
Cochlicopa
Cepaea / Arianta spp.
Limacidae
Trichia hispida
Vertigo pygmaea
Abida secale
Pupilla muscorum
Vallonia costata
Vallonia excentrica
Helicella itala
Helix aspersa
Introduced Helicellids
Cecilioides acicula
Mollusc Zone
Shade-loving species
Intermediate species
Open country species
7
6
5
4c
4b
4a
3
2
1
MJA 93

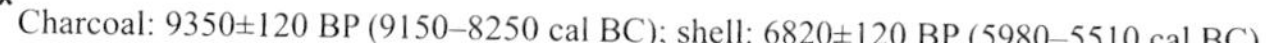

* Charcoal: 9350±120 BP (9150–8250 cal BC); shell: 6820±120 BP (5980–5510 cal BC)

TREES & SHRUBS
HERBS
SPORES
TOTALS
BETULA
PINUS
ULMUS
QUERCUS
ALNUS GLUTINOSA
TILIA
TILIA (degraded)
FRAXINUS EXCELSIOR
JUNIPERUS COMMUNIS
CORYLUS AVELLANA TYPE
RANUNCULACEAE UNDIFF.
RANUNCULUS TYPE
SINAPIS TYPE
CHENOPODIACEAE
PAPILIONACEAE
ROSACEAE UNDIFF.
FILIPENDULA
UMBELLIFERAE
FALLOPIA CONVOLVULUS TYPE
RUMEX
SCROPHULARIACEAE
PLANTAGO LANCEOLATA
RUBIACEAE
TUBULIFLORAE
CENTAUREA UNDIFF.
LIGULIFLORAE
CYPERACEAE
GRAMINEAE
CEREAL TYPE
PTERIDIUM
DRYOPTERIS TYPE
POLYPODIUM
TREES/SHRUBS/HERBS/MARSH
SPORES
Zone
Strat.
Depth cm
% Total Dry Land Pollen
% Sum+Spores
DURR:4
DURR:3
DURR:2
DURR:1
Fen Peat
Pot
Humified Peat
Rob Scaife

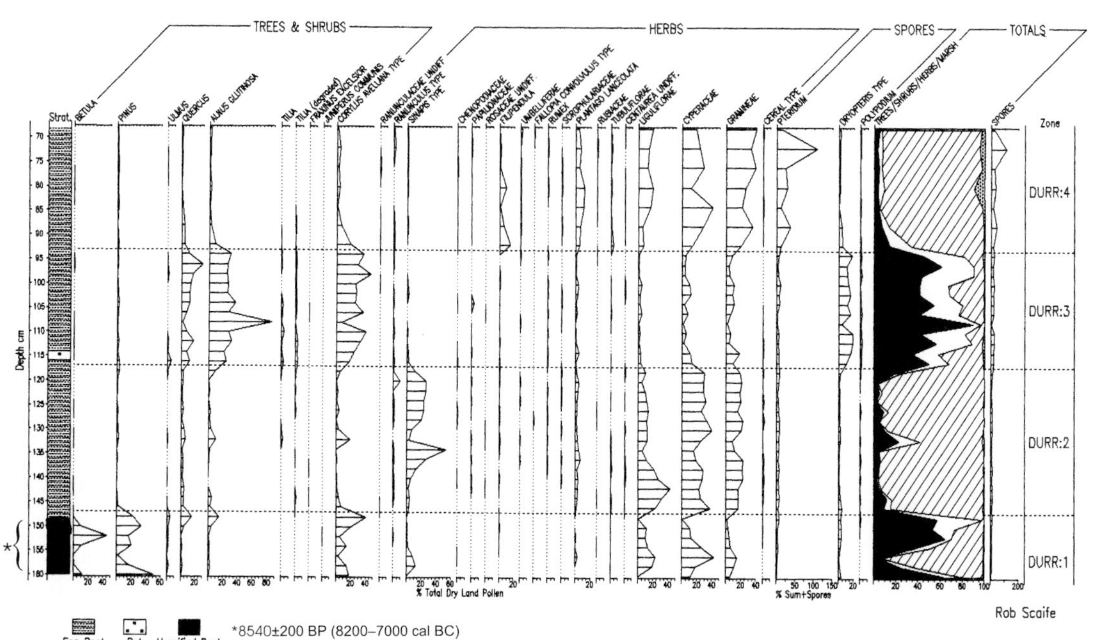

*8540±200 BP (8200–7000 cal BC)

FIGURE 4. Land snail diagram of the Mesolithic woodland (layers 14, 11), clearance (layer 10), Iron Age occupation (layer 8), Roman agriculture (layers 6 to 3) and medieval pasture (layer 1) at Strawberry Hill, Wiltshire.

FIGURE 5. (*below opposite*) Pollen diagram from the Avon floodplain near Durrington Walls, Wiltshire. (Scaife 2004)

FIGURE 6. Interpretation of Windmill Hill early Neolithic causewayed enclosure set within a woodland clearing. (Whittle *et al.* 1999) by kind permission of J. Pollard.

populations because of their openness, the presence of wild fruits and berries, and their concentrations of herbivores (*cf.* Allen 2002). Evidence of open park woodland and these interactions between humans and nature are explored further in Allen (1997b; forthcoming), Scaife in French *et al.* (2003) and French *et al.* (2007).

Woodland clearance

The presence and clearance of woodland has been shown from pollen evidence in Kent (Godwin 1962) and Sussex (Thorley 1971; 1981) and from long land snail sequences in colluvium at Brook and Holywell Coombe in Kent (Kerney *et al.* 1964; 1980), in Sussex (Bell 1983; Allen 1995a; 2005a) and in Wiltshire (Allen 1992). John Evans demonstrated these phenomena in many Wessex archaeological landscapes (Evans 1971; 1972). We can still assume that much of the chalkland supported woodland; we will now briefly consider the history of its clearance. On the scarp slope of Salisbury Plain, at Strawberry Hill, Wiltshire, a colluvial sequence 3.4 m deep provides a 10,000-year history of downland land-use (Figure 4), showing Boreal woodland (5700–7000 BC) with charcoal indicating the presence of pine, juniper, oak and hazel, with widespread clearance, probably in the Bronze Age. A similar picture emerges from the impressive pollen diagram from the Avon Valley, near Durrington Walls (Figure 5) showing early post-glacial woodland clearance and the development of fen peat in the river valley, but extensive open downland on drier land. Work on colluvium and land snails from Dorset to Sussex indicates that, despite local clearances in the earlier Neolithic period around monuments such as causewayed enclosures (e.g. Thomas 1982; Fishpool 1999) (Figure 6), large tracts of downland were probably cleared during the Early

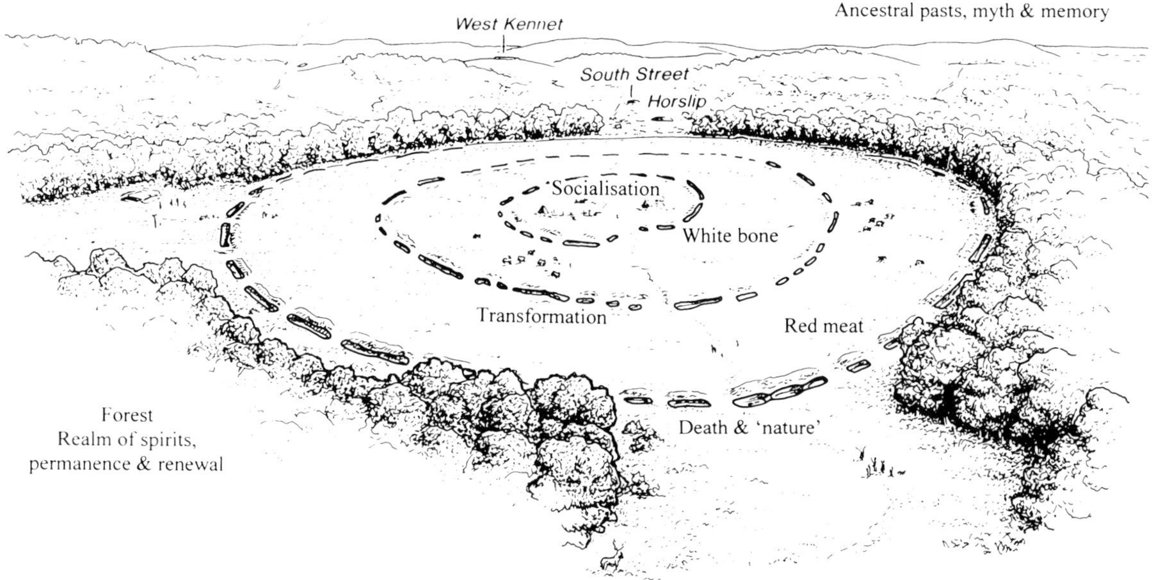

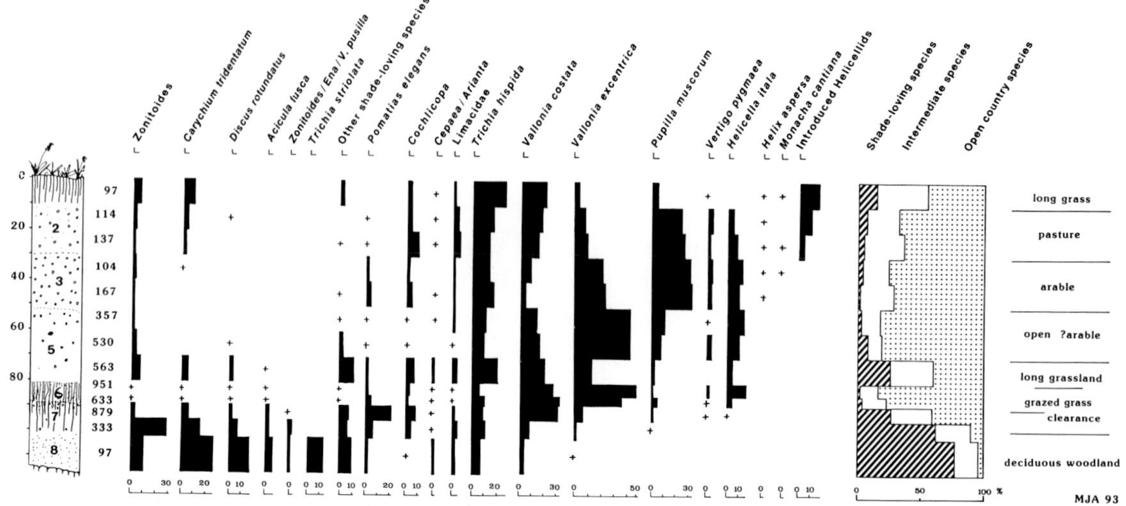

Bronze Age. This is suggested by the large number of Bronze Age barrows constructed in open landscapes, a series of colluvial deposits indicating clearance and established downland by the Beaker period *c.*2000 BC (Allen 2005a; 1995a) (see Figure 7). By the Middle Bronze Age, very large areas of downland in Sussex and on Salisbury Plain were clear-felled and open for pasture and tillage. Thus the basis of our 'natural' downland was largely created in prehistory.

FIGURE 7. Land snail diagram showing woodland clearance (layer 7) prior to Beaker occupation (layer 6), and prehistoric agriculture (layers 5 and 3) and medieval pasture (layer 2) at Southerham, Grey Pit, near Lewes, East Sussex. (Allen 1995a)

Prehistoric farming and the erosion of a natural landscape

Prehistoric farming not only led to the creation of now-fossilised fields, but inadvertently changed the soils, ecology and shape of the chalk downs. This is demonstrated by the extensive occurrence of colluvium across southern England, a product of the erosion of downland soils, largely in prehistory. Just as the post-glacial closed woodland cover was a complex mosaic, so was the distribution of soils. Thicker loessic and less calcareous soils have been suggested for parts of Sussex (Allen 1988), Wiltshire (Allen 1995b) and Dorset (Staines in Allen 1997a); these might have supported open woodland with pine. Elsewhere, there are thin calcareous rendzina soils under Bronze Age barrows (see the detailed work on Cranborne Chase, Dorset – French *et al.* 2003; 2005). Both soils are, however, less calcareous and more silty than the thin grey and brown rendzinas that are almost ubiquitous today; they are predominantly loamy (Wooldridge and Linton 1933), being characteristically silt-rich (60 per cent; Hodgson 1967, 313) as a result of insoluble, non-calcareous, silt-sized minerals resulting from Late Devensian loess deposits (Catt 1978). These early soils were fertile and easily tilled; but they were also subject to erosion (Allen 1988; 1991; Bell 1983). This erosion had been considered to be an incipient, frequent, small-scale process resulting from rainsplash and seasonal soil creep, which would have been accelerated by human interventions such as deforestation and tillage (Dimbleby 1976; 1984), resulting in the gradual accumulation of appreciable thicknesses of hillwash in dry valleys (Kerney *et al.* 1964; Bell 1983; Allen 1992). However, excavation of colluvium has recovered horizons that suggest higher energy erosion events, examples of which have been seen in landscapes ploughed in recent times.

Lenses of small rounded chalk pieces are commonly seen in chalkland colluvium (Allen 1992, table 4.1), and have often been considered to be a result of earthworm sorting in former soils (Bell 1981; 1992). Iron Age colluvium at Strawberry Hill, Wiltshire, showed a number of these in section (Figure 4). When excavated in plan, however, they were not simply concentrations of chalk, but a series of 'fingers' of chalk pieces that had washed downslope (Figure 8a), and which could be paralleled by modern erosion deposits witnessed at Ashcombe Bottom in 1984 (Figure 8b). These chalky lenses often represent chalk fan deposits, probably originating from rilling of the A and A/C horizons within an arable field (*cf.* Allen 1991, 44). Similarly, thin stone-free horizons are often considered a product of earthworm-working and thus to represent *in situ* soil formation; but at Strawberry Hill, soil micromorphological analysis by Macphail demonstrated otherwise. Field interpretation of a stone-free horizon with a quantity of sherds of an Early Iron Age carinated bowl suggested an earthworm-worked horizon, representing stabilisation and cessation of erosion. Soil micromorphological evidence cast doubt on this, however; Richard Macphail reported that the stone-free horizon was 'a massive chalky "slurry" of weathered chalk, sand, silt, and mollusc fragments, arionid granules, fine charcoal and organic matter'. This was, then, chalky mud that had eroded from an intensively cultivated rendzina soil in prehistory; again, parallels can be seen in modern agricultural erosion (Boardman 1992) (Figure 9). Finally, lenses of flint gravel are commonly seen in chalky colluvium, and these were particularly noted at Kiln Combe (Bell 1983, fig. 3, plate 17), and Ashcombe Bottom (Allen 2005a, figs 7 and 9). A large-scale and more rapid erosion from tilled land was observed after a storm on the night of 14 September 1984 (Figure 9). Here a delta mass of soil and mud up to 17 cm thick, estimated to contain several tons of large flint nodules, was deposited in the valley. The nodules were deposited in a location comparable to that of a Bronze Age gravel fan recorded during archaeological excavations (Allen 2005a) (Figure 10). Hillwash studies have long shown the extensive distribution of thick colluvial deposits on the downs.

Modern erosion analogues have thus suggested that prehistoric cultivation has created gradual accumulations resulting from rainsplash and small-scale soil creep, but was also associated with occasional but recurrent mass erosion events. Erosion changes soil types and distributions, alters the shape of the landscape by infilling valleys and erodes hilltop sites, exposing artefacts preferentially while burying those in slopefoot and valley locations (Allen 1991). Whole classes of prehistoric site, such as the elusive Beaker settlements, may be buried in dry valley locations (Allen 2005b).

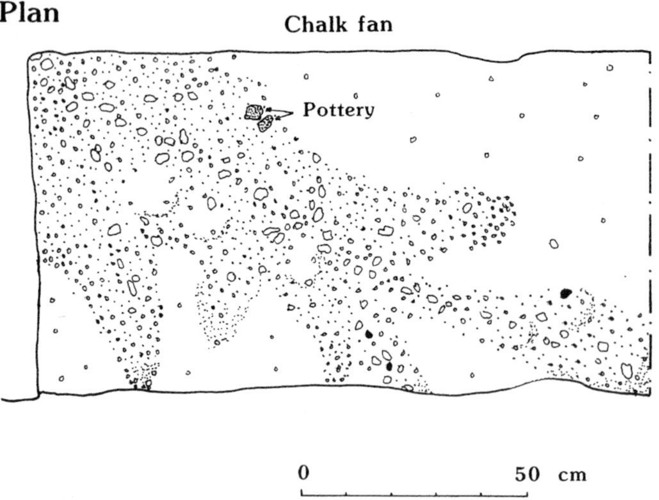

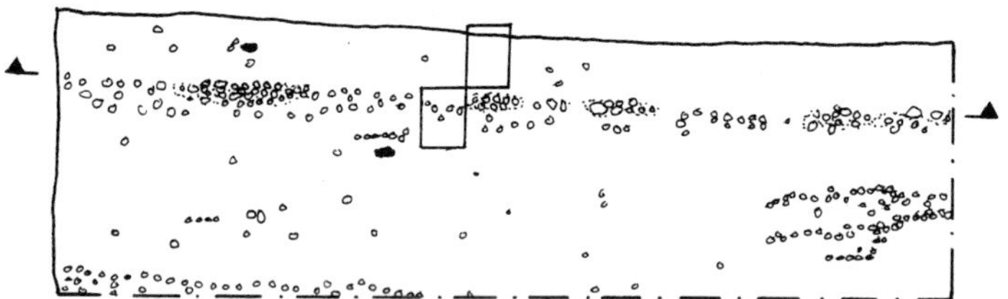

FIGURE 8.
a. Plan and section of a chalk fan excavated at Strawberry Hill, Wiltshire; the rectangular boxes are the positions of soil micromorphology samples. (Allen 1992)
b. Chalk fan as a result of rill erosion from an arable field: September 1984 at Ashcombe Bottom, East Sussex. (Allen 1992)

FIGURE 9.
a. (above) A view of the excavation at Ashcombe Bottom, East Sussex, in July 1984.
b. (below) The same view showing a fan of mud concealing a gravel fan after the erosion event during a storm on 14 September 1984. (Allen 1988; 1991)

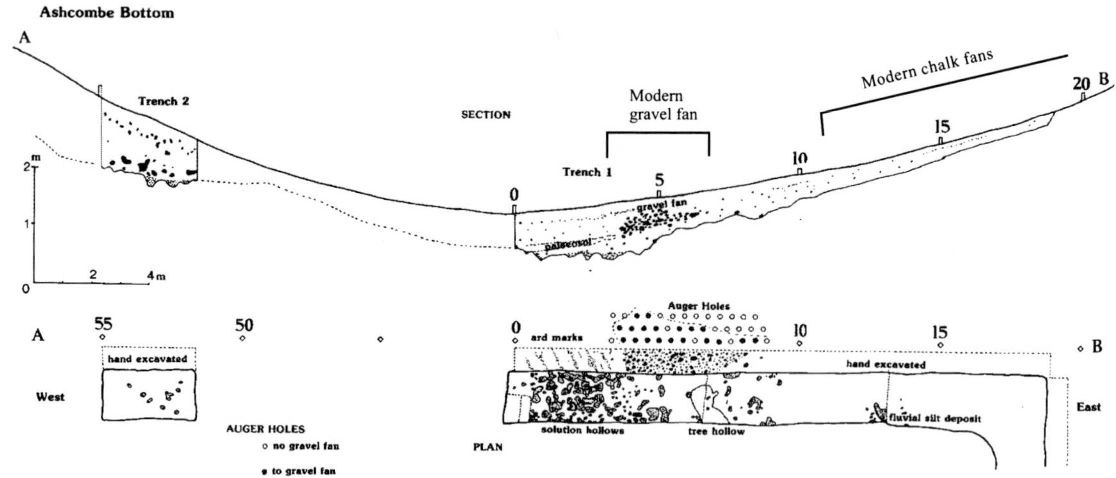

FIGURE 10. Summary section and plan of the excavated hillwash at Ashcombe Bottom, near Lewes, East Sussex, showing the prehistoric gravel fan and location of the modern gravel fan and chalk rill erosion events. (Allen 2005a)

Extensive evidence from snails, pollen and hillwash studies now allows us to 'map' some prehistoric landscapes (Allen 1997b; 2005c). Although an open downland had been created by the Middle Bronze Age, this need not have presented the close-cropped downland lawn which we see today. Grassland would have been long and tussocky, with bushes scattered across the landscape.

In conclusion: the creation of the downs

Downland landscapes have always been variable, and their environmental history cannot be presented as a single, universally applicable narrative. A general overview was available by the mid-1970s. Now, however, as we examine individual landscapes and take archaeological findings into account, we see a mosaic, in which differences in natural development and human modification both carry significant consequences for patterns of human history, and ultimately for the landscape we see today. The natural beauty of the downlands finds expression through rare plants, distinctive ecologies and open landscapes; but what we see today is the inadvertent creation of human action, commencing 9,000 years ago, but largely manifest over the last 4,000 years. Indeed, most of the 'downland' was created as long as 3,500 years ago, following the recurrent, piecemeal opening of park woodland, the clearance of denser woodlands and ensuing tillage and consequent erosion. It was only with the advent of large rabbit populations that the familiar grassland baize was created. The downs are considered to be fragile ecosystems today. Changes in vegetation and soil as a result of human activities have demonstrated that they were fragile systems in prehistory too, and were changed rapidly by agricultural operations.

CHAPTER THREE

Making Strange: Monuments and the Creation of the Earlier Prehistoric Landscape

Richard Bradley

If we are to talk about the making of landscapes, we must begin with a question. What were the elements out of which they were formed? At first sight this is an easy question to answer: so easy, in fact, that it is rarely asked. The landscapes studied by Hoskins were made out of houses and villages, roads and fields, and from the raw materials that went into their construction. These are familiar features. That is not to say that they had a continuous history or that the landscapes that Hoskins wrote about with so much eloquence were the same as those of later prehistory. There is no need to suppose that they experienced an unbroken development, but it does seem as if they were formed from similar components.

It is all too easy to project those preconceptions onto still earlier landscapes. On the one hand, prehistorians have tried to identify the same features from the origins of agriculture onwards – fields, land boundaries, habitations, farms – and, on the other, they have often assumed that the terrain was organised according to a logic similar to that of the landscapes of later periods (Fowler 1983). This is a mistake, for the earliest insular landscapes were made out of quite different elements. They developed according to different processes from those familiar from the historical period, or even from the last millennium BC. The process followed in this article is described in Seamus Heaney's poem 'Making strange' (1984, 32–3). It accepts the existence of the unexpected and analyses it in its own terms.

This paper focuses on the period between about 4000 and 1500 BC and particularly on the earlier part of that sequence. In nearly every area one point is absolutely clear: fields and land boundaries are extremely rare, houses are ephemeral and often difficult for archaeologists to find, and the landscape is dominated by great stone and earthwork monuments of no practical significance whatsoever. Their construction consumed as much labour as clearance and cultivation, and the traces of these endeavours have lasted to this day.

That is not an accident of survival. It is an indication that the priorities of Neolithic communities were very different from our own – and just as different from those discussed by Hoskins in *The Making of the English Landscape.*

The cursus and its implications

This has not always been apparent. To illustrate my argument I shall consider one type of field monument: the elongated earthwork enclosures known as cursuses (Barclay and Harding 1999). There are two reasons for doing so. First, the archaeology of earlier prehistoric monuments is deceptive, for it is generally written around structures that were too large for later generations to destroy, or those which lay outside the limits of more recent land use. That is why the literature is dominated by the burial mounds that survive on the higher ground, rather than their equivalents whose remains have been ploughed out. Like those mounds, many cursuses have been levelled, but they

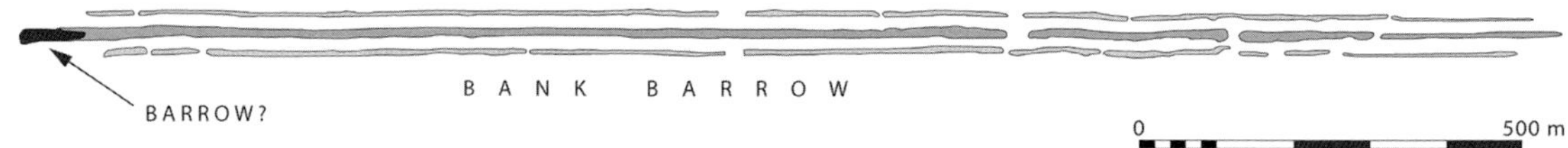

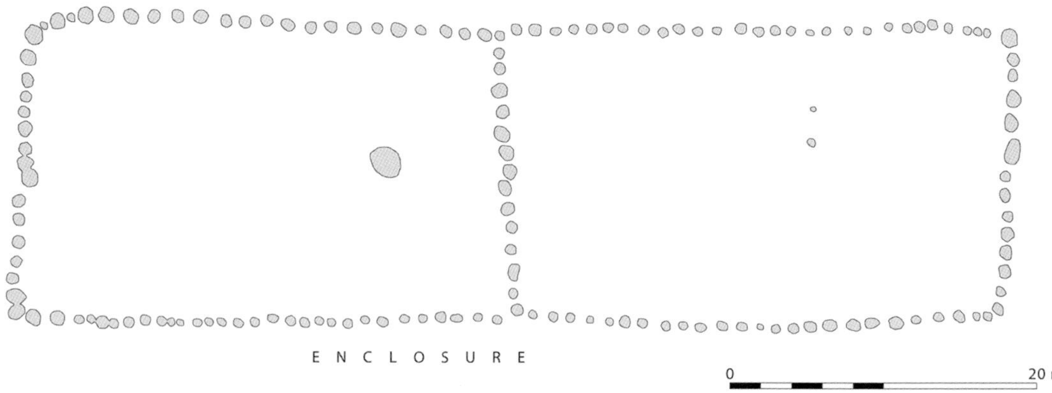

are representative of a wider pattern because they were usually in river valleys. A second reason for considering these monuments is that they were an insular development. Unlike other early enclosures, long barrows or megalithic tombs, they have no Continental counterparts.

A word on the definition of this type. To say that cursuses are elongated earthwork enclosures is an over-simplification. These monuments are long and narrow and approximate to a rectangular or oval outline, although they can show subtle changes of orientation. They resemble wide ditched roadways, but they are normally closed off at both ends. There are also a few examples with a low mound along their central spine. In fact they are occasionally interchange-able with the extended mounds known as bank barrows. The shortest cursus runs for approximately 50 m; the most imposing extends for 10 km. Nor are all these monuments represented by earthworks, for some of the earliest sites in Scotland were built of wood (Brophy 2000).

Figure 11 illustrates several of these points. It shows three early Neolithic monuments in Scotland, where some of the oldest of these monuments are found. Douglasmuir was a wooden enclosure defined by massive posts (Kendrick 1995). It was divided into two approximately equal sections. Cleaven Dyke was first built as a burial mound of conventional form, but during subsequent phases it was lengthened until it extended for 2 km (Barclay and Maxwell 1998). The mound was flanked by two wide-spaced ditches exactly like those of a cursus, and a long cairn (outside the area shown in Figure 11) was aligned upon its terminal. Auchenlaich was another enormously elongated mound, but in this case there is evidence that it contained a burial chamber (Barclay *et al.* 2002, 114–19). A monumental timber setting was found nearby at Claish (Barclay *et al.* 2002, 65–106). This resembled a much reduced version of the site at Douglasmuir. All three monuments date from the fourth millennium BC.

One might suppose that the oddity of these early structures would have commanded attention from the outset, but the first people to study them were keen to seek practical reasons for their construction. In doing so they were unconsciously importing later concerns to the past. These monuments were called cursuses because in the eighteenth century they were compared with Roman racecourses. Indeed, William Stukeley, who first recognised this phenomenon, also called them Hippodromes. They have been mistaken for the remains of Roman or later roads, and the largest of these monuments in England, the Dorset Cursus, was recorded by Sir Richard Colt Hoare as a 'British trackway'. That is not the only source of confusion. Until recently the long mound of Cleaven Dyke was interpreted as a Roman military earthwork attached to the legionary fortress at Inchtuthill. Even now I receive letters from people who have convinced themselves that these were territorial boundaries, deer fences or, for some reason, ploughed fields. In every case there seems to be a nostalgia for the farming landscapes of later periods.

FIGURE 11.
The bank barrows at Cleaven Dyke and Auchenlaich and the rectangular enclosure at Douglasmuir. After Barclay and Maxwell (1998), Barclay *et al.* (2002) and Kendrick (1995)

Figure 12 shows how mistaken such assumptions can be. It illustrates the two largest groups of cursuses in England: the Rudston complex on the Yorkshire Wolds (Stoertz 1997, 25–30), and the Dorset Cursus in Wessex (Barrett *et*

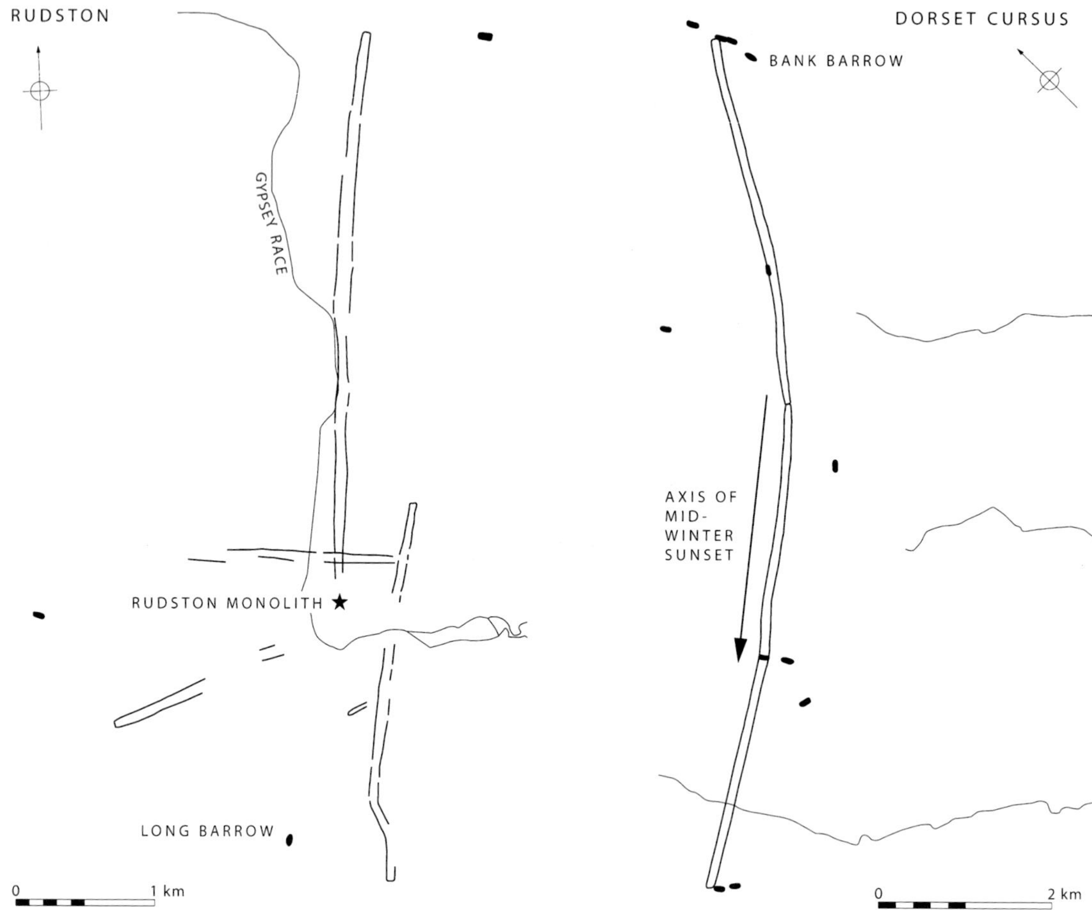

FIGURE 12.
Outline plans of the Rudston and the Dorset cursuses, showing their relationship to long barrows and watercourses. After Stoertz (1997) and Barrett *et al.* (1991)

al. 1991, 35–58). Aerial photography suggests that there may have been as many as five cursus monuments at Rudston. They vary considerably in scale, but their combined length totals no less than 10 km. Long barrows can be seen on the skyline from some of these enclosures (Chapman 2005), although it is not clear whether they were built in open country. More importantly, the terminal of the southernmost cursus was built on an enlarged scale so that it resembled a mound of this type. The main axis of these monuments followed the lie of the land and conformed quite closely to the position of a seasonal watercourse, the Gypsey Race, and the Great Wold Valley. Four of these monuments converged on the Rudston Monolith, the tallest standing stone in Britain.

The Dorset Cursus shared some of the same features. Like Cleaven Dyke, it may have grown incrementally, so that the final monument consisted of two, or possibly three, of these structures built end to end. Like the components of the Rudston complex, the earthwork extended for 10 km. In this case it ran between the headwaters of a number of streams and rivers and again it seems to have been closely integrated with the distribution of long barrows in the surrounding area. It incorporated several examples in its path and its southern terminal was built on the same scale as one of these monuments. A bank barrow was constructed at the northern end of the Dorset Cursus. The middle section of this monument was erected between 3360 and 3030 BC (Barclay and Bayliss 1999, 22–3).

There are other elements that illustrate the individual character of such monuments. The main section of the Dorset Cursus was aligned on the mid-winter sun, which set behind a long barrow in the centre of the monument (Barrett *et al.* 1991, 56). Similarly, the Stonehenge Cursus faced the equinoctial sunrise (Burl 1987, 44) and that at Dorchester on Thames pointed towards the rising sun at midwinter (Bradley and Chambers 1988). Such earthworks did not lead to settlement sites, but a number of examples did run between burial mounds of the same period. Figure 13 illustrates a recently excavated example at Eynesbury in East Anglia, where a typical cursus is associated with two of these sites (Ellis 2004). Cursuses are not associated with large collections of artefacts of the kind found on living sites, but occasionally they do produce finds of human bone. The largest structures consumed enormous amounts of human labour. It took half a million worker hours to create the Dorset Cursus (Barrett *et al.* 1991, 45–6).

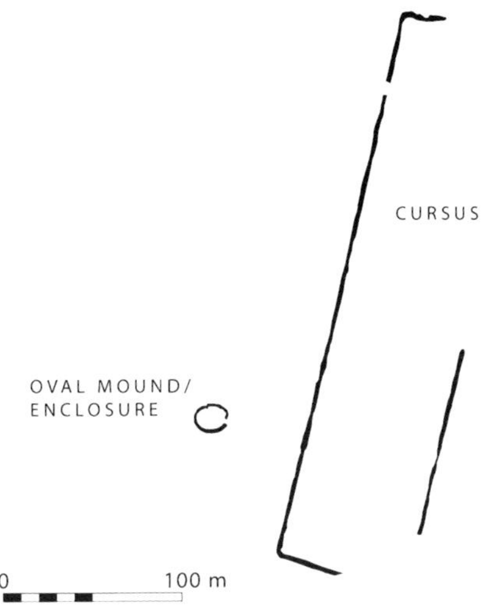

FIGURE 13. Cursus and two Neolithic mortuary monuments at Eynesbury. After Ellis (2004)

It has become the conventional wisdom that these were like the avenues attached to later monuments such as Avebury and Stonehenge – processional ways leading between significant points in the landscape (Burl 1993, chapter 5). But even this approach encounters problems. Individual cursuses were constructed in stages, and some examples cut across one another. If they were processional ways, it is hard to apply the same idea to the bank barrows which took the form of raised mounds. Moreover, cursus monuments have very few entrances and most of them are blocked at both ends. Of course, this could have happened when they went out of use, but there is nothing to show that this occurred. In many ways they were entirely cut off from the world around them. Given their association with mortuary monuments and human remains, they may have been populated by the dead rather than the living.

At the same time they were related to the local topography in a significant way, and for that reason they sometimes provided the axis around which the ancient landscape was organised. It was once supposed that prehistoric monuments were on hills. Aerial photography has shown that this was wrong, but cursuses and bank barrows do sometimes run across valleys, so that their terminals command a continuous view over the lower ground. That is clearly illustrated by the Dorset Cursus and by most of the monuments at Rudston. More often they are laid out so that they run parallel to a nearby stream or river. The layout of these monuments reflects the structure of the local terrain, but also gives it greater emphasis. There may be a link between these natural and cultural elements, for the layout of most of these monuments seems to presuppose some kind of movement from one end to the other. At times a cursus monument is aligned on a specific feature, usually a mound, an enclosure or an area of higher ground, and this suggests both a starting point and a destination.

Figure 14 illustrates this pattern. It shows two monuments in lowland England and one in Scotland which share the same basic features. At Dorchester on Thames the cursus followed an existing alignment of monuments and incorporated a small enclosure at one end (Bradley and Chambers 1988; Whittle *et al.* 1992). This seems to have been the destination of the monument, as its earthwork followed the axis of the midwinter sunrise. This monument was probably built between 3380 and 2920 BC (Barclay and Bayliss 1999, 22). A very similar pattern has been identified at Brampton, where the cursus runs up to an oval structure which may have been a burial mound (Malim 1999). The Scottish monument at Balneaves illustrates the same relationship, but in this case the entire monument may have been built of wood (Brophy 2000). The enclosure in its terminal is rather like the site at Douglasmuir (Figure 11).

In some cases people would also have travelled in the same direction as the water in a nearby river (Brophy 2000); in that sense they would have been moving 'downstream'. The link between the earthwork and the water might have been metaphorical, but it is difficult to suggest what it meant. What matters here is that these earthworks became the dominant elements in the

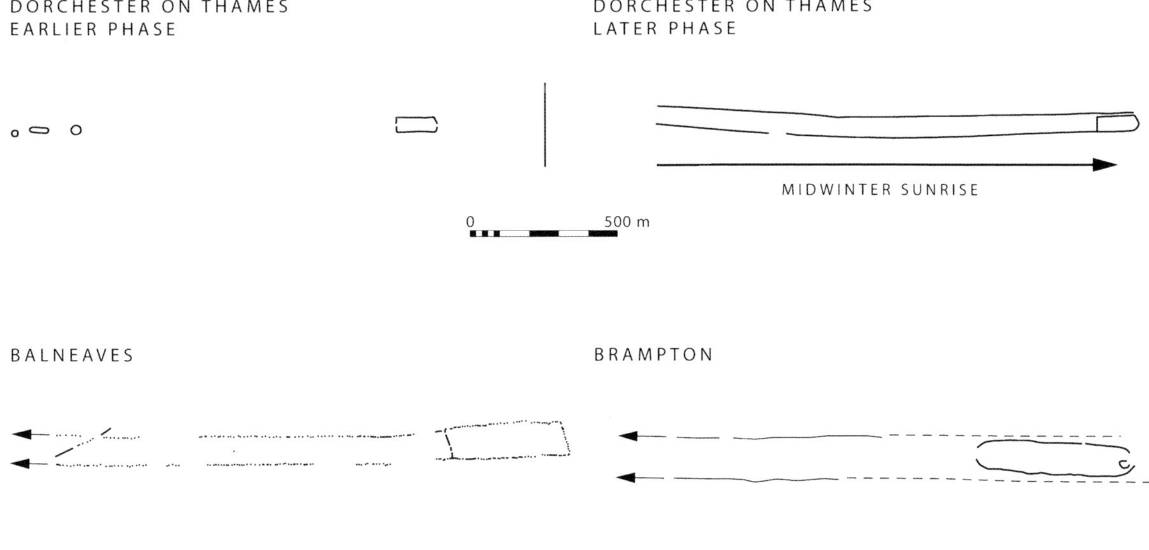

FIGURE 14. Outline plans of three cursus monuments and the enclosures associated with their terminals. The plan of Dorchester on Thames summarises its sequence of construction. The arrows indicate that a cursus is known to extend beyond the area illustrated here. After Bradley and Chambers (1988), Brophy (2000) and Malim (1999)

local landscape. They emphasised the importance of natural features such as watercourses and valleys but they supplemented them with an artificial design that incorporated a variety of smaller monuments. That design was to prove extraordinarily long-lived.

It is important to work out how the construction of these earthworks would have affected human experience. Their construction must have influenced conceptions of time and space. Time is relevant because certain of these monuments, admittedly a small minority, were aligned on specific astronomical events which punctuated the course of the year. The sun was very important and there is no convincing evidence of lunar orientations. If the cursuses occasionally acknowledged such events, the long mounds with which they were associated were generally directed towards the sunrise.

Space is even more important. The longer cursuses divide up the ancient landscape and provide it with a dominant axis. This may been influenced by the course of a nearby river, but that is not always true. At the same time, their construction also created an obstacle to free movement across the terrain. The Dorset Cursus, for instance, divided the fertile lowlands from a major source of raw materials, and this distinction is shown clearly by the distribution of Neolithic surface finds. Beside the monument was a series of settlements, some of them containing objects of exceptional quality (Barrett *et al.* 1991, chapters 2 and 3) Beyond it occupation sites were located at important flint sources and the inhabitants engaged in artefact production. Something similar seems to have happened with the Rudston Cursus complex (Pierpoint 1980, 271–7; Durden 1995).

Such earthworks stamped a new identity on their immediate surroundings and, while they were often aligned on mortuary monuments, there are other cases in which they cut across an older enclosure as if to put it out of use.

This pattern is illustrated in Figure 15. At Fornham All Saints, a site which is known from aerial photography, it seems as if two curvilinear enclosures had been built side by side (Oswald *et al.* 2001, 135). Each of them was defined by discontinuous ditches. These monuments were built in sequence, but both belong to a tradition of earthwork building that was established in the second quarter of the fourth millennium BC. They were cut by a cursus monument which ran parallel to a nearby river. It was one of a pair following that alignment, whilst a third example crossed it at right angles, as if to approach the river bank. At Etton a similar enclosure was bisected by another cursus which seems to have followed the edge of a river channel, whilst a second example adopted almost the same axis and ended beside the older monument (Oswald *et al.* 2001, 134–5).

The same pattern is illustrated by the construction of the bank barrow at Maiden Castle. In this case it seems as if a long barrow had been built just outside an enclosure (Sharples 1991, 253–7). Both monuments may have been in use together, but when the enclosure went out of use parts of its earthwork were levelled and the burial mound was extended at both ends. In one direction it followed the summit of a chalk ridge and, in the other, it crossed the site of the older earthwork. Although such monuments acknowledged the positions of their predecessors, their construction may have signified a fresh beginning. In each case linear monuments cut across a pattern of circular

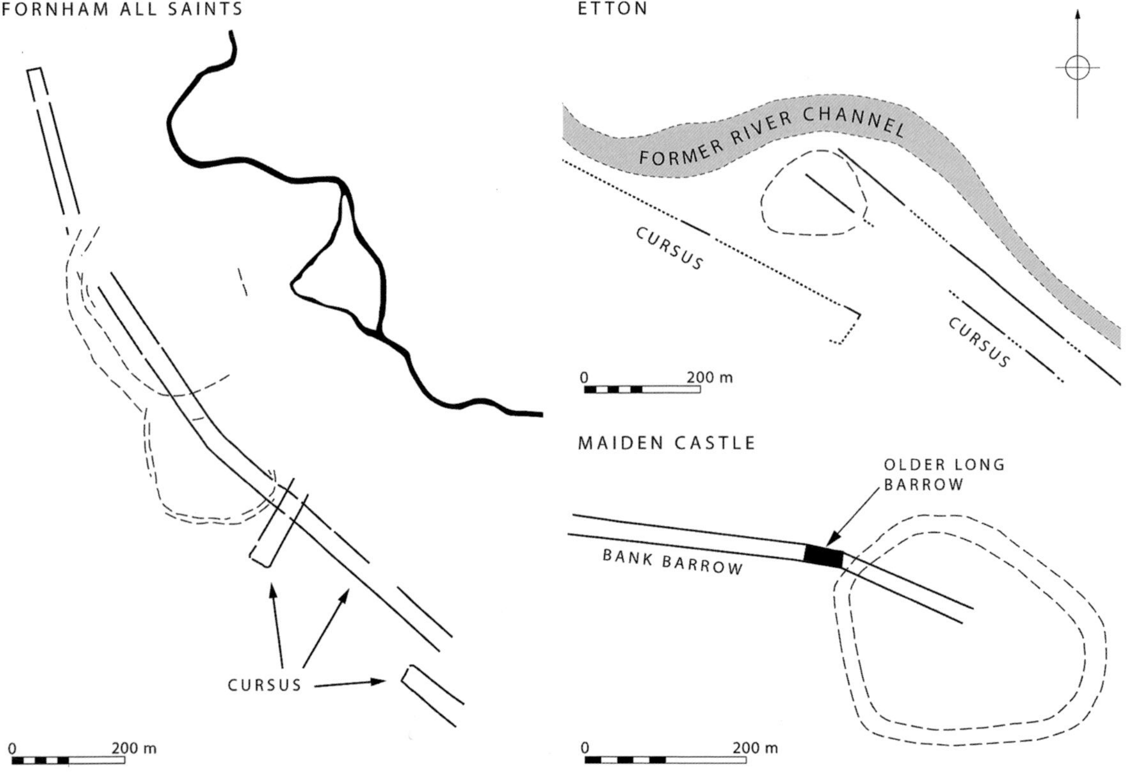

enclosures and seem to have imposed a new conception of space on the prehistoric landscape.

This is seen in many different ways, and what is especially striking is how the presence of these monuments seems to have influenced the organisation of human activity for nearly 1,500 years after they were built. There is a paradox here, for these monuments were normally respected, yet their ditches and banks were seldom renewed. Rather, deposits of artefacts, food remains and sometimes human bones were made in and around what were becoming ancient monuments in their own right.

That process applied to the construction of other forms of monument. These often occupy the sites of cursuses, although by that stage those ancient earthworks would not have been such prominent features of the terrain. It seems possible that their remains could be identified because they had been colonised by vegetation. A whole variety of small enclosures or burial mounds were constructed in and around the sites of some of the cursuses. Where the newly built monuments had one clearly-defined entrance, it normally echoed the long axis of the older monument (Bradley and Chambers 1988). Even where larger enclosures were built, including the massive constructions known as henges, the new monument often acknowledged the position of its predecessor. Thus henges were built beside a number of examples, including the Dorset Cursus and those at Rudston and Dorchester on Thames, whilst at Thornborough in north-east England a monument of similar type was built over an older cursus (Harding 2000).

FIGURE 15. The relationship between cursuses, causewayed enclosures and bank barrows. At Fornham All Saints a major cursus cut across the sites of two enclosures, and smaller monuments were built nearby. At Etton two cursuses were constructed running parallel to one another; one of them bisected an earlier causewayed enclosure. At Maiden Castle a long barrow was built just outside a similar enclosure. In a subsequent phase it was lengthened at both ends. The resulting 'bank barrow' cut across the remains of the older earthwork.

In other cases the relationship between these features is perhaps more subtle. The monoliths of Stonehenge are visible from one short section of the nearby cursus, but they can also be seen from both its terminals. On the other hand, one of the major groups of Early Bronze Age round barrows, the aptly-named Cursus Barrows, is laid out parallel to that earthwork (Richards 1990, 271–5). The same relationship is apparent from excavation on the Dorset Cursus, where a row of cremation burials without any covering mound was located just outside the existing monument (Barrett *et al.* 1991, 128–32). Again, it echoed its alignment.

Other features might be associated with cursuses. At Dorchester on Thames, for instance, there was not only a major henge, but also a series of free-standing timber circles which were built several centuries after the original construction (Bradley and Chambers 1988; Whittle *et al.* 1992). Where they have a clearly identified alignment, it followed that of the older monument. Similarly, round barrows often clustered around the terminals of these monuments. Even though the prevailing tradition favoured the building of other structures, the linear configuration of the cursus still had a lasting influence.

When did that come to an end? The disuse of cursus monuments is just as revealing as their first creation. It happened from approximately 1500 BC and forms part of a much wider phenomenon which is described in David Yates's contribution. There were two main possibilities. The remains of Neolithic cursuses, their earthworks much reduced by erosion, could be disregarded as the landscape was reorganised around a network of fields. That is what occurred at Dorchester on Thames during the Middle Bronze Age, where a newly created field system cut across the remains of the cursus at an angle (Bradley and Chambers 1988; Whittle *et al.* 1992). The alternative scenario is the reuse of the Neolithic earthworks as field boundaries, even, perhaps, providing the baseline for a network of land divisions. That seems to have happened to two of the best-known monuments, the Dorset Cursus and the Stonehenge Cursus, and in both cases their remains came under the plough (Barrett *et al.* 1991, 186; Richards 1990, 275–80). In the case of the Dorset Cursus cultivation impinged on the site of a nearby cemetery and disturbed some of the deposits only a few generations after they had been made.

In other instances the remains of cursus monuments were reused in the network of linear ditches that characterised the Later Bronze Age and Iron Age landscape. The five cursuses that make up the Rudston complex illustrate this relationship, for individual sections of these earthworks were incorporated in a later prehistoric boundary system, whilst others were integrated with enclosures and fields. The smallest of these monuments was obliterated altogether (Stoertz 1997, 73). The Dorset Cursus has a similar history and at its southern limit it was extended to form a major land division (RCHME 1975, 24–5).

Conclusion

This paper has discussed the process that Seamus Heaney calls 'Making strange'. Archaeologists should accept that the earliest prehistoric landscapes may have expressed quite different concerns from those which are familiar today. Cursus monuments are real structures that were built at a particular time and structured the landscape in a particular way, and yet they bear a disquieting resemblance to the wholly imaginary features that are described as ley lines (Williamson and Bellamy 1983). In this they pose a challenge to contemporary ways of thinking about landscapes and their making. They were built by farmers who produced their food according to techniques that became established across the *longue durée*, and yet they lack the seeming familiarity of the fields and boundaries, settlements and roads that Hoskins knew so well. The same is true of other earlier prehistoric monuments, and landscape archaeologists have still to devise appropriate ways of coming to terms with their histories.

Acknowledgements

I must thank Andrew Fleming for presenting the original paper when I was prevented from attending the Leicester conference. Thanks are also due to Aaron Watson for the illustrations.

CHAPTER FOUR

Geophysical Survey and the Emergence of Underground Archaeological Landscapes: The Heart of Neolithic Orkney World Heritage Site

Nick Card, John Gater, Chris Gaffney and Emma Wood

> The student of the English Landscape faces at times the possibility of underground evidence; though in this book I have striven to analyse what can be seen on the surface today as an end in itself. The visible landscape offers us enough stimulus and pleasure without the uncertainty of what might lie underneath.
>
> (Hoskins 1975, Introduction)

In this paper we will be entering Hoskins's 'uncertain world' and delving into a buried landscape which until recently had remained invisible to the human eye. We will consider the role of archaeological geophysics in identifying and mapping buried archaeological remains. In particular, we will be looking at a region outside Hoskins's England, the landscape associated with the Heart of Neolithic Orkney World Heritage Site (WHS). This is an archaeologically rich landscape, dominated by some of the most remarkable upstanding monuments surviving in Western Europe.

Historical perspective

Back in 1958, only three years after the publication of *The Making of the English Landscape*, Martin Aitken, doyen of archaeological geophysics, writing in the first volume of *Archaeometry*, reported on the successful use of a magnetometer to detect not only kilns, the initial target, but also other features of archaeological interest:

> the value of magnetic surveying in locating whatever archaeological remains are buried in an unknown region can be gauged from the experience

> that in one field 20 random trial holes all proved blank whereas 4 holes dug on magnetic anomalies revealed archaeological features in 2 cases, a geological feature in the third and a horseshoe in the fourth. (Aitken 1958, 25)

At the time of Hoskins's first edition, the concept of landscape investigation using geophysical techniques was a long way off. In fact, it was not until the 1980s that geophysics started to take on this role (see Gaffney and Gater 2003, 20–4). The organisation of the first major British conference on the subject, entitled 'Geoprospection in the Archaeological Landscape' and held in the late 80s, was an attempt to combat the use of geophysical techniques in the restricted role of following walls (Spoerry 1992). In the ensuing publication, Aston argued for the introduction of 'remote sensing' into landscape studies in general and the then nascent Shapwick Project (Somerset) in particular. He expressed the archaeological need for geophysical survey at the landscape level (Aston 1992, 147). Frankly, at that time this was a forlorn hope; the use of geophysics on large-scale projects was limited, and it was very rare for these techniques to be fully integrated within the research methodologies of individual projects. The end product for the Shapwick Project was an inevitable compromise based around need and economic reality (Gaffney and Shiel in press). At this time there were problems associated with the available technology which, although reliable, did not lend itself to the collection of the large data sets required for landscape studies. However, large-scale archaeological field survey projects had been common in the previous decade, when geophysical techniques were increasingly used to investigate small-scale artefact scatters, for example at Maddle Farm, Berkshire (Gaffney and Gaffney 1986). For university archaeologists studying in countries where permits were required for *any* archaeological fieldwork, geophysical techniques were attractive in that they were favoured by the local archaeological authorities because they did not involve excavation; academics liked the fact that they often obtained significant results quickly and at great speed or reduced cost. Sarris and Jones (2000) have charted the widespread use of survey work from this period in Mediterranean countries, and the techniques then available. It is interesting that few, if any, of the large-scale 'regional' surveys common in the 1980s have really produced geophysical evidence at that scale. This is probably because many of the regional field survey projects described in the Sarris and Jones review integrated geophysics *after* the start of fieldwork; the non-invasive component was often tagged onto the research design and appears piecemeal in its use.

Similar criticism may be levelled at the survey work reported in another important paper by David and Payne (1997), in which they chart geophysical work by many different groups in and around the World Heritage Site at Stonehenge. Here, much of the research-led work has been concerned with the study of individual monuments, while more recent work has investigated large swathes of landscape within a developer-led framework. In particular, several potential routes have been surveyed in advance of proposed new road construction, and potential sites for new visitor facilities have been investigated. As David and Payne point out, there has been no integrated approach to this survey work; their success in summarising the results of the individual surveys is a major achievement. They also present proposals that they believe should be considered in any programme of future geophysical survey at Stonehenge and within the landscape of the WHS. As they rightly state, any future investigation should be 'not just of the grander monuments and their groupings and alignments, but of the provocatively empty spaces between'. It is the ability speedily to transform apparent data lacunae into data-rich landscapes that makes non-invasive techniques so important in areas that are archaeologically sensitive.

This large-scale but piecemeal approach spawned an increasing confidence in both the robustness of the techniques and the interpretability of data; by the end of the twentieth century, markers for non-invasive investigation had been put down in many aspects of fieldwork. In landscape studies, where geophysical techniques had reduced the 'need' for intrusive excavation, a bandwagon had been formed where the use of geophysical techniques often went unchallenged.

Projects are now emerging where archaeological geophysics is firmly embedded in the research strategy. Of particular note is the work by Powlesland and colleagues at Heslerton, North Yorkshire (http://www.landscaperesearchcentre.org) and the South Cadbury Environs Project, Somerset (Tabor 2002). The latter is particularly important in this context. The project, which is attempting to produce chronological maps of former land division in the landscape that surrounds the Iron Age hillfort of Cadbury Castle, is committed to the use of geophysical survey as its main tool, coupled with ploughzone sampling techniques. Despite having obtained long-term funding, this project is still sampling – rather than surveying in its entirety – an admittedly very extensive landscape.

However, in principle a fully formulated research project is much more flexible than, for example, the developer-funded lottery that characterises the analysis of the Stonehenge WHS. The Heslerton project is of interest for its use of geophysical techniques to locate the archaeology of the post-Roman period, which is often difficult to find, let alone map. This has been achieved mainly by large-scale survey that can discriminate even small sites within a landscape survey. As it happens, the Heslerton project has revealed a landscape with considerable time depth. While the inability to define individual phases or periods of a multi-period landscape using geophysical techniques alone may be seen as a drawback, the structured archaeological approach and a fundamental knowledge of the present-day landscape has circumvented this problem. At Heslerton the features which constitute the buried landscape are complex, numerous, diverse and evidently multi-period. In short, this is a landscape that can only be *delineated* by non-invasive means; it requires traditional archaeological endeavours to understand the detail.

Only a few years into the twenty-first century, we can appreciate that the role of archaeological geophysics in landscape studies has entered a new era. Surveys have become larger, more efficient and better integrated within mature landscape studies. It was at this stage in the history of our discipline that our work on the Orkney WHS began.

Orkney World Heritage Site

The Heart of Neolithic Orkney was inscribed by the United Nations Educational, Scientific and Cultural Organisation (UNESCO) as a World Heritage Site in 1999. The title applies to six discrete sites in West Mainland: the chambered tomb of Maes Howe; the stone circle and henge at Stones of Stenness; nearby stone settings known as the Watch Stone and the Barnhouse Stone; the stone circle, adjacent standing stone and burial mounds at the Ring of Brodgar; and the settlement of Skara Brae. Excluding the last-named site, an area of over 200 ha, referred to as the *inner buffer zone*, incorporates the monuments and their immediate landscape. Although the actual WHS has been documented, many of the surrounding monuments and much of the landscape in which they lie have not.

The recently published Research Agenda (Downes *et al.* 2005) aspires to an improved understanding of the WHS and its setting. The most recent archaeological geophysical survey has been carried out within the aims of this agenda, which has been set out in detail (Downes *et al.* 2005, 22).

The aim of the ongoing geophysical mapping project is to survey an extensive area of the landscape, providing detailed information about individual sites, to enhance our knowledge of their setting within the wider landscape and to determine the nature and extent of previously unknown sites. The Orkney landscape is largely flat and treeless and fortunately under little development pressure. While geophysical techniques are clearly on the agenda, research in the WHS must be largely driven by academic rather than commercial considerations (see discussion of Stonehenge WHS, below).

Before this project started, geophysical survey here had been somewhat sporadic. Early investigations (in the 1970s) were performed by the late Tony Clark and other members of the Ancient Monuments Laboratory at English Heritage (e.g. Clark 1973; Bartlett and Clark 1973). Bradford University had also carried out pioneering surveys in the wider WHS landscape, led initially by Arnold Aspinall. However, being largely experimental in nature, few of these surveys were published, except as footnotes or occasional images: for example, the survey at the Stones of Stenness (in Clark 1996; Ritchie 1976). This site was resurveyed in the 1990s (GSB Prospection 1999), but none of the other main monuments had been investigated geophysically in recent times. While extensive resistance survey was carried out in the vicinity of the Barnhouse settlement near Stenness (Richards 2005), the location or extent of other surveys in the inner buffer zone has not been fully recorded. It is important to stress that these surveys were all very site-specific. We learnt that magnetic survey had become predominant in Orkney, producing numerous good surveys, including 'classic' responses such as those obtained by Clark at the Stones of Stenness.

A comparison with the WHS of Stonehenge indicates that the English example has had considerably more archaeological geophysics carried out within its boundary. However, as stated earlier, the majority of the geophysical work here is the result of developer-led funding undertaken in the last ten years, especially in advance of the upgrading of the A303 trunk road. Stonehenge itself was not surveyed until 1993, a full twenty years after Clark and Bartlett (two surveyors employed at the Ancient Monuments Laboratory) surveyed the Stones of Stenness. David and Payne (1997), commenting on the level of geophysical work in the area around Stonehenge, stated: 'our assumption is that the entire surveyable area should be covered in as much detail ... but it is necessary to be more selective' (David and Payne 1997, 107). Given the largely favourable geological and pedological conditions on Orkney, there is no reason why total coverage should not be the ultimate goal, if political support remains strong.

In fact, there are many strategies that can be used to investigate large areas with magnetic techniques. They have been discussed in detail elsewhere (Gaffney and Gater 2003, 88–101), and include: rapid assessment by volume Magnetic Susceptibility (followed by detailed Fluxgate Gradiometry (FG)); random or semi-random sampling, using detailed survey (variable percentage); systematic sampling, using detailed survey blocks or transect (variable percentage); rapid assessment ('scan') by FG (followed by FG detailed); and 100 per cent detailed survey.

There is an implied confidence within this structure, which progressively increases down the list; however, there are many reasons why this impression may be deceptive. What is important is that the strategy in the Orkney WHS is firmly encompassed by the description 'detailed survey'; that is, all areas that are investigated should use a consistent methodology of regular, close-spaced measurements over the survey area, without recourse to sampling. It is considered neither practical nor financially possible to consider 100 per cent survey of the WHS, at least not in the immediate future. However, for the Orkney WHS it was decided at the outset that detailed survey should be adopted, with the ultimate aim of investigating all areas in their entirety as funds and permission become available.

Technological advances in instrumentation since Clark's work in 1973 have made this strategy feasible. The advent of Geoscan Research's FM series of instruments produced the first commercial instruments that enabled large-scale surveys to become commonplace, and in the late 1990s many strategies and innovations were tested to speed up data collection. The most successful British approach has been to collect two adjacent data traverses simultaneously; this reduces collection time dramatically. Throughout the lifetime of the project, magnetic measurements were collected using different types of fluxgate gradiometer instruments: Geoscan Research's FM36 0.5m separation instruments were used in the first few sessions, followed by Bartington Grad601–2.

Invariably the survey area was set out and tied in using an EDM. The grid was subdivided into 20 x 20 m grids for convenient data capture. The grids were walked along grid east–west; traverses were spaced 1.0 m apart and data was collected at 0.25-m intervals along each traverse. Subsequent data processing and reporting followed accepted standards and will not be discussed in detail here (see Gaffney and Gater 2003).

Results

To date six stages of geophysical survey covering nearly 125 ha have been undertaken by GSB Prospection Ltd (GSB) and Orkney College Geophysics Unit (OCGU). Here the results from the surveys will be discussed by location, rather than period, starting in the north-west of the inner buffer zone and extending south-eastwards to Maes Howe (Figure 16).

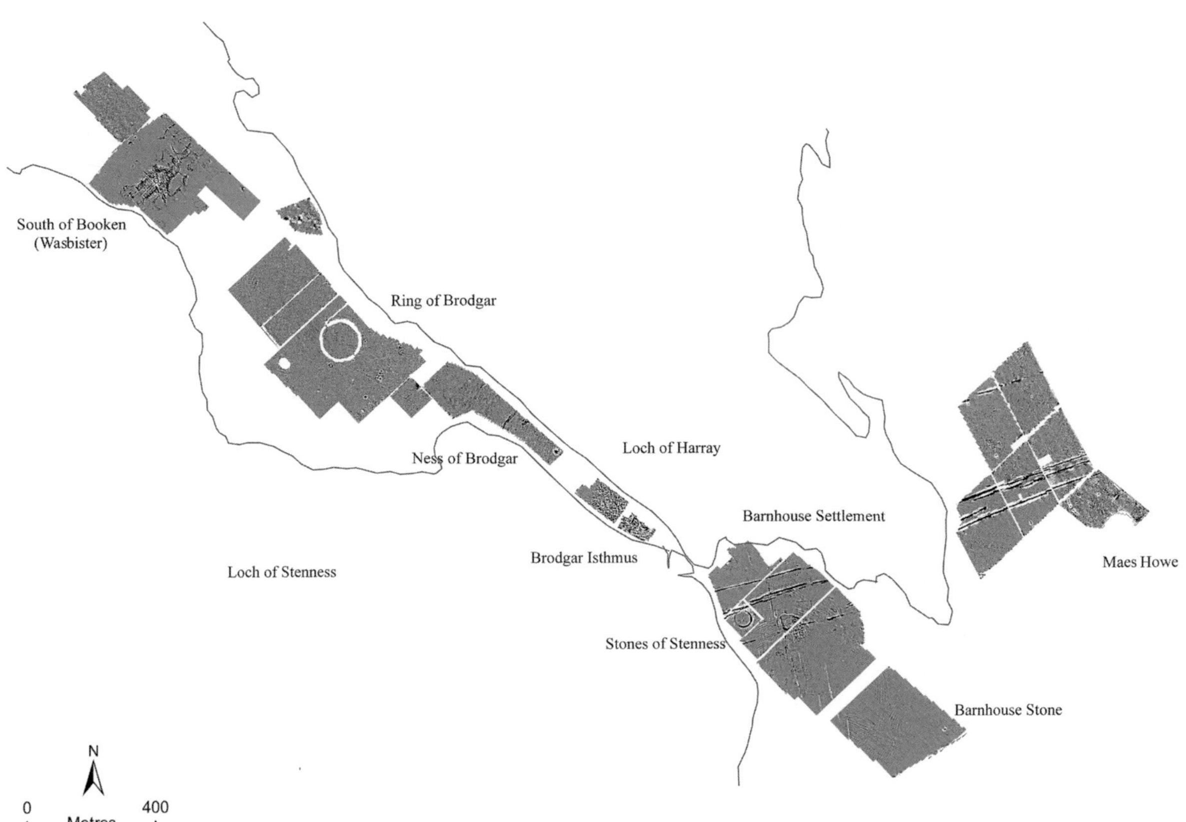

FIGURE 16. The Orkney World Heritage Site.

Wasbister Area

A major settlement site of around 4 ha in extent has been detected at Wasbister (Figure 17). The strong anomalies associated with an area of dense occupation are thought to represent an accumulation of midden, burnt structures, building remains and debris. The limits of the site to the north, south and west have been determined, but it is thought that occupation features might extend eastward to the shore of Loch of Harray. A pattern of discrete anomalies has been identified; a direct relationship between this and existing monuments is suggested. A Bronze Age 'house' (which survives as an earthwork) has produced magnetically strong and clear anomalies at the centre of the occupation area and a similar but smaller group of structures may have been located some 70 m to the east. A number of lesser buildings may have also been identified, with the suggestion of a complex arrangement of 'cells' forming larger structures. The interpretation of these anomalies is speculative; the data are complex and far from clear. They suggest the presence of buildings accompanying the Bronze Age 'house'. Two further magnetic responses have

FIGURE 17.
The Wasbister Area.

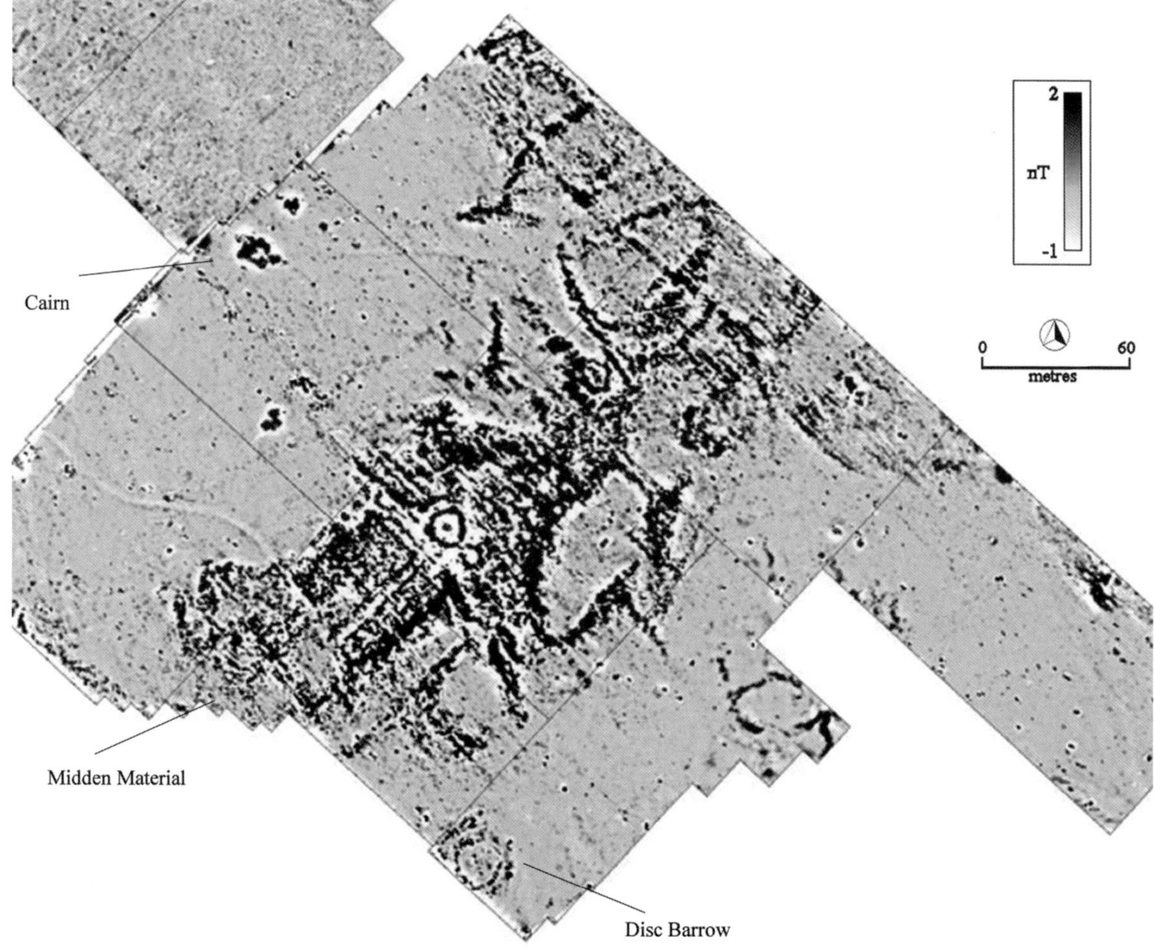

been identified that relate to structures already recorded on Ordnance Survey maps and the National Monuments Record Scotland – a disc barrow that has indications of revetted walls as well as embankments, and a cairn. The data suggest that small cells might be present within this structure. In the east, linear responses are thought to represent collapsed walls or revetments. Survey has also confirmed that a small grass-covered mound recorded in the NMRS is unlikely to be a burnt mound (a mound of burnt stones often associated with an early cooking site), since there is no magnetic signature.

Ring of Brodgar

The survey at the Ring of Brodgar (Figure 18) identified an absence of the magnetic enhancement which might normally be expected on a ceremonial and funerary site. Except for possible pits or areas of burning, there are few anomalies of interest within the henge, and no other indications of activity. Similar results were obtained in the immediate vicinity of the henge, where, apart from anomalies associated with the cairns surrounding the monument and also with the Comet Stone, there is a general lack of magnetic enhancement.

Gradiometer survey of two fields lying to the south of the Ring of Brodgar towards the shore of Loch of Stenness has, on the whole, also produced a low level of magnetic response, which is consistent with results from surveys around the Ring of Brodgar. However, a concentration of responses which

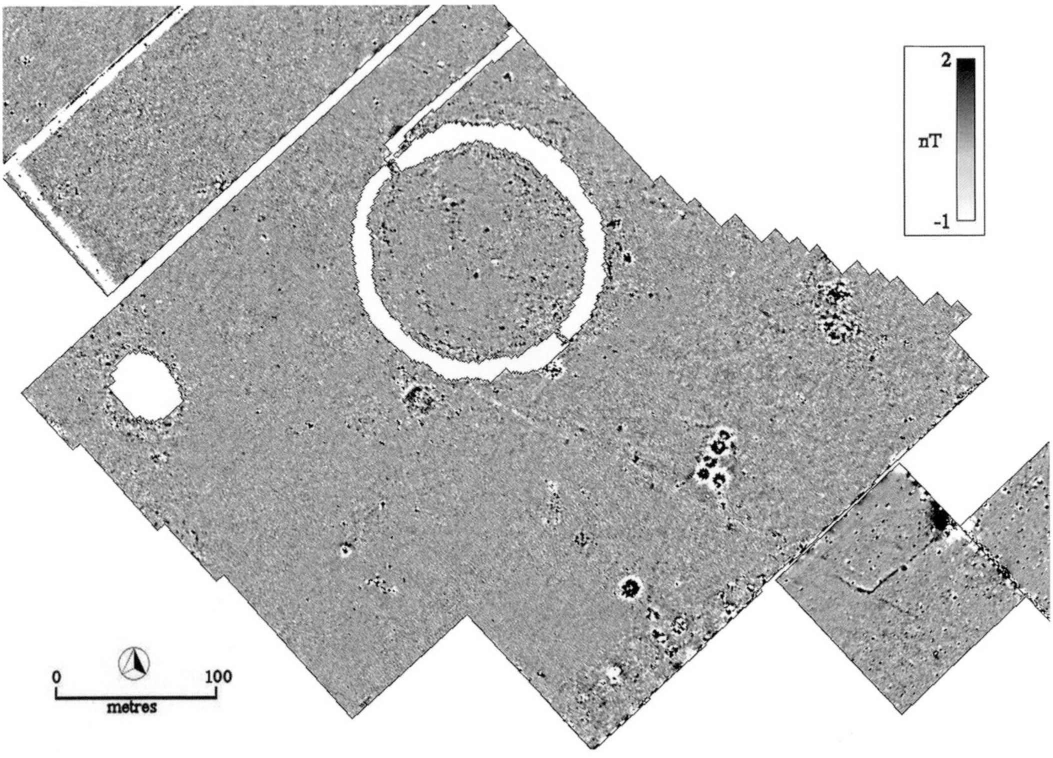

FIGURE 18.
The Ring of Brodgar.

may be archeologically significant has been recorded leading to the shore of Loch of Stenness; these include responses that may represent burnt mounds and associated features. Although the responses on the peninsula are diffuse in nature, it is a promising location for the discovery of archaeological sites.

Ness of Brodgar

Survey of the isthmus of land between the Ring of Brodgar and the Stones of Stenness produced a range of gradiometer results (Figure 19). To the north, a low level of magnetic response was observed, as at the Ring of Brodgar. However, the remains of two burnt mounds or possible ploughed-out barrows have been detected on the eastern side of the peninsula.

Survey at the southern end of the isthmus over a large mound has located a dense complex of archaeological features. Trial excavations (Ballin Smith 2003; Card 2004; Card and Cluett 2005) showed that the dense concentration of features revealed by geophysical survey was only the tip of the iceberg. The preliminary results appear to indicate that much of this substantial mound is artificial, comprising structures, middens and deep midden-enhanced soils dating to the Neolithic. In one trench part of a previously unrecorded

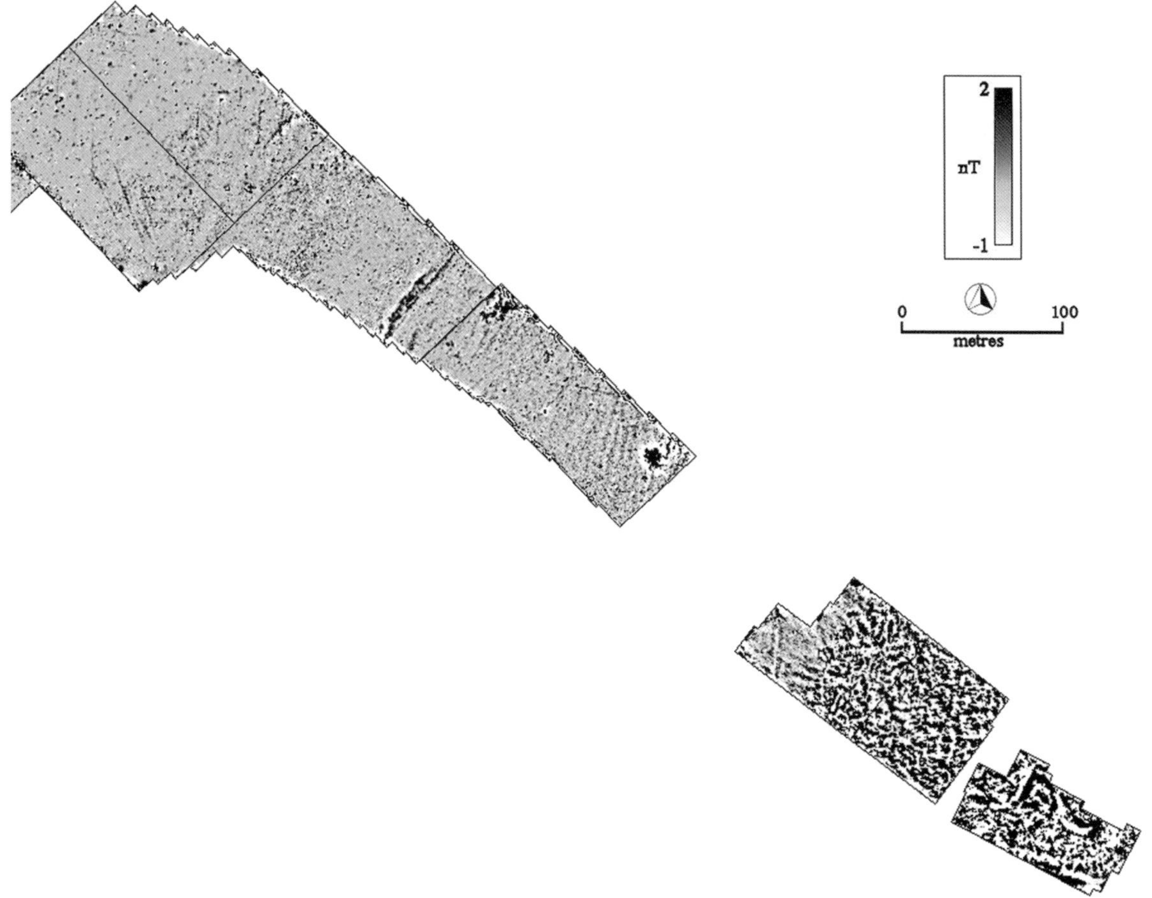

FIGURE 19.
The Ness of Brodgar.

chambered cairn was revealed. The settlement revealed by the geophysics is very extensive, being *c.*240 m long.

Several isolated anomalies of interest were encountered on the isthmus; these might represent isolated cist burials or the footings of former standing stones. Sadly, there are no indications of an avenue or formal layout of features suggesting a link between the Ring of Brodgar and the Stones of Stenness.

Stenness

To the north of the Stones of Stenness, a cluster of responses recorded immediately to the south of Odin Cottage appears to be part of a possible settlement site (Figure 20). Recent study by Richards (2005) discovered flint scatters, burnt soil and a hearth considered to be associated with specialised activity in this area. There are no indications in the magnetic data that occupation activity extends westwards from the Barnhouse Neolithic settlement discovered by Richards in 1984 (Richards 2005). However, groups of strong anomalies suggest that occupation does extend to the south along the shore of Loch Harray, supporting the view put forward by Richards.

The survey at Stenness provided some of the most dramatic results. The data are dominated by strong linear anomalies, both magnetically positive and negative, that often produce responses in excess of +/- 100nT. At first glance they appear to indicate some major division of the landscape. However, the nature and strength of the anomalies indicate that they are geological in origin, corresponding to a series of igneous dykes. These may be seen to extend across the landscape to Maes Howe.

To the east of the Stones of Stenness is the most notable evidence for Iron Age activity within the WHS – a probable broch, Big Howe. Survey of this conspicuous mound recorded responses indicating a probable interior bank/ditch *c.*40 m in diameter enclosed within a larger 'light-bulb-shaped' bank/ditch. The elongated and squared-off northern end suggests a defended entrance like those recorded at other broch sites. The interior produced a very strong level of magnetic response, suggesting midden heaps and hearths. The exact position of the broch itself is unclear, but it is noticeable that the strongest magnetic activity within the enclosure lies on the southern side, furthest from the postulated entrance. Very strong responses to the south may relate to magnetically enhanced debris strewn over the downward slope. This may represent excavation debris and/or plough damage.

In Stenness a complex of anomalies of archaeological interest was revealed that highlight a contrast with the nature of ancient land use suggested around the Ring of Brodgar. The gradiometer survey recorded strong magnetic responses associated with the supposed broch site of Big Howe, additional anomalies suggesting that the Barnhouse settlement extends further south, and other magnetic responses suggesting occupation features to the north of the Stones of Stenness. To the south of Big Howe, the results mostly reflect the old field systems indicated on mid-nineteenth-century maps (Thomas 1852), and presumed medieval ploughing.

FIGURE 20.
Stenness.

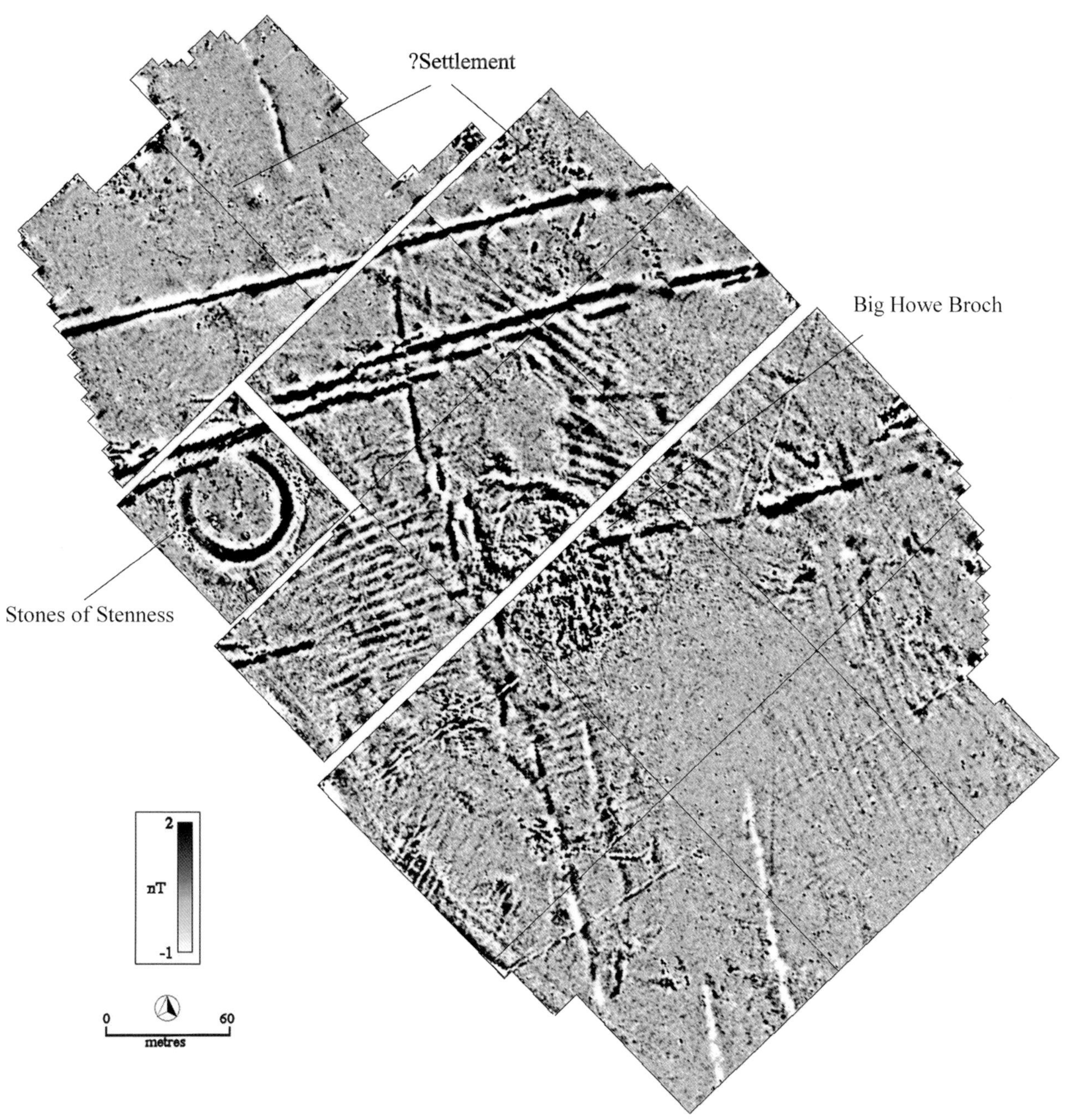

The survey around the isolated Barnhouse Stone, to the south-east of the Stones of Stenness, provides no indication that it represents part of a larger and more complex monument (Figure 21). The stone appears, then, to be an isolated megalith. The data from the area are dominated by responses associated with old field systems and medieval ploughing. There are a few

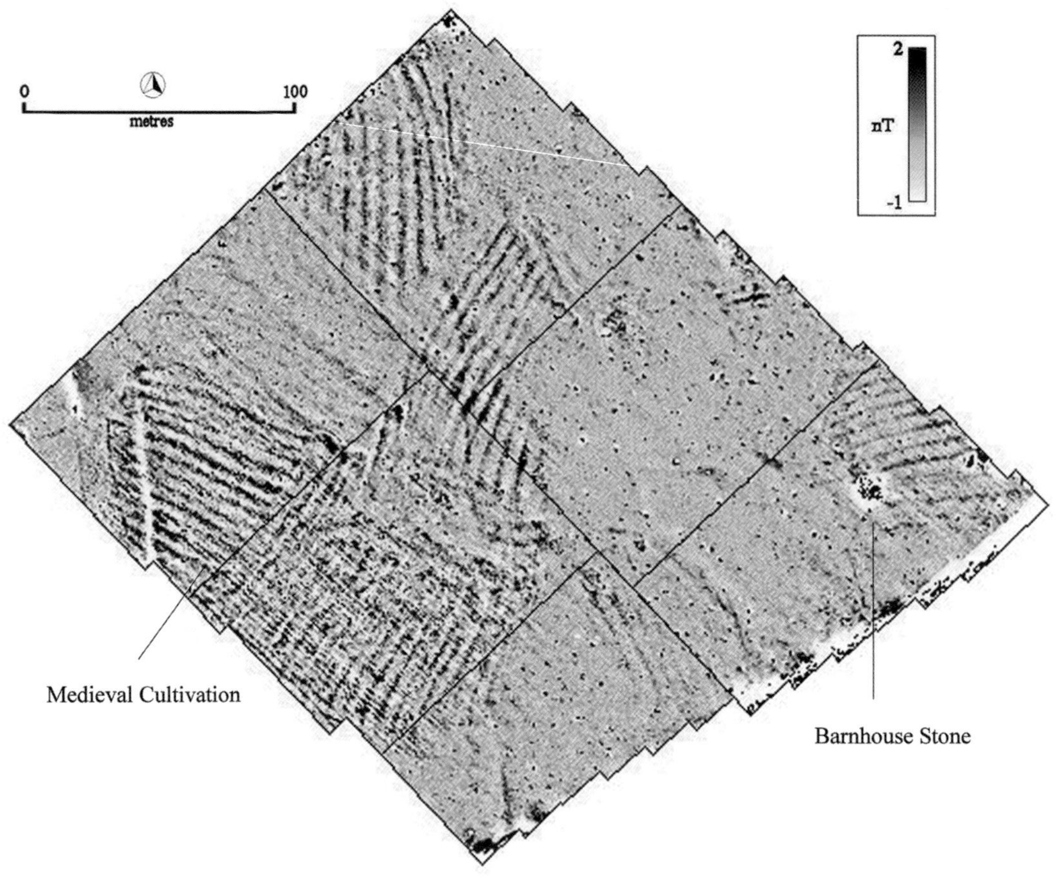

FIGURE 21.
Around the Barnhouse Stone.

anomalies suggesting ditches or perhaps trackways, and hints of possible plough-damaged deposits perhaps associated with former settlement.

Maes Howe

Extensive survey work has been conducted to the north and south of Maes Howe and westward to the shores of the Loch of Harray (Figure 22). The courses of igneous dykes have been traced and can be seen to be continuations of those recorded at Stenness. An enclosure, recorded as a cropmark, has been detected to the north, though it is barely visible above background noise levels. There is some suggestion of an entrance in the south-eastern part, defined by increased magnetic enhancement in the ditch terminals. Elsewhere, responses of archaeological potential have been few and are often adjacent to anomalies likely to be modern in origin. In the west there may be the remains of more recent settlement, removed only when the land was enclosed. To the south, suggestions of further enclosures are apparent; however, their proximity to the Burn of Heddle points to a possible natural origin, such as a former pond. In the parcel of land adjacent to Maes Howe magnetic responses have been affected by debris associated with World War II military buildings.

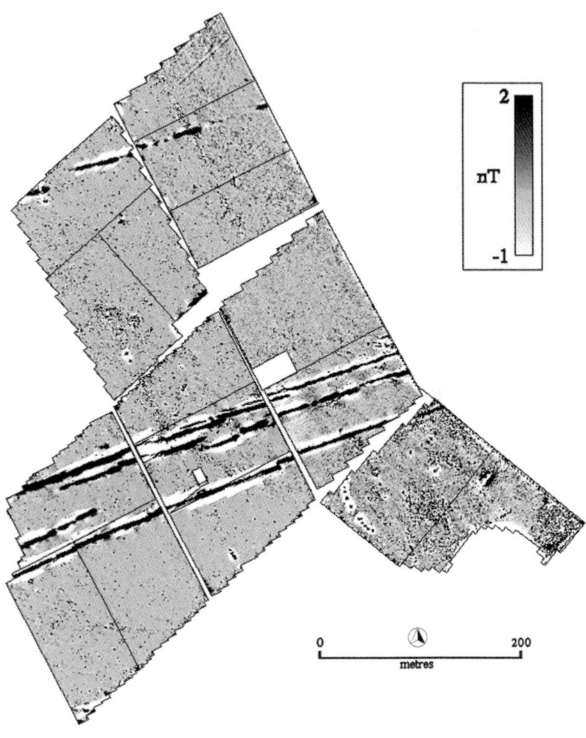

FIGURE 22.
Maes Howe.

Discussion and conclusion

The ongoing gradiometer survey within the inner buffer zone of the WHS is proving successful in a number of ways. Work on the narrow isthmus of land between the Ring of Brodgar and the Stones of Stenness has revealed a dense occupation area. These results highlight a previously unknown and unexpected high density of occupation in the Brodgar area. At Wasbister similar dense areas of occupation activity have been recorded. Here, however, a pattern of discrete anomalies has been identified and a direct relationship between this and existing monuments is suggested. In the context of the WHS, these sites are of international importance. Survey has also provided more detailed information regarding the nature of features visible as earthworks, and in some instances has suggested a different interpretation of them. This is particularly true when considering whether or not a mound is 'burnt'. While the large-scale gradiometer surveys of the buffer zone continue to expand, additional non-invasive survey techniques, such as resistance survey and ground-penetrating radar, will be used to provide detailed information on specific sites.

Subsequent excavations by Orkney Archaeological Trust have confirmed that an extensive, deeply stratified and well-preserved settlement is present on the Brodgar isthmus (Card 2004; Card and Cluett 2005). From a curatorial stance the identification of occupation within what David and Payne would describe as 'provocatively empty spaces' is heartening, especially because, within a WHS, excavation cannot be regarded as a prospecting tool in its own right, and non-invasive strategies come to the fore. The settlement responses here are strong but often confused; this lack of definition is frequently the result of the dense occupation typical of such sites in the area. In such cases excavation must play a significant role in a staged approach where the thrust is to establish the anthropogenic origins of the geophysical response and to add the temporal dimension.

Hoskins spoke of the fine borderline between *landscape history* as he conceived it and *archaeology*; we wonder what he would think about the role of *geophysics* in landscapes studies. We would like to believe that he would have found some stimulus and pleasure in the *underground* landscapes revealed by archaeological geophysics.

Acknowledgements

This project was undertaken on behalf of Orkney Archaeological Trust, funded by Historic Scotland and Orkney Islands Council. The authors would like to acknowledge the help and financial support given by the following organisations: Historic Scotland; Orkney Archaeological Trust; Orkney College; and Orkney Islands Council. Thanks are also due to all the landowners and tenant farmers who granted access for the survey work.

CHAPTER FIVE

Bronze Age Field Systems and the English Channel–North Sea Cultural Region

David Yates

European communities 3,000 to 4,500 years ago experienced the first golden or international age. It was a time of rapid economic growth, with the development of sophisticated and competitive long-distance exchange networks. During this European Bronze Age, widely spaced regions of the continent were drawn together by alliances which ensured safe travel and the rapid spread of new ideas, material wealth and people (Harding 2000; Kristiansen and Larsson 2005, 28). In the English archaeological record, an extraordinary wealth of bronze metalwork marks this era. Bronze artefacts first appeared in the Early Bronze Age (2300–1500 BC), rapidly increasing in number during the Middle and Late Bronze Age (1500–1000 BC and 1000–700 BC respectively). More significantly, it was during the Later Bronze Age (a term which encompasses the traditional Middle and Late Bronze Age phases) that parts of the landscape of southern England were transformed by the construction of regimented field systems. The scale, chronology and significance of that land partitioning have only become apparent in the last two decades.

Coaxial field systems

Bronze Age communities in southern England used a distinct form of land division. Rectilinear land plots were constructed, each forming a component of a large grid of fields. Extensive blocks of this form of regimented land tenure carpeted much of the chalk downland of southern England.

Field systems have been defined as being either coaxial or aggregate. Coaxial field systems have one prevailing orientation, with most of the field boundaries following this axis or alignment or running at right angles to it (Fleming 1987). The size of coaxial systems and their inherent inflexibility tends to make them terrain oblivious: their dominant axes rarely respect topographical obstructions. Integrated droveways, with paired ditches, hedgerows or walls, are often incorporated to enable the movement of livestock through the partitioned field plots. The reconstruction painting of a coaxial

FIGURE 23. South Hornchurch Late Bronze Age ringwork and field system. A ringwork or high-status enclosure encroaches on a droveway that leads toward the River Thames. Its occupants controlled movement through this highly ordered landscape. Reconstruction painting by Casper Johnson. (Yates forthcoming)

field system at South Hornchurch in Essex, shown in Figure 23, is based on a detailed archaeological investigation. It shows the ordered nature of Later Bronze Age landscapes. Straight banks, hedges and fences divide the land into closely rectilinear fields and pastures.

Rectilinear field systems in which one layout axis is not dominant over the other are referred to as aggregate field systems. Field blocks were clearly added on a piecemeal basis rather than in adherence to one original plan (Bradley 1978, 268). Excavation may show that the aggregate field system results from a number of phases of boundary realignment.

A century of archaeological investigation

Sustained archaeological interest in English prehistoric coaxial field systems started just over 100 years ago. Sussex archaeologists pioneered much of the early work. Foremost amongst them was Toms, who developed methods of analytical field survey to work out chronological relationships by surface observation (Bradley 1989, 32). His interests were not confined to Sussex, for he returned to his native Dorset and reinvestigated Angle Ditch and South Lodge Camp, originally excavated by Pitt-Rivers. He was able to demonstrate that Middle Bronze Age enclosures at both sites overlay earlier field systems (Bradley 1989, 34; Toms 1925). Dr Eliot Curwen and his son E.Cecil Curwen also made significant contributions to the study of early land division. With O.G.S.Crawford, they introduced the term 'Celtic field' to denote the widespread occurrence of this type of prehistoric field in southern England (Crawford 1923; Curwen and Curwen 1923, 64).

Ordered landscapes – droveways, field systems, linear ditches – were being recognised in increasing numbers, and not just in Sussex. Air photography revealed their scale nationally, and the striking imagery in major publications alerted a wider public to their existence (Crawford and Keiller 1928). The discovery, observation, classification and excavation of earthwork farm boundaries proceeded throughout the 1920s and 30s, when it was still possible to map their distribution in relation to settlement and associated droveways (Holleyman 1935, 444). From the 1940s to the 1990s there was an added urgency to upland investigations, as deep ploughing erased more earthworks.

Bowen (1961) spelt out the importance of studying the vanishing upland landscape, which contained numerous lynchets or cultivation terraces. His work inspired a series of research projects on the chalk downlands. These included work on the Marlborough Downs (Gingell 1992; Fowler 2000; McOmish 2005), the South Dorset Ridgeway (Woodward 1991), and the Salisbury Plain Training Area (Bradley, *et al.* 1994; McOmish *et al.* 2002). Each of these studies concluded that coaxial field systems, once referred to as *Celtic fields*, were mainly a Bronze Age phenomenon. Construction of these gridded land blocks lapsed for several hundred years after the end of the Bronze Age. They were not a major feature of Iron Age agriculture. Late in the Iron Age and particularly after the Roman Conquest, there was renewed interest in land control, again using coaxial design principles (Bradley and Yates in press).

Discoveries were not, however, confined to the chalk downlands. In Devon, the rediscovery of the Bronze Age Dartmoor reaves added to the number of ordered landscapes of second millennium BC origin. Work on Dartmoor by Fleming (1988) encouraged further research on Bodmin Moor (Cornwall) and Exmoor (Devon and Somerset) (Johnson and Rose 1994; Riley and Wilson-North 2001). It also stimulated interest in Cornish prehistoric field systems, including those at Chysauster (Smith 1996), Kit Hill (Herring and Thomas 1990) and the Lizard peninsula (Johns and Herring 1996).

Lowland field systems

The highly visible upland earthworks of prehistoric farms dominated investigations for much of the twentieth century. However, by the 1970s there were clues which suggested that Bronze Age field divisions were also widespread in the English lowlands (Fowler 1978, iv). Pioneering work by Pryor at Fengate (Cambridgeshire) proved that deeply buried prehistoric field systems still survived (Pryor 2001, 6). Developer-funded excavations have confirmed their existence in the English lowlands and have enhanced our knowledge of their distribution and complexity. The vast majority of archaeological investigations since 1990 (close on 50,000) have been developer-funded, greatly expanding the archaeological database for England. Landscape history research has been aided not only by the sum total of sites discovered, but also by the extensive use of open-area excavation. By removing topsoil overburden (sometimes over several hundred hectares of ground) it is possible to record how successive generations have worked to shape and reshape a cultural landscape.

Ancient lowland boundaries long masked and hidden from view are now being revealed. In the lowlands, the stone boundaries and earthworks of the uplands are absent, and while some traces of land division can show up as soil marks during air reconnaissance, most are undetectable. However, open-area excavation exposes ditched lowland coaxial field systems. Ideally, dating is achieved by rigorous sampling. In addition to the linear boundaries, post-holes, stake-holes and fence-lines may survive, together with evidence of roundhouses and burnt mounds. Sections cut through the ditched boundaries may reveal that they were variously embanked, double-ditched and banked, reinforced by hedging/posts or constructed as foundation trenches for stout fencing (Yates forthcoming).

In southern England it appears that coaxial field systems were the favoured method of land division in two separate eras: first, during the Bronze Age and, after a gap of several hundred years, late in the Iron Age and during Roman rule. Three lowland zones, namely the Thames valley and estuary, the English Channel coast, and the Fenlands of East Anglia, have particular concentrations of Bronze Age coaxial land division, metalwork finds and settlement.

The Thames and its estuary

One of the key areas defined in recent fieldwork is the Thames valley and the banks of its estuary. Land divisions have been found on either side of the estuary, the river mouth and on the gravel terraces. Away from the main river course, groups of fields have been located along the major tributaries, including the Lea in the east end of London, the Wandle (at Carshalton), the Colne (at Heathrow) and the Lower Kennet (Figure 24). These organised landscapes are associated with settlement and river metalwork finds. Much of the ostentatious weaponry from the Thames entered the river from the later Middle Bronze Age onwards (York 2002, 81), when a subdivided landscape was emerging. It suggests that as competition to acquire land increased, armed conflict escalated.

Farmsteads were integrated into these formal landscapes. A settlement generally consisted of a single farming household occupying several unenclosed post-built roundhouses. Increasingly during the course of the Later Bronze Age more elaborate forms of enclosed settlement were constructed, suggesting the emergence of social elites. Along the course of the Thames routeway an increasing number of ringworks have been recorded. These were circular compounds, which offered segregated living- or meeting-places, and were often associated with metalworking. Ringworks may be of particular significance as

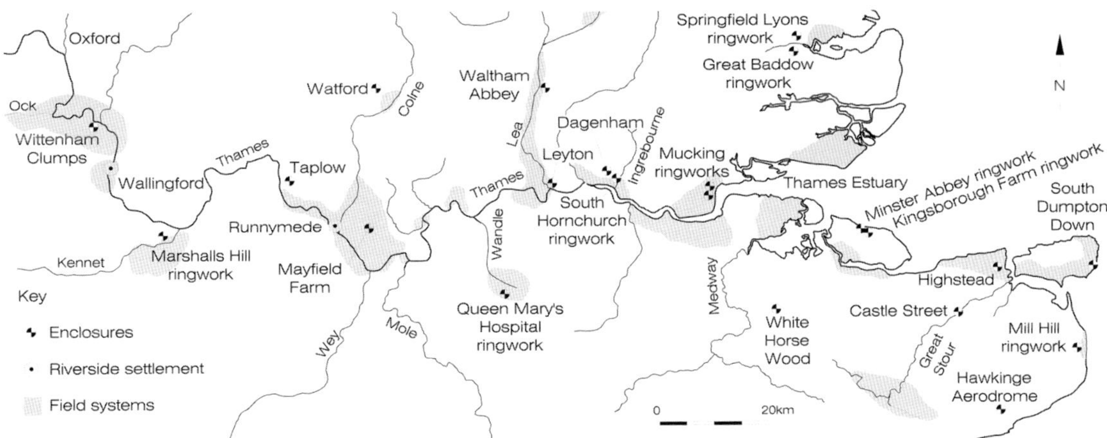

FIGURE 24. Later Bronze Age fields and enclosures along the Thames Valley.

they occupied strategic positions such as low hills or terrace bluffs overlooking farmlands and major routeways. For example, the vantage point of the ringworks at Mucking (Essex) provided a commanding view over the head of the Thames estuary (Figure 24). As I have suggested elsewhere, a ringwork may also be regarded or described as an aggrandised enclosure – that is, an impressive base for those who exploited the new opportunities presented by farming surpluses and long-distance exchange.

In addition to the distinctive ringworks, other forms of settlement are found along the Thames valley. Amongst these are two Late Bronze Age settlements on islands or eyots in the Thames – Runnymede Bridge (Surrey) and Whitecross Farm, Wallingford (Oxfordshire) (Cromarty *et al.* 2006). Both were foci for high-status activity, locations offering access to the social and political relations that went with exchange (Needham 2000, 242). The enclaves of metalwork, enclosure and land division along the Thames (Figure 24) represent areas of productive intensification (Yates forthcoming; Robinson 2006, 141). The evidence suggests that livestock rearing took precedence within mixed farming regimes.

The English Channel coast

The choice of strategic locations for farming settlement along the Thames compares well with the siting of lowland field systems along the English Channel coast (Figure 25). There is increasing evidence of land divisions on the Sussex coastal plain, clustering around the River Arun and the Selsey Bill peninsula. These brickearths have produced a significant number of metal finds. It is now apparent that the downlands may have been peripheral to a core area of farming and settlement on the coastal plain. Rising sea levels (Scaife *et al.* 2000, 32–3) have erased the original extent of these coaxial land holdings. It is a stretch of coastline that has produced a concentration of bronze ornaments and axe-heads. Highdown Hill in Sussex, the site of a Middle Bronze Age high-status enclosure, dominates much of this coastal plain, and several high-status settlements are found on the downlands nearby.

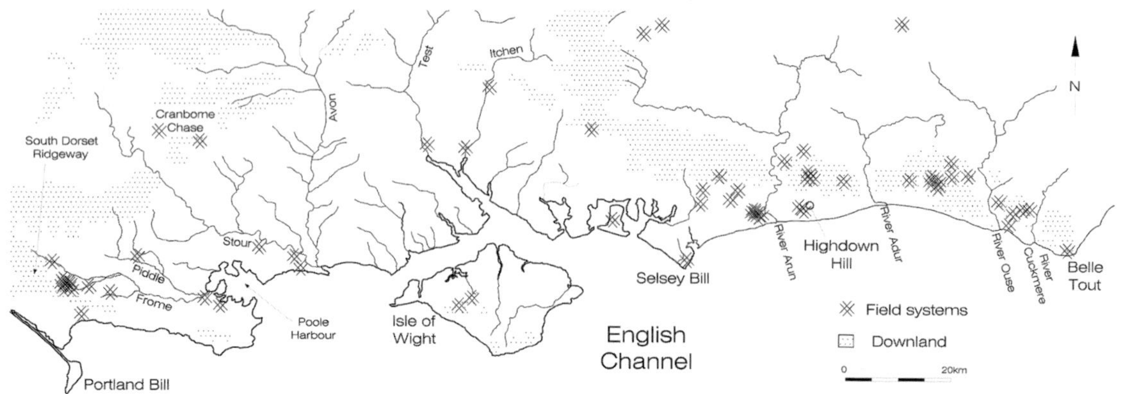

FIGURE 25. Sussex and the Hampshire Basin.

Areas around the mouths of the Test and the Stour attracted farming settlements (Figure 25). Land divisions have also been recorded around Poole Harbour. Inland in Dorset, land division extends along the River Frome. Further along the English Channel, traces of ditched and banked field boundaries (contemporary with the Dartmoor reaves) have been found in the Exe Valley and Castle Hill at Feniton (Devon), overlooking the River Otter (Yates forthcoming). Work on the outskirts of Plymouth and along the Devon coast indicates that settlement and land tenure was concentrated in the southern half of Devon, from Dartmoor down to the sea. It suggests that land was enclosed and exploited from the channel foreshores up onto the moorland heights (Yates forthcoming).

In Cornwall, there are instances of coaxial field systems ascribed to the late second and early first millennia BC, but they are few and far between. Those that have been identified often enclose prime lands, as, for example, at Chysauster, East Moor and St Keverne (Yates forthcoming). This last zone of regimented boundaries is particularly interesting; this was evidently an area that was associated with long-distance exchange. The Trevisker style of pottery, made from gabbroic clay outcropping at St Keverne, has been found as far away as Kent, Picardy, Normandy and Ireland. The coaxial fields are only one type of late second/early first millennium BC field system found in Cornwall; the majority of prehistoric fields in the county have irregularly-shaped perimeters. The relative paucity of coaxial field systems in Cornwall is matched by a relatively small number of bronze weaponry finds. It suggests that the political economy dominating south-eastern England was less influential in this part of the West Country, or took another form.

East Anglia

Along the North Sea coast in Essex, land beside the rivers Chelmer, Blackwater and Colne was parcelled up. This is another area associated with Late Bronze Age ringworks. Two were sited on either side of the river Chelmer at Springfield Lyons and Great Baddow (Figure 24). Later Bronze Age coaxial fields are also found on the Tendring peninsula (Essex), which dominates

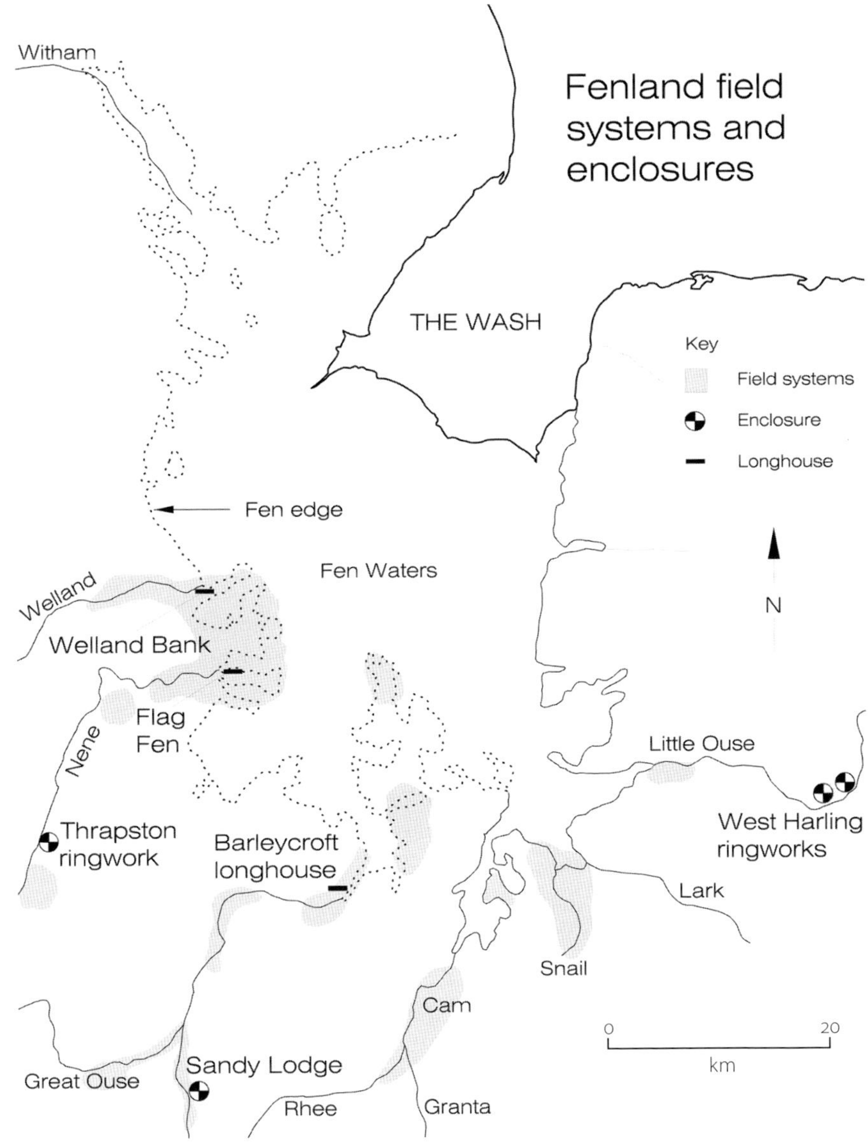

FIGURE 26.
The Fens and feeder rivers.

the entrance to the River Stour (see Figure 27). Inland, the Fenlands were important at this time, although it is clear that the field systems occur along the lower reaches of major rivers as well as in the wetland itself (Figure 26). Concentrations of Bronze Age coaxial fields, stock enclosures and droveways have been found where the Welland, Nene, Great Ouse, Rhee/Cam/Granta, Lark and Little Ouse join the Fens. These field blocks are associated with a concentration of bronze metalwork which reflects the extraordinary wealth of the Fenland communities; indeed, there is evidence for the development of a social hierarchy by the end of the Bronze Age. Ringworks were sited on rivers feeding into the Fens at Thrapston (Northants) and West Harling (Norfolk).

The general design of these ringworks is very similar to those encountered in Kent and along the Thames valley. High-status Late Bronze Age longhouses have also been recorded at Welland Bank (Lincs.), Flag Fen (Cambs.) and Barleycroft (Cambs). The Barleycroft example was set in a ditched compound surrounded by an extensive coaxial field system.

Fenland people were exploiting environments rich in natural resources, and in habitats capable of sustaining a growing population they were establishing land claims to the best soils. Social change was being enacted through the new medium of economic intensification.

An English Channel–North Sea cultural zone

When the distribution of upland earthworks is combined with the results of recent lowland excavations, a significant pattern emerges (Figure 27). Bronze Age rectilinear fields as a rule are confined to southern England (south of a line drawn between the Bristol Channel and the Wash) and especially the South East. Their occurrence is restricted to particular parts of this area. They are commonly found in distinct enclaves on the coast, beside estuaries or along major rivers and their tributaries – areas where communities were well placed to participate in long-distance exchange. This pattern suggests that there was a distinct cultural region in southern England.

This zone may have included communities on the other side of the English Channel. Suggesting a special affinity and exchange links between communities on either side of the Straits of Dover, Clark draws attention to the strong cultural similarities between Middle Bronze Age settlements in Kent and those in the Pas-de-Calais, particularly sites such as Fréthun and Étaples (Clark 2004, 7). Much further west the discovery of a Later Bronze Age coaxial field system at L'île de Tatihou in Normandy (Figure 27) provides potential evidence of cross-channel exchange within an extended regional economy (Marcigny and Ghesquière 2003). It may be that the distinctive form of rectilinear landscaping adopted in southern England and parts of northern Europe may be used to delineate and define an English Channel–North Sea cultural region (Figure 27).

FIGURE 27. Late second and early first millennium BC rectilinear field systems in the English Channel–North Sea Region.

In England there is a marked change in land control along the 'north-western frontier' of this English Channel–North Sea region. Starting in the Midlands of England (Clay 2002; Mullin 2003; Knight and Howard 2004) and extending north of the Wash, a different pattern of land tenure dominates the archaeological record for the first millennium BC – a practice of enclosing large tracts of land with linear boundaries and pit alignments (Bradley and Yates in press).

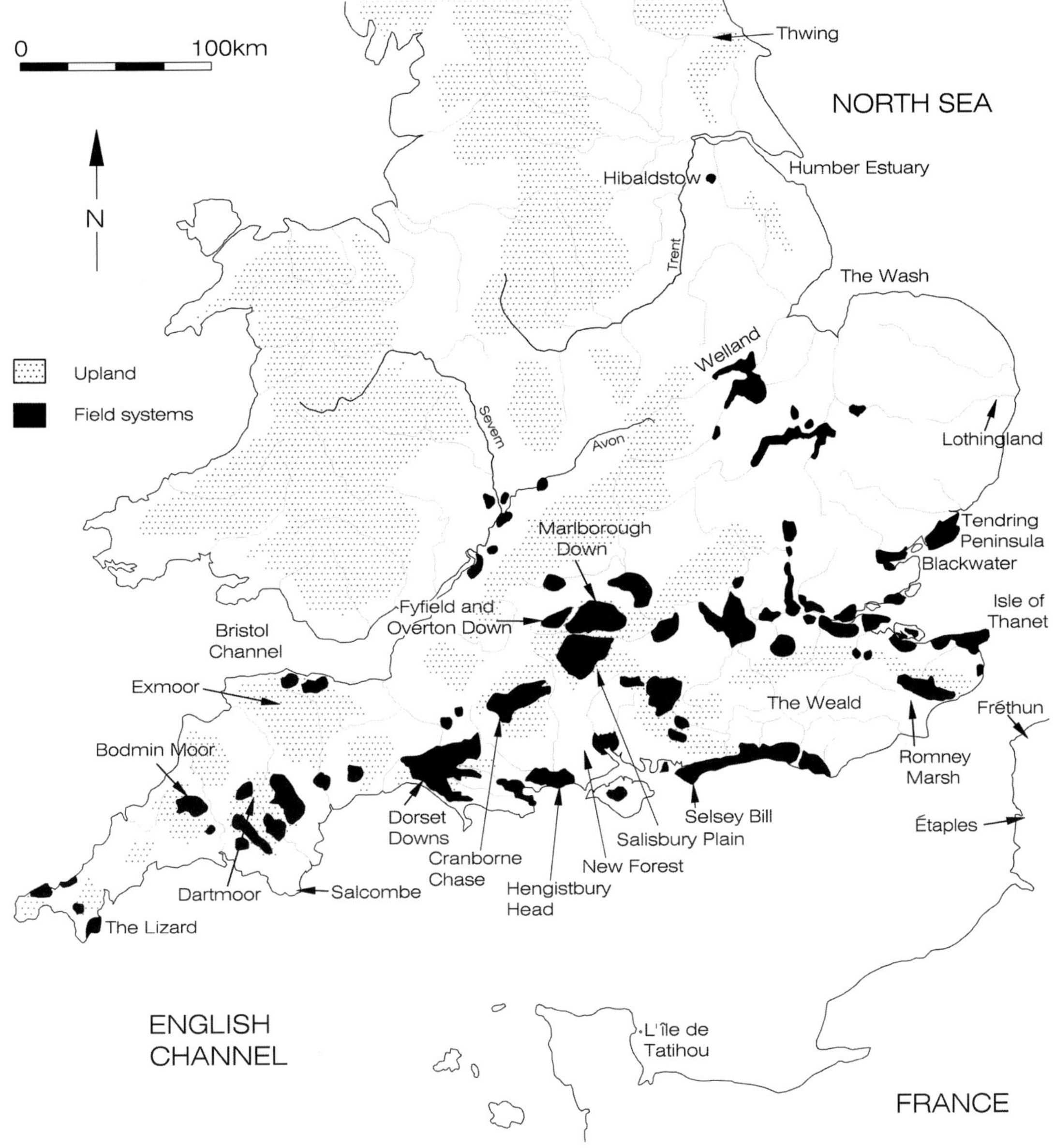

The socio-political importance of the distribution of coaxial field systems

Over twenty years ago, Rowlands (1980) offered a theoretical model of the social structure of southern England designed to explain how this country was linked into a wider European exchange network. Given the newly available data from commercial archaeology, his model may now be reconsidered. For Rowlands, southern England formed one part of a larger economy (which he called the Atlantic Region) uniting south-east England and north-east France. This was a region of varying economic fortunes, in which communities of different size and power competed to gain political and economic advantage. Despite fierce rivalry, people on either side of the English Channel were closely bound within a highly stable and expansionist hierarchy of alliance and exchange. So close were those ties that the south-east effectively became more 'Europeanised' and increasingly segregated from other parts of southern and northern England (Rowlands 1980, 37). This resulted in a community of people united by a common culture occupying both shores of the English Channel.

Within the south-east corner of England, Rowlands suggested that there was a hierarchy of exchange. Occupying the upper reaches of this hierarchy may have been exchanges between 'twinned' coastal populations on either side of the Channel, using established sea routes for the flow of specialist resources, people and new technology. Lower down may have come exchanges between centres along specific coastlines; further still down the hierarchy, inland networks linked the coasts and river valleys to their hinterlands (Rowlands 1980, 38). Location at key points was essential to ensure access to the widest possible exchange and alliance network and to the best possible soils (Rowlands 1980, 34). The better the location, the greater the likelihood of local political dominance. Rowlands used the evidence of pottery, metalwork and burial distributions to suggest flourishing and densely populated zones of riverine settlements along the Thames, the English Channel coast and the East Anglian Fens (Rowlands 1980, 34).

These specialist enclave economies enjoyed varying degrees of dominance and success. Their political power ultimately depended on their ability to accumulate, display and distribute wealth. Successful management of available resources, including the mobilisation of labour, would have transformed the nature of the lived environment. For Rowlands, it was the coastal and river elites which engaged in long distance alliance formation and exchange. These densely populated niches or enclaves benefited from more centralised wealth and power than was possible in comparable upland settlement zones. Rowlands admitted that there was little evidence, apart from the metalwork, which might allow us to estimate the success of these long-distance relationships, although he did suggest that 'they must have been producing some kind of surplus in exchange' (Rowlands 1980, 34). Evidence now suggests that part of that surplus must have been derived from large-scale animal husbandry (Yates forthcoming).

The occurrence of a recurrent and uniform type of land division within the English Channel–North Sea region supports Rowlands's model. The concentration of lowland coaxial land division in the Fenlands, Thames valley and south coast areas suggest that the political ascendancy of these zones was based on productive intensification. Perhaps these distinctive field blocks were a form of conspicuous production instigated by ranked societies.

Subtleties in the landscape

Arguably, one of the greatest achievements of developer-funded excavation has been the detection of lowland Bronze Age land divisions. The problem is no longer one of trying to find them. With growing experience, it is becoming apparent that they are intricate creations. The present-day challenge is to unravel the complexity of their design.

Chronological subtleties

These developments did not all occur at the same time; greater chronological precision is now required. That will enable us to look more closely at the first phase of construction of coaxial fields, a phenomenon which endured in overall terms for 800 years. Chronological precision will provide a clearer insight into different building and maintenance phases, claims and counter-claims to land, and the longevity of settlements, perhaps in part reflecting the fluidity of changing political fortunes.

Determining the origins of this distinctive form of field construction poses particular problems; the task is complicated by the actions of Later Bronze Age people, who customarily placed Neolithic and Early Bronze Age artefacts in their field structures. Already there is some evidence to suggest that the ditch-defined rectilinear fields of the Later Bronze Age represent the formalisation of earlier land claims and agreed access points. Boundaries may have been marked out initially by pits and posts in the Early Bronze Age. Subsequently, boundaries were consolidated by the construction of linear ditches (Knight 2002; Chapman *et al.* 2005, 19; Hülka 2006, 112).

Subtleties of stock management

Evidence for droveways and stock handling systems is now plentiful in the layout of most British prehistoric field systems, implying livestock farming on a large scale involving a considerable degree of sophistication and organisation during the Bronze Age (Pryor 1998). At several sites the drove roads had metalled surfaces, suggesting the frequent passage of large herds of cattle; and at South Hornchurch (Essex) and Round Pound, Kestor Rocks (Devon) there were chicaned droveways close to aggrandised enclosures (Guttmann and Last 2000; Fox 1954). A series of waterholes, wells and ponds (on the chalk downlands) enabled the confinement of large herds, and composite fencing comprising ditches, banks and fence posts are evidence of the strength of the stock pens. Discoveries of sheep bridges on marshland, and wattle fencing, imply further subtleties of shepherding practices (Wilkinson and Murphy 1995, 150).

Subtleties of soil management

There is a recurrent pattern of coaxial field construction in areas with alluvial and brickearth deposits. After the claiming of the most fertile soils, the next priorities were to conserve and improve them. Pressure on the land was intense, with progressive erosion of the soils occurring on the uplands, for instance on the South Downs (Favis-Mortlock *et al.* 1997; and see Allen and Scaife, this volume). To counteract that loss, lynchet banks were constructed at the edges of fields. On the lowlands, soils were threatened by flooding; it is interesting that the value of the land could apparently justify the construction of flood prevention dams (Wessex Archaeology 2000). Waterlogging could also be addressed by digging drainage ditches through the brickearths into the underlying gravel terraces.

Improving these soils involved ground clearance, weed control and regular ploughing. There is some evidence of bean propagation, which would have improved soil nitrogen levels (Brooks 2002, 61). The field layouts also suggest controlled grazing; there is evidence of manuring on lowland sites. The establishment of massive middens at East Chisenbury (Wilts.) and Potterne (Wilts.) by the end of the Bronze Age (McOmish *et al.* 2002, 73; Lawson 2000; Guttmann 2005) shows the interest in soil enrichment.

Field boundaries may represent an increased desire to claim the best farming lands – especially when they became more scarce. The great explosion of land enclosure on the lower/mid slopes of Dartmoor and the first gravel terraces around the Fenlands may have resulted from a wish to exploit the best remaining land as seasonal pasture declined (French 2003, 77, 150). A similar drive to demarcate land ownership may have occurred on the northern shoreline of Kent and along the coastal plain of Sussex as relative sea levels rose.

A framework for ritualisation and cosmological beliefs

Within the grids there is evidence for ritualisation – in other words, for actions which reflect some of the dominant concerns of society (Bradley 2003, 12). Farming people were governed by the changing seasons of the year; the recurrent agricultural cycle of growth, decline and renewal may have come to dominate their own perceptions of the world. In consequence, certain dominant elements of farm life (those critical to the survival of the community) were selected and given added emphasis (Williams 2003; Bradley 2003). One such concern would have been the welfare of the breeding herd. A range of offerings has been recovered from Bronze Age watering holes and wells within the field systems. This includes Neolithic polished stone axes, quern stones, spindle whorls, bronze metalwork, axe hafts and complete pottery vessels (Barrett *et al.* 2001, 224–5; McFadyen 2000). Such ritualised activity may have increased in times of drought (Masefield *et al.* 2003, 114).

Recent fieldwalking and excavation is starting to indicate that the burial of Later Bronze Age metalwork deposits (single finds and hoards) can be directly related to the construction of the formal landscapes (Dunkin 2001). Many of the answers to questions about people's engagement in the new world of farming, and what the world meant to them, may lie scattered among their fields (Ingold 2000, 208).

In 1987, Fleming discussed the powerful ideological or symbolic meaning of coaxially aligned land. He suggested that it is difficult to avoid the elusive notion of the ritual landscape, which involved the conscious creation and maintenance of a special terrain, full of symbolic meaning (Fleming 1987, 197). The discovery of common north-east to south-west alignments for the field systems on the Wessex chalklands (McOmish *et al.* 2002; Gingell 1992, fig. 96; Fowler 2000, 25) gives weight to the argument of 'ritually correct' landscaping, the knowledge of which may have been held by ancestral guardians (Fleming 1987, 201). The ditched field systems along the Thames valley and the south coast shared a similar alignment. Like their upland counterparts, they show a subsidiary axis from north-west to south-east that matches the orientation of some of the houses in the associated settlement (Bradley and Yates in press). However, there are variations within southern England, especially in the Fens where the base line followed the riverbanks and the dividing lines were perpendicular to the river course or fen edge. Conformity to agreed bearings might have represented acknowledgement of the life-giving permanence of the sun (Williams 2003, 242); many field systems are aligned to face the direction of the sunrise. It suggests that we are studying a complex cultural landscape, in which formal land tenure was not solely an impersonal expression of demographic and economic forces (Fokkens 1999, 41). It was a supernaturally charged landscape in which people, their livestock and their cultivated land were closely linked in a complex cosmology (Kristiansen and Larsson 2005, 54).

Evidently the way later Bronze Age farmers shaped the land suited their ideological needs. In comparison with historically known peasant societies (Kristiansen and Larsson 2005, 32), these communities may have had a very different perception of the world and their role within it (and see Bradley, this volume). Numerous rescue excavations have now revealed the rich detail of the later Bronze Age organised landscapes of southern England, providing the evidence which should definitively establish the Otherness of their creators.

Acknowledgements

Richard Bradley, Tim Phillips, Andrew Fleming, Frances Healy, Tim Malim and Francis Pryor encouraged and helped me throughout this study. Field archaeology teams in England provided invaluable access to new material. Many shared their own research findings, particularly: Stuart Needham, Tim Champion, Mark Knight, Chris Evans, Terry Manby, David Field, Martyn Barber, Joanna Bruck, Jill York, J. D. Hill, Richard Cross, Colin Pendleton, Roger Thomas, Alistair Barclay, Gill Hey, Mike Allen, Jonathan Last, Jonathan Hunn, John Barrett, Mike Williams, David Dunkin, Catriona Gibson and Cyril Marcigny. Without the financial assistance of English Heritage this research would never have been completed. Jane Russell prepared the illustrations and Casper Johnson created the reconstruction painting: both greatly assisted my research efforts.

CHAPTER SIX

Claylands Revisited: The Prehistory of W.G. Hoskins's Midlands Plain

Patrick Clay

Introduction

The underlying geology of most of the east midlands comprises clay substrata including Liassic clays, Mercia Mudstone Group and, most commonly, glacially derived boulder clay. These areas were long considered to have had little settlement during prehistory (Fox 1932; Wooldridge and Linton 1933; Clark 1945). W.G. Hoskins, writing in 1957, felt that the midlands were largely avoided by prehistoric settlers and were not densely settled until the medieval period. In his assessment of the landscape history of Leicestershire, for example, he states: 'in Leicestershire we have a county, perhaps characteristic of the inner Midlands as a whole, which under natural conditions was very largely a region of thickly forested and heavy clays. This inhospitable landscape attracted early man only in small numbers, and even the Romans made comparatively little impression on it ... The human history of Leicestershire only really begins in the second half of the fifth century (AD) with the penetration, by the first waves of Anglian settlers, along the larger rivers and to some extent along the Roman roads' (Hoskins 1957b, 2). This view was echoed to some extent by Heather Tinsley (1981, 249), who suggested that the 'lowlands of Britain, except the chalklands of the south and the east were subject to only temporary clearance during the Bronze Age. The exploitation of the large areas of dense forest which covered the Midland plain ... was not accomplished until the development of more sophisticated tools.' In the same volume Judith Turner (1981, 264) came to broadly similar conclusions: 'At the beginning of the Iron Age there was a marked contrast between areas in the southeast of England with light calcareous soils which were already being settled and farmed and which only retained a fraction of their original forest cover, and most of the rest of Britain where the forest was more or less intact, except where open moorland existed in the uplands.'

Where fieldwork had been undertaken in the east midlands this traditional picture seemed to be supported. From his fieldwalking surveys in

Northamptonshire, David Hall concluded that 'experience has shown that sites earlier than the Iron Age *do not* [my emphasis] occur on clay soils' and based on this he suggested modifying fieldwalking techniques, to examine areas with clay soils with a less intensive method (Hall 1985, 28).

These views raise the question of why these landscapes, so successfully exploited in the medieval and post-medieval periods, were so very different in prehistory, and whether the success of later agricultural regimes has rendered evidence for prehistoric settlement less visible. Is this a true picture of absence, or are we seeing biases in the record due to visibility, research interests and funding? Nigel Mills (1985) identified four main biases in the British Isles database: first, a bias towards particular classes of evidence (for example, upstanding monuments and cropmarks); secondly, a bias towards 'sites' rather than archaeological landscapes (see below); thirdly, within a given period, a bias towards particular types of site (for example, ceremonial sites for the Later Neolithic/Earlier Bronze Age or hillforts for the Iron Age); and fourthly, a bias towards particular landscape zones within given regions. Many of these biases are interlinked and can be predicted to operate in regions with poorly visible archaeology, as in the case of the claylands of the east midlands.

Standing monuments are poorly represented in this area, and the survival of prehistoric earthworks is rare. The geology is not very conducive to the formation of cropmarks, although it has produced some results of a faint and often fleeting nature, including remarkable recent discoveries on the Bedfordshire clays (R. Palmer pers. comm.). The area examined is essentially a plough zone, with ongoing erosion of archaeological deposits; pasture, woodland, colluviation and alluviation have masked much of the evidence. Artefact scatters in areas of arable cultivation are likely to be the primary evidence for prehistoric activity. Even these are not always easy to discern in clayland areas, owing to the 'drag factor' found during ploughing and cultivation (Clark and Schofield 1991, 94). This can lead to greater dispersion than would occur on lighter soils, making artefact concentrations harder to detect. It is, therefore, the long subsequent history of successful arable and pastoral farming which has made the identification of pre-Iron Age evidence difficult (Mills 1985, 41).

Another factor which affects the perception of how a region has been exploited is the amount of fieldwork undertaken. Much archaeological fieldwork takes place in response to threats to sites from development, and is thus concentrated in zones of urban or village expansion or infilling, areas of quarrying for gravel, limestone, granite, ironstone or coal, and along the routes of roads and pipelines (Cooper and Clay 2006, 6). The integration of archaeological recording into the planning process (Department of the Environment 1990) may serve to compound this bias, with fieldwork being concentrated where most development is taking place, and where previous SMR information is available to provide justification for further work. While the Aggregates Levy sustainability fund offers an opportunity for more fieldwork, it does concentrate on areas already well served by PPG16 – further compounding the biases. The main threat to the east midlands claylands comes from ploughing, and despite English Heritage's 'Ripping up the past' initiative (English Heritage 2003), for political reasons an 'agricultural levy' to alleviate destruction by agricultural practices is highly unlikely to materialise.

Understandably, academic research has concentrated on areas containing high concentrations of visible late prehistoric ceremonial monuments, such as Wessex, Orkney and the Boyne valley, and, for the Iron Age, on regions featuring the most conspicuous hillforts. Whilst these have undoubtedly been important areas, they were not necessarily any more special than others which have left less visible evidence. Much of their perceived status has been a result of the weight of research focused upon them (Barclay 2001). The way in which certain areas have dominated research conjures up the image of footballers chasing the ball instead of using all of the pitch.

Clay soils

To understand how clayland areas were exploited we need to know more about the nature of clay soils. Modern clay soils are often poorly permeable, or impermeable, and suffer from inadequate drainage (Jacks 1954, 21). Chemically they are usually quite rich in plant nutrients, but owing to poor aeration these may not be in a condition available to plants. Additionally, they do not respond to applications of manure and fertilisers as readily as sandy soils. Clay soils are liable to waterlogging, which can lead to the clay particles swelling, resulting in a loss of structure. When cold and waterlogged, these soils take longer to warm up in the spring than sandier soils (Limbrey 1975; Curtis *et al.* 1976). They do retain fertility longer than some sandy soils, however, and crops that do well include wheat, oats, barley, beans and grass.

These *modern* clay soils are the result of agricultural exploitation over many centuries, however, and will be different from the soils which confronted prehistoric communities. Under natural woodland, given relatively uniform climatic conditions, soils in north-west Europe tend towards the brownearth type irrespective of the substrata (Evans 1975, 136). These early soils would have had a friable and well-drained upper humus horizon and would have been just as cultivable as soils on other geological formations. Only following cropping or grazing without liming or manuring would the soil structure have degraded and the problems of loss of nutrients and poor drainage become apparent (Clay 2002, 3; Evans 1975, 136).

Regional study

By the late 1980s, traditional perceptions of prehistoric settlement patterns on the east midlands claylands were changing. In contrast to Hall's results, fieldwalking by community archaeology groups in Leicestershire (Liddle 1985; Clay 1989) was finding flint scatters on clay substrata. It seemed, therefore, that the traditional model of minimal clayland settlement and land use might be an over-simplification, and other models needed to be proposed. In order to investigate these issues, a regional study was undertaken. It was based on Sites and Monuments information, and incorporated four sub-regions which had been subject to detailed survey. The east midlands do not form a coherent regional unit, and many different interpretations of its limits have been suggested (McCullagh 1969; Dury 1963). In order to include significant areas of clayland and samples of different geologies, an area of 4,200 sq. km was selected on the basis of the Ordnance Survey Grid, bounded by NGR SK 400 300 to the north-west and SK 000 600 to the south-east (Figure 28). Four areas where detailed survey information was available were also examined as case studies. These consisted of the Raunds Area Survey, Northamptonshire (Clay 1996, 120–80; Parry 1994; 2006), the

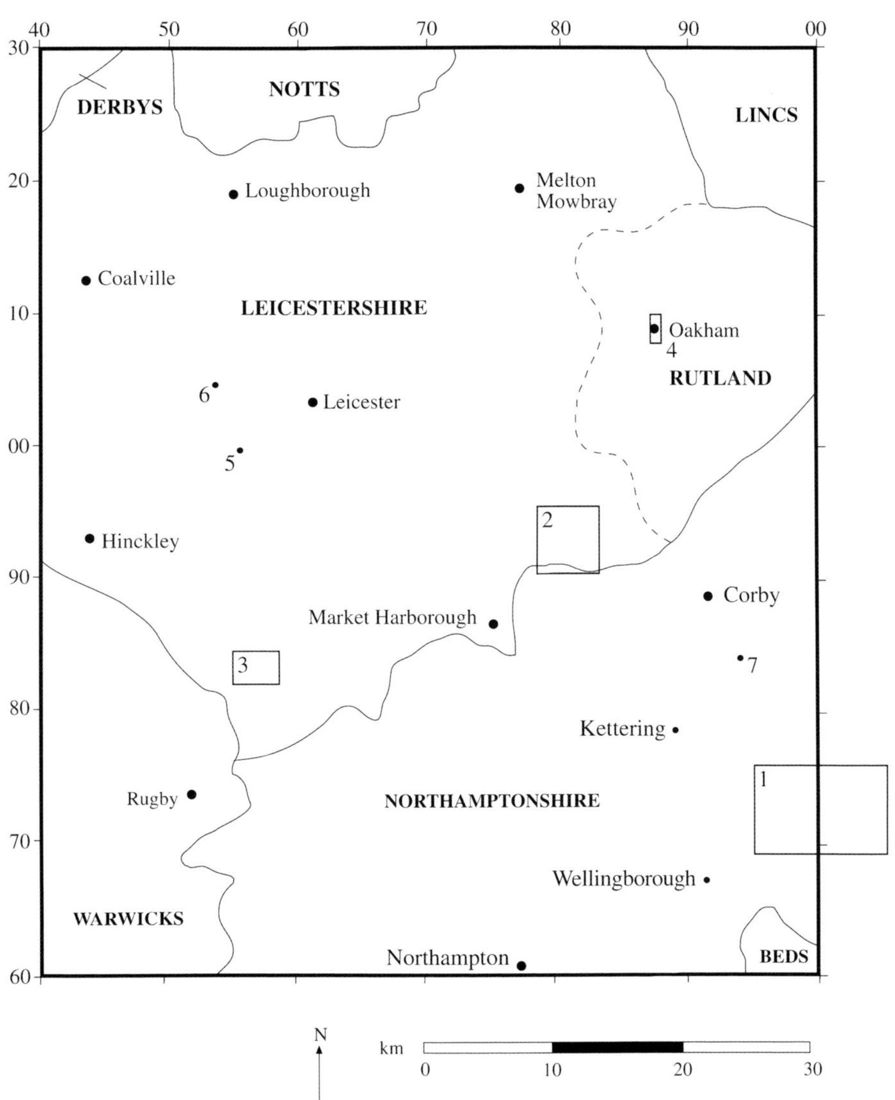

FIGURE 28. Area of regional survey, showing the present counties, major towns and survey areas. 1: Raunds; 2: Medbourne; 3: Swift Valley; 4: Oakham. (Clay 2002, fig. 2)

middle Welland valley at Medbourne, Leicestershire (see Figure 30; Clay 2002, 51–84; Liddle 1994), the Swift valley at Misterton, Leicestershire (see Figure 31; Clay 2002, 85–104) and the Upper Catmose valley at Oakham, Rutland (Clay 1996, 262–96; 1998).

The character of the region is largely dictated by widespread Pleistocene and later deposits, with over 50 per cent being covered by unevenly deposited glacial drift. The river terrace gravels constitute the latest geological formations, with significant terrace gravels in the valleys of the major rivers (Avon, Trent, Soar, Nene, Welland, Ouse). With the retreat of the Weichselian glaciation *c.*12,000 BC the topography of the region had been established essentially as a lowland, well dissected and separated by the major rivers, with areas of small irregular hills, soft in outline and at present often partially masked by hedges and trees. There was little truly flat land, with the exception of narrow bands of floodplain, terrace and scarp crest (Dury 1963; Pye 1972).

For the regional survey, the Sites and Monuments Record (SMR) entries for the Neolithic and Bronze Age were plotted against the underlying geology, altitude, watersources, primary and secondary surface geology, aspect and land-use capability. For the Neolithic and Bronze Age, virtually all the information comes from surface scatters of lithic material. Although these are indicative of 'activity', there are problems in defining what type of activity is represented; often a lack of diagnostic material means that the scatters are difficult to date or interpret with any degree of reliability. Dispersion by more recent ploughing also affects field scatters (Yorston *et al.* 1990). However, following Schofield (1991), it was possible to identify 'core areas' on the basis of higher proportions of cores and retouched lithic material.

The evidence for the Earlier Neolithic from the regional and case studies has much in common with the rest of the country, in that clear evidence of agricultural activity is absent (Kinnes 1988). The regional survey confirmed that there was no evidence of clayland areas being avoided; over 30 per cent of 'core areas' and 40 per cent of Early Neolithic artefacts were located within them (Figure 29; Clay 2002, 111). Whilst the case studies at Oakham (Clay 1998) and the Swift valley (Clay 2002, 185) have identified Earlier Neolithic *foci*, these are less clear from large-scale extensive surveys using less intensive collecting methodologies. At Medbourne (Figure 31) and Raunds the earlier Neolithic pattern appears to have been essentially the same as that for the Mesolithic (Clay 2002, 112), with low-density scatters. Three core areas could be identified from the intensive survey in the Swift Valley, all situated on boulder clay substrata at *c.*120 m OD on one south- and two north-facing slopes overlooking the River Swift (Clay 2002, 101). This area is notable in that lithic densities were comparable to those found in surveys of chalkland areas – for example, the Vale of White Horse, Maddle Farm and East Berkshire surveys (Figure 32; Tingle 1991; Gaffney and Tingle 1989; Ford 1987). An earlier Neolithic core area could also be postulated for the same Liassic clay area of the Oakham survey, which contained a Mesolithic core area (Clay 1998).

FIGURE 29.
The study area, showing clay substrata and Earlier Neolithic core areas, ritual areas and findspots. (Clay 2002, fig. 9)

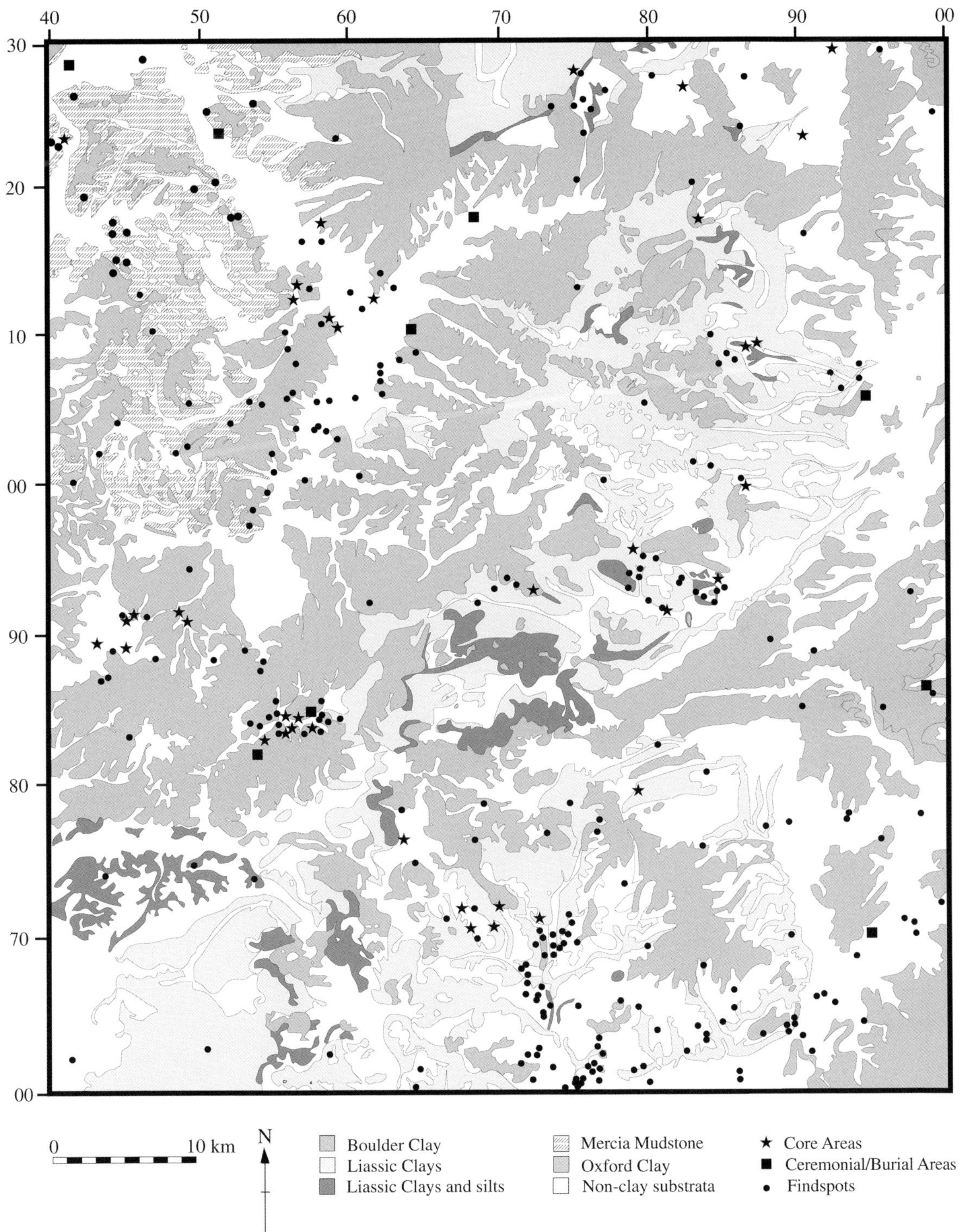
40
50
60
70
80
90
00
30
20
10
00
90
80
70
00
0
10 km
N
Boulder Clay
Liassic Clays
Liassic Clays and silts
Mercia Mudstone
Oxford Clay
Non-clay substrata
Core Areas
Ceremonial/Burial Areas
Findspots

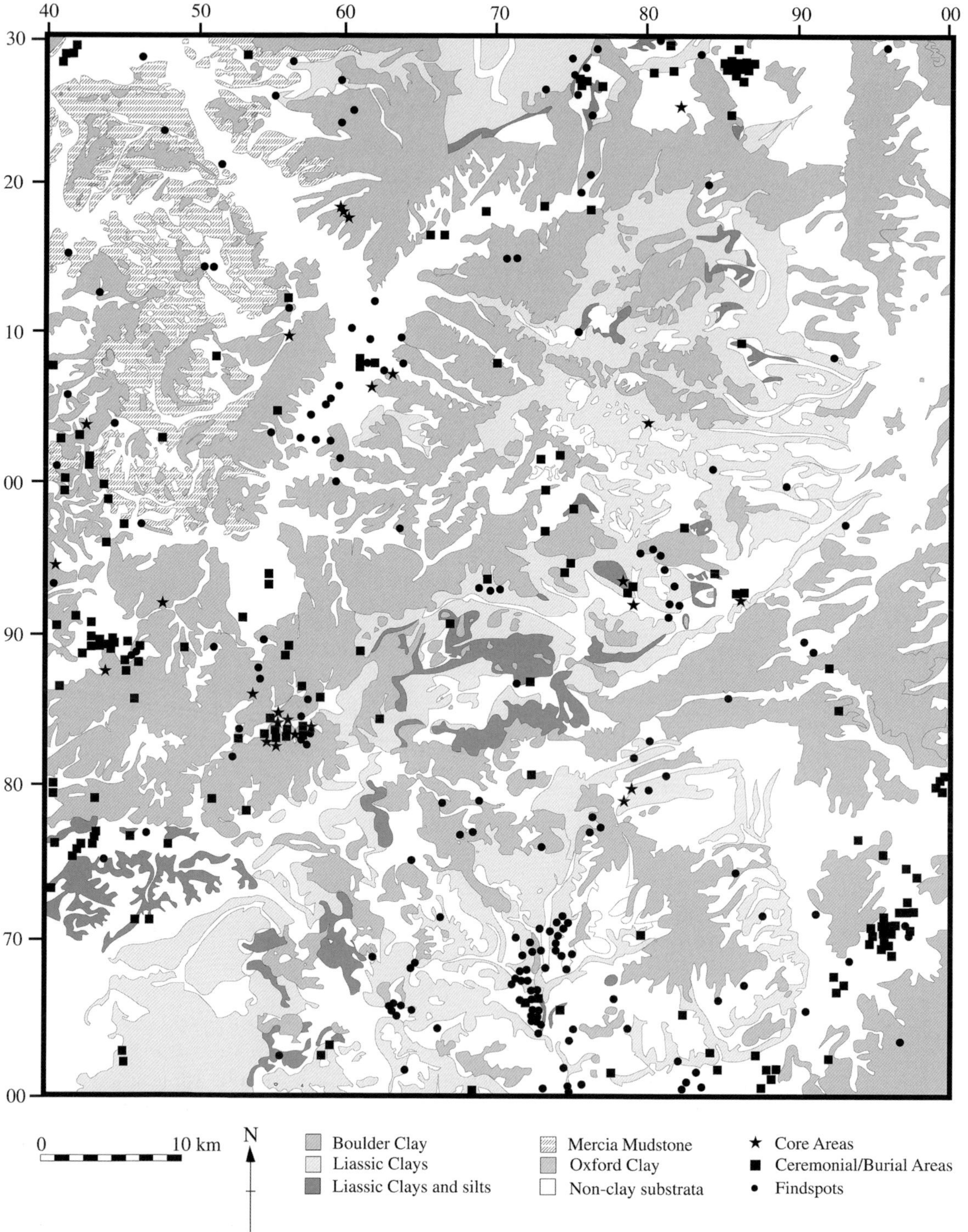
40
50
60
70
80
90
00
30
20
10
00
90
80
70
00
0
10 km
N
Boulder Clay
Liassic Clays
Liassic Clays and silts
Mercia Mudstone
Oxford Clay
Non-clay substrata
Core Areas
Ceremonial/Burial Areas
Findspots

FIGURE 30.
The study area, showing clay substrata and Later Neolithic–Earlier Bronze Age core areas, ritual areas and findspots. (Clay 2002, fig. 10)

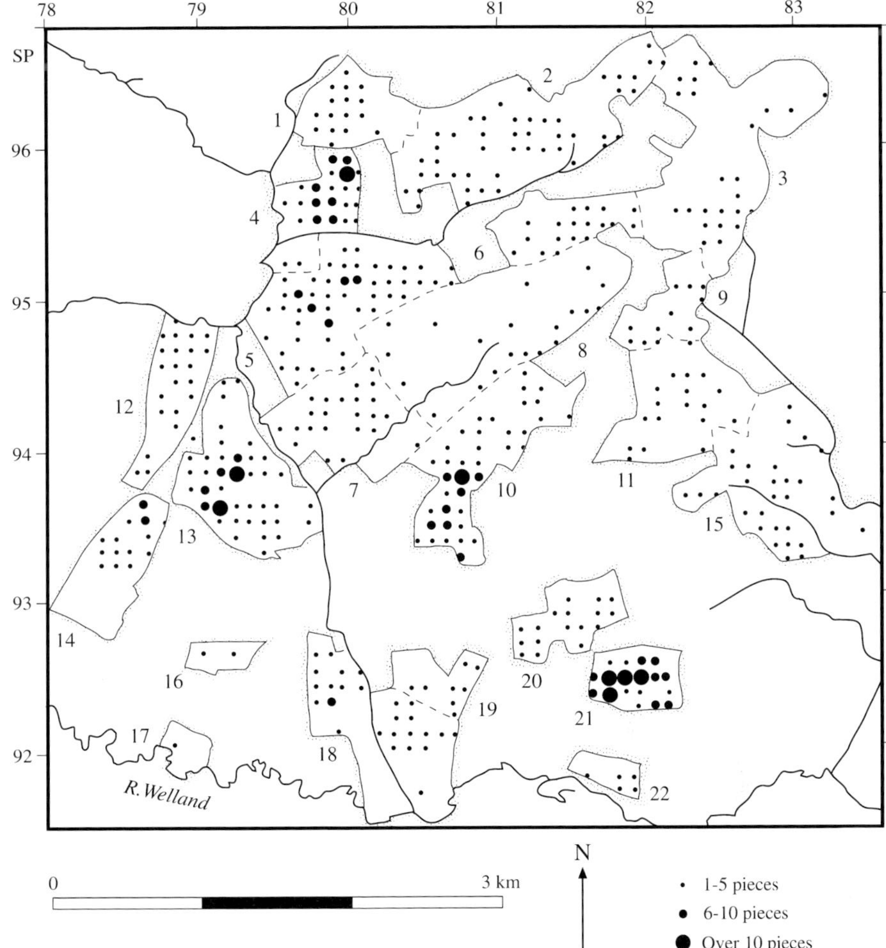

FIGURE 31.
The Medbourne area survey, showing the distribution of all lithics. (Clay 2002, fig. 18)

How does evidence from the east midlands claylands accord with present models of Early Neolithic settlement in Britain? Traditional models suggested a rapid pioneering phase of agriculture commencing in the late fifth millennium BC, with a slow-down later in the third millennium BC (Whittle 1978). Other interpretations (Thomas 1991, 28; Barrett 1994) have questioned the importance of arable farming and permanent settlement in the earlier Neolithic, arguing for mobile hunter-gatherer communities adding non-intensive agricultural practices of long-fallow horticulture and some animal pasturing to the hunting, fishing and gathering already undertaken by Mesolithic groups (Whittle 1996). However, this mobility model appears to be at variance with those put forward on the Continent and in Ireland (Cooney 1997). The apparent absence of evidence for agriculture in the claylands of the east midlands would fit the mobility model quite well, but may simply be a product of survival conditions.

During the Later Neolithic–Early Bronze Age some preferred locations within the study area seem to have continued in use, with some expansion onto previously unexploited land (Figure 32). This evidence appears to support Barrett's (1994) interpretation of agricultural expansion. Findings from the case studies differ from those from the regional survey; core areas appear to decrease in the latter, whereas the case studies all suggest an increase in their numbers. At Raunds there were perhaps seven identifiable core areas, three of them on clay substrata (Clay 1996, 140), while at Medbourne six core areas can be identified, three on clay substrata, with four sharing the same location as Mesolithic/Early Neolithic groups (Clay 2002, 81). In the Swift valley survey six areas, all with boulder clay substrata, are interpreted as core areas, and two further areas may have been procurement locations; four areas include cropmarks of ring-ditches, indicating locations for burial or ritual (Clay 2002, 101). Two possible core areas on Liassic clay and Marlstone Rock Bed substrata could be identified from the Oakham survey, where environmental information from the excavation of a pit circle complex suggested arable and pastoral farming in the area (Clay 1998). If the increased use of clayland areas during the Later Neolithic/Early Bronze Age suggested by the area surveys is a true reflection of past activity, one contributory factor may have been the contemporary 'climatic optimum', which may have been accompanied by lower rainfall. If we were to extrapolate the relatively low rainfall characteristic of this region today to the Later Neolithic/Early Bronze Age, we might conclude

FIGURE 32.
The Swift valley survey, showing the distribution of lithic blades. (Clay 2002, fig. 32)

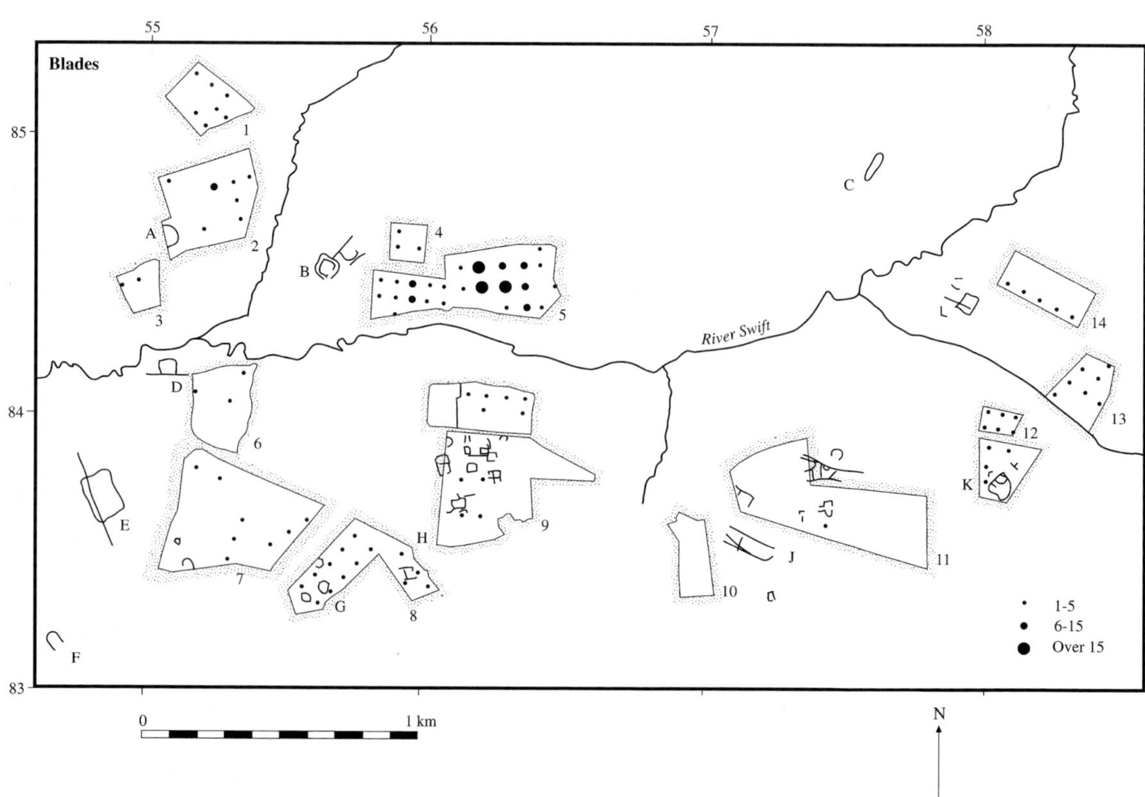

that dryness of the soils may have been an important factor in the success of arable and pastoral farming. The higher water retentiveness of clay soils may have increased their desirability, especially for pasture, outweighing any drainage problems experienced during the winter. Based on his examination of land allotment along the fen edge, immediately east of the study area, Francis Pryor (1998) suggests that sheep farming was a major part of the economy in the Later Neolithic/Early Bronze Age.

Were soils above clay substrata all equally attractive to pioneer farming communities? Did other constraints influence site selection? From the examination of SMR data for both the Early Neolithic and Later Neolithic/Early Bronze Age, there appears to be a preference for possible core areas in boulder clay locations rather than Liassic clay, Liassic clays and silts, Oxford clay or Mercian Mudstone. The case studies, however, show a different pattern. Whereas the predominantly boulder clay area of the Swift valley apparently contains core areas, such an interpretation is doubtful for the boulder clay areas in the Medbourne and Raunds surveys. Here the Liassic clay valley sides appear to be preferred locations, with some home-range activities suggested for the boulder clay areas. A possible explanation for this discrepancy involves the different types of boulder clay encountered throughout the region. Whereas the basic clay matrix is often very similar (Shotten 1953) the inclusions within it vary greatly, with, for example, a very high proportion of chalk pebble flint evident from the boulder clay areas in the Swift valley (Poole *et al.* 1968, 57). This may have provided an important flint resource and a more permeable soil with better drainage qualities, perhaps making it more conducive to arable farming. Such factors may have influenced the selection of this micro-region for core areas during the Neolithic and Bronze Age. It is perhaps significant that this is the only area examined which has lithic densities comparable to those produced by field studies in the south of England. The high densities of the Swift valley, then, may result from the procurement of flint supplies, whilst the large quantities of flint tools may indicate prolonged use of this area.

Conclusion

Despite gaps in the data, the study of this area of central England has demonstrated that the question of clayland land use during the Neolithic and Early Bronze Age is more complicated than had been previously suggested. Claylands were neither avoided nor consistently exploited, but show exploitation patterns which vary widely from area to area. This is not surprising, as it mirrors many similar landscape studies of prehistoric settlement patterns in Britain and the continent (e.g. Bogucki 1988). Boulder clay plateau areas do seem to be the last to be occupied systematically, only showing significant exploitation during the first millennium BC. These would have been no more intrinsically difficult to cultivate than other clay soils, such as Liassic clays on valley sides which show evidence of having been farmed in earlier periods. It is evident from this study that other environmental factors, notably slope and proximity to water, are likely to have been more significant than the underlying clay substrata. This is especially true for the first farming communities, who would have been clearing and cultivating a forest brownearth or loessic soil which would have been fairly uniform whatever the underlying substrata (and see Allen and Scaife, this volume).

Environmental factors are the most predictable influences on the areas where people chose to live, hunt, forage, farm and generally exploit regional resources. Prediction of preferred locations through a consideration of environmental factors has sometimes been attempted (e.g. Kvamme and Jochim 1988; Pilgrim 1987). In such studies, the relative importance of different environmental variables can be assessed; but it is more difficult to take into account less predictable factors, some of which are now impossible to measure.

A less tangible but arguably more significant influence on the activity of prehistoric groups might be described as their social knowledge of the landscape. Information on the qualities of a particular section of landscape could have been passed on through each group's relationship with its neighbours (Mithen 1990; Edmonds 1999); the actions of one group may have been influenced by the activities of others. Historical knowledge of an area may have been significant, with previous sequences or events influencing a group's responses. Positive experiences in an area might lead to its being frequently revisited; negative experiences might result in its avoidance. This kind of historical knowledge might be reflected in the archaeological record, indicated by contexts where recurrent use of one location is evident. It might also have a symbolic significance. An area with its own 'mythology' or ritual importance might be visited by several prehistoric groups. All of these factors might lead to the use, reuse or avoidance of different areas, and should be considered as complementary to environmental factors such as soils.

The examination of this region has enabled changes in land use to be detected and comparisons to be made with other studies (Clay 2006). For the Early Neolithic, in the fourth millennium BC, long-fallow horticulture and some animal pasturing appears to have been added to the activities undertaken by Mesolithic groups, with, in many cases, an apparent preference for traditional Mesolithic locations, which were often close to the headwaters of streams and rivers. Later, an expansion downstream from these 'core areas' appears to have taken place. Communal monuments were constructed, perhaps at the interface of the groups' home ranges, while some low-lying confluences were also being occupied; the interfluves were only exploited intermittently (Brown 2000).

By the later third millennium BC, many of the Early Neolithic 'core areas', then, may have become ceremonial centres. The Later Neolithic/Early Bronze Age 'core areas', now the locations of more intensive short-fallow agriculture, were more commonly situated at slightly lower altitudes, further downstream. This gradual expansion downstream continued into the second millennium BC, some ceremonial areas being further developed in former 'core area' locations. Confluences and riverside locations continued to be significant, perhaps linked to ritual practices which have left their signature in the form of burnt mounds – heaps of fire-cracked pebbles used to heat water, possibly for 'saunas' or 'sweat lodges' (Hodder and Barfield 1997).

The pattern for the Later Neolithic/Early Bronze Age suggests occupation of locations many of which had already been used in the Mesolithic and Early Neolithic. The change from long-fallow to short-fallow agricultural systems suggested by Barrett (1994) may have produced this pattern of more intensive use. It is also possible that lower rainfall at the time of the climatic optimum may have encouraged farming on clay soils, with their greater qualities of water retention. Larger social groups may have lived more permanently in one place, with some flocks and herds being moved out to preferred pasturing areas. Cleared land was maintained for longer periods, and zones for burial and ritual were chosen; areas where communal monuments had been established in the earlier Neolithic were respected and sometimes reused. The maintenance of cleared land suitable for cultivation or stock-herding would have increased the significance of certain areas; a key consideration may have been reverence for the groups' ancestors, who would have been seen as important in the establishment of territories (Bradley 1984).

Looking forward

The perception of clayland exploitation is changing. Prehistoric settlement was frequently located in clay vales, with lower densities on boulder clay plateaux.

FIGURE 33. Fragment of a stone plaque with incised decoration, depicting a stylised face, found during excavations in 2005 on a Late Neolithic clayland site at Rothley, Leicestershire.

Since the completion of this research, nearly ten years ago, more evidence for Neolithic and Bronze Age activity on clay substrata has been recovered (e.g. Albone 2000). A good example of a prehistoric clayland site comes from Rothley in Leicestershire. This was situated on a north-facing slope of Mercia Mudstone – an unforgiving clay marl – in an area allocated for industrial development. There was no known archaeology, no results had been obtained from geophysical survey, and fieldwalking had located a low density of flint. At this stage the site could have been consigned to 'no further action' or a token watching brief. However, a small concentration of flint tools located by fieldwalking was targeted by trial trenching, and pits and post-holes associated with flint, Peterborough ware and Grooved Ware were discovered. Subsequent excavation uncovered a Late Neolithic occupation site with a possible sunken-floored building within which was evidence of structured deposition, including a carved stone plaque with a decoration interpreted as a stylised face (Figure 33; Cooper and Hunt 2005).

So clayland archaeology is now coming of age, and we are beginning to people the prehistoric landscapes of Hoskins's midland plain. Regions such as the east midlands may still hold significant evidence, although this may be less visible and accessible than in areas which have seen less agricultural exploitation over the last three millennia. However, as the site at Rothley indicates, prehistoric research into these landscapes can still produce important and unexpected results.

CHAPTER SEVEN

Hillforts and Human Movement: Unlocking the Iron Age Landscapes of Mid Wales

Toby Driver

Introduction

The Iron Age is traditionally understood as the time when hillforts rose to dominate the landscape, from sometime after 700 BC until the Roman invasion of Britain. Decades of research since the end of World War II have taught us how complex the landscape really was: that hillforts and defended farms have their origins in the preceding Later Bronze Age and sometimes continued in occupation until the early medieval period; and that regionally, across Britain, patterns of settlement could be extraordinarily diverse and fragmented. Certain myths remain, however, in the study of the British Iron Age. Hawkes's original 1931 study of hillforts was hugely influential, and his now outdated models of successive waves of invasion and immigration from Europe giving rise to different phases of the British Iron Age have become partially ingrained in the popular consciousness. The idea of the noble Celtic warrior clashing with Roman troops is equally attractive and dramatic. Here, we find Hoskins's original text a model of restraint, founded in field archaeology rather than myth. The prehistoric landscape serves mainly as a background to the main text, and hillforts are not especially mentioned; Hoskins (1985, Chapter 1) prefers to impress upon the reader the deep antiquity of the field systems and settlement patterns preserved in parts of western Britain. He describes a busy, populous, well-farmed landscape before the Roman conquest, alive with villages and smaller defended enclosures – some revealed only by aerial photography. In this respect, Hoskins's treatment of the later prehistoric landscape was forward-looking, and his themes of movement between population centres, and the permanence of trackways, boundaries and lines of human movement, are reflected in this paper.

The study of hillforts in Britain has commonly focused on the military capabilities and grand defences of some of the largest and best-preserved examples in the Welsh borderlands, Wessex and southern England. Statistics on rampart volume and slope angle are compared, while the chronological development of defensive schemes is linked to advances in Roman attack strategy. Such perspectives often seek to generalise or standardise approaches to the study of hillforts and their landscape settings without due cognisance being paid to local and regional subtleties of design and construction, and considerable variation through time in the relationships of monuments to the landscape. Within such approaches, which are still very much in vogue (e.g. Ralston 2006), architecture is seen as a tactical development, a functional and sober response to the problem of attack.

Recent years have seen a reorientation of Iron Age studies and new research perspectives targeted at defended settlements, with a wealth of results (e.g. Hill and Cumberpatch 1995; Champion and Collis 1996; Gwilt and Haselgrove 1997; Bevan 1999; Haselgrove *et al.* 2001). Away from the monumental English hillforts, with their abundance of excavated data and established regional chronologies, how can one advance the study of the Iron Age in a region of largely unexcavated defended settlements?

A recent study (Driver 2005) of a region of coastal Mid Wales, North Ceredigion (formerly Cardiganshire: the coastal region north of the Aeron Valley, south of the Dyfi Estuary and west of the Plynlimon range; Figure 34) sought to revisit an interesting group of hillforts sited in a strongly demarcated landscape bounded by coast, estuary and mountain and dissected by deep valleys. As in other regions of Britain, traditional approaches (e.g. Savory 1976; Hogg 1994) had focused on the application of generalised classificatory systems and

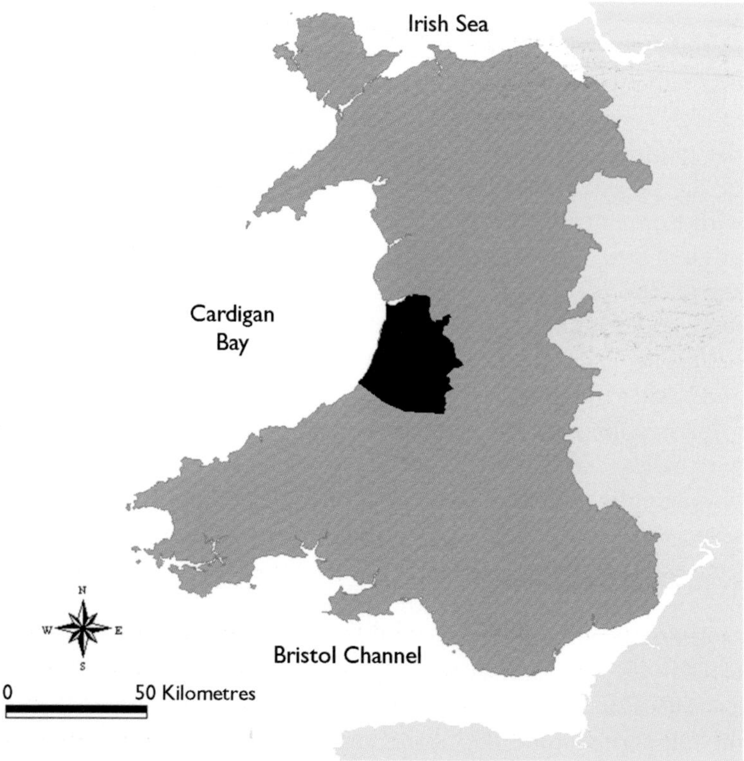

FIGURE 34.
North Ceredigion. Location of the study area within Wales. © Crown copyright. All rights reserved. Royal Commission on the Ancient & Historical Monuments of Wales. Licence number: 100017916, 2007

FIGURE 35. Monumental display, but on a budget: Pen y Bannau hillfort near Strata Florida. In common with neighbouring hillforts built within the Cors Caron façade scheme, short lengths of steep, overlapping ramparts block direct access to the main gateway, sited at the tip of an outcrop, while the sides of the ridge are largely undefended. The hillfort façade does not look out over the surrounding lowlands, but instead faces inland, towards high ground and the route of a mountain pass. © Crown copyright RCAHMW, DI2005_0213

the analysis of distribution of hillforts, divided into size categories on the basis of their internal areas. Such approaches barely addressed the specific characteristics of architecture and topography which make this region's hillforts so interesting. The North Ceredigion study examined the hillforts and defended enclosures as complex, three-dimensional architectural spaces, and made these static monuments more dynamic by placing them in their landscape contexts. New interpretations regarding monumentality in hillfort facades have been developed. Extensive evidence of *architectural complexity* has shown a society bent on achieving monumental display (Figure 35; see Figures 41 and 42). The identification of potential shared *façade schemes* has shown evidence for wider architectural traditions, informing us about the promulgation and sharing of regional (and wider) design concepts in hillfort architecture. This regional study has considerably improved our understanding of the Iron Age in this part of western Britain.

Rediscovering complex hillfort architecture in North Ceredigion

Nearly 100 defended enclosures of later prehistoric type have been recorded in North Ceredigion. The great variety of hillforts, from the very small (less than 1 ha) to the large (more than 4 ha), from the unelaborated to those clearly enlarged during one or more episodes, points to a chronological sequence spanning several centuries. As in other regions of Wales, there have been few modern excavations. Save for the 'classic' excavation of Pen Dinas, Aberystwyth, by Professor C. Daryll Forde in 1933–7 (Forde *et al.* 1963; Browne and Driver 2001), recent work has been far more small-scale (Murphy 1989; Murphy 1992; Driver 1996; Timberlake and Driver 2006).

The lack of a robust chronological framework, artefactual data or ceramic assemblages is frequently seen as a hindrance to understanding Iron Age monuments in Mid Wales (e.g. Davies and Lynch 2000, Haselgrove *et al.* 2001; Gwilt 2003, 105, 109–12). On the other hand, the hillforts and defended enclosures themselves are abundant and very well preserved; in the author's view they have been under-researched. Rather than deriving conclusions from two-dimensional plans and morphology, as many regional studies still do (e.g. Jackson 1999), we should examine the forts as three-dimensional 'artefacts' in their landscape settings, viewed at a human scale. This approach must be able to incorporate design elements too unusual, subtle or experiential (for example, the physical method by which access to or from a hillfort is sought) to be included in traditional classificatory schemes, which tend towards generalisation.

Research on these subtle and diverse design elements came together with the identification of a suite of building techniques, collectively termed 'architectural complexity'. Another significant discovery has been the recognition of shared 'façade schemes', interpreted as the construction or remodelling of a given hillfort along certain required architectural lines, governing both the overall spatial arrangement of defences and gateways, and the details of defensive style and technical characteristics. This results in a hillfort with an appearance and structural arrangement which apparently belongs to a distinct architectural tradition, regardless of the physical constraints of topography. Patterns were observed in the use of certain structures (for example, gateway bastions, wide-spaced terraces, outworks) and spatial arrangements of key elements (the positioning of the gateway on the defensive circuit; whether the gateway is obvious or hidden on the approaches; whether the gateway is 'open' or blocked), which allowed regional groupings of potentially contemporary hillforts to be identified for the first time. These themes will be briefly explored here.

Harnessing the landscape: architectural complexity and symbolic projection

The North Ceredigion research has shown that the monumental hillfort façades in Mid Wales were chiefly devised to maximise visual impact and the projection of appropriate symbolism to those approaching or encountering the hillforts. This 'symbolic projection' was carefully contrived and controlled in relation to the approach to the fort in two main ways: through the direct orientation of a coherent monumental façade; or through more complex combined schemes of topographic incorporation and monumental aggrandisement of particular points on the defensive circuit, termed collectively 'architectural complexity'. Crucially, all such developments would have appeared bold and often at odds with the natural environment and terrain. Techniques of architectural complexity fall into five categories, summarised below.

Structured internal building techniques and façade display
Important, forward-facing façade ramparts, or those which were particularly visible on key approaches or flanked main gateways, were better built in terms of their internal construction than other ramparts in less visible or less prominent locations around the defensive circuit. This is shown by their modern-day survival, with steeper faces and fewer signs of slippage or erosion than in other parts of the hillfort (Figure 35).

Revetment walling as a method of display
Stone walling is applied differentially to more and less important parts of the defensive circuit. Walls on display, or those forming the façade, may be better built, from neat stone blocks, or may incorporate conspicuous quartz elements (Figure 36), contrasting with those walls in 'rear' or less visible positions.

Levelling of ramparts and terraces
There is evidence that a number of hillfort ramparts and terraces were engineered to form level lines against the distant horizon, at odds with the undulating, natural terrain, thus heightening an artificial appearance in the landscape.

Topographic incorporation
This involves the use of existing, impressively sited outcrops for hillfort

FIGURE 36. Conspicuous use of a massive quartz block at the south gateway terminal of Darren hillfort with excavations in progress by the Early Mines Research Group in July 2005 (see Timberlake and Driver, 2006). The dramatic discovery of the large quartz block at the front corner of the terminal has similarities to gateway arrangements at Cnwc y Bugail, a small North Ceredigion fort (Driver 2006) where quartz blocks lined the entrance passage on one side. This discovery reinforces the occurrence of ostentatious, elaborate display techniques at regional hillfort gateways. © Crown copyright RCAHMW, DS2005_108_001

construction, and the incorporation of pre-existing high outcrops or cliff lines within the artificial circuit of the hillfort defences (Figures 39 to 42).

Conspicuous construction and false multivallation
Higher, stronger or more impressive stretches of rampart were constructed in places away from main gateways or at strategically weak points; these appear to serve no utilitarian role, but rather were designed to overlook key approaches to the fort, or to enhance particular views of the defences from afar (Figure 35).

Monumental facades and landscape approaches: two case studies

Methods of architectural complexity employed at the forts vary considerably from site to site, depending on the nature of the terrain and local approaches to the monument. Accordingly, one of the few ways to describe the subtleties of architecture and monumentality employed at these forts is to illustrate them in some detail. Here, two case studies are presented.

Symbiosis between lowland and upland: Caer Lletty Llwyd and Pen Dinas, Elerch
Caer Lletty Llwyd and Pen Dinas, Elerch, represent two potentially contemporary forts, each apparently reacting to expected human 'traffic' from the other, as shown by the reactive construction or modification of their respective monumental defences. Both hillforts share elements of the regional Pen Dinas façade scheme, employing wide-spaced terraces as an integral part of their design (see below). This may suggest they were occupied contemporaneously. However, both also appear to incorporate non-utilitarian aspects in

their defences which are difficult to explain without considering their particular landscape settings.

Caer Lletty Llwyd sits on the perimeter of a lowland basin (Figure 37), but its vastly disproportionate trivallate façade faces away from the lowlands towards a blind hillslope. This would appear to be a non-utilitarian expenditure of construction effort, if one were to make the assumption that the façade should be 'on show' to passing traffic in the lowlands. Further, due to the choice of a natural, partly defensible knoll, the fort is highly visible from the surrounding lowlands, but its interior is also exposed to view. Monumental defences here would certainly have concealed the interior to some extent, but evidently the builders of Caer Lletty Llwyd wanted to orientate the most impressive façade eastwards, towards the hillslope.

This skewed orientation is explicable only when viewed within the landscape context (Figures 38 and 39); the façade faces a well-marked routeway linking lowland with upland, perpetuated today by farm tracks and paths and the place-name Bwlch-y-ddwyallt (Pass of the/on the two slopes). The *bwlch* or pass gives access to a high plateau above the fort. The only evidence for later prehistoric settlement and activity on this plateau is the major hillfort of Pen Dinas, Elerch, which lies almost due east of Caer Lletty Llwyd, occupying a prominent outcrop. One potential reason for the orientation of Caer Lletty Llwyd's massive façade upon Bwlch-y-ddwyallt would have been the facilitation of encounters – friendly or combative – with visitors descending from this upland plateau.

FIGURE 37. Caer Lletty Llwyd. An elevated view from the west. This view looks across the lowlands which surround the western side of the fort, directly east to the high ground and the well-marked line of the pass or cleft in the hillside beyond, giving access from the valley floor to the upland plateau. This view illustrates the high visibility of the hillfort interior, and the pronounced terraces which define its western side.
T. DRIVER

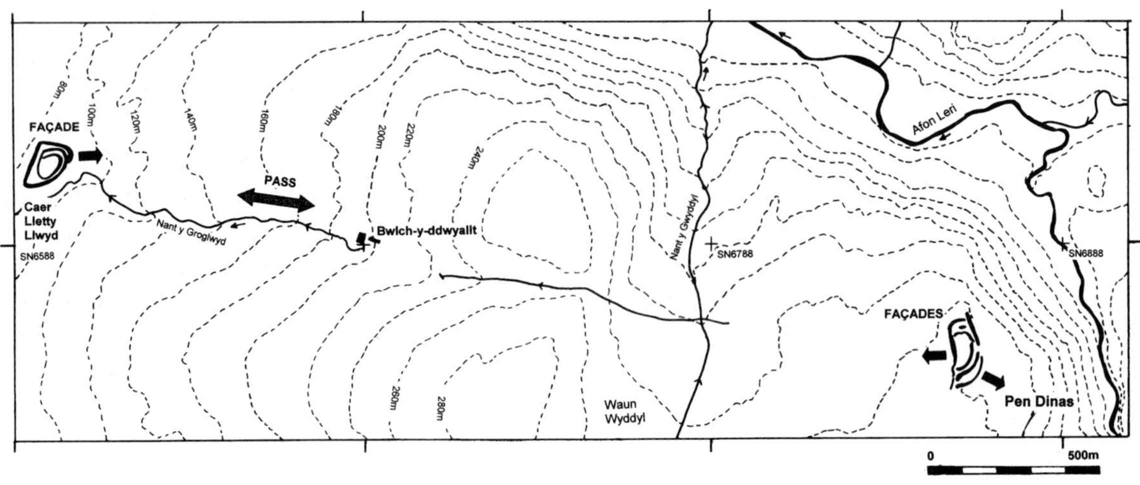

FIGURE 38.
Map showing the relationship between Caer Lletty Llwyd (left) & Pen Dinas, Elerch (right) in the landscape. The forts are connected by the pass or 'bwlch' which runs between them, and the monumental facades of both forts are orientated to face this routeway accordingly. © Crown copyright. All rights reserved. Royal Commission on the Ancient & Historical Monuments of Wales. Licence number: 100017916, 2007. DI2005_0147

FIGURE 39.
The western face of Pen Dinas, Elerch. Interpretative sketch from ground photography illustrating the western slopes of the fort which have been embellished with revetment despite their precipitous nature. This is a view of the side of the fort, which is orientated broadly north-south having its main gate at the southern tip of the outcrop (right) dominated by a free-standing bastion. (labelled).

T. DRIVER

What evidence is there that the defences of Pen Dinas react to this westerly traffic in any special way? Once on the upland, one approaches Pen Dinas from the west (Figure 39). This is the less monumental side of the hillfort, which has its main gate and entrance approach to the south, and its main terraced façade to the east. The west side of the Pen Dinas outcrop is very steep and so has few artificial defences. Despite this, it is embellished with a stone revetment with a capping line or palisade footing, still visible in places through the grass, apparently intended to heighten the appearance of this steep slope to visitors from the west. This west side of the hillfort also has a minor gateway or postern, which may have been later modified or blocked up. Such a relationship between the defences of these two hillforts may suggest that they were broadly contemporary, and may in part fossilise the otherwise transient and frequently invisible activity of human movement between two centres of upland/lowland population in the Iron Age landscape. Here the interpretation of subtleties of architecture at both forts, coupled with a close reading of the landscape evidence, is crucial to understanding the potentially symbolic role of these neighbouring monuments.

Incorporating topography: the approach to Castell Grogwynion

Castell Grogwynion ('the castle of the white pebbles') is a complex rectangular fort which overlooks the gorge of the River Ystwyth in the south of the study area (Figure 40; Driver 2006). The architecture and defences of the fort can be understood at a number of levels. The hillfort is divided into two distinct, though unequal, parts by a steep rock outcrop. Two sets of ramparts enclose this western outcrop, but it is questionable whether this highest point ever provided much suitable ground for settlement. However, it is highly visible, and is the first part of the hillfort that comes into view when approached from the north. The elaboration of the outcrop with ramparts, even though

FIGURE 40. Castell Grogwynion, aerial view from the east, showing the striking setting of the fort, on the precipitous edge of the Ystwyth gorge. The higher western outcrop can be seen centre-right, and sunlight strikes the prominent entrance bastion at the bottom-left narrow end of the fort. The finely executed and regular character of the terraced façade, with the upper rampart driven through in virtually a straight line despite the rocky terrain, can be fully appreciated in this view. © Crown copyright RCAHMW, DI2005_0218

FIGURE 41.
Castell Grogwynion: Close view from the west-northwest, on the main approach route. Here the deceptive characteristics of the defended western outcrop can be appreciated. The pair of ramparts which encircle the summit are clearly marked and seem to define a rugged, towering fort founded on a high outcrop. The main bulk of the hillfort remains hidden on the lower saddle beyond the outcrop. © Crown Copyright RCAHMW, DI2006_2002

there is little space to settle on its summit, appears to suggest an important monumental role which is only explained when one approaches the fort on the ground.

Castell Grogwynion is not visible until one drops down into the small valley it commands on its 'landward' side (Figure 41). From these approaches, only the towering western outcrop can be seen; the main body of the fort is largely hidden from view save for the prominent bastion of the main gate far down the slope, which signals the way in (Figure 42). The well-built bivallate defences which encircle the outcrop combine with slight cliffs in the natural rock above (possibly artificially cut back) to mimic multiple defences. Palisades, if present, would have enhanced this view. The impression from below, with the main lower fort hidden from view, is that this is the entire fort; that Grogwynion is a steep, towering, multivallate stronghold on the edge of a gorge. It is only on reaching the fort that it becomes clear that the fortified outcrop forms but a small part of the total defended area.

While Castell Grogwynion would have been a truly strong hillfort in its day, this high outcrop perhaps conveyed a more awesome first impression to strangers than would the larger, lower fort beyond. In incorporating a prominent outcrop, the builders harnessed topography to great effect, proclaiming the strength of the fort over a wide area.

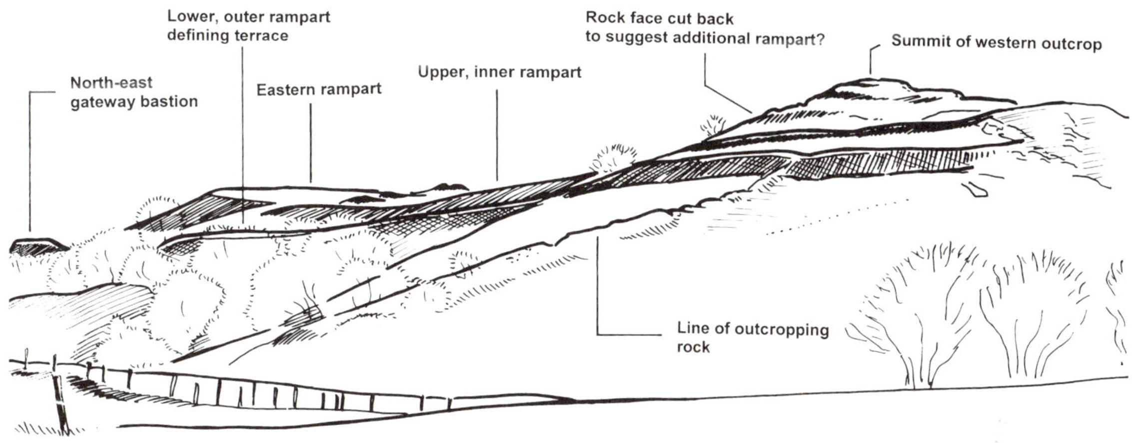

FIGURE 42.
Castell Grogwynion on closer approaches: Interpretative sketch from ground photography (not the view in Figure 41) from the north showing the true extent of the defences below the high western outcrop. The eastern extents of the main hillfort can now been seen on the left side. The entrance bastion of the main northeast gateway is just visible at the far left. This view also shows the main terraced façade which defines the northern (nearside) boundary of the fort, and the way the twin ramparts climb several metres from the low saddle, to enclose the western outcrop.

T. DRIVER

FIGURE 43.
Gaer Fawr, built within the Pen Dinas façade scheme. Aerial view from the east, with the main gate in the centre foreground and the terraced northern façade connecting, in the background, to the west gate. The main gates are open to the summit of the ridge, and unblocked by outworks. The impenetrable façade, also seen at Castell Grogwynion, blocks direct access to the hill summit and instead forces visitors to follow a 'correct path' of approach.

Wider networks of alliance – façade schemes and overland contact

The 'façade schemes', or regional architectural traditions, tell us about networks of contact well beyond the west coast of Mid Wales. The two major façade schemes identified in the study area, the Pen Dinas and Cors Caron schemes, are very different (Driver 2005). Evidence for other schemes was also recorded both within and beyond the study area, but these are not described here.

The Pen Dinas façade scheme

The hillforts classed within the Pen Dinas façade scheme (Figures 40 and 43) share common characteristics. They are all set against a precipitous edge which forms one long side of the fort, utilising the steep natural slopes for defensive purposes. They feature a wide-spaced terrace or terraces running the length of the fort on the long opposing side. There is no direct access through these terraces in the form of purpose-built gateways; therefore, access is only possible at the narrow end/s of the ridge. The gateways sited at these narrow ends are 'open', in the sense that access is unhindered by blocking outworks or overlapping banks and ditches. The gateways employed regionally 'exotic' technology, such as stone-lined passages, bastions or command posts, and crossing-bridges, although the guard chambers common on the Welsh borders appear to be absent here. Three main hillforts share these characteristics: Pen Dinas Aberystwyth (Browne and Driver 2001); Gaer Fawr Lledrod (Figure 43); and Tan y Ffordd. Certain key components of this façade scheme can be

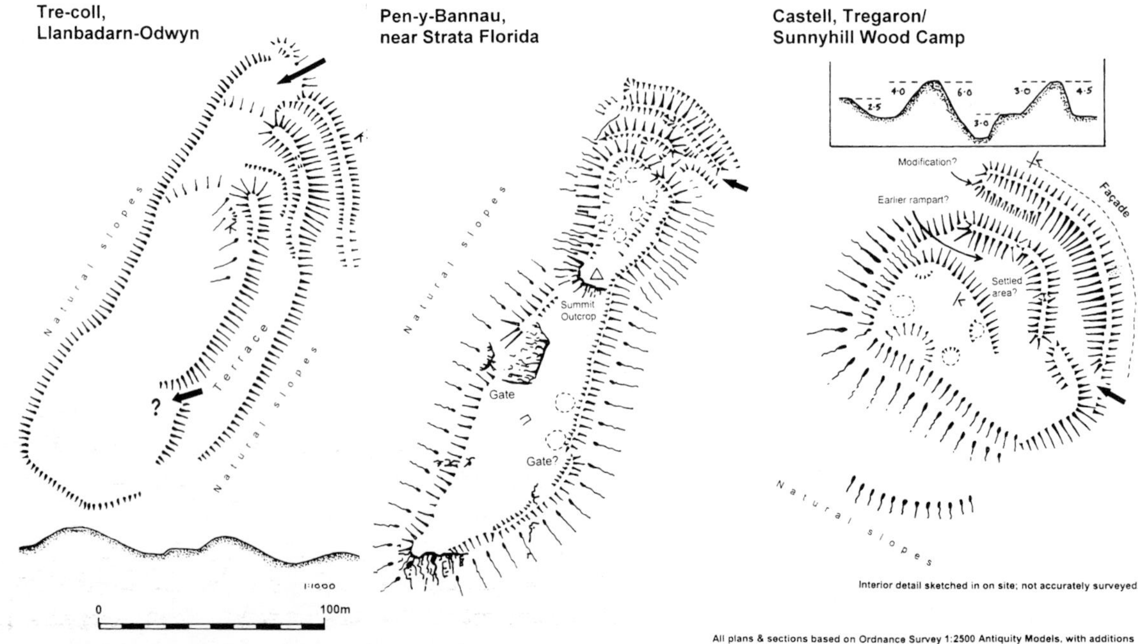

found among some of the larger and more complex hillforts north of Cors Caron (including Castell Grogwynion and Caer Lletty Lwyd). Indeed, the occurrence of pronounced terraces on one side, along with the siting of the gateways at the narrow ends, are the more consistently traceable elements among forts which occupy different topographic settings, including narrow or broad ridges, knolls and outcrops.

The Cors Caron façade scheme

Hillforts sharing the Pen Dinas façade scheme contrast markedly with those within the Cors Caron façade scheme (Figure 44), the distinctive architecture of which is exemplified by Pen y Bannau hillfort, but is also well demonstrated at the hillforts of Trecoll, Castell Tregaron and within key components of Penyffrwdllwyd. In summary, these hillforts are all sited around prominent outcrops or ridges, and have few artificial defences along their sides. Instead, the main ramparts are sited at the narrow end of the promontory or ridge, are steep and close-set, and serve to block direct access to the gateway. The implementation of this scheme is variable. Although the topographic situations of all forts vary and have influenced the spatial layout of some features, the visual characteristics of the defences remain very similar.

Architectural parallels with Pen Dinas façade scheme, east of the study area

Terraces are a fairly common defensive feature across Wales; indeed, the throwing of material downslope to form a wall or rampart is one of the most straightforward techniques of façade construction. Not all terraces exhibit the distinctive traits of the Pen Dinas façade scheme, and similar hillforts are largely absent in the landscapes of south-west Wales. Those which lie to the east, however, along the Upper Severn Basin in Montgomeryshire and along the Welsh borderlands, have considerable parallels with the Pen Dinas façade scheme.

In the upper Severn basin, Cefncarnedd is a major ridge-top fort, enclosing some 6 ha in its final stages (Spurgeon 1972, 339–41); it appears to share many characteristics with the forts displaying the Pen Dinas façade scheme. Gaer Fawr, Guilsfield, in the Upper Severn Basin (Spurgeon 1972, 337; Burnham 1995, 64–58 and 81; Davies and Lynch 2000, 154 and plate 22), is so similar in design, and sophisticated in its execution, that one could infer direct cultural links with Pen Dinas, Aberystwyth. Gaer Fawr is an impressive hillfort which commands a steep hill with precipitous slopes along the south-east side. It has a complex terraced façade on the north-west side which, before the hill became densely wooded, must have appeared bold and artificial, reinforcing a powerful visual presence across a wide tract of the Montgomeryshire countryside. Such occurrences suggest established networks between the Welsh borderlands and the west coast along which people, and ideas, travelled.

Trading or exchange contacts beyond the boundaries of North Ceredigion are demonstrated by the single, but important, discovery of an imported Malvernian vessel at Pen Dinas, Aberystwyth (Figure 45). This provides good

FIGURE 44. The Cors Caron façade scheme, showing Trecoll, Pen y Bannau and Castell, Tregaron. Although there are variations in the execution of the scheme, all forts occupy outcrops or promontories, and feature short lengths of steep ramparts at the narrow end which serve to block, or conceal, direct access to the interior. All plans and sections based on Ordnance Survey 1:2500 Antiquity Models, with additions by T. Driver

evidence for human movement, whether cultural or commercial, over the *c.*130 km between the Malvern Hills and the far west coast of Wales, and implies that Pen Dinas had a role in long-distance trade during the second or first century BC (also noted by Davies and Hogg 1994, 229). In discussing the success of the traded wares, Peacock noted that 'if the pottery was distributed

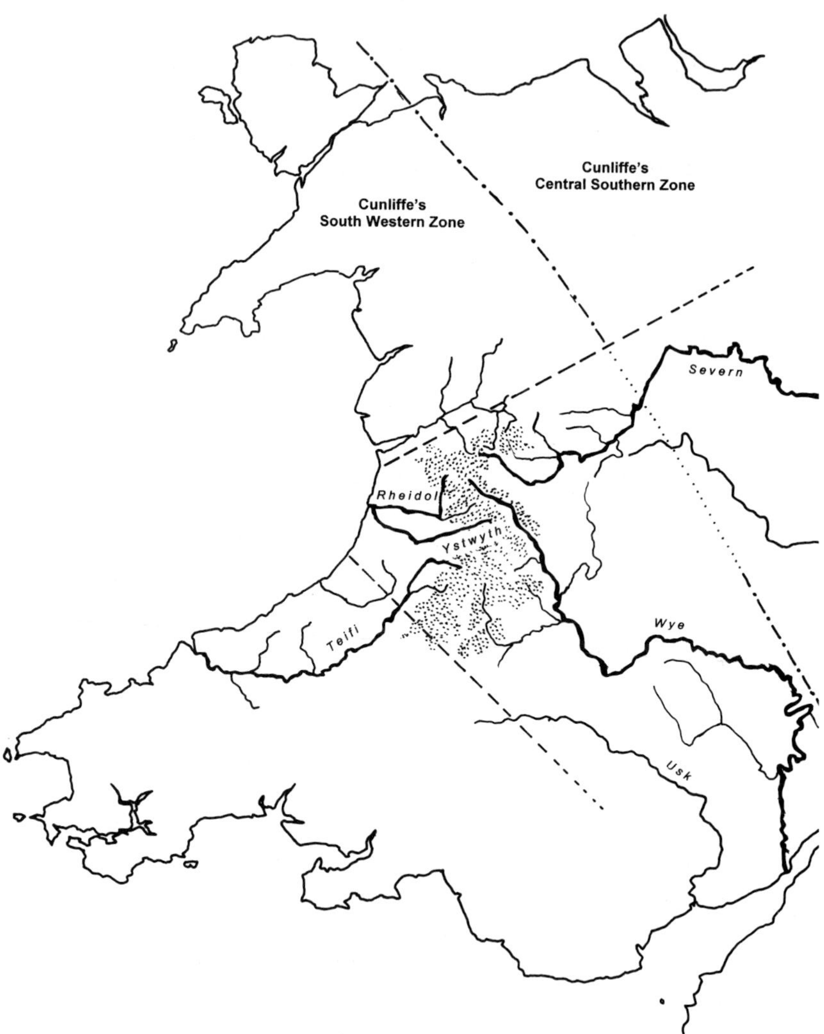

FIGURE 45.
The Central Wales Zone of Cultural Contact, showing major river routes in the context of the high ground of the central Cambrian Mountains (stippled) and the west coast of Wales. The broadly demarcated zone between the dotted lines reflects perceived spheres of influence, trade and communication between the Iron Age communities of North Ceredigion and those of the Usk, Wye and Severn valleys, east to the plains of Herefordshire, Shropshire and Cheshire, chiefly seen through evidence for ceramic and salt trading and the architectural development of the main hillforts. The north-west/south-east bisecting dot and dashed line represents the schematic boundary between two of Cunliffe's (1991, Figure 20.2) zones of Iron Age Britain. Clearly these zones are very generalised and retain little flexibility for east–west overland contact, and the spread of cultural influences, between the west coast of Wales and central England.

T. DRIVER

to a particular people other evidence of their culture should be discernable, for example, in hill-fort architecture' (Peacock 1968, 424). His short discussion constitutes an invitation to find evidence of a flow of cultural ideas in the hillfort architecture, one which has only been followed up in recent research (Driver 2005). It is likely that area excavations in the region would reveal additional evidence for imported ceramics which would place the Pen Dinas find in a more realistic context.

The salt trade would have established an important long-distance link between west and east. While evidence suggests that both the Cheshire and west midlands (Droitwich) production centres may have competed during the Iron Age, it is the Very Coarse Pottery (VCP) salt containers from Cheshire which are the best indicator of trade; they were being distributed as far west as Merionethshire and Anglesey by the second century cal. BC (Davies and Lynch 2000), with trade intensifying during the Middle–Later Iron Age (Morris 1994, 385). Morris (1994) notes that containers originating from Droitwich have been found at sites up to 75 km away, while those from Cheshire have been found up to 100 km distant. They are well represented in the Welshpool area of the Upper Severn Basin, with discoveries at a number of sites including Collfryn (Britnell 1989) and The Breiddin (Musson 1991; see Morris 1985, fig. 10 and table 5). However, two bodies of the VCP containers are also recorded from Cefncarnedd hillfort above Caersws (Guilbert and Morris 1979), which is far closer to the study area (50 km from Pen Dinas, Aberystwyth). The scarcity of excavated Iron Age sites in North Ceredigion prevents us from drawing more definite conclusions about the extent of east–west cross-mountain trade in fine ceramics and salt.

Façade schemes in the landscape

In their most impressive and extensive manifestations, the hillforts which shared recognisable façade schemes stood as monumental symbols in the landscape, contrived so that the main façades and embellished ramparts commanded particular vistas, even where these were concealed among valleys, passes and lowland basins. Prime landscape positions or even major topographic features such as outcrops were harnessed to enhance the visual presence and artificiality of the forts. The development of the different façade schemes no doubt centred on a clear desire to demonstrate a radical departure from existing cultural traditions with the inception of a new 'symbolic vocabulary' of architecture. This would dominate the landscape, emulating the physical appearance of distant, 'exotic' hillforts found in wealthier, more cosmopolitan or technologically advanced parts of the Iron Age world, such as the Welsh borderlands, thus establishing or implying the existence of alliances and networks with more complex societies to the east (e.g. Kristiansen 1991, 39). Referencing these external sources of power, inaccessible to others, would in turn have reinforced and legitimised the chiefly power of the elite in North Ceredigion (Earle 1991, 7). Architectural symbolism had thus become a powerful component in social control.

Front/rear symbolism and duality in the hillfort defences of Mid Wales

In this region we see 'complete' hillforts, but not 'comprehensive' monuments of the scale of those on the Welsh borderlands or in Wessex. These Mid Wales hillforts appear to have been finished, but they did not necessarily have complete or homogenous defences on all sides of the enclosure. In many senses they were built 'on a budget' (see Figure 35). *Duality* played an essential part in their construction, with a public front and a private interior and rear (Table 4). At the most public, visible points there was a heavy investment of design and labour, at the expense of less crucial parts of the defensive circuit, where the bare minimum of care and effort would suffice for enclosure.

Front	Rear
Monumental Architecture	Utilitarian building
Façade	Rampart
Visible	Invisible
Symbolic	Not symbolic
Artificial/contrived	Natural/unremarkable
Formal	Informal
Public	Private
Main gateway	Postern/rear or no gate
Most effort	Least effort
Structure	No structure
Closed/blocked	Unenclosed/open
Defensible	Indefensible

TABLE 4 The duality of monumental hillfort architecture in North Ceredigion as encountered in the field. In practice, at a complex hillfort, there may be several 'fronts' and 'rears' present in any single defensive circuit.

The extent of this duality in the field is presented in Table 4. We can envisage the conscious tensions, Collis's (1994) 'binary oppositions'; monumental and non-monumental parts of the fort would be treated, built, and worried over in different ways by those in charge. Thus we have a way of 'reading' the defensive arrangements that we might encounter at a Mid Wales hillfort, and, no doubt, at forts in other regions of western Britain. We may now interpret contiguous complete and incomplete rampart sections not necessarily as poor or unfinished workmanship (e.g. Hogg 1975, 54) but as part of a wider practice of monumental symbolism. We can appreciate the symbolic role and importance of the façade, or 'front', of the hillfort, and it is reasonable to assume that the orientation of these main façades was carefully considered and contrived. Façade orientation may well indicate the direction of key lands which fell within the visual command and territorial control of the hillfort and also, clearly, routes approaching or bypassing the fort (for example, long-distance overland routes). Despite the author's view that most forts were probably finished monuments, it is quite possible to interpret them originally functioning as ongoing socio-political 'projects', whereby the construction work in progress would have acted as a conspicuous if intermittent display of status and vigorous activity to outsiders. From this perspective, what looks like an 'incomplete' monument today nevertheless played a significant role during its lifetime.

Conclusions

This paper has begun to show that hillforts and defended enclosures of all kinds in coastal Mid Wales were built with a more complex and impressive architecture than was necessary to provide defence. In a region where resources (human, agricultural, natural, territorial) may have been under stress during certain periods of later prehistory (Driver 2005), the introduction of architectural complexity and what must have seemed like difficult construction projects signifies the socio-political importance of this method of monumental display. At hillforts where architectural complexity was implemented, a utilitarian approach to building had to be drastically modified. Hillfort designs which did not closely follow the prevailing topography made construction more difficult, more 'exclusive' and non-utilitarian, through reference to a higher symbolic purpose. In a potentially risk-laden, relatively impoverished environment, the act of building and creating iconic monumental architecture may have played a role similar to the chiefly feast as described by Dodgshon (1998, 15), where 'conspicuous consumption' may have been replaced by 'conspicuous construction', or the 'consumption' of labour and the 'destruction' of easy access to a hill summit by the creation of complex and ostentatious structures. This detailed examination of hillfort architecture has also suggested cross-regional influences and contact in the Mid Wales Iron Age, on a scale not previously considered in insular, single-county studies (e.g. RCAHMW 1986).

We cannot yet tie the North Ceredigion hillforts to a coherent regional chronology which could demonstrate changing trends in monumental architecture through time, as has been demonstrated by Collens's (1988) study of the Upper Severn Valley, or studies of the hillforts of Sussex by Hamilton and Manley (1997 and 2001). We should expect that social systems, methods of working and living in the landscape, and ideas of symbolism and monumental architecture were in a state of flux from at least the Early Iron Age to the Roman conquest of Wales (Hill 1995), and were subject to regional variation (e.g. Woolf 1993a, 215). It is no longer sufficient to apply overarching, rudimentary classificatory schemes to unsorted landscapes of Iron Age settlements, whose positioning, design and very existence were all products of a dynamic regional environment. Only by studying the monuments in their landscapes can we forge new understandings of Iron Age architecture in Britain.

Acknowledgements

I am grateful to the Secretary and Commissioners of the Royal Commission for their long support of my doctoral research, and to Professor Andrew Fleming both for his advice and insight as supervisor during my programme of research, and for the opportunity to contribute this paper to the volume.

CHAPTER EIGHT

The Roman Landscape of Britain: From Hoskins to Today

Richard Hingley

Hoskins's Roman Britain

Hoskins's main source in interpreting the landscape of the Roman period was R.G. (Robin) Collingwood's contribution to *Roman Britain and the English Settlement*, published jointly with the Anglo-Saxon specialist J. N. L. Myres in 1936 (Collingwood and Myres 1936, 161–273). Hoskins used the first edition, despite the fact that there had been several reprints prior to the mid-1950s. At the time of writing *The Making*, Collingwood's work was the best general source available for understanding the towns and countryside of Roman Britain. It was a balanced account that aimed to examine the entire population of the province, including the rural populations. Ian Richmond's *Roman Britain* (Richmond 1955) was first published in the same year as *The Making* and contained an up-to-date but relatively brief account of the Roman countryside. Richmond's main focus was on the military and administrative organisation of the province, including the major towns and villas, emphasising the topics that fascinated most of the archaeologists who studied Roman Britain during the first three-quarters of the twentieth century (Hingley 2000, 138–9). Records of excavations of Roman-period sites in Britain have been kept since 1920 and, between this time and 1959, there was a significant emphasis on the excavation of military sites, walled towns and villas (Figure 46; Hingley, 2000 149–51).[1] Collingwood's account of the countryside would evidently have appealed to Hoskins since it not only examined the available evidence for the villas of Britannia but also that for peasant settlements.

Drawing upon Collingwood's ideas, and reacting against the strong tradition of military and administrative history, Hoskins assessed the character of the settlement of the Roman landscape, paying no attention to the incoming Roman army and showing relatively little interest in the urban centres of Roman Britain. The incomers to the Roman province were of little relevance to Hoskins, who perceived that pre-Roman and Roman populations had relatively little impact on what he called the 'natural' landscape of England. He argued that a major dislocation occurred at the end of the Roman period and that the landscape was transformed as a result of the large-scale abandonment that was thought to accompany the fall of the Roman empire.

Hoskins communicated a minimalist view of the impact of prehistoric and Roman populations upon the landscape and also suggested that even this had been diluted by the regeneration of the landscape by the time of the Anglo-Saxons arrived during the mid-fifth century. For Hoskins, the most important lasting commemoration of the Roman occupation was provided by the Roman roads, villas and canals; these, he argued, left a clear physical impact, which influenced the post-Roman landscape (Hoskins 1955, 29). Hoskins considered that the occupation and clearing of the landscape during prehistory and from the first to fourth centuries AD was of far more limited significance in historical terms.

Hoskins drew upon population estimates made by Collingwood, Mortimer Wheeler and Grahame Clark to suggest that between 500,000 and 1,500,000 people were living in Roman Britain (Hoskins 1955, 34–5). He emphasised the rural character of the province, drawing upon the division between villas and 'villages' which Collingwood had elaborated almost twenty years previously (Hoskins 1955, 30–3; Collingwood and Myres 1936, 209), which itself drew upon historical roots dating back to Richard Colt Hoare in the early nineteenth century (see discussion of Knook Down (Wilts.) in Hoare 1810, 83–5 and Gussage Down (Dorset) in Hoare 1821, 31–4). Hoskins argued, following Collingwood's observations on the area around Cranborne Chase, that the distributions of villas and native villages were generally distinct from each other, although he noted that, in north Oxfordshire, where he lived, the two types of sites appeared to be intermingled (Hoskins 1955, 33 and fig. 2). While the use of Collingwood's interpretation for the villas and villages of southern Britain was excusable in 1955, in view of the scarcity of relevant contemporary synthetic work, Hoskins's repetition (1955, 31) of Collingwood's ideas about 'pit-dwellings' is more problematic. Victorian and later excavators had uncovered later prehistoric pits in some numbers on sites in southern Britain and, observing the pottery and animal bones in their fills, had argued that these were underground dwellings (Evans 1989). This resulted in generations of archaeologists referring to these pit dwellings as the homes of pre-Roman and Roman 'peasants'. Collingwood had written of 'huts, not houses: one-roomed, nearly always circular in shape; sometimes pit-dwellings sunk into the ground, sometimes stone-built structures standing wholly above it ...' (Collingwood and Myres 1936, 209). Since these pits often occurred in groups, the idea of the Roman 'village' came about. However, since Bersu's careful excavation during 1939 of the substantial timber roundhouse at Little Woodbury and the prompt publication of the results (Bersu 1940), ideas of pit dwellings had been increasingly dismissed by Iron Age archaeologists (Bowen and Fowler 1966, 43; Evans 1989). Excavators began to recognise the impressive and elaborate

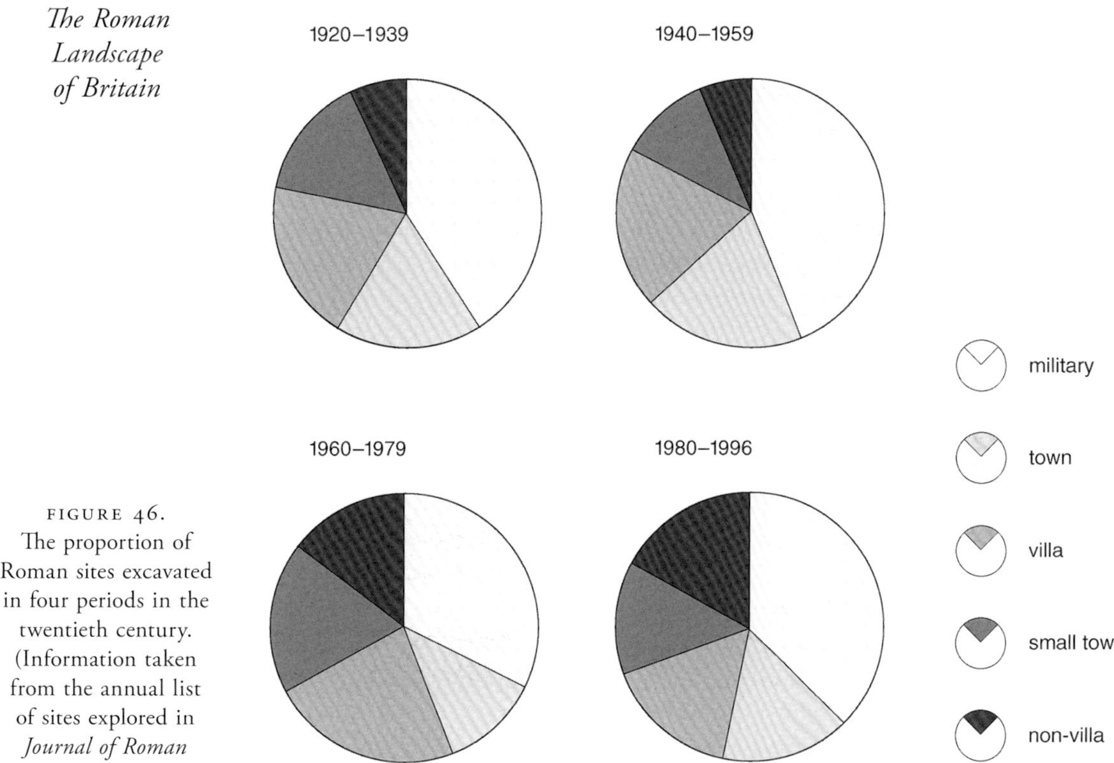

FIGURE 46.
The proportion of Roman sites excavated in four periods in the twentieth century. (Information taken from the annual list of sites explored in *Journal of Roman Studies* and *Britannia*)

remains of substantial prehistoric buildings in some numbers, but Hoskins did not address this changing knowledge.

In view of the transformation of understanding of the pre-Roman and Roman monuments of Britain that was to emerge in the 1960s, it is too easy to be critical of the way in which Hoskins omitted the complexity of the prehistoric and Roman landscape from his account (Taylor 1988). Knowledge of the extensive evidence for cropmarks across certain areas of southern Britain only became widely available in 1960, with the publication of the Royal Commission's volume *A Matter of Time* (RCHME 1960). It was relatively easy for a medieval landscape specialist to overlook or play down the evidence that had already emerged, as a result of aerial photography and earthwork survey, for dense patterns of settlement across some areas of Britain. Hoskins did review the evidence from aerial photography for 'close settlement' of the Fens of southern Lincolnshire and Cambridgeshire (Hoskins 1955, 33–4), but did not address in any detail the increasing evidence for dense complexes of cropmarks revealed by aerial photography on chalk downlands and in some of the river valleys of southern Britain (see, for example, Crawford 1928; Allen 1938; 1940; RCHME 1960, 9). This had enabled Hoskins to write, in the context of Roman settlement, of 'the open downs and some of the valleys dotted with hamlets and isolated farms' (Hoskins 1955, 35), but he also emphasised the relative rarity of settlement, estimating (and allowing for discoveries still to be made) that there might have been some 2,500 rural settlements across the whole of England, together with 100 towns (Hoskins 1955, 34). He guessed the number of native villages, noting that the 1931 edition of the Ordnance Survey *Map of Roman Britain* marked around 500 villas and 700 'native villages' (Hoskins 1955, 35). As a result of his computations, Hoskins proposed that only 750,000 acres 'rescued from the waste' at this time was used for arable and pasture. Noting that the total acreage of England and Wales under crop and grass in 1914 amounted to 27,000,000 acres (Hoskins 1955, 36), he suggested that, although locally important, Roman communities made generally 'little impression on the natural scene' (Hoskins 1955, 35).

Roman towns were also comparatively easy to fit into the agenda that Hoskins was pursuing, since Collingwood had created an essentially minimalist view of them (Hingley 2000, 133). Hoskins, drawing upon Collingwood's arguments, suggested that some 200,000 people lived in the 'small' Roman towns of Britain (that is, all of the towns, since these were all small) and, also following Collingwood, proposed that they were 'quite foreign to the mode of life of most of the population ...' (Hoskins 1955, 34). Hoskins noted the twelve tribal capitals and the thirty-three 'civil towns' (Hoskins 1955, 34), but did not discuss classification any further. He recorded that Collingwood had written extensively on Roman towns and would have been aware of his proposal that one reason for their decline during the third century was a 'sense of hostility toward the towns' by the 'peasants' (that is, the indigenous Britons: Collingwood and Myres 1936, 205). A more fundamental point, however, is that the minimalist view of the pre-Roman and Roman settlement of Britain, together with the idea of decline and fall, suited Hoskins's purposes, since it enabled him to develop his main proposition, the Anglo-Saxon origin of the patterns of settlement across the English landscape.

Hoskins's view of a transformed post-Roman landscape drew upon both authoritative accounts and a powerful English myth of origin, with roots that went far back in history. The Anglo-Saxon myth of origin for the contemporary populations of England drew upon late Roman and post-Roman accounts of the conquest of the lowlands of Britain by Germanic peoples during the fifth century, recorded by Bede and other early writers. The image of Teutonic origins drawn upon by Hoskins was one of a number of powerful ideas about the ancestral roots of the English which had been developed during the seventeenth century, dominated nineteenth-century ideas of cultural origins, and survives to the present day (Floyd-Wilson 2002, 106–7, 112–13; Floyd 2004). Hoskins also drew upon the powerful idea, also derived from classical writings, of a late Roman decline and fall. His idea of the depopulation of late Roman Britain and the abandonment of sites and landscapes was in keeping with many gloomy late-nineteenth- and early-twentieth-century accounts of the end and aftermath of the province (Hingley 2000, 28–37). These ideas drew upon classical writings which had been significantly reinterpreted for the contemporary context by Edward Gibbon, in his highly influential *History of the Decline and Fall of the Roman Empire* (1776–88; see Porter 1988). The fall of Roman Britain was developed as a political analogy for the contemporary British empire, drawing significant moral lessons for the contemporary British (Hingley 2000).

By the time Hoskins wrote his book, the British empire was in terminal decline, but ideas of Anglo-Saxon origins were still seen as having value in explaining the origins of Englishness. In this case, Hoskins did not draw directly upon Collingwood's writings, since the latter had viewed the condition of change in late Roman and 'sub-Roman' Britain as a gradual process from Roman to post-Roman (Collingwood and Myres 1936, 316–17). Collingwood's alternative myth of origin is much more in keeping with those that have been articulated by many landscape historians and archaeologists over the past forty years (e.g. Rackham 1976, 51; Taylor 1988, 9; and see below). In his contribution to the same book, Myres wrote of a beginning, during the fifth to sixth centuries AD, to the 'strenuous conversion' of the 'primeval forests' of central and southern England (Collingwood and Myres 1936, 325), an idea that was developed by Hoskins. In the mid-twentieth century, scholars did not agree about the nature of the transition from Roman to post-Roman Britain and Hoskins drew upon one of the dominant traditions of thought to elaborate his interpretation.

In order to supplement his claim for the limited impact on the English landscape that he attributed to pre-Roman and Roman peoples, Hoskins developed a rather negative view of a late Roman decline of the province prior to its eventual fall in the early fifth century. He argued that much of the limited area which had been cleared by this time had reverted or was reverting to waste when new populations took over (Hoskins 1955, 36). Villas and estates were decaying, resulting in much of the 'work of taming and shaping the landscape ... [being] lost in weeds, scrub, and ruins' by the mid-fifth century (Hoskins 1955, 36–7). In certain cases, Hoskins noted potential survivals from Roman sites to medieval villages (Hoskins 1955, 45). Mentioning Seebohm's *The English Village Community* (Seebohm 1883), which he called 'a neglected and under-valued book' (Hoskins 1955, 45), Hoskins discussed cases in which Roman remains had been found in close proximity to medieval villages, suggesting that a number of villages may have had a continuous existence since Romano-British times (Hoskins 1955, 46). Seebohm had also made the more dramatic assertion that the 'tribal' system of the pre-Roman 'Celts' in Britain was transformed by Rome, becoming the origin of the English manor (for the context, see Hingley 2000, 92). He argued for a continuity between the Roman and English systems of land management (Seebohm 1883, 418), which was taken to indicate the survival of substantial proportions of the pre-Roman population. Hoskins's emphasis on post-Roman discontinuity effectively dismissed Seebohm's tribal model, although we shall see that a number of other authors, in the years following the publication of Hoskins's book, were more willing to consider a substantial continuity from British (pre-Roman) to Roman and post-Roman landscapes.

To summarise, Hoskins drew on appropriate sources to reconstruct the

Roman landscape, but he did this with certain ideas in mind. He emphasised the Anglo-Saxon origin of the medieval and modern landscapes of England and this required a substantial fifth- to sixth-century taming of an effectively 'natural' landscape. The available information was changing as Hoskins was writing and this altering database was to require a swift re-evaluation of his claims over the succeeding thirty years. Other traditions existed in English (and British) landscape studies, but these did not suit Hoskins's purposes. It is notable that his ideas about the pre-Roman and Roman landscape continued to be published, in unchanged form, in revised editions of *The Making* into the 1970s (Hoskins 1973b, 17–44). For example, the text of Chapter 1 in the 1973 reprint is almost identical to the original, even retaining the reference to 'pit-dwellings'. Although a few new publications, including Charles Thomas's edited volume *Rural Settlement in Roman Britain* (1966), had been added to the select bibliography of the 1973 edition, the text had not been revised to allow for changing perspectives arising from the collection of new data.

Roman Britain since Hoskins

The impact of Hoskins's book on various disciplines was the main topic of the 2005 Leicester conference and the three edited books that are being published from the proceedings. It is interesting, in the context of Hoskins's contribution to the debate, that knowledge about the Roman countryside was transformed during the 1960s and 1970s as the result of archaeological prospection, fieldwork and excavation, and also through the holding of conferences and the publication of archaeological surveys and other books. Changing perceptions and the collection of new data had, by the mid-1970s, created a 'quantitative explosion' of archaeological sites (Taylor 1975, 107), indicating dense prehistoric and Roman settlement across the variety of soil types that characterised southern Britain.

A 'quantitative explosion' of information

It would be highly simplistic to suggest that this work occurred as a reaction to the minimalist views of the prehistoric and Roman landscape communicated by Hoskins in *The Making*. Archaeologists who focused on the prehistoric and Roman periods were emphasising the significance of their materials to the study of the British landscape, arguing that these past peoples had made a substantial contribution which justified the spending of public money on the excavation of threatened sites. In the context of the development of rescue archaeology, the minimalist view of the prehistoric and Roman landscapes that had been communicated in *The Making* was inappropriate and unacceptable, although it did serve to emphasise the significance of the medieval archaeology of England (the Society for Medieval Archaeology was founded in 1957: Christopher Dyer, pers. comm.).

The explosion of archaeological information occurred alongside the revision of ideas about the clearing of trees from the landscape. Hoskins was writing before the availability of dated sequences of pollen in the 1960s and 1970s, evidence which forced landscape historians and archaeologists to re-evaluate the idea of a substantial post-Roman clearing of the landscape. Oliver Rackham and Christopher Taylor, for example, pointed out the need to recalibrate the date of the substantial clearance of trees from the British landscape, much of which we now know (as a result of pollen analysis and the application of carbon 14 dating) to have occurred well before the Roman invasion (Rackham 1976; Taylor 1988, 8; see Dark 1999, 247–8 for early works on the Romano-British environment). The far greater historical depth in the British landscape was stressed in works that allowed for the development of a greater degree of continuity throughout prehistoric and historic times (see below).

Some of the evidence for the complexity of pre-Roman and Roman landscapes in areas of the southern British landscape was communicated in a dramatic fashion in the Royal Commission on the Historical Monuments of England's seminal volume, *A Matter of Time* (RCHME 1960). This study helped to create and articulate a new conception of the richness of the surviving archaeological landscapes across certain areas of southern Britain, and pursued the developing aims of the Commission, which reflected changes in knowledge of the English landscape. In 1956, the Commission undertook a new 'task', involving the recording of prehistoric and other earthworks threatened with afforestation, mining and agriculture (RCHME 1960, 3). It was noted that a special problem arising from this commitment was what to do with the early occupation on the river gravels. It was becoming evident at this time that many areas of river gravel in southern Britain were 'almost as thickly settled in prehistoric and Roman times as were the chalk downs' (RCHME 1960). The volume was intended to aid archaeologists and potential excavators in appreciating the resource and also to provide a basis for local planning policy. It classified monuments into easily definable types, including 'enclosures', 'circles', 'cursuses', 'pit alignments' and 'ridges' and discussed excavated examples. These major classes of sites were prehistoric and Roman in date and, by contrast, early medieval and medieval settlements appeared to be relatively rare in the river gravel landscapes. Landscapes of cropmarks were addressed through case studies in the Deeping and Newark areas of the East Midlands. Some of these areas appeared to have supported a density of later prehistoric and Roman settlement that was rather greater than that imagined by Hoskins.

Over the following fifteen years, a number of regional studies appeared which developed the idea of the mapping of cropmark landscapes (e.g. Benson and Miles 1974; Webster and Hobley 1964). These emphasised the potential complexity of ancient landscapes and the development threat to these resources, an observation which was picked up by the rescue movement, particularly during the 1970s (Jones 1984). With the increased recognition of the threat posed by construction work and aggregate extraction to these sites and landscapes, excavation also became far more common, revealing the types of information that would transform ideas about the pre-Roman and Roman past. The traditions of research that have formed archaeological databases have gradually changed as a result of rescue archaeology in the 1970s and the introduction of *Planning Policy Guideline 16* during 1990. A changing appreciation of the character of the Roman province is also reflected in changing academic frameworks of thought (Hingley 2000; Hingley 2005a, 40–2; Mattingly 2006).

Classifying sites

New information from survey and excavation fed back into the classification of later prehistoric and Roman sites. In 1965, the Council for British Archaeology organised a conference to address Roman rural settlements, and *The Pattern of Rural Settlement in Roman Britain* was published the following year under the editorship of Charles Thomas (Thomas 1966). A number of papers in this book explored the extent of the emerging evidence from archaeological survey and excavation, emphasising the complexity and intensity of later prehistoric and Roman settlement. Significant papers included George Jobey's 1966 summary of the evidence from his campaign of survey and excavation on the 'homesteads' and 'settlements' of roundhouses in the frontier area of northern England and southern Scotland. This work was of fundamental importance, since it illustrated the density of sites and their variability in a region that had been previously dominated by studies of the Roman military. H.C. Bowen and P.J. Fowler (1966) provided an equally significant and detailed description of the distribution and classification of rural settlements in Dorset and Wiltshire, drawing upon the extensive survey work of various earthwork sites undertaken by the Royal Commission in this area.

Classifications of the sites represented during the Roman period in Britain developed as researchers sought to understand these settlements. Charles Thomas's volume had shown the complexity and variety of some of these sites, emphasising that there were many settlements that fitted into the category of sites identified as 'villages' by Collingwood and Hoskins. Some of these appeared to be isolated farms, but villages were also observed as a result of the nucleation of a substantial number of buildings in a single location (see Bowen and Fowler 1966). In 1970, Malcolm Todd explored the concept of the Romano-British 'small town' in some detail (Todd 1970), enabling a distinction to be established between Roman towns (including colonies, *municipia* and *civitas* capitals) and small towns which remains fundamental today, despite the problems inherent in these concepts (Millett 2001). A significant collection of papers on small towns was published in 1975 (Rodwell and Rowley 1975), enabling a focus to be developed on these sites, which has resulted in further excavations, studies and publications (Burnham and Wacher 1990; Burnham 1993). Discussions of towns and small towns have often, until recently, been dominated by considerations of administration and the legal definitions placed on these places by Roman administrators and governors (Wacher 1995). During the past forty years, excavation, survey and research have, however, provided a wealth of additional evidence about the complexity of the settlements across Britain at this time, indicating the dangers of over-simplistic classifications (Hingley 1989; Hingley and Miles 2002; King 2004; Miles 1982; Taylor 2001; Fowler 1975).

In the context of the developing knowledge of the density and complexity of the settlement evidence for Roman Britain, a change can be observed in the direction of excavation. After 1960, the proportion of excavations on non-villa settlements and unwalled small towns increased (Figure 46), accompanied by a general increase in the excavation of Roman-period sites of all types (Hingley 2000, 149–51). A change in focus was occurring in the study of Roman Britain, with a broadening-out of interest from a fixation on the military, the administration and the relatively 'Romanised', to the population in general, including relatively poor (or 'un-Roman') settlements (Hingley 1989; Hingley 2000, 151–2; Hingley 2005a, 268). In the Mediterranean areas of the empire, a comparable development occurred as a result of the large-scale survey work that took place from the 1960s onward, uncovering whole landscapes of settlement and placing the more 'Roman' sites in a wider landscape context (Mattingly and Witcher 2004).

The landscape and the environment

Changes in understanding arising from the collection of new classes of information have gradually transformed the interpretations of Roman Britain and its landscapes (Hingley and Miles 2002; Taylor 2001). A relatively limited amount of work has occurred on the Roman roads and canals which featured significantly in Hoskins's account (but see Rogers, this volume, for an account of the significance of canals in the Fenlands of East Anglia and Witcher 1998 for the potential impact of roads on the environment). Some publications of the 1960s and 70s explored the idea that the British landscape was characterised by a far greater degree of continuity through later prehistoric, Roman and post-Roman times (Jones 1984, 162), an interpretation that remains influential today. Some researchers, emphasising the density of later prehistoric and Roman settlement and the evidence for continued agricultural use of the landscape during the fourth and fifth centuries, started to redefine ideas of a late Roman and post-Roman abandonment and subsequent Anglo-Saxon conquest and clearance of 'natural' land. For example, Taylor (1975, 118), discussing the Nene Valley, proposed that:

> It seems clear that the incoming Saxon settlers of the fifth and sixth centuries, to judge from the relatively few pagan-Saxon finds in the area, were in a considerable minority. The Saxons came to a very densely populated area, intensively occupied and cultivated for many centuries. Whatever political and tenurial control they achieved, most of the population is likely to have remained basically Celtic rather than Saxon for many generations.

Other authors – such as Fowler, in his work in Wiltshire, Somerset and Gloucestershire (Fowler 1975) – looked for evidence for continuity from Roman to Saxon landscapes. Although this idea of the general continuity of the occupation of the southern British landscape from Roman, or even pre-Roman, times to the present day has been challenged in some studies, it remains significant for some researchers.

An increasing appreciation of the density of settlement in certain areas has gradually led to projects and publications that explore the character of the occupation of various parts of the Roman province. Studies of particular Roman landscapes have explored the distribution of settlement, land boundaries and activity areas, emphasising the complexity of the ways in which people exploited the landscape (for some examples, see Taylor 2001, 53). A few attempts have been made to assess the extent of villa estates (Hingley 1989, 105–8; Hingley and Miles 2002, 160–1), while some work has occurred on the extent and nature of the fields that accompanied settlements of Roman date (Bowen and Fowler 1978).[2] Pollen analysis has also enabled a far fuller understanding of the extent of the clearance of trees across much of Britain, leading to the dismissal of ideas of late Iron Age and Roman Britain as a heavily wooded landscape (Dark 1999 summarises the evidence). Though much of the land was cleared of trees, the forests, woods and wetlands remained vital resources, particularly for food and building materials, while studies of later prehistoric and Roman sites show that people were good at managing woodland (Hingley and Miles 2002, 147–8). Individual projects have considered the relationship between people and the environments in which they lived, including soils, plants and animals. Useful work has also focused on the development of methods for the analysis of botanical and animal remains recovered from archaeological excavation; these have helped to transform our knowledge of the environment and economy of Roman communities, both on individual sites and across the landscape as a whole (Dobney 2001; Grant 2004). Comparable high-quality data on various classes of finds are enabling new comprehensions of the character of individual settlements and the relationship between people across the landscape (e.g. Evans 2001).

Population numbers and the identity of the province

From the evidence for known sites, recent accounts have emphasised the density and complexity of the Roman rural and urban landscapes across Britain (e.g. Burnham *et al.* 2001; Hingley and Miles 2002; Taylor 2001). Population estimates for Roman Britain have increased from the levels suggested by Hoskins and his informants, and currently stand at around 2,500,000 to 3,600,000 people, emphasising the density of rural settlement across much of Roman Britain. The vast majority of the population of the province, perhaps 80 per cent, are likely to have lived in the countryside, while approximately 20 per cent may have occupied the towns and small towns, with the 4 per cent that constituted soldiers and their dependants occupying forts and towns (Hingley and Miles 2002, 153–4). The military population of Britain is of considerable significance, since it represented a significant proportion of the entire army of imperial Rome (James 2001 and Mattingly 2006, 166–98 provide stimulating new perspectives).

Looking at the areas emphasised by Hoskins, it is thought that only 15 per cent of the Roman settlements in the lowland zone, at the very most, were supplied with villa buildings (Hingley and Miles 2002, 161). It is now evident, after decades of survey and excavation, that the vast majority of the population lived in rural settlements and small towns that do not fall into the categories of town, villa and fort/fortress that previously dominated accounts of the Roman archaeology of Britain (Hingley 1989; Taylor 2001). This realisation has been accompanied by a growing interest in the less 'Roman' but numerically far commoner types of rural settlements and small towns. Although the past forty-five years have seen a change in the focus of archaeological work, with increasing attention paid to the non-villa settlements and unwalled small towns, the forts, walled towns and villas still receive more excavation and emphasis in publication than their relatively lower frequency alone would warrant (Figure 46; Hingley 2000, 155), indicating that research traditions continue to emphasise the more apparently 'Roman' sites of the province.

The collection of new types of information from the 1960s onward, however, has led to the challenging of old ideas about the character of the Roman conquest and domination of Britain. A critique of the ideas of 'Romanisation', which had dominated studies throughout the twentieth century, emerged during the second half of the 1990s (Hingley 1997a; Hingley 2000; Webster 2001; Mattingly 2006) in response to the publication of Martin Millett's influential book *The Romanization of Britain* (Millett 1990). Many recent accounts aim to decentre our understandings of the Roman province, as ideas of the identity of its population have been redefined in more complex terms (Hingley 2005a, 47–8; Taylor 2001; Mattingly 2006). One particular area of focus is the developing emphasis on the ways that different peoples and individuals in the province defined their own lives, resulting in a much more variable pattern of identity (Hill 2001; Mattingly 2004, 14–15; Mattingly 2006). In these terms, questions of settlement classification and hierarchy become far more complex and difficult to define, since people are allowed agency in creating their own variable interests and fashions (Martins 2005). The potential of studies of human remains to examine issues of identity and health is also being currently developed (Roberts and Cox 2004).

Economy challenged by ritual

In the 1970s, the analysis of the towns of Roman Britain in terms of their economic function was popular (Hodder 1972; Hodder and Millett 1980), a tradition of study that has also influenced the analysis of villa estates, pottery marketing and other areas of life in the Roman province (Taylor 2001, 49; see Fulford 2004 for a continued focus on the Romano-British economy). The types of economic models outlined in Ian Hodder's study of location and marketing areas appears, however, to relate more to marketing models derived from the contemporary world, and their relevance in the Roman context appears unclear (see Rogers, this volume). Recent writings on roads, urbanisation and the settlement of the rural landscape have begun to emphasise the difficulty with the overall economic models which continue to dominate Roman studies, emphasising the potential significance of different approaches relating to power and ritual (e.g. Burnham *et al.* 2001; Taylor 2001; Witcher 1998).

One way of interpreting both urban and rural landscapes is to focus on the symbolic and ritual significance of place and region. Several new accounts explore symbolic and ritual aspects behind the foundation and topography of oppida and towns (Creighton 2006; Woodward and Woodward 2004), while accounts of the landscape, coast, waterways and roads take comparable perspectives (Witcher 1998; Willis, this volume; Willis 2007; Rogers, this volume). These works seek to explore the beliefs, rituals and power that lay behind the way previous populations occupied and exploited the landscape, drawing inspiration from phenomenological analysis, social anthropology and studies of prehistoric settlement and landscapes (e.g. Brück and Goodman 1999).

Conclusion

This brief summary has explored the ways in which understandings of the Roman landscape have changed over the past fifty years. Hoskins's ideas have been placed in context through the exploration of the quantitative explosion in our knowledge about the settlement of the landscape during later prehistoric and Roman times. Changing concepts about the significance of the Roman empire have led to an increasing focus upon the less 'Roman' and/or the less wealthy populations of the province, as some archaeological attention has turned away from the towns, villas and forts and toward the unwalled nucleated settlements ('small towns') and non-villa settlements of the Roman landscape. The pioneering publications of a variety of organisations and individuals, including the RCHME, George Jobey and Charles Thomas, have played a significant role in the development of our understanding of the province. New classes of information have encouraged academic approaches to change, leading to an increased understanding of the variability and complexity of Roman-period patterns of occupation, which, in turn, has helped to challenge earlier assumptions.

Notes

1. Figure 46 updates the information provided in Hingley 2000, 150; see Hingley 2005b.
2. Examination of the three recent summaries of the archaeology of Roman Britain (James and Millett 2001; Salway 2002; Todd 2004a) indicate that this is a neglected area of study, with only limited observations in these works about Roman land allotment.

Acknowledgments

I am grateful to Chris Dyer, Andrew Fleming and Christina Unwin for comments on earlier versions of this paper. It was written in the autumn of 2006, while on research leave funded by Durham University.

CHAPTER NINE

Beyond the Economic in the Roman Fenland: Reconsidering Land, Water, Hoards and Religion

Adam Rogers

Studying the Fenland: an economic bias

Early accounts of the Fenlands (Figure 47), such as Babington's *Ancient Cambridgeshire* (1883) and Fox's *The Archaeology of the Cambridge Region* (1923), were mainly descriptions of archaeological discoveries, but with the foundation of the Fenland Research Committee in 1932 at the University of Cambridge by Grahame Clark and C.W. Phillips archaeological studies were combined with the environmental and scientific for the first time. This legacy can be seen in the 1970 volume *The Fenland in Roman Times*, published by the Royal Geographical Society and edited by C.W. Phillips, who had been on the Fenland Research Committee. It is also evident in the Fenland Project, initiated in 1970 with the intention of gathering and documenting evidence for occupation and activity through time across the Fenland (Hall and Coles 1994, 7). Scientific and economic approaches dominated both of these studies and although the Fenland Project resulted in the beneficial discovery of much evidence for previously unknown Roman and prehistoric activity, it was with an emphasis on the land as an economic resource. Of course, the Fenland would have been exploited for land and salt production, amongst other things, but this does not mean that we can overlook alternative or additional ways in which the Fenland was understood.

One of the major recent publications concerning the Fenland is Fincham's *Landscapes of Imperialism: Roman and Native Interaction in the East Anglian Fenland* (2002), which attempts to explore the area, and especially settlement evidence, by applying post-colonial theory to the archaeological evidence. Although this study makes a valuable contribution to our understanding of the Fenland, it inherits much of its theoretical approach from earlier publications with no attempt to go beyond modern conceptions of landscape, economy, exploitation and value; there is no consideration of the wetland

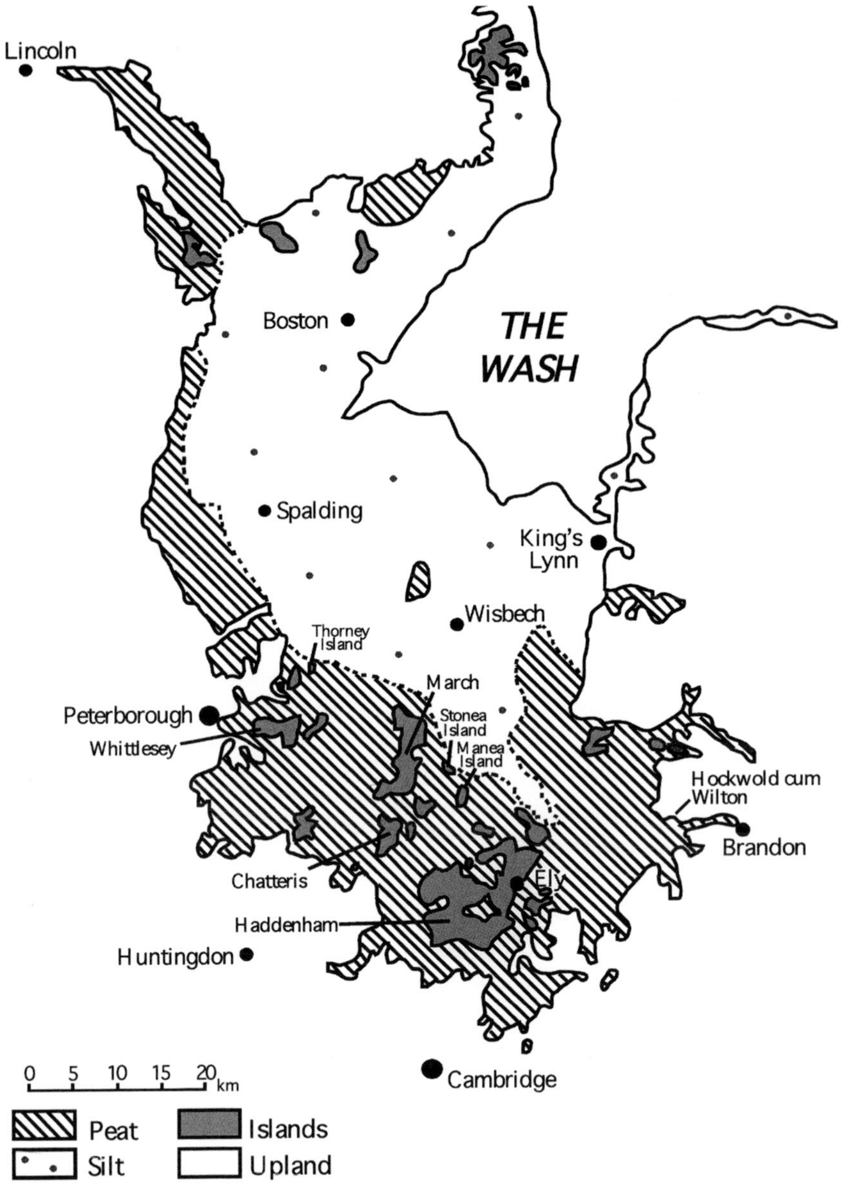

FIGURE 47.
Map of the Fenland. This map shows the various environments of the Fenland with some of the islands and modern towns highlighted. Redrawn by the author from Skertchly 1877

landscape as a possible sacred place/space. This economic reductionism can be seen in many studies and there is a general lack of impact of other approaches towards landscape.

Hoarding and deposition in the Fenland

The first part of this paper provides an examination of the evidence for Roman hoards and other religious material that have been found in the Fenland. Evidence for over 400 groups of finds and individual items from across the

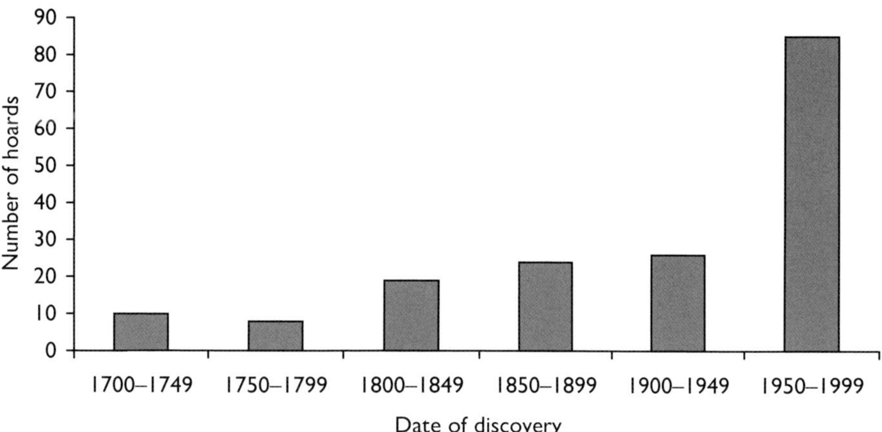

FIGURE 48.
The dates of hoard discovery in the Fenland. A large number were found before 1950; this may be through the ploughing of reclaimed land and drainage and dredging operations – a product of 'rationalising' the Fenland. After 1950, metal detectorists and more intense agriculture have contributed to the peak in discoveries.

Fenland and its edge were recorded by the author in a database for this analysis. It is clear from this that there is a concentration of such items in this area. The scale of the evidence, moreover, suggests that there is value in a detailed assessment of archaeological material in the context of an evaluation of attitudes towards the Fenland in Roman times.

Before the Fenland data is explored further, however, it is necessary to highlight the caveats. Figure 48 displays the date in which all of the finds of hoards and other religious material within the Fenland were made and from this it is clear that many were found in the nineteenth and early twentieth centuries, often accidentally, with few being excavated to modern standards, making the context and date of deposition often difficult to identify. This problem is intensified with the watery context of many of the finds, since stratigraphic details are even rarer here (Roymans 1990, 87; Wait 1985, 17). It is also difficult to judge whether a find represents the whole deposit or merely what was recovered or has survived (Johns 1996, 7); indeed, single finds, including coins, add further complication since they also may have been deposited purposefully (Haselgrove 1987, 13; Hingley 1990a, 108) and therefore studies of the deposition activities within an area can never be comprehensive.[1] There is, however, much to merit further study of the Fenland hoards and religious material, which have traditionally been interpreted in economic terms, and the context of their deposition.

The finds

The traditional emphasis on hoards and deposition as the storing of 'wealth' had often resulted in the concentration upon items of 'value', such as precious metalwork and coin hoards, but a more thorough examination of the types of finds from the Fenland show that this approach provides a very narrow understanding of the items deposited. Figure 49 shows that many different types of material, representing a wide range of objects, have been found. The necessity of studying the deposition of such items as ceramics has been highlighted by Reece (1988, 262) but these still remain neglected when contrasted with items of metalwork. Within the Fenland, however, Figure 49 does suggest that coin hoards were the most common hoard type. Whether coin hoards can be considered purely in terms of their monetary value and their role in the economy (Greene 1986), however, is debatable (Johns 1994, 114; Millett 1994, 100). Traditionally, Roman coin hoards placed within prehistoric monuments have been considered to be savings placed at recognisable markers for easy recovery (e.g. Robertson 2000, xxiv), but alternative views have suggested that the monuments may have been involved in ritualised activity in the landscape which included the deposition of possessions (Dark 1993; Hingley 1996; 1999; Williams 1998). A small number of groups of gold and silver objects have been found within the Fenland, and these have received the majority of the attention. These include the so-called Mildenhall Treasure from the eastern edge of the Fenland in Suffolk, which consisted of thirty-four silver items including the 'Great Dish' which depicted Oceanus (Toynbee 1962, 169), and the hoard of silver drinking cups found in a crushed state within peat near where Little Ouse river opened out into the Fen in Hockwold-cum-Wilton (Norfolk) (Johns 1986; Toynbee 1964).

Items of other metals have, however, been found within the Fenland, including much pewter and bronzework. There are numerous examples of large pewter hoards (considered in Appendix 1). Poulton and Scott (1993) have argued for a 'Celtic' revival origin for these objects, suggesting that they may have come from temples or shrines or were even acquired specifically for votive purposes. Petts (2003), in contrast, supports the Christian use of pewter and has suggested that deposition may have played an unproblematic part in Christian worship at this time. These arguments, however, may be simplistic, as they ignore the other materials deposited, and sometimes associated, with the pewter in the Fenland.

Many bronzes have also been found in the Fenland, especially statuettes

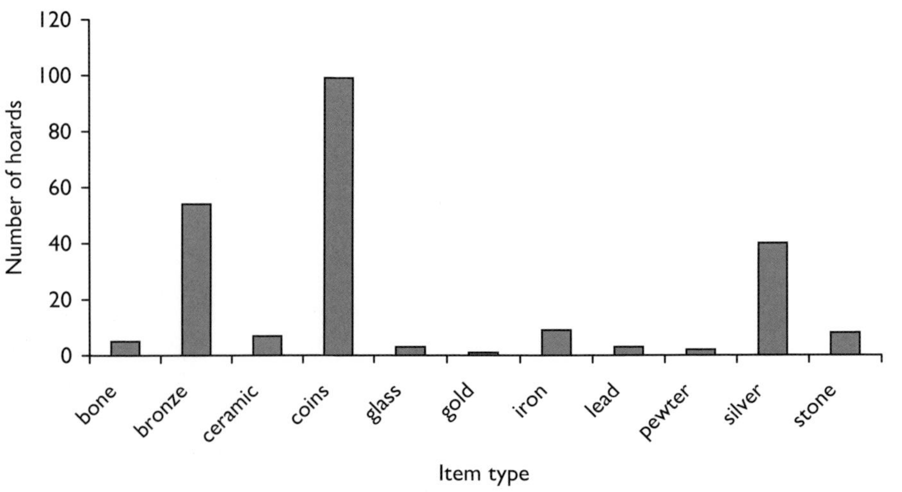

FIGURE 49.
The types of material deposited in the Fenland. The coins, despite being of different metals, have been classed together. Both hoards and single items are included here.

and other religious regalia, which probably represent many and varied beliefs, but also vessel hoards, with a notable example being the eighteen items from Burwell in Cambridgeshire, which consisted of eight bowls of 'Irchester type', three carinated cauldrons, one carinated bowl, a handled skillet, a semi-spherical fluted bowl, two penannular rings with incised decoration and two incomplete vessels (Browne 1976; Gregory 1976). The many statuettes found include ones of both classical and more local artistry (Pitts 1979, 19–20). One of the most well-known hoards was found in Willingham Fen (Cambridgeshire) in 1857 and consisted of a bust of Antoninus Pius in the form of a staff terminal, numerous baton lengths, a baton/mace terminal, a decorated baton sleeve and horse and rider statuettes within a wooden box (Babington 1883, 83–4). Similar items, including batons, have been found at Haddenham (Cambridgeshire), Bullock's Haste, Cottenham (Cambridgeshire), and Sawbench, Hockwold-cum-Wilton (Norfolk), all seemingly associated with shrines along the fen-edge (Babington 1883, 87; Evans 1984; Evans and Hodder 2006; Gurney 1986, 92). Examples of the statuettes found in isolated contexts in the Fenland are listed in Appendix 2. Again, the iconography has dominated studies of these objects (e.g. Alföldi 1949; Heichelheim 1937) over the circumstances of their location in the landscape.

Ironwork was also deposited, such as the hoard of tools, including axes, chisels, hammers and sickles, found in a field at Worlington in Suffolk (Liversidge 1956, 81), as was pottery and stonework, which could also have been used in ritual deposition (Hill 2002; Merrifield 1987; Willis 1997b). Deposits of lamps have been found, such as the collection of twenty-four ceramic examples at Whittlesey in Cambridgeshire found in the old course of the river Nene and the single inscribed lamp discovered on the edge of Stuntney Island in Cambridgeshire, where an old course of the River Ouse ran by (Hall 1996). Lamps were used in ritual activities, with artificial light often having symbolic meaning, and it was also a luxury because it required the burning of a food resource (Eckardt 2002, 15, 95). The importance of lamps and pottery in funerary rituals (e.g. Niblett 2000) might further highlight their significance. That pottery vessels seem to have been considered suitable for deposition in the same way as metal vessels is illustrated by the hoard of twenty unused and complete pottery vessels placed within a pit at Leverington (Cambridgeshire) and dated to the fourth century; the vessels had been stacked one within the other like a pewter hoard (Hall 1996, 172). Willis (2005) has recently drawn attention to the many unusual samian vessel assemblages known from sites across Britain, which he suggests may have been the result of structured deposition, such as the curious pit deposit at Stonea. Here, Pit 10 contained a number of complete and semi-complete vessels showing little or no wear; they were found along with pipeclay figurine fragments and other objects (Jackson and Potter 1996, 219). Other studies have shown that many different types of objects could be deposited together in ritual activity (e.g. Perring 1989). Stonework items that may have been deposited include a large number of quern stones found together in a site on the east side of March Island (Cambridgeshire) by the side of the Old Croft River that linked with the River Nene at Coldham (Hall 1987, 34).

It has been demonstrated, then, that many different types of material were deposited in the Fenland and the concentration on one or two is misleading and has perhaps been influenced by modern concepts of value (Millett 1994, 99). In many cases different materials were deposited together or in close proximity, such as the collection of two pewter plates, one pewter bowl and two copper alloy bowls from a field in Coldham (Cambridgeshire) (Potter 1981, 95) and the pewter vessels with the pottery beakers in the bed of the 'Old Slade' in Isleham Fen (Wedlake 1958, 90). Recent discussions of ritual deposition in Roman Britain have put minor emphasis on materials – the act of deposition was important (e.g. Clarke 1997; Fulford 2001; Woodward and Woodward 2004). Woodward and Woodward (2004) have suggested, for example, that a wide variety of objects were used in the same town foundation rituals. This may be simplistic, however, because it denies an individual significance given to materials or objects. Hill (1995b) has suggested that a conscious decision may often have been made when choosing an item for deposition, which highlights the need to give balanced attention to all items. All items deposited in the Fenland may have been chosen deliberately and thus it is important not to concentrate solely upon the 'precious' metalwork or to divide up deposits by material where mixed hoards are found.

Hoarding

The study of hoarding within the Roman period remains relatively neglected; the presence of hoards has always been acknowledged but they have never been explored in detail and interpretation is often simplistic. In 1987, Merrifield stressed the need to recognise ritual within the Roman period, and its continuity from prehistory, but it is only much more recently that papers have begun to question assumptions of a 'rational' Roman Britain, especially contributions in the Theoretical Roman Archaeology Conferences (e.g. Clarke 1997; Dungworth 1998; Williams 1998; Willis 1997b). On discovery, the group of indented pottery beakers and two small pewter jugs from the 'Old Slade', the extinct river course in Isleham Fen, were considered to have resulted from 'a capsized barge cargo or a place where barges commonly anchored' (Lethbridge 1934, 93). Similarly, it was suggested that the collection of quern stones found in Crowland Common, in the context of the Roman course of the River Welland, resulted from a sunken boat, as had the collection of pottery and large stones from an extinct meander of the Cam found in 1942 (Hall and Coles 1994, 109). Other attempts to explain the hoards have placed them within historical narratives, such as the collection of pewter plates and cups in the river at Mildenhall (Suffolk), which was said to have resulted from the hiding of possessions during the 'great Pict War' in the late fourth century (Lethbridge and O'Reilly 1933, 166).[2] In a similar way, the cut and folded pewter bowl found with a pewter jug and pewter dish engraved with a chi-rho emblem in the 'Old Croft' river at Welney (Norfolk) was interpreted as representing loot that, when discovered not to be silver by the robbers, was 'all thrown into the river in disgust' (Lethbridge 1951, 19–20).

The issue of value is also important since the straightforward nature of hoard deposition is especially emphasised for gold, silver and other 'treasure'. This is particularly clear in writings concerning coin hoards where they were deposited either to save money, as in a bank, or for safety (Kent 1974, 185; Mattingly 1932; Robertson 1988, 14; 2000, xxv). Classical texts, which have traditionally had an influence within Roman archaeology, do describe treasure and the value of materials[3] but it is unlikely that all inhabitants of the Roman Empire would apply similar values or importance to the same materials or objects (Millett 1994, 101). Salway (1970, 16) described the Fenland hoards as items hidden from tax collectors while Hingley (1991, 79) argued that the hoarding in this area was a form of wealth-display. Economic interpretations predominate in most studies of hoarding activities in prehistory, which are most often seen in terms of conspicuous consumption – the activity of the elite – to ensure social and political advantage (Veblen 1925). Such views have also been influenced by the anthropological concept of the gift (Mauss 2002 (1925), and were popular within archaeology in the 1970s and 1980s, when economic interpretations and systems theory were dominant. Veblen's initial theory of conspicuous consumption has subsequently been critiqued (Campbell 1995; Corrigan 1997), on the grounds that it denies the importance of the individual and assumes that all peoples consider wealth and wealth display as the most important factor in life (Mason 1981, 26–31; Martins 2003, 85). Fincham's (2000) suggestion that the elite deposited metalwork, 'portable wealth', in the Fenland as a way of expressing power and gaining status, then, puts an emphasis upon issues of wealth, value, economics and status which would not necessarily have been so important in the past.

The contexts of deposition

The context of the finds within the Fenland is an important factor to consider and this evidence might indicate whether the whole or just elements of the landscape saw deposition. Certainly, studies of activities within other contemporary wetlands, such as The Vale of York, the Ancholme Valley, Holderness and the Essex Marshes, have not identified such quantities of deposited artefacts as occur in the Fenland, which might indicate the special nature of this area. Figure 50 shows that, where a context is known, many hoards and single items found in the Fenland came from watery contexts such as meres and marshes; the finds that have been interpreted as lost cargoes have already been highlighted. The three pewter plates placed within Whittlesey Mere, found while draining this large watery area (Hall 1992, 30), and the pewter jug from an extinct course of the Ouse at Quaveney in Cambridgeshire (Lethbridge and O'Reilly, 1933, 165), are further examples. Other finds were less obviously from watery contexts but this remains a possibility as many drier areas today are the result of centuries of draining; the vicinities of the Hockwold and Mildenhall finds, for example, were once watery locations. Hutcheson (2004) has shown for Iron Age Norfolk that many types of 'natural' locations, not only watery contexts, could have been chosen for the deposition of metalwork. While there is perhaps a danger in categorising 'natural' and 'domestic'/'non-natural' in prehistory and the Roman period, this can perhaps be seen in the Fenland with the interaction between watery and non-watery locations. The Fen 'islands' and especially the higher surrounding fen-edge, important parts of this socially significant landscape, were also subject to deposition and much religious activity. The Fenland was more than a venue for conspicuous consumption. It was a significant, socially constructed and religious place/space embedded in the history of human action, as seen at locations such as Stonea Island, which contains monuments dating from the Neolithic to the Iron Age (Fincham 2002, 53) and, during parts of the year, would have been surrounded by water. It may be more stimulating to see Stonea as a ritual complex fully integrated into its landscape setting. One area of the Fenland that does seem to have received less deposition than other areas is the expanse of silt near the Wash; the peat areas, and the islands within them, surrounding this silt were where the majority of the artefacts were found.

It is also noticeable that the fen-edge, a transitional zone marking the boundary between the 'treacherous wild Fenland' and rich drier upland (Taylor 1985, 46), and still greatly susceptible to flooding (Bromwich 1970), saw a particular high concentration of finds of religious artefacts and hoards. Boundaries seem to have had a special significance amongst indigenous peoples and Romans (Bowden and McOmish 1987; Hingley 1990b) and the fen-edge may, then, have had an importance beyond the natural resources to be exploited. Rivers and bogs were also regarded as liminal places where contact with the supernatural world could be made (Wait 1985, 249). The concentration of depositions from prehistory onwards at areas on the edge of the Fenland, such as Fiskerton (Lincolnshire) and Hockwold-cum-Wilton (Norfolk), support notions of its importance. Fincham's suggestion that the fen-edge was wealthier and less

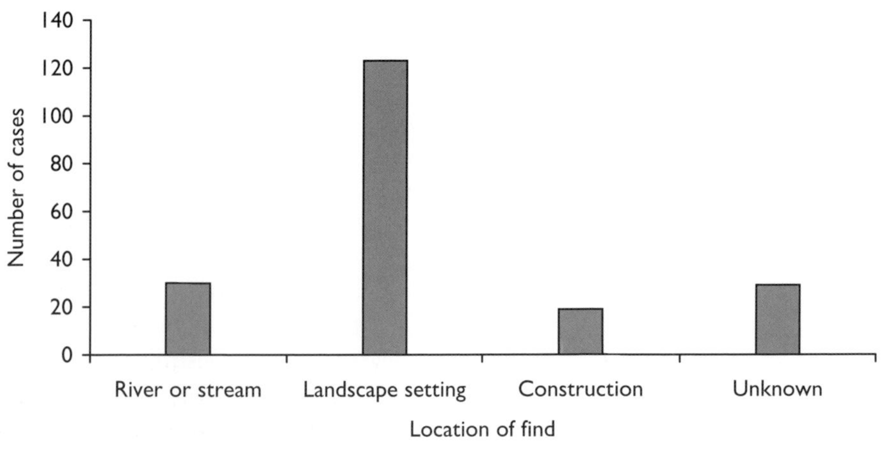

FIGURE 50.
The contexts in which the hoards have been found in the Fenland. The 'landscape setting' category is broad, but signifies items deposited away from watercourses and buildings; many of these may have been deposited in land that was once wet.

traditional than the centre, and those living there expressed themselves with Roman-style material culture (Fincham 2002, 69), may be valid but it neglects the possible religious importance of the fen-edge and the impact this would have had on the lives of Fenland inhabitants and upon patterns of deposition. Sixty-two out of seventy-six bronze objects of a definite religious nature found in the Fenland came from along the fen-edge, and there was also a number of temple or shrine-like buildings here.

The hoard of religious regalia from Willingham (Cambridgeshire), on the south-west fen-edge, for example, may have been connected with a shrine building in the vicinity, but the material itself seems to have been deliberately collected together and deposited in the Fenland landscape setting away from this shrine. Similar material was found nearby at Haddenham, also on the south-west fen-edge, where excavations have shown that a Roman shrine had been constructed directly above a Bronze Age barrow (Evans and Hodder 2006, 339), suggesting that the significance and history of the area was being drawn upon; this interaction with the past was a complex process which can be explored in different ways (e.g. Hingley 1999). This excavation has also highlighted the shrine's apparent isolation, with no evidence for a means of long-term self-support. This may suggest that the building played a role in religious activity that moved within the Fenland landscape: ritual performance within the culturally significant religious space. Indeed, Evans and Hodder (2006, 446) have suggested that, acknowledging the prehistoric mound under the shrine, movements within the Fenland landscape may have been drawing upon and developing ways in which monuments were used in prehistory. Religion involving movement within the landscape setting is also suggested by the large number of mace/batons found in, and largely unique to, the Fenland. Such movements within the landscape may also be the reason for the discovery of so many bronze statuettes that were seemingly deposited in isolated locations.

A watery setting also seems to have been important for other religious complexes, such as that at Prior's Meadow, Deeping St James (Lincolnshire), on the western fen-edge (Hayes and Lane 1992, 135), and Leylands Farm, Hockwold-cum-Wilton (Norfolk), on the eastern fen-edge (Gurney 1986, 49). Both sites have yielded ritual crowns and diadems; one, having been excavated to modern standards, had been placed within a pit. Other crown fragments and religious bronze finds, possibly associated with the Hockwold silver cups, have been identified at Sawbench in Hockwold-cum-Wilton, and may also have indicated the site of a shrine along the fen-edge (Gurney 1986; Silvester 1991, 49), suggesting that bounding the Fenland with religious activity was important.

Drawing on its prehistoric past, the temple building at Stonea in the central Fenland may have been an important focus, but material was also deposited in the surrounding landscape. This was also the case for other shrine sites, suggesting that the structures may have been reflecting behaviour that had been, and was still, taking place within the landscape (Figure 51). That the

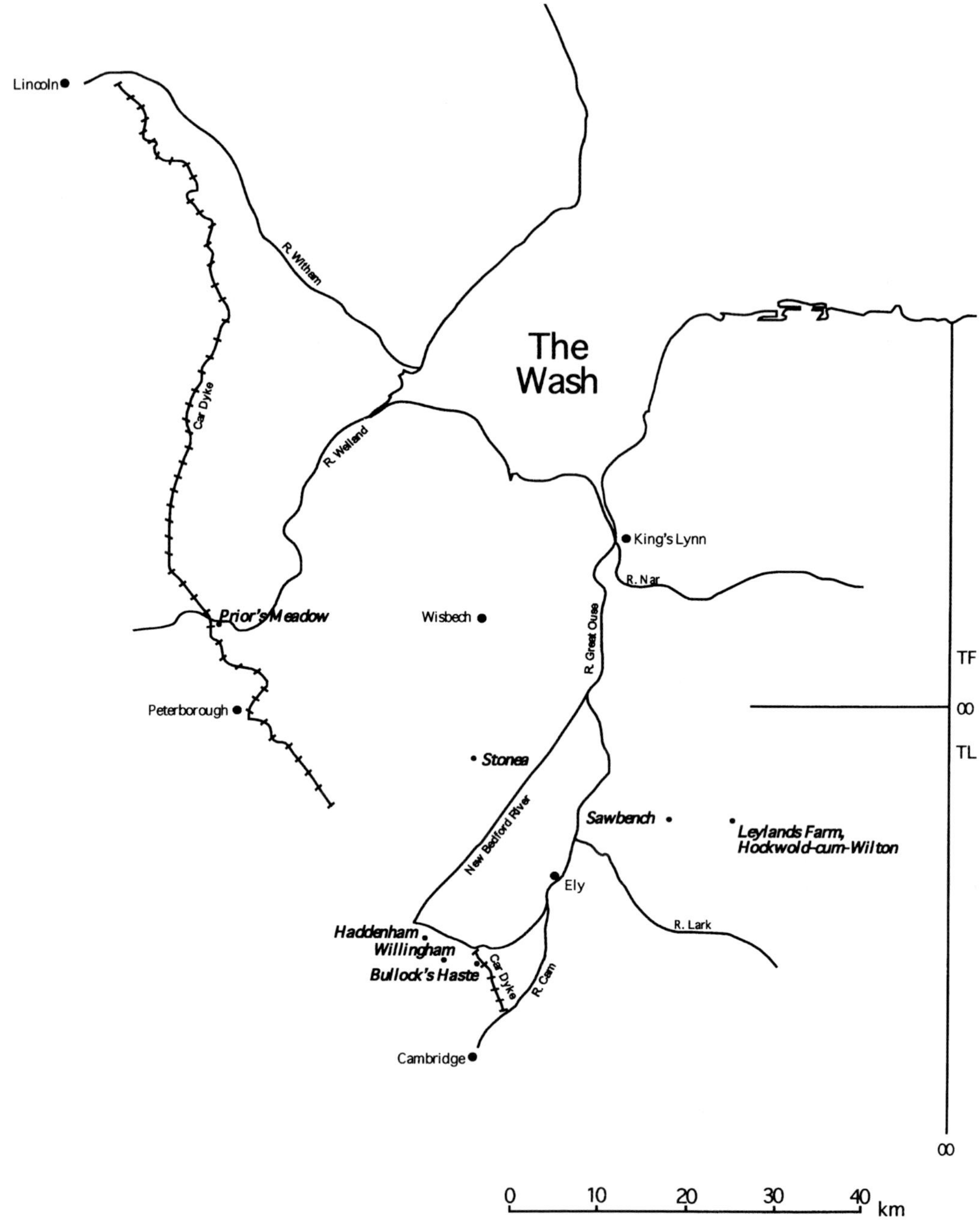

buildings and enclosures at temples or shrines were not necessarily always the most important focus for religious belief has been suggested by Willis (2007) for the Iron Age, where he has highlighted the concentration of temples in close proximity to the sea, perhaps drawing on the significance of the tides. Isolated finds such as the miniature axes found in Lode (Cambridgeshire), which are rarely found outside the context of temple sites (Taylor 1985, 47), might also indicate a similar interpretation. The parish of

Hockwold-cum-Wilton includes shrine complexes at Leylands Farm and Sawbench, together with many hoards, including the silver cups and numerous hoards of pewter vessels that have been found in the environs of the shrines. Many of the finds of metal items in the Fenland have been made by detectorists, and frequently no contextual information is recorded. Although this raises the possibility that some finds were associated with buildings that have not been discovered it does not deny the importance of their concentration within the Fenland. Moreover, the number of finds suggests that it is unlikely that all would have been associated with shrines or other buildings. The examples discussed above do seem to support the notion that depositions, and the related religious activity, occurred within the landscape, away from buildings, possibly because the Fenland itself was special. By the time of the Roman conquest, the Fenland was a significant historical landscape. It was a socially important and constructed religious place and space which demanded veneration. Over time, along with the threat from the Romans, the significance of the Fenland may have increased and it is clear from the many pewter items found (a material not evident in Britain before the mid-third century (Peal 1967) that deposition continued into the later Roman period. The Fenland may have been much more than an area to be controlled, drained and exploited.

Beyond the economic

This examination of objects from the Fenland attempted to add another dimension to our understanding of the area in the Roman period. Economic reductionism within studies of the Fenland has led to a particular emphasis in understandings of the Fenland landscape. This can itself be placed within its historical context since it is perhaps only from the post-medieval period that economic thinking and consumerism have begun to dominate thought. Industrialisation and the exploitation of the colonies from the eighteenth century onwards was perhaps especially influential and it was this period that also witnessed developing interest in the Roman period (Hingley 2000, 145; Todd 2004b). That the Fenland seems to have been imagined in alternative ways in earlier times is hinted at by the actions of incoming Christians in the post-Roman period who, according to Bede, sought to convert the area by the symbolic washing of St Oswald's bones in the River Witham (Stocker and Everson 2003, 282). The monasteries that were then founded in the Fenland transformed the landscape through construction and drainage activities (Aston 1993, 20; Purseglove 1988, 41) and the exploitation of the natural resources (Bond 2000, 63; Darby 1983, 10–26; Hall and Coles 1994, 1–2).

FIGURE 51. The major bronzework hoards found within the Fenland. Many of these were also found near a shrine or temple. Drawn by the author

Drainage and economic development intensified in the post-medieval period, with the passing of Acts of Parliament intended to turn over much of the land to cultivation (Purseglove 1988, 46). This was a time when society was becoming increasingly commodity-driven and the possession of material wealth was an important social indicator (Porter 2000; 2001, 99 and 205; Wood 2002, 2 and 206). Nature was increasingly commoditised, being seen in terms of value that should be exploited (Beinart and Coates 1995, 5). With a growing interest in classical texts from the post-medieval period onwards, early modern and often aristocratic views about the importance of owning productive land drew upon Roman elite attitudes and influenced the way in which land was viewed. Cato's work *De Agricultura*, for example, focuses upon the investment potential of the farm and negates other forms of money-making (Cato trans. Dalby 1998, 24). Virgil's *Georgics* also has farming as its main theme and land ownership and agricultural activity are described in such a way as to portray a new golden age within Rome (Johnston 1980, ix). Similar attitudes can be seen clearly in the post-medieval aristocratic estates of western Europe; indeed, the architect and designer Inigo Jones was described by a contemporary as 'the Vitruvius of his age' (Summerson 2000, 6). Through stately homes and especially their estates, many of which appeared to be 'natural' landscapes but were in fact the product of much artificiality, direct parallels between the present and the Roman past were made (Taylor 1983, 41; Turner 1999; Weiss 1995).[4] From the Enlightenment onwards, the 'transition from *homo civilis* to *homo economicus*' (Porter 2000, 396) will have altered attitudes towards economic matters in such a way as to transform perceptions and understandings of 'landscape'; this is important when attempting to understand the ways in which Roman archaeology has been studied and understood.

It is uncertain, however, how far the concept of the market economy existed in Roman Britain and the rest of the Roman world. In 1957 Polanyi suggested that within primitive societies the economy worked differently; exchange was 'embedded' in social relations and therefore terms such as 'economic life' and 'economy' had no meaning (Polanyi 1957). In an important but often neglected paper, Hodder (1979) advanced similar ideas for the British Iron Age and went on to suggest, as has Salway (1993, 437–9), that such an 'embedded' economy continued after the Roman conquest and that the economic system of the Romans themselves was far from its modern Western counterpart. Temin (2001), however, studying the Roman economy as an economist rather than ancient historian, suggested that there was market exchange and a market economy, even if the parts of the economy were not tied together as tightly as they are today. Temin's study, though, concentrated on the Mediterranean region and may be less supportable for areas such as Britain. Studies of other periods of the past – for example, the Neolithic and Iron Age – are now increasingly stressing the need to think beyond the economic when interpreting ways of life (e.g. Hill 1989; 1995b; Hingley 1997b; Thomas 1991). Thomas, for instance, in his book *Rethinking the Neolithic* (1991), argued that too often the term 'Neolithic' has been seen as synonymous with 'mixed farming economy', with the consequent neglect of other aspects of human life, including ritual behaviour.

It seems logical that similar approaches should be attempted for Roman Britain, and perhaps especially for areas such as the Fenland, although of course the Roman period would have differed in many aspects from earlier periods. The notion that the Fenland had been a Roman Imperial Estate, which has often dominated studies of the area (e.g. Hall 1987; Hall and Coles 1994; Salway 1970), may have been at least partly based on the concept that economic and material wealth was universally desirable. That this was not obviously visible in the Fenland, given the absence of villas, has been taken to indicate that the land was exploited in a different manner. That Imperial Estates existed is clear (Kehoe 1988; Thompson 1987), but there have always been uncertainties concerning the Fenland (Taylor 2000); rather than being an estate centre, the tower at Stonea Grange may have been built to keep control of an important indigenous political and religious focus (Taylor 2000, 656). Although Fincham argued against the Imperial Estate model for the Fenland, the economy is still central to his arguments, suggesting the possibility of mixed ownership and exploitation between the local population and the Roman authorities (Fincham 2002, 75). These writings appear to project attitudes of economic rationality that emerged with the Enlightenment; they also draw on certain concepts derived from the classical texts. Instead, we can seek to understand the Fenland in different ways, pursuing ideas that emphasise alternative aspects of the available information.

Indigenous and Roman attitudes towards water

Before modern drainage there would have been a constant, or near constant, presence of water in the Fenland; today, even after drainage, the water table lies not far below the surface (Hall *et al.* 1987, 2). Wetlands are transitional zones between land and water, being neither one nor the other, but part of both, and are constantly transforming – at times water would even seemingly try to dominate the land (Dinnin and Van de Noort 1999, 69; Giblett 1996, 3). The possible religious significance of water in prehistory in Britain and western Europe is well discussed and this has also been acknowledged for the Roman period (e.g. Casey 1989, 37; Green 1986, 138; 1995, 89; Merrifield 1987). The deposition of objects within wetlands during prehistory is firmly attested; areas in Britain which have produced finds include the wetlands of the Ancholme and Lower Trent Valleys, Holderness and North Lancashire (Van de Noort and Ellis 1995; 1998, 296; Middleton *et al.* 1995, 205). Within the Fenland such sites include Flag Fen (Coombs 1992; Pryor 2001) and Fiskerton (Field and Parker Pearson 2003), while there are also numerous isolated hoards of late Bronze Age and Iron Age date (see Appendix 3). There are also precious-metal hoards in north-west Norfolk and some, at least, of these came from watery contexts, such as the Sedgeford hoard, which probably consisted of at least thirty gold Iron Age coins, twenty of which remained *in situ* within a cow bone deposited in a pit (Dennis and Faulkner 2005).

The Romans, too, had complex ideas concerning water and wetlands; divine presences were considered to exist in springs, pools and other watery locations (Romm 1992, 144; Scheid 2003, 72). Bronze plaques found at York were inscribed with dedications to Ocean (Braund 1996, 12), and Rome itself was situated near the marshland of the river Tiber, which required considerable drainage. Ammerman's (1990) study of the origins of the *Forum Romanum* has shown that the *Forum* basin could originally have been subjected to much flooding, both from the overflowing of the Tiber banks and from natural springs in the area; the basin was infilled in order to create an improved space for the establishment of the *Forum*. Purcell (1996) has suggested that this was thought by the Romans to demonste their mastery over nature, but considering the significance applied to water, there may have been other meanings behind these activities. Roman engineering works within the Fenland, such as the construction of the Car Dyke (Simmons 1979), which have generally been considered solely in terms of their economic function, may also have had the effect of alienating people from their land and managing the water in such a way as to lessen its power, perhaps even as a form of religious desecration. This may also be the case for other wetlands in Britain, where studies have so far taken a very economic stance, such as the Severn Estuary with the Somerset and Gwent Levels (Rippon 1997; 2000). The Roman drainage and engineering projects that have been focused upon are likely only to represent those that are most visible today and, although drainage would also have occurred in the Iron Age, this does not detract from the possibility that Roman impositions in the Fenland were, at least in part, ritually motivated, and represented an attempt to create a new symbolic order. Roman activity in the Fenland may have been a means to dominate the religious and supernatural forces that permeated the whole landscape and ways of life within it (*cf.* Purcell 1991). It may have been this perceived power of the Fenland, and the evident threat that the Romans brought through increased human impact on the land (as well as other factors such as guilt amongst the local peoples, and possibly some incomers, concerning this meaning-laden landscape), that encouraged the increase and concentration of religious activities here during the Roman period.

'Natural' landscapes

When addressing the significance of the Fenland, the other half of a wetland, the land, also needs to be reconsidered. Techniques such as fieldwalking and mapping, though of course necessary and highly useful, have been criticised for the effect that they have of distancing the land from the people and actions within it (Thomas 1993, 25) and they often artificially assume that there are patterns to be recovered (Chapman 1997a, 10). New geography and new archaeology considered space as a distinct entity, 'a container in which human activities and events took place' (Tilley 1994, 9). Postmodernist approaches have since been adopted for the study of landscapes in some periods of archaeology, most notably the Neolithic and Bronze Age. Through concepts such as phenomenology, attempts have been made to approach the way in which space may have been constructed and experienced and the ways in which it could vary through human feeling, thought and interaction (Bender 1993, 3; Cosgrove 1984, 35; Knapp and Ashmore 1999, 7; Tilley 1994, 1–3, 11).

Within Roman archaeology, however, most discussions of the Roman countryside and landscape in Britain have put an emphasis on the economy and economic ways of exploring social behaviour and relationships (e.g. Branigan 1977; Dark and Dark 1997; Hingley 1989). Rare exceptions such as Hingley and Miles (2002, 167), who acknowledged the ritual aspect of Roman landscape, often provide only brief discussions and more is needed to alter our perceptions of landscape in the Roman period. The term and concept of 'landscape' only originated in Europe in the fifteenth century and reached Britain by the late sixteenth century, amid social change and the rise in the predominant importance of the economy. That the word 'landscape' originated from the Dutch painting term *landschap* (Cosgrove 1984, 20; Hirsch 1995, 2) and was part of Cartesian perspectivalism which viewed space as rectilinear and abstract (Chapman 1997a, 4) highlights its distant, elitist and specifically Western perspective of viewing and understanding land.

There is evidence that some non-Western societies today view land in different ways, with the concept of 'sacred landscapes' being an important way in which the land is understood, such as with the Aborigines (Bender 1993, 2–3). The concept that natural places could have been equally significant to the monumental environment in the past was central to Bradley's *An Archaeology of Natural Places* (2000), which draws upon examples both from ethnography and prehistoric archaeology. Early medieval Irish texts also suggest that the inhabitants viewed the landscape in which they lived as having a mythical and sacred nature (Dark 1993, 141). That vernacular landscapes could be considered significant was also proposed by Chapman (1997b, 148) in his study of prehistoric eastern Hungary; here he demonstrated that certain so-called flat-sites (that is, non-monumental) were continuously chosen for occupation over time and consequently accumulated 'place-value'. The meaning that people ascribe to a landscape is, then, not always represented by highly visible monuments and it is therefore possible that the Fenland, due to its special nature and perceived isolation and boundedness, carried special significance in the Roman period. This may have been intensified by the history of activity in the area over time, creating a special 'place-value'.

This depth of activity within the Fenland may have played an important part in shaping communal experience within the landscape (Alcock 2002, 31). From the Bronze Age, the Fenland appears special but, although preservation and discovery issues may be factors, there appears to have been an increase in the deposition of items during the Roman period. Salt production – utilising tidal water and interacting with the sea – was also carried out in prehistory and throughout the Roman period in the Fenland, and is considered to have linked production and magic (Lane and Morris 2001; Morris 2007); Willis's paper (in press) also considers the possible special nature of these inter-tidal areas and the production of salt. These locations may have been magical places and this is perhaps further indicated by the fact that the sea does not seem to have been used as a food resource at this time (Morris 2007).

Memory and myths of the past seem to have played an important role in religious practices in Roman Britain (Dark 1993; Williams 1998), and the religious activity within the Fenland at this time may have been drawing upon the past. The Romans, too, may well have recognised the significance of natural places. It is possible that the notable intensification of artefact deposition in the Fenland at this time may have been a response to the changes and threat to the Fenland that the Roman period brought, through both drainage activities and increasing exploitation, probably by incomers as well as the local population.

Conclusions

Studies of the Fenland in the Roman period have been preoccupied with economic explanations and issues of cultural domination and resistance, and the rationalisation and exploitation of the Fenland from the post-medieval period have had a major influence. Landscape is a socially constructed term resulting from cultural changes dating to the post-medieval period, but from the phenomenological perspective landscape is not a single entity but depends on individual perceptions, experiences and beliefs (Tilley 1994, 11). The evidence discussed in this paper suggests that modern economic theories are not the only or even the best way to study such landscapes. It has been shown that a concentration upon the economic aspects of life has created a bias in understanding of the past, as other factors, such as religious belief in watery landscapes, have often been neglected. The combination of land and water in the Fenland would have made it a special locale in which people lived their lives, interacted and constructed their identities.

Studies of the hoarding within the Fenland have not addressed the specific and special context in which the acts occurred. Arguments have traditionally centred on the need to express status and wealth through conspicuous consumption or the need to hide wealth for safekeeping. There is an assumption in this work that 'value' and 'wealth', as the terms are understood today, can be applied uncritically to the Roman period. Through an examination of all the different types of materials deposited in the Fenland it is clear that alternative theories are needed to help to explain this phenomenon. The concentration of special deposits along the fen-edge implies that this was a meaning-laden and powerful place, or a marginal and dangerous place, perhaps because it bounded the culturally significant wetland. The presence of shrines on the fen-edge has led to the divorcing of this evidence from everyday life. It is clear, however, that much ritual activity took place within the landscape setting and was part of 'being' in that environment. Different people would have had different experiences but, combined, this would have created a hugely powerful timemark – a place where significant social action occurs (Chapman 1997b, 158) in an area with a long history. The Romans, whose attitudes towards water and land were as complex as those of the indigenous Britons, may have recognised the importance of the area and the possibilities of acculturation in such a meaning-laden landscape.

Social interpretations of the past also reflect trends towards the social in the present but through a thorough and considered discussion of the archaeological evidence, together with theoretical issues, new suggestions can be made. The Fenland would have meant many things to many different people, holding significances beyond modern economic interpretations, but with careful analysis these meanings can perhaps begin to be approached.

Appendix 1: Pewter finds from the Fens

These include the collection of two jugs, three bowls, two tazze, one dish and one pedestalled bowl, together with pottery beakers, from the bed of the 'Old Slade' at Isleham Fen (Cambridgeshire), the six large platters from a field in Sutton (Liversidge 1959, 7; Wedlake 1958, 90), and three plates, excavated to modern standards, at Willingham (Cambridgeshire). Here the excavation showed that the plates had been deliberately placed within a pit on top of cattle skulls and other animal bones (Denham *et al.* 1995, 178). Discussions of the role of pewter vessels have ranged from dinner services (Liversidge 1959, 7) to church plate, with the observance of chi-rho and other religious symbols sometimes engraved on them (Toynbee 1962; 1964); the tazza found in isolation on the Isle of Ely (Cambridgeshire) has been described as a font (Clarke 1931).

Appendix 2: Isolated statuettes from the Fenland

Examples include the six statuettes from Stuntney on the Isle of Ely (Cambridgeshire) (Heichelheim 1937), the bust of Luna from a field in Cottenham, Cambridgeshire (Taylor 1985, 31), and the numerous statuettes from Earith, also in Cambridgeshire (Babington 1883, 76–7; Taylor *et al.* 1980).

Appendix 3: Late Bronze Age and Iron Age hoards from the Fens

These include the late Bronze Age hoard of 6500 items of bronzework at Isleham and the 163 late Bronze Age items found at Wilburton in 1882, which included 115 spearheads (Hall 1996, 71, 82–6). Numerous swords, shields and bronze vessels have also been discovered within Fen contexts, including three shields at Coveney Fen (Coles 1998, 38) and swords at Wisbech and Mildenhall (Wait 1985).

Notes

1. Hingley's study of the context of iron 'currency bars' suggested that single finds had been deposited deliberately since it is unlikely that a complete bar would be lost or discarded (1990a, 108); they also occur in the same types of context.
2. Lethbridge and O'Reilly (1933, 166) also suggested that 'pewter services were placed in closets and sunk in the rivers with a small buoy to mark the place much as fishermen now keep lobsters alive in the sea'.

3. Strabo (4.1.13), quoting Poseidonius, for instance, wrote 'the treasure that was found in Tolosa amounted to about fifteen thousand talents (part of it was stored in sacred enclosures, part of it in sacred lakes), unwrought, that is, merely gold and silver bullion'. Diodorus Siculus wrote that 'in the temples and precincts made consecrate in the land, a great amount of gold has been deposited as a dedication to the gods' (5.27.3–4).
4. As commonly occurred in the eighteenth and nineteenth centuries, the fourth Earl of Cardigan removed the mosaics from the Roman villa at Cotterstock (Northamptonshire) near his estate and placed them within the garden buildings of his home at Deene Park (Upex 2001, 63). By doing this he was appropriating the Roman remains and associating them with himself and his lifestyle.

Acknowledgements

I would like to thank the following people for much useful discussion, comments and for reading various drafts of the paper: Dr Richard Hingley, Dr Anna Leone and Dr Tom Moore at the University of Durham, Professor Colin Haselgrove at the University of Leicester and Dr Steven Willis at the University of Kent. I would also like to thank Dr Christopher Evans at the Cambridge Archaeological Unit for useful discussion and unpublished information, Dr Steven Willis for access to his 2007 paper prior to its publication, Dr Christopher Martins for references connected with the economy, and staff at the Sites and Monuments Record offices at Cambridge, Lincoln, Norfolk and Northampton. The Arts and Humanities Research Council funded my Masters programme, on which this research was based.

CHAPTER TEN

What Did the Romans Ever Do For Us? Roman Iron Production in the East Midlands and the Forest of Dean

Irene Schrüfer-Kolb

Introduction

Since the publication in 1955 of W.G. Hoskins's *The Making of the English Landscape* 'archaeologists, too, have added enormously to our knowledge of the antiquity of the present landscape' (Hoskins 1985, 10). In his introduction to the 1985 reprint (written in 1976) Hoskins notes that now 'even the claylands of the Midlands, once thought so inhospitable to early settlement, have produced an average of four Romano-British settlements per mile [in certain areas], including arable fields of the same period.' He concludes that 'our knowledge of how much of our land had been cleared and brought into cultivation by, say, Roman times if no earlier, needs complete revision, for people imply farming systems for their material needs' and that 'one can hardly over-estimate the contribution of archaeologists in this field ... Not only have archaeologists greatly enlarged our time-scale in the making of the English landscape, but they have also shown how complicated a pattern of past landscapes we may have to take into account' (Hoskins 1985, 11). 'The student of the English landscape therefore faces at times the possibility of underground evidence ... In other words, the borderline between landscape history and archaeology is a fine one' (Hoskins 1985, 12).

The following paper will illustrate how integrated landscape archaeology has contributed to our understanding of settlement and landscape development in the east midlands in antiquity, a region that has a particular relationship with Hoskins's work at Leicester University. However, Hoskins remained sceptical about the lasting contribution of Roman Britain to the present landscape: 'In the first place we must not overestimate the total impression made by the Romano-British generations upon the landscape. Their clearances, fields and settlements were locally important, but considered as a whole they made little impression on the natural scene ... Moreover, much of this cleared and tamed landscape had reverted, or was reverting, to its natural state when the Anglo-Saxons were taking over' (Hoskins 1985, 42–3).

And still Hoskins cites, somewhat contradictorily perhaps, Roman roads and urbanisation as being among the most shaping factors in the English landscape at that time. This shows that there is indeed more to landscape development than the rural, agricultural focus which Hoskins maintains in his first chapter on 'The landscape before the English settlement'. Many villages and towns in Britain are known to have Roman or even pre-Roman origins and the lines of Roman roads such as Watling Street survive as modern roads. Roman urbanisation – on a scale unknown before the conquest – brought about for the first time an urban society dependent on goods produced in the surrounding countryside and a close, two-way consumer–producer relationship between town and country. Better living standards caused by surplus production and centralised provincial administration gave rise to an increasing market for goods produced farther away. The road network all over Roman Britain helped the provincial economy to reach a previously unknown level of productivity: trade and exchange were widespread and an essential part of daily life in the province. These market and infrastructure developments are particularly relevant to those branches of industry, beyond farming, which make use of natural resources, the products of which need to be transported from their manufacturing place to the end consumer. Mining and metalworking are one such industry and in this paper we will see the impact that Roman period iron production in the east midlands had on the present landscape.

Roman iron production in Britain

There were three major iron production areas in Roman Britain: the Weald of Sussex and Kent, the Forest of Dean in west Gloucestershire, and the east midlands region (Figure 52).

More accurately, the east midlands are defined by the Jurassic Ridge, which runs from south Humberside to Oxfordshire. The Jurassic Ridge has long been recognised as an area with exploitable iron ore deposits, and from the Industrial Revolution the east midlands have been among the most important regions in the country for iron and steel production. In addition, extensive archaeological evidence of earlier iron-working activity has been noted in the region. Although some archaeological information is now lost due to modern mining, recent research has shown that the east midlands represented a significant region for iron production in antiquity (Schrüfer-Kolb 2004). Detailed analysis and interpretation of the widespread remains of this industrial activity indicate that the socio-economic framework of iron production in this area had much in common with that in the Forest of Dean, but differed somewhat from that in the Weald. Therefore, another aspect of this paper will be a comparison of Roman-period iron production in the east midlands with that in the Forest of Dean, focusing on the various similarities and discussing some differences.

FIGURE 52. Roman iron mining regions in Britain.

Geology and natural resources

Iron production is closely linked to natural resources and in antiquity the local geology was the dominant factor. The geology of the east midlands comprises the Jurassic escarpment, a crescent of sedimentary lime and sandstone that runs from the Humber estuary to Oxfordshire. Iron ore deposits belong to the carbonate type. They are generally not as pure as the Forest of Dean ores, but contain a similarly high amount of iron oxide and are characterised by their phosphorus content, which is beneficial to iron smelting since it hardens the iron (Tylecote 1986, 125, table 67). In the Forest of Dean, iron ore deposits within the stratigraphy of carboniferous rocks mainly comprise outcrops of limonite. Forest of Dean ores are comparatively free of elements detrimental to iron smelting and provide the high iron oxide content that is needed for the bloomery process (Fulford and Allen 1992, 186–8, table 3).

Both the Forest of Dean and the east midlands landscapes provided ample raw material for iron production: in addition to easily accessible ore deposits, the soils and woodlands covering the higher parts of the regions supplied clay for furnace construction and fuel for the smelting process. Evidence for extensive charcoal burning in post-Roman times survived both in the east midlands and the Forest of Dean, and parts of both areas were designated as medieval royal hunting forests.

The archaeological evidence

Unlike the Weald (Cleere and Crossley 1995) and the Jurassic Ridge (Schrüfer-Kolb 2004), the Forest of Dean still lacks a comprehensive, integrated assessment of the evidence for Roman iron production. Some significant data collection (Jones and Mattingly 1990, 193–5) and detailed research has already been carried out (Walters 1992) and, to date, there are around ninety-five published sites with evidence for Roman iron production in the Forest. In the east midlands, around 230 Roman iron production sites are known, situated mainly along the Jurassic escarpment, with a particular concentration in Northamptonshire and south Lincolnshire. However, the two study areas differ in size, so that site density over a given area is a more representative way to appreciate the intensity of iron production (Figure 53).

In both areas the iron ore was exploited by opencast mining, leaving shallow pits that can be seen to the present day (Figure 54). In the east midlands, only one mining trench has been recognised, in the Scunthorpe area, and the Forest of Dean is home to the only ironstone mine known in Roman Britain, at Lydney (Wheeler and Wheeler 1932, 18–22). It is, however, doubtful if this was actually operating or was merely a test shaft. One striking feature of opencast mining in the Forest of Dean is the numerous, sometimes linear, pit alignments called 'scowles', following ore deposits. A survey in 2003/2004 of these quarry-like features by Gloucestershire County Council has shown that they are often geological features originating from underground cave systems, used later to extract iron ore. In both regions, where mining pits are preserved in woodlands, they can be seen to pockmark the landscape and, even if dating evidence is scarce, at least some of them can be safely assumed to have been worked during the Roman period. The scars that ancient mining and quarrying left on the landscape show that there are indeed cases where prehistoric and Roman industrial activity irrevocably changed the landscape, making a lasting impact on how it looks today. At first glance, individual mining and quarry sites may appear to be only of local importance, as Hoskins claims (1985, 42), but as a whole the evidence for Roman mining in Britain is substantial (Mattingly and Schrüfer-Kolb 2003) and there are sites, such as the lead-mining centre at Charterhouse-on-Mendip, where a lack of post-Roman activity has preserved the evidence.

As far as the location of smelting sites is concerned, there appears to be a significant difference between the two regions. In the east midlands, like

FIGURE 53. Distribution of Roman iron production sites along the Jurassic Ridge.

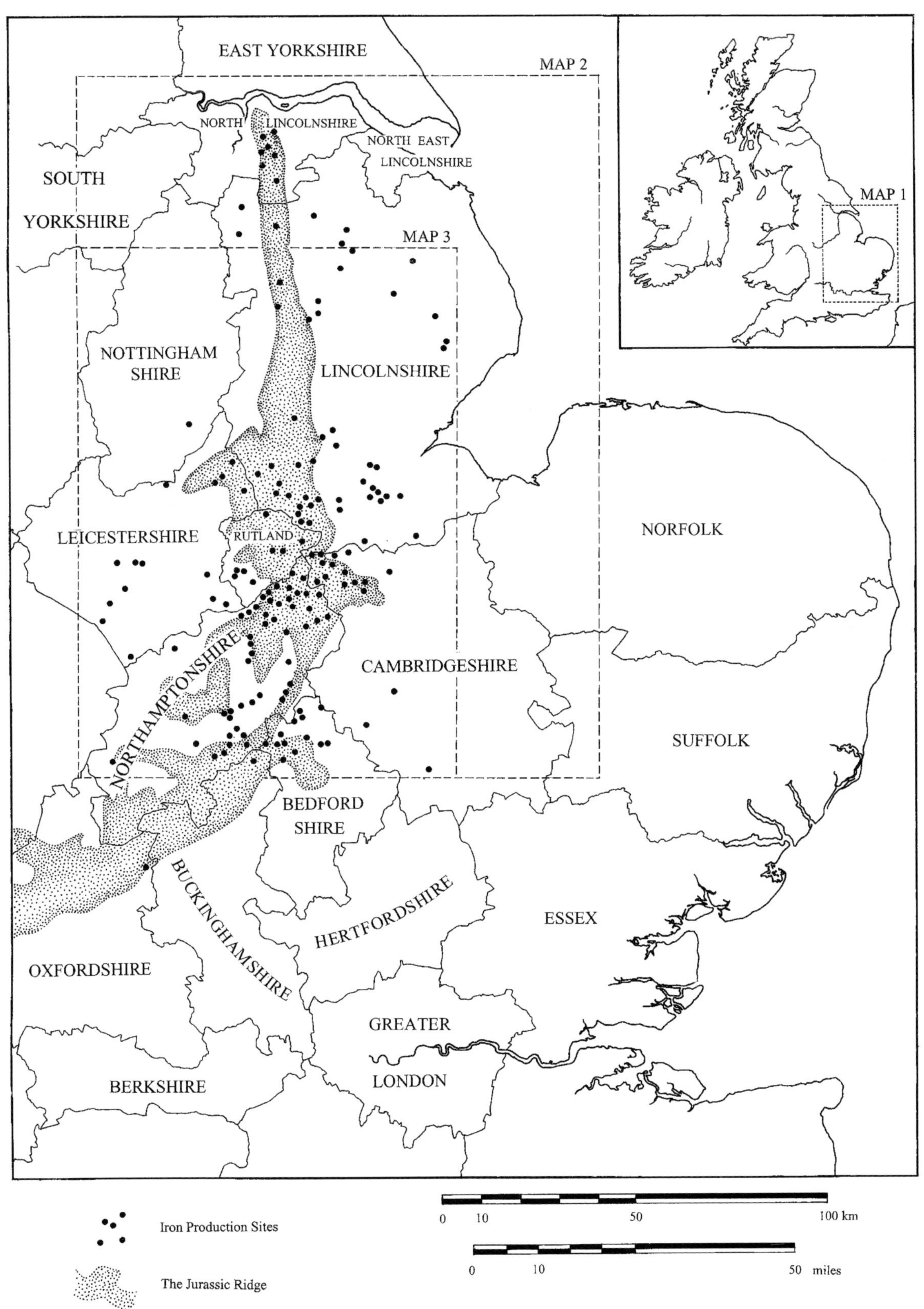
EAST YORKSHIRE
MAP 2
NORTH LINCOLNSHIRE
NORTH EAST LINCOLNSHIRE
SOUTH YORKSHIRE
MAP 3
MAP 1
NOTTINGHAM SHIRE
LINCOLNSHIRE
LEICESTERSHIRE
RUTLAND
NORFOLK
NORTHAMPTONSHIRE
CAMBRIDGESHIRE
SUFFOLK
BEDFORD SHIRE
BUCKINGHAMSHIRE
HERTFORDSHIRE
ESSEX
OXFORDSHIRE
GREATER LONDON
BERKSHIRE
0 10 50 100 km
0 10 50 miles
Iron Production Sites
The Jurassic Ridge

FIGURE 54. Wakerley Wood, Northants – opencast mining pits.

many other metal-producing regions in antiquity, the ore was smelted in close proximity to the mining site to minimise transport costs (Figure 55). This was due to economic considerations; iron ore is a raw material that creates a lot of waste before the finished product is obtained. In the Forest of Dean, however, most iron-smelting sites are situated some distance away from the mining sites, and the major iron-smelting centre of *Ariconium* (Weston-under-Penyard) lies outside the Forest (Figure 56). The reason behind this is not yet fully understood, but it has been suggested that the central area of the Forest was kept clear of industrial sites to preserve managed woodlands (Walters 1992, 131–2).

Little research has been published to date detailing the technology by which bloomery iron was produced in the Forest of Dean, and the evidence for Roman iron smelting at Chesters Villa, Woolaston, is the most accessible to date. At this site, mostly slag-tapping shaft furnaces (Cleere 1972) constructed of clay were in operation (Fulford and Allen 1992, 192–3), and this is supported by the analysis of iron production debris elsewhere in the Forest. This particular furnace type was also widespread in the east midlands (Jackson and Ambrose 1978, 164–5), as it represents a common furnace type during the Roman period (Tylecote 1986, 132–42). In both regions, the archaeological evidence points towards multiple use of this kind of furnace. Alongside the slag-tapping shaft furnaces, the prehistoric low shaft domed or advanced

FIGURE 55. Roman iron production sites in the east midlands in relation to ore deposits and the road/river network.

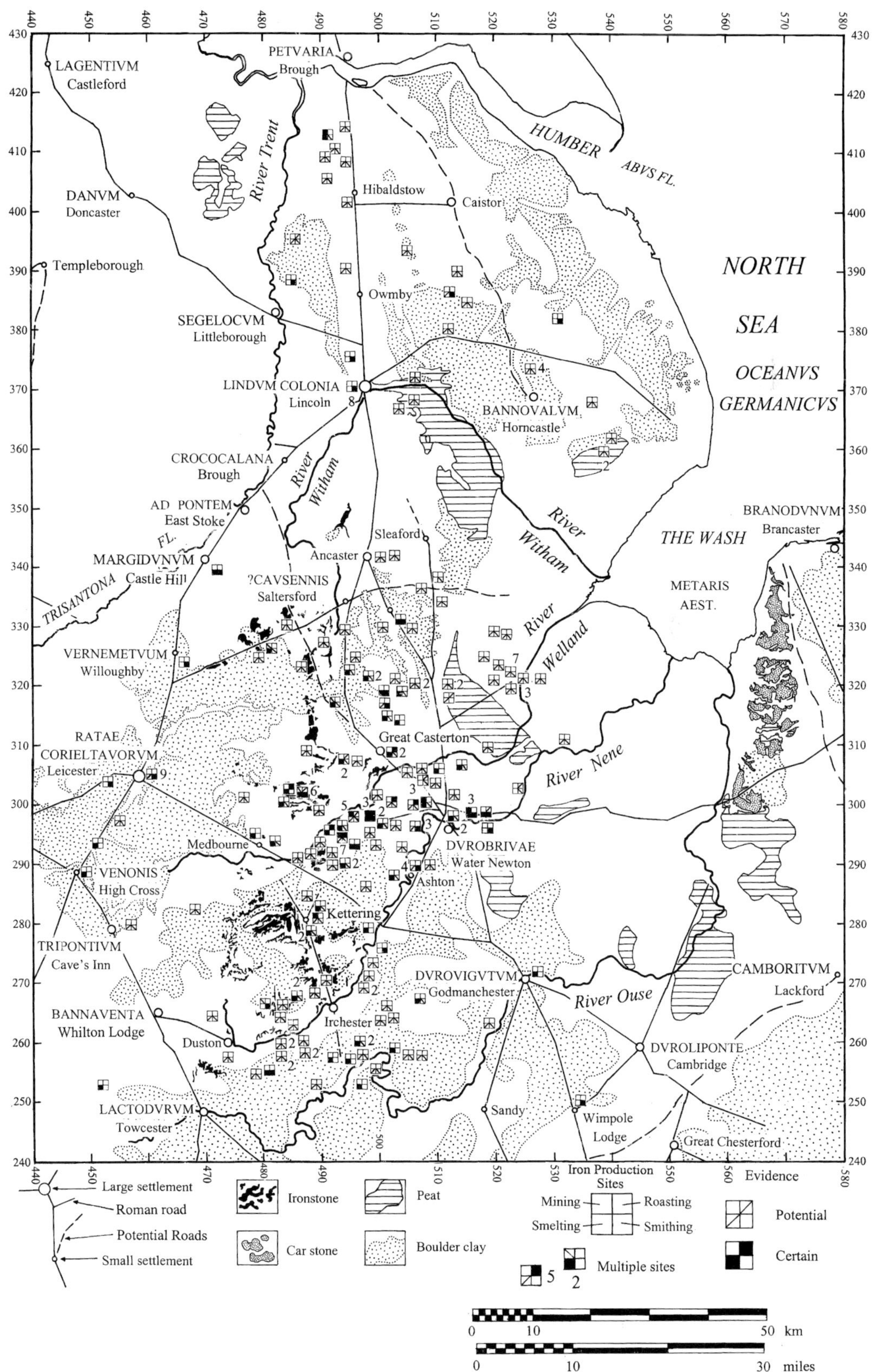

PETVARIA
Brough
LAGENTIVM
Castleford
HUMBER
ABVS FL.
River Trent
DANVM
Doncaster
Hibaldstow
Caistor
Templeborough
NORTH
SEA
OCEANVS
GERMANICVS
Owmby
SEGELOCVM
Littleborough
LINDVM COLONIA
Lincoln
BANNOVALVM
Horncastle
CROCOCALANA
Brough
River Witham
AD PONTEM
East Stoke
Sleaford
BRANODVNVM
Brancaster
THE WASH
MARGIDVNVM
Castle Hill
Ancaster
TRISANTONA FL.
?CAVSENNIS
Saltersford
METARIS
AEST.
River Welland
VERNEMETVVM
Willoughby
Great Casterton
RATAE
CORIELTAVORVM
Leicester
River Nene
Medbourne
DVROBRIVAE
Water Newton
VENONIS
High Cross
Ashton
Kettering
TRIPONTIVM
Cave's Inn
DVROVIGVTVM
Godmanchester
River Ouse
CAMBORITVM
Lackford
BANNAVENTA
Whilton Lodge
Irchester
Duston
DVROLIPONTE
Cambridge
LACTODVRVM
Towcester
Sandy
Wimpole
Lodge
Great Chesterford
Large settlement
Roman road
Potential Roads
Small settlement
Ironstone
Car stone
Peat
Boulder clay
Iron Production
Sites
Mining
Roasting
Smelting
Smithing
Multiple sites
Evidence
Potential
Certain
km
miles

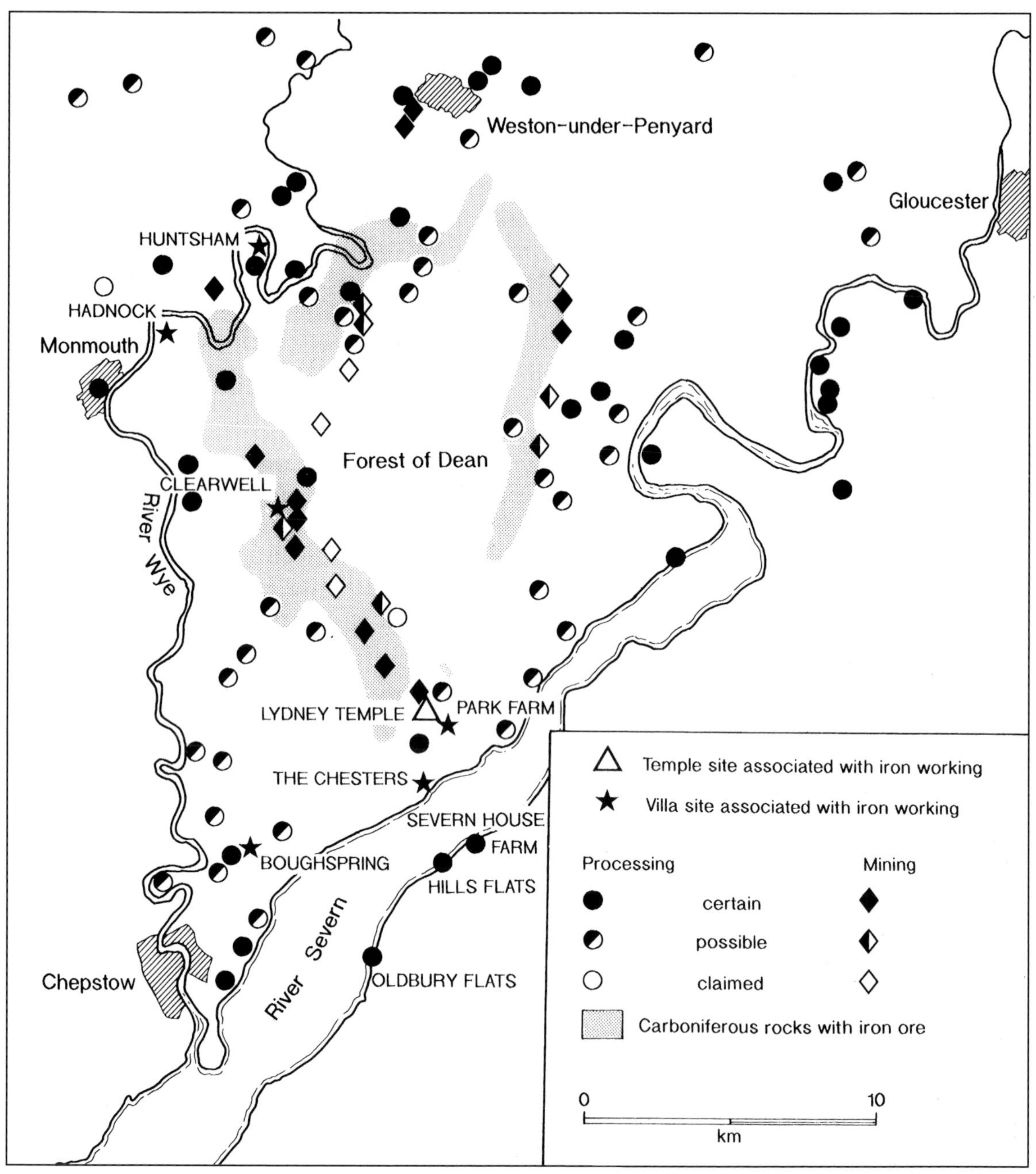

bowl furnace (Cleere 1972) remained in use in the east midlands (Jackson and Tylecote 1988, 279–84, 293–6). We do not know to what extent this was the case in the Forest of Dean too, although at Chesters Villa there is potential evidence for at least one furnace of this type (Fulford and Allen 1992, 192, 193). It may not have been the only one in the region.

Evidence for ore benefication (enrichment) is generally poorly preserved. For the Forest of Dean nothing is known to date and it is possible that the ore chemistry made enrichment obsolete. In the east midlands, however, the ore had to be roasted to drive off impurities before it could be smelted. This way, the iron content in the ore was increased. This process was undertaken in roasters either of circular or trench-like shape (Schrüfer-Kolb 2004, 20–4).

Equally, little information is available to date about the subsequent forging of iron in the Forest of Dean and it is hoped that the publication of detailed slag analyses will address this problem at some point in the future. In the east midlands, such analyses have made it possible to identify a substantial number of smithing sites (Figure 55), sometimes in association with smelting, and several stone-built smithing hearths. They typically had an oblong bulbous shape with an internal clay lining (Schrüfer-Kolb 2004, 31–5, 46–7).

Chronological developments

Both in the east midlands and the Forest of Dean there is evidence for small-scale Iron Age production of iron (Walters 1992, 150; Schrüfer-Kolb 2004, 51–4). Demand increased considerably with the arrival of the Roman army in both regions in the first century AD. The military benefited from the existing Iron Age metallurgical tradition and is likely to have transferred additional technological knowledge to the local population. In the east midlands, there were substantial industrial developments from *c.* AD 47: first-century iron production is well documented in the context of the early military forts in the region, and entirely civilian iron production is equally attested. A further increase in the number of iron production sites can be observed from the second century and during the third century a network of industrial sites exploited the local ironstone at a persistently high level. A considerable number of sites operated well into the fourth century AD. Iron production continued during the Saxon and medieval periods and the remains of the modern industry can still be seen.

FIGURE 56. Roman mining and iron production sites in the Forest of Dean and Severn Estuary. From Fulford and Allen 1992, fig. 25; reproduced with the kind permission of M. Fulford and the Society for the Promotion of Roman Studies

In the Forest of Dean, output was stimulated notably in the early military phase of the later first century AD and iron production continued to flourish during the second century. A stabilisation of productivity occurred in the third century, which gradually led to a decline in late antiquity (Walters 1992, 150–153). Iron production of some scale was taken up again in the Middle Ages and many bloomery slag tips were used for resmelting in blast furnaces on the other side of the Bristol Channel.

Socio-economic frameworks

Roman iron production in the Forest of Dean has much in common with that in the east midlands when it comes to the ways in which the industrial activity was organised and administered. Both regions are also much alike in their economic potential and the way this potential was exploited. An integrated view of this industrial activity against a broader background of the entire

Roman-period archaeological evidence in both regions allows us to interpret the archaeometallurgical data within a socio-economic framework of ancient settlement organisation and landscape development.

In both the east midlands (Schrüfer-Kolb 1999) and the Forest of Dean, Roman iron production was essentially settlement-related and constituted an important part of the regional economy. Three levels of settlement associated with iron production are known in the Forest: major nucleated settlements like *Ariconium*, villa estates like the Chesters Villa, and minor rural settlements (Walters 1992, 1–28). The situation is similar in the east midlands, but there production took place mainly at rural and suburban settlements. Forging, but also some smelting, was undertaken in small towns and sometimes on villa estates.

This raises the question of the degree of industrialisation of individual sites in the east midlands and the region as a whole. On the basis of furnace types, the number of furnaces present, their chronological interrelationship and the process stages present we can establish levels of industrialisation from household iron-working – that is, primarily smithing or repair work – to highly productive industrial units. In between, we find rural settlements operating on a more efficient basis with several furnaces working at one time. Still, on this level, there is evidence for a mixed economy together with pottery production and/or agriculture (Jackson and Ambrose 1978). The transition to specialised iron production is on this level. At several locations in the east midlands we also find nuclei of smaller production sites which may have cooperated as parts of one bigger enterprise. At the top scale of industrialisation are sites with a number of smelting furnaces aligned in rows, and slag heaps of considerable size (Jackson and Tylecote 1988).

The great individuality in applied technology among the individual production sites shows clearly how iron in the east midlands was produced at varying economic levels. In the Forest of Dean, the archaeological evidence for settlement-related iron production suggests that, with an integrated study linking iron production to the Roman-period settlement patterns, a similar model of production levels could be established to help to better understand the organisation of iron production in the region. At present, a hierarchy from production at minor rural settlements to villas and up to major settlements seems most likely.

Although in Roman times mineral resources were usually vested in the *patrimonium* (imperial chest), neither in the east midlands nor in the Forest of Dean is there evidence for direct imperial control of the iron production. On the basis that the central part of the Forest is void of smelting sites, major settlements and villa estates (Figure 56) it has been speculated that this area was an Imperial Estate (Walters 1992, 146–50), but to date there is no convincing evidence to support this hypothesis. The interpretation of the settlement pattern suggests for both regions a model of independently operating production sites. These were probably organised around one or a small number of family units, or one part of a larger community that devoted itself to iron production, whereas others specialised in farming or other industrial activities. Presumably, a system of communal responsibility by *collegia* (guilds) or *societates* (cooperatives) took over the administration of the trade in iron after early military control of the local iron production had ceased. This would have made artisans independent from the mercantile power of centralised town administration and even might have enabled them to sell their goods beyond the nearest small town. More detailed site investigations are needed for the Forest of Dean to establish firmly the potentially important role of villas within the organisational and administrative framework of iron production, especially in its later phases. In the east midlands, on the contrary, the archaeological evidence suggests that villas did not play a major part in the region's iron production, as little of the production debris comes from this type of site. Still, this aspect remains to be further investigated, as their influence may have been on an administrative level or through ownership of the resource.

The substantial Roman-period technological development in the east midlands and the Forest of Dean indicates that the overall production process was clearly market-orientated. The excellent infrastructure of major roads and waterways in the east midlands (Figure 55) stimulated trade not only on a local level but also with regional markets in small towns. Important long-distance roads encircled and crossed the region and rivers led to the region's major Roman towns – Leicester, Lincoln and *Durobrivae* (near Peterborough), and to the Wash. These facilities made inter-regional trade with a specialist market, such as the Roman army on Hadrian's Wall, a distinct possibility. Iron products could have been extensively traded, possibly in close connection with the Nene Valley pottery that was produced in the region in Roman times. The Forest of Dean was equally well suited to establishing flourishing trade networks for both local and regional supplies. Several roads and the rivers Wye and Severn led to major Roman settlements such as Gloucester, *Ariconium* and Worcester, while access to the sea was provided via the Severn estuary. This, again, made seaborne trade to the northern garrisons a possibility.

Conclusions

A comparison of the archaeology of Roman iron production in the east midlands and the Forest of Dean reveals many similarities but also a few distinctive differences. The archaeometallurgical data refer to similar mining and furnace technologies. Chronological developments differ slightly, with the east midlands iron production developing more slowly but operating well into the fourth century AD and beyond. Organisation and administration need further investigation, but are largely civilian. Both regions made full use of their economic potential and had a rich supply of all the raw materials needed for iron production. It is hoped that fresh research into the Forest of Dean industry will add some new knowledge to the rather patchy picture we still have of this important Romano-British iron production centre (*cf.* Meredith

2006, 29–60), and that eventually an integrated study will bring the many results of local investigations together.

In the Forest of Dean, little is known about post-Roman iron production, but many ancient slag heaps were used as charges for the blast furnaces across the Bristol Channel. Along the Jurassic Ridge, iron production continued throughout Saxon and medieval times and a second peak occurred in the twentieth century, when huge amounts of iron and steel were produced at centres such as Kettering and Corby. Ancient iron production from the Iron Age onwards laid the foundation for this modern industry. Even if the archaeological evidence for this is not visible above ground, Hoskins's benchmark for landscape history (Hoskins 1985, 12), it nevertheless had a lasting impact on the modern landscape in that it provides testimony for the beginnings of an industrial landscape. The impression of Roman iron production on the east midlands is one of large-scale economic development and industrial continuity – less visible but perhaps even more important than the mining sites preserved in Northamptonshire woodlands for 2000 years.

Acknowledgements

I wish to thank Henry Cleere, Ian Standing and Tim Young for discussing evidence from the Forest of Dean. Thanks are also due to draughtspersons Lucy Farr, for Figure 52, and David Hopkins, for Figures 53 and 55, and to Michael Fulford and the Society for the Promotion of Roman Studies for granting copyright permission for Figure 56.

CHAPTER ELEVEN

Roman Towns, Roman Landscapes: The Cultural Terrain of Town and Country in the Roman Period

Steven Willis

Introduction: town, people and landscape

There is a long tradition in Roman studies of investigating town–country relations. This paper pursues this theme by looking at various aspects of that relationship. Hoskins states that towns were an 'important Roman contribution to the landscape' (1975, 41), and he considered Roman London in terms of its economic relationship with its hinterland. Towns played a novel and fundamental role in the inter-relationships of people, landscape, society and empire in north-west Europe at this time. This paper discusses their social, political and ideological significance.

Towns were a defining feature of the Roman episode in north-west Europe; towns in this region (Gaul, Germany and Britain) differed from anything that had existed before, or what was to exist subsequently. Yet towns of the Roman era are problematic. At one level they are familiar to us, with repeated well-defined elements, but on the other hand they were complex entities, variable as a category from site to site and over time, requiring careful explanation beyond description (*cf.* Daniels and Cosgrove 1988). There is a great deal about these towns that is for us in the twenty-first century alien and different; this should not be underplayed. They were, to varying degrees, an imperial imposition, played a crucial centralising role, and promoted Roman ways of living. Roman towns were mechanisms for ordering people and environments. Yet combined with these aspects were elements that made towns attractive to the populations around them in the *civitas*; these offset tensions around the new *status quo*. Degrees of acceptance may have come in part via the consumables and possibilities that towns offered. In addition, towns incorporated spaces that had indigenous cultural resonances: places of religious and ceremonial activity and, presumably, of entertainment,

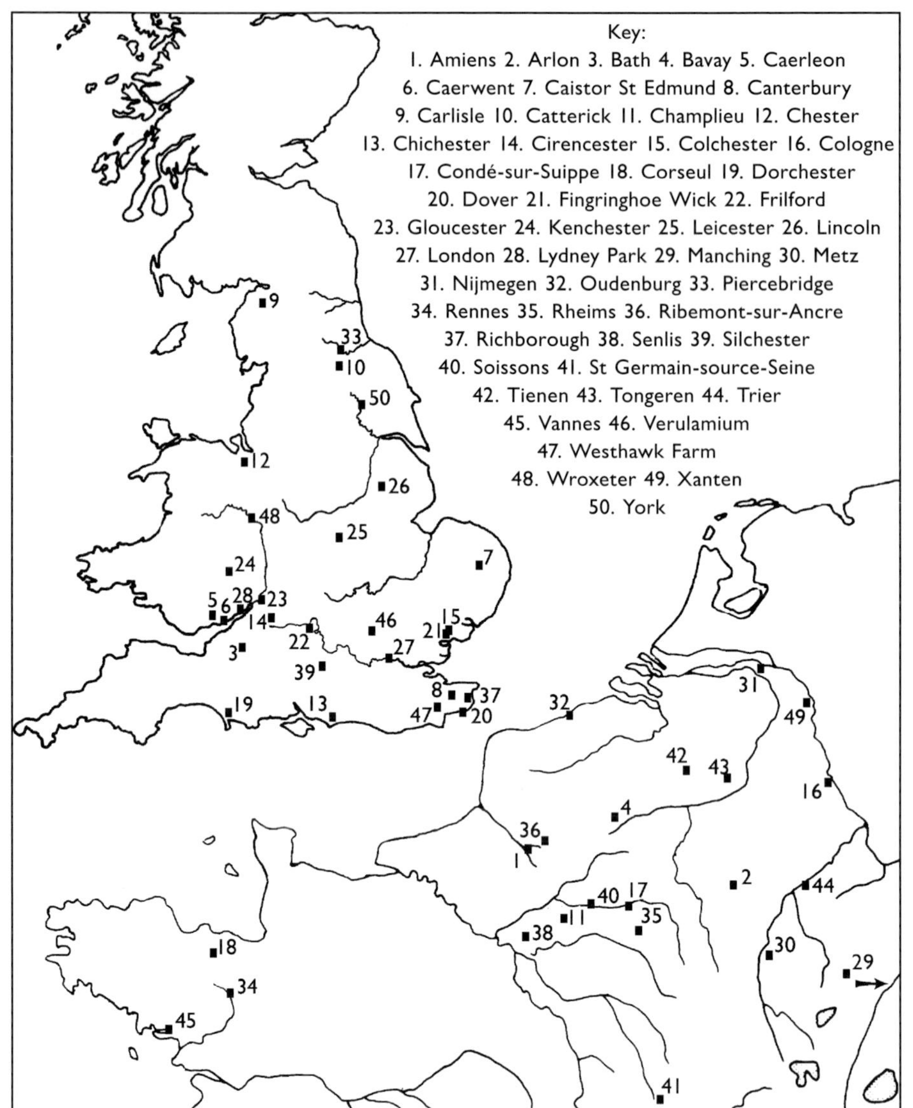

FIGURE 57. Sites mentioned in the text. For brevity Roman names for sites are not specified here. The map was prepared by Ges Moody of the Trust for Thanet Archaeology

which we see especially in the suburbs (Esmonde Cleary 1987). Suburbs of Roman towns are an understudied domain, but were crucial in the mediation of social relations between town and country. These elements, in terms of the activities that occurred and the social relations that were played out in their constructed places, made towns meaningful places for perhaps most of the 90 per cent of the population who would have occupied the countryside. Towns played a pivotal role between Rome and local traditions and between incomers and the indigenous, representing physical contexts for mediating these relations.

In the past, archaeologists tended to see Roman towns in terms of street plans, structural coherence, buildings and walls, with the stratified footprint of town cores being the focus of attention (e.g. Rivet 1964; Wacher 1974; 1995; *cf.* papers in Greep 1993). Documenting these typically complex elements was the priority, while 'explanation' for their existence was treated as axiomatic. More recently, towns have been examined as a manifestation of a Romanisation process (Millett 1990; Woolf 1997; 1998; Carroll 2001; or otherwise in the case of 'small towns' (Hingley 1989; 1997a)), or as centres of consumption (Cooper 1996; *cf.* Perring 2002), while Roskams (1999) and Witcher (2005), looking at York and Rome respectively, outline the rich interchange of city–hinterland relations. In the case of the latter, the study highlights degrees of symbiosis and integration in economic and social affairs (*cf.* Millett 1992). With York this was almost certainly the case too, but this is less clear from the material culture in the hinterland of the site (for example, as manifest in the circumscribed distribution of Ebor ware). The pattern at Wroxeter may prove to be similar to that at York when the findings of the Hinterlands Project (White in press) are available. An interactive relationship between town and countryside is to be expected, even if this may not be directly visible via archaeological evidence. A key perspective in interpreting towns and what they represent is to conceive of a town (including its suburbs and hinterland) as essentially a set of relationships between people, reflecting cultural processes that were often changing.

The fact that many Roman towns are overlain by modern urban development has influenced the way they have been perceived, adding to the tendency to see parallels between these towns and modern urban phenomena. Increased physical exploration of Roman towns, added to changes in both governmental policy and modern urban development, mean that archaeological investigations take place in the suburbs of modern towns at a more frequent rate, creating fresh data. Recent studies and fieldwork show Roman towns to have been more extensive entities in the landscape than hitherto recognised. Their suburbs, cemeteries and semi-urban elements were socially significant environs, arguably as important for understanding towns of the era as the traditionally pawed-over monumental 'cores'. Changing information requires an updating of our understandings of Roman towns. Fortuitously, this has coincided with a fresh appetite for theoretical advances (supported by methodological developments) in approaching towns and landscapes, interpreting evidence in terms of wider cultural processes.

Previous characterisations of Roman towns have taken too narrow a view of what towns were (*cf.* Rivet 1964; Wacher 1974; 1995; see Burnham *et al.* 2001). The view has been too limited in physical terms, focusing traditionally on walled 'core' areas, and missing key elements in the geography and anatomy of towns in the immediate vicinity of the 'inner urban area'. Secondly, Roman towns must be seen in terms of their social relationship with the countryside and the people in proximity to them. Finally, the interpretations have been conceptually restricted, influenced by inappropriate models of medieval and modern towns and our own experience of contemporary urban existence. A curious intellectual tradition (pertinent to observe given the series that this publication belongs to) is that towns tend to be accorded an *a priori* significance that elevates them above the countryside and other foci.

The Roman era was a period of intense change, with marked cultural impositions on land in terms of settlement patterns, road and infrastructure formation, and monument construction (Mattingly 2006). Yet new archaeological work is also revealing surprising dimensions of continuity, following forms and trajectories established during later prehistory (Millett 1990; Haselgrove and Millett 1997; Creighton 2006). This configuration of old and new ideologies and uses in the land demands investigation.

Roman towns and their hinterlands in society: evolving relations

Defining towns is not straightforward. What they represent depends upon the perspective from which they are viewed. They are culturally contingent: the Roman town was a set of distinct formations. Hence comparison with towns of other times and cultures cannot be direct (as it has sometimes been assumed to be). Towns are physical and social entities that exist through sets of internal relations, *and in relationship to other places* beyond the specific town; they are the context within which certain actions, normative and sanctioned, can take place, where both possibilities and power exist that do not occur elsewhere. The idea that they are essential for any developed society is an idea that has imposed itself on western thought (as we can see in the work of Marx, Weber, Veblen, Mumford and Jane Jacobs (*cf.* papers in Abrams and Wrigley 1978; Williams 1973; Jacobs 1970; 1984)). Functions associated with towns and cities in the modern world have been thought to be 'fundamental and uniform'. Combined with this is the idea that organised societies have 'central places' that are about economy, politics and other key dimensions in the re-creation of society.

Hence cultural historians and archaeologists have looked for central places in past societies to which they can ascribe such functions; the hillforts of temperate Iron Age Europe have traditionally been seen in such terms. From this background of viewing towns as both essential and central comes the modern expectation that such places have a close relationship with elites, the keepers of cultural hegemony. This combination creates a model that is projected back onto towns of the past. That Roman towns had 'cores', as manifest in street-girded areas, substantial buildings, town walls, and often a forum-basilica at the centre, plus distinct spatially marked legal rights and status, has instituted ideas of their modernity and parallels with modern western towns. This enabled them to be cast as Roman central places *par excellence.*

Towns, then, from this view, might not necessarily be about people as such, nor be defined by the presence and habitation of large numbers of people. They may include these aspects, but significantly have more to them than demographics. Towns have come to be about key phenomena in the existence of societies. They are places in the landscape where political, economic, judicial and religious power is stored, enacted, negotiated and radiated in relationship to the land and people around them. Towns of the Roman era had all these dimensions.

Roman towns, however, did not monopolise these roles in the manner of certain Greek city-states or modern towns and cities in Europe; they had these functions, but they were also nodes within wider structured systems of economics, politics and religion. Within the empire in temperate Europe alternative centres existed for most of these functions. Forts and fortresses with their *canabae* settlements, for instance, were centres of power, population, production and consumption, with an equal significance to towns, as with Chester and Oudenburg. Equally, in terms of economy and politics the alternatives of the 'small towns' and roadside settlements ('*vici*' as they are called in Continental Europe) existed, which developed as something novel, and in an organic manner, across the provinces through the Roman years (Drinkwater 1985; Burnham 1986; Brulet 1987; Hingley 1989; Burnham and Wacher 1990; Millett 1995; Vermeulen 1995). Furthermore, in northern Gaul, Britain and Germany there existed religious and recreational foci in 'the countryside'; places that evidently developed from 'sacred groves' and other special places during the Iron Age. Such locations are well known, as at Ribemont-sur-Ancre, Somme (Faudet 1993; Faudet and Bertin 1993), Frilford, Oxfordshire (Hingley 1985; Gosden and Lock 2003), and Lydney Park, Gloucestershire (Wheeler and Wheeler 1932; John Casey, pers. comm.). At Champlieu, for example, set in countryside between the major towns of Senlis and Soissons, a temple, theatre and baths complex assimilated classical and indigenous elements; the complex was every bit as substantial as the structures seen in the major contemporary towns, but evidently this was not a place where people resided in any number. Manifested within a bucolic environment, its placement in the landscape and the actions and public dramas undertaken within the complex will have reflected ideas that were independent of, and perhaps prior to, Roman towns. Doubtless such places and their associated human interplay contained political and power elements, but these existed in evident ease with towns.

In terms of political power, by the mid and late Roman period it seems that across the north-west provinces towns may have lost certain *gravitas* as elites moved out of towns to villas in the countryside (*cf.* Millett 1990), albeit these were situated in halos around the towns. This can be observed at Rennes, Corseul and Vannes in eastern Armorica (Langouët and Jumel 1991; Naas 1991). So towns in the Roman era did not have a monopoly of the roles that are associated with towns in our world. At its extreme, the capitol was where the emperor happened to be.

Any definition of Roman towns and Roman countryside needs, necessarily, to acknowledge that throughout the Roman era both were in a process of unfolding change, changes that affected their functions and relationship. Towns developed with stunning rapidity in the early Roman era in the north-west provinces. During the Flavian to Antonine period they were especially vibrant. The sequences of occupation and frequent redesign at Watling Court

(Newgate Street) and Leadenhall Court, London (Perring and Roskams 1991; Milne and Wardle 1993) and, famously, at Insula 14 at Verulamium (Frere 1972) are clear examples of this, as too are the sequences at Tongeren (Vanderhoeven 1996) and Rheims (Berthelot *et al.* 1994). Yet this testimony to occupancy and flourishing town life begins to fade from the archaeological record by the advent of the later Roman period.

This aspect was examined by Reece in a seminal paper (Reece 1980). In this cogent contribution, Reece documented the evidence for the demographic and economic contraction of towns in later Roman times. He did not deny that they retained important functions at a political, administrative and cultural level. However, he made the telling contrast between towns in Britain in the early Roman decades and their nature in the late Roman era, that is, the later third and fourth centuries. He argued that in the late Roman period there was 'life in towns' and the construction and use of large buildings, but this was not 'town life' as characterised the period *c.* AD 50–250. The biographies of Roman Colchester and Tongeren provide examples of this evolution (*cf.* Verhulst 1999). Millett (1990) took a similar line to Reece, and this became an orthodoxy (*cf.* Woolf 1998): towns of the north-west provinces remained important central places within the *civitates* into the late Roman period, being vital to the infrastructure of the empire while retaining ties to the people of the localities. While, for instance, few people may have inhabited these late Roman towns, the large late Roman inhumation cemeteries outside the towns (as with London (Barber and Bowsher 2000)) suggest that people were brought there for burial. This would seem to testify to their continuing physical and ideological significance.

FIGURE 58. Tongeren, Belgium. A view of the Plinius site in 2006, looking to the south-east towards the modern town, which over lies the Roman town; on the horizon is the basilica church. Archaeological investigations in town suburbs have become routine in recent years revealing new data on the character and extent of settlement and land use in Roman times. The photo was supplied by Alain Vanderhoeven and Geert Vynckier of the Flemish Heritage Institute

Casting town–county relations

In many texts, through plans and 'reconstructions', the reader is confronted with the neat lines of Roman towns. These convey the impression of planning and ordered urban living: of the Roman town as the architecture and defining landscape of civilisation. The town can be understood as the apex of classical civilisation and a metaphor for, in north-western Europe, a new society.

The coming of Rome disrupted landscapes; it changed places and made new ones, and, hence, profoundly impacted upon lives and human possibilities. This occurred through the appropriation of land for the erection of towns and their varied components, for military bases, for resources needed to build towns and the new infrastructure, for land allotments associated with the *coloniae* (*centuriation*), and for roads that linked country to town.

As in other eras, the town was fed in many ways by the countryside; there may not have been an even reciprocity. For example, eighteenth- and nineteenth-century London was famously known as 'The Great Wen', and Hoskins uses the appellative for Roman London (1975, 37), identifying its probably parasitic relationship with its hinterland. The relationship was more complex than this view suggests, though it conveys a fundamental truth.

Roman towns were different from what had passed before. Some towns were (on current evidence, at least) built from scratch where no settlement had previously existed. Cirencester and Piercebridge (Holbrook 1998; Millett 1990; Mattingly 2006) belong to this category, as do Soissons (although there was shifting late Iron Age settlement nearby; Haselgrove 1996) and Tongeren (Vanderhoeven 1996). More typically, though, they were constructed over or within existing major late Iron Age foci, as at Colchester, Silchester, Verulamium, Canterbury, Rheims, Arlon and (seemingly) Amiens. Yet, whether constructed at virgin or previously important settlements, what was brought into being was a new creation expressing changed human relationships, practice and ideology. Roman towns were transforming: they were not ideologically neutral, they were political (Hingley 1997a; Creighton 2006). None of these dimensions existed in isolation, but were broadcast into their hinterlands. The town and its functions penetrated the regional social landscape via the road network, through taxation, in the dissemination of imperial policy, through the diffusion of culture and people, and through the flow of exotic commodities and disease. Roman towns were pivotal in these dynamics (*cf.* Adams and Laurence 2001). The radial pattern of roads surrounding Roman towns accelerated accessibility, communication (of all sorts) and specialisation within and between towns and suburban spaces, thereby integrating them.

During the 1960s to 1980s there had been a view that the oppida of late Iron Age temperate Europe represented proto-towns (*cf.* Cunliffe 1974; Collis 1979). Caesar's account of his conquest of Gaul seemed to equate oppida with towns, as they existed in the Mediterranean world. Their archaeology showed on the one hand that the variable layouts of oppida defined something that could be interpreted as 'town-like', and on the other that certain activities occurred at such places on a large scale (such as industry, coining and consumption). However, this view implied a direct continuity that has subsequently been questioned.

Roman towns were unprecedented in so far as they were massive monumental statements that impacted on the lives of the peoples who lived in and about them (*cf.* Laurence 1994; Millett 2001, 64). The scale of many structures was colossal; in some cases in wood initially, then obdurate stone – for instance, the forum basilica complexes at Bavay, Silchester and London, the circus and temple of Claudius at Colchester, the Black Gate at Trier, the baths and temple complex at Bath, and also the town walls, arches and arterially placed mausolea. New configurations of social relations were created, bound up with the ideology and politics of the empire, and were played out, for people of the *civitas*, principally in the towns (Revell 1999). Within a generation or two after the incorporation of the western provinces towns were manifest as a new highly visible statement of changed times. They were technologies for new social relations; and for provincial populations they were never very far away in terms of geography and, one presumes, they will have felt metaphysically close too, even for those living in the countryside.

Developments leading to new understandings of 'town and country'

Three unfolding trends have engendered changes in understanding sites and settlements of the period. First, the nature of archaeological fieldwork in north-west Europe has altered as a consequence of both the shifting focus of development in and around modern towns, and changes in planning controls and issues around heritage, most clearly manifest in PPG16 in Britain and developer-funded contract archaeology in France and The Netherlands. As a result, Roman-period archaeology has been found in many types of place in the modern landscape where it had not previously been sought, or possible to look. This is especially true of the extensive suburbs of large modern towns, as well as in and around current market towns and smaller towns. Changed circumstances, including modern infrastructure development and 'out of town' shopping and industrial parks have led to sustained archaeological investigations (as at West Hawk Farm, Ashford, in Kent (Booth and Lawrence 2000; Williams 2003), and Tienen, Belgium (Vanderhoeven *et al.* 2001)). Indeed, the quantity of new evidence emerging for settlement of the Roman era in the past 15–20 years is remarkable. This has led to the intensification of discoveries relating to the Roman townscape *beyond* the walled 'core'. Work on the 'outskirts' of modern towns is revealing and exciting, for it demonstrates that so many Roman settlements were far more expansive and multi-focal than hitherto realised.

Second, there have been significant advances in refining our understanding of the character of towns (see Laurence 1994, for Pompeii). In north-west Europe recent archaeological work has confirmed that townscapes contained great variations in terms of the compositional elements. They included functionally diverse areas: market gardens, farming and derelict places sat side by side with large, used, structures. This was so both within and outwith the walled core. Additionally, comparative and intra-site studies looking at material culture have helped fulfil the processualist promise of finding differing functional and status areas across settlements both within and outside the walled areas. This is apparent through the work of, for example, Cool (e.g. Cool and Baxter 1999), Eckardt (2007) and van der Linden (forthcoming).

Third, our increasing knowledge of the archaeology of towns underscores how different individual sites actually were. A major development emerging in the 1980s and 1990s, thence, was the realisation that Roman towns had much more marked individuality than had been appreciated. Earlier studies had tended to emphasise similarity of design and function. Now it can be recognised that towns of the Roman period had their own taxonomy, unique identities and status. Nonetheless, the category of 'town' is still valid. They typically shared a series of key imperial, economic, political and ideological roles (that other entities such as 'small towns' did not), containing types of edifice and 'places' in common. These roles threaded them and the Roman phenomenon together as a piece, creating a fabric across the landscape that bound people to empire and each other through various configurations. Towns were central in the day-to-day materiality of the people within the provinces. A citizen from the East entering a 'town' in the Roman West would recognise it as a familiar place: a town; while the reverse would be true, if a citizen from the West entered a town in the East (*cf.* Alcock 1997).

During the 1990s increasing attention was paid to Roman towns as constructed spaces that will have had an intimate dialectic with the structuring of everyday relations of people using and living in towns. At the heart of such explorations have been considerations of the Roman town as a manifestation of power relations (e.g. Creighton 2006), structuration theory approaches (Abrams 1982; Giddens 1986; Revell 1999; 2000) and the phenomenological experience of such milieux (*cf.* Berger 1972; Yegül 2000).

Towns beyond walls

The collection of data from areas skirting town centres has shown that many towns of the era were far more expansive than hitherto realised, with 'suburbs', cemeteries, ceremonial and recreational places, and covered a wide landscape, perhaps for kilometres (*contra* Hoskins 1975, 40). While Roman towns had defined civil, legal and political boundaries and physically defined limits in banks, ditches, arches and walls (the triumphal arch at the Balkerne Gate, Colchester, evidently marks a legal limit (*cf.* Abbott and Johnson 1926; Crummy 1984; 1997)), many in actuality spread beyond these limits. One need only recall the new pictures we have of the extents of Carlisle, Chichester and Colchester and the roadside complexes through Yorkshire. The settlement at Catterick, North Yorkshire, for instance, extended for more than a kilometre south along Dere Street (Wilson 2002).

The emerging picture suggests zoning and functional variety across areas, high and low density occupation and, importantly, overall, constructed space containing many key elements and milieux for the mediation and reproduction of social and economic relationships and ideologies. Many towns appear to have had a halo of foci outside their walled core. These often included elements that were key features in Roman urban and *civitas* life. Colchester exemplifies this phenomenon (Table 7). This is not a 'sprawl', but a structured environment of locations with differing, though integrated, functions, tied into the needs of Roman society.

At Colchester there is design apparent in the configuration of this close hinterland to the town, as evident in the placement of the circus (Crummy 2005), and in the reflection of Gallo-Roman/Romano-British ideas of the relationship of religion and 'social drama' in a non-urban setting in the Gosbecks temple and theatre complex (Crummy 1997; Creighton 2006). By contrast, the Southwark suburb of London appears to have been a much more organic development (*cf.* Watson 1998). At Colchester many of these components arose within the context of previous developments during the late Iron Age. In the Roman period Colchester seems to have been much more than a town in any modern or medieval sense of the term, representing a multi-focal, multi-faceted

Location of functional area beyond the town walls	Type of site/function, and date
Immediately to the NW, at Middleborough	Elaborate 'town housing' (Crummy 1984). Mid Roman
To the NW, at Sheepen and beyond	Extensive industrial and religious zone (Hull 1958; Niblett 1985; Crummy 1980). Late Iron Age/early Roman
Immediately to the W, at the Balkerne Gate	Extra-mural settlement and temples (Crummy 1997). Early to late Roman
To the W, in vicinity of Colchester Royal Grammar School	Cemeteries (e.g. Hull 1958)
To the W, at Stanway	Enclosure cemetery seen as 'high status' (Crummy 1997). Late Iron Age/early Roman
To the SW, at Gosbecks	Temple and theatre complex (Dunnett 1971; Crummy 1997; Creighton 2006). Early to mid Roman
To the S, at Butt Road	Church and cemetery (Crummy *et al.* 1993). Later Roman
To the S, at site of the Colchester Garrison	Circus and cemetery (Crummy 2005). Mid Roman
To the E, in the Hythe Hill/Hythe area	Likely settlement and possible quay by the lowest crossing point of the river Colne (Crummy 1997)
To the N, by the site of the Old Hospital and Railway Station	Cemeteries (unpublished). Early to mid Roman

TABLE 7: The suburbs of Roman Colchester

complex serving both the urban and rural population. Evidently many Roman towns had satellite centres that were not necessarily residential, fulfilling a variety of functions.

Roman towns retained a distinct rural dimension that linked them to Iron Age origins and their economic base. The margins of many Roman towns seem to have graded into the countryside, with evidence for farms on the urban fringes and for farm buildings within town cores. There was a continuity here. For instance, excavations at the Marlowe car-park in central Canterbury demonstrated that at the time when the settlement was receiving exotic imports from Italy and Gaul (often taken to be an index of status) through the first century AD, the site comprised principally farmland related to low-density indigenous farmsteads (Blockley *et al.* 1995). Yet clearly power resided here too. Later, on the south-west side of Canterbury, by the site of the Roman town wall, one or more farms existed during the heyday of the town (Bennett *et al.* 1982). Similarly, a domestic building of some pretension on the fringe of Kenchester was related to agricultural processing (Wilmott and Rahtz 1985). At Leicester, the Norfolk Street villa, located a little way outside the walled town, had a farming element (Liddle 1982, 37–9), although whether this site should be categorised as a villa or a town house outwith the town is a moot point. At Culver Street, Colchester, excavations in the mid-1980s revealed a small stone-founded granary, later overlain by an apparent drying oven (Crummy 1992), located in a part of the enclosed town where an open and perhaps cultivated area lay next to substantial town houses. Environmental samples from Colchester have, in addition, indicated that seaweed was brought into the walled area in some quantity, presumably as fertiliser (Murphy 1992). Richard Brewer (pers. comm.) has interpreted several buildings within the walls at Caerwent, South Wales, as likely farms.

Major distinctions may be made between the elements we see in suburbs based on their function, meaning and development: (i) suburbs and elements that emerged, or already existed, in proximity to the core of the town; (ii) suburbs and elements that developed along the major arterial roads leading to/from the town core; and (iii) locations in the immediate hinterland of towns that were a little removed from town 'cores' and had specialist functions either as newly instituted places or due to an *a priori* cultural significance. In the case of (i), suburbs may have emerged because of limited land within town cores, or because land prices were cheaper; this may account for the town house at Middleborough, Colchester (*cf.* Table 7). It might be contended that living outside the town walls was not necessarily significant or 'problematic' for people in the Roman era, but this ignores the fact, highlighted above, that the enclosed area will have been associated with certain rights, laws and legal definitions (all subject to change over time). The *canabae* that emerged outside forts and fortresses as settlements for 'camp followers' – that is, merchants, families, non-military specialists and so on, who provided services for soldiers – often became enduring settlements as, for instance, fortresses were developed as *colonia*, as at Colchester, Gloucester and Lincoln (Hurst 1999), or where a complex and dynamic relationship emerged between major military and civl presence in the landscape, as at Caerleon, Nijmegen, Oudenburg, Xanten and York. Clearly differing in terms of character, function and consumption vis-a-vis forts (Willis 2005; Eckardt 2007), the *canabae*, as elements of later settlements, evidently continued to retain a degree of separateness in terms of function and identity from the town 'cores'. Likewise, the temples present outside the Balkerne Gate at the site of the former *canabae* by the main entrance to Colchester on the London side (Crummy 1984; 1999) occur at a significant boundary location where religious activity was customary.

With (ii), the presence of properties along arterial roads leading to/from the towns is explicable for practical and economic reasons. This may explain the linear developments south of Catterick along Dere Street (see above) and at Carlisle. It may also in part explain the emergence of the important Southwark suburb at London. Also extending along the arterial roads were cemeteries, mausolea, other funerary features, shrines and altars, as at London, Wroxeter, Colchester and Tongeren (Perring 1991; White and Barker 1998; Vanderhoeven 1996; Vanderhoeven *et al.* 2001). This visibility of the dead, and of religion, as one approached the town was a familiar expression in Roman culture, while Roman law was a factor too, forbidding the burial of the deceased within the town. Such a visible configuration will have represented a landscape 'event', emphasising the town as a central place.

Apropos (iii), constructed elements in and around towns will have developed because they required certain terrain and space or as a result of cultural ideas about place. With regard to the latter, it was noted above that the temples to the north-west and west of the walled town at Colchester, at the Royal Grammar School and Sheepen (Table 7), may relate to pre-existing (Iron Age) shrines sited intentionally by the river Colne and the adjacent springs. The religious significance invested in environments is likely to have been a determining factor in the emergence of shrines and temples outside some urban cores. However, it may well be the case that Roman towns emerged out of Late Iron Age religious centres, rather than religious foci being a consequence of town development; the view that oppida and other sites of the later Iron Age emerged from meeting and market places, perhaps by water and where there was a religious dimension, is a persuasive one; with some oppida in turn becoming Roman towns, the prominence of temples and shrines in and around Roman towns in the north-west provinces is all the more explicable. The siting of both a temple and a theatre at Gosbecks is highly significant, since these two elements are often paired in the Roman world for cultural reasons. Aerial photography and some excavations have indicated that Gosbecks was a location of substantive occupation in the late Iron Age – with some even claiming that Cunobelin's residence was here; but, in any case, something of erstwhile significance was located at this spot prior to the construction of the temple and theatre (*cf.* Creighton 2006). Requirements of space were clearly to the fore with the siting of the circus at Colchester (though it seems to have been a part of the original design of the town), and the large *horreum* outside Tongeren (Vanderhoeven 1996).

So both within and outside the town walls, in certain spaces, the dramas of the *civitas* were played out in temples, churches, theatres and at the circus, through burial, shipping, and agricultural processing. We need to reconceive the extent of settlements and the experience of their multiple environments by past actors. Suburbs were integral components of a whole, part of the everyday lived environments of Roman Britain, Roman Gaul, and so on. In this skirt of areas of activity and clustering of low-density occupation around towns, the terms 'rural' or 'urban' may not be helpful; such suburbs were neither. This new understanding of their extents necessitates a refinement of what Roman towns looked like and what they represented.

The Roman town as a landscape event

We are accustomed to visualise the Roman town in terms of a plan of its street pattern, insulae and stone-founded structures, in a one-dimensional way. Reconstruction illustrations are more common these days but more three-dimensional thinking is required, bringing forward the cultural implications of the town as a social construct (*cf.* Ingold 1997). The physical scale of towns, in terms of breadth, height and monumentality, will have exercised a strong visual and phenomenological impact, added to which would have been their colour(s) in the landscape. Cirencester (96 ha), Tongeren and Amiens (*c.*72 ha), and especially Trier and London (together with the Southwark suburb), were vast settlements (*cf.* Hurst 2005; Vanderhoeven 1996; Wightman 1970; Rowsome 1998; Watson 1998). Amiens, Bavay, Silchester, Trier and Wroxeter included some massive buildings and building complexes – visually stunning and awe provoking even today (Wightman 1970; 1985; Fulford and Timby 2000; White and Barker 1998).

FIGURE 59. Canterbury, Kent. A view looking south-east. The medieval and modern city overlie the Roman town which sits in the valley of the Great Stour. Photo: Spencer Scott, University of Kent

While some buildings and structures in and around towns will, when viewed from 'up close', have seemed extremely impressive, from a distance the townscape in many instances would have appeared either cluttered or obscured by a variety of structures in the foreground, mid and far distance. Colchester is a case in point. Furthermore, some towns sat in valleys, meaning that if they were approached from points other than within the same valley they were hidden until one was quite close (as with Canterbury, if one was approaching along the roads from Dover, London or Richborough; Cirencester and Lincoln are further examples). The implication here is that towns of the Roman era were not necessarily sited with a view to their visual prominence (unlike many villas).

It has been fashionable to talk of past people 'moving through landscapes' and to speculate upon why they followed the routes they did, what they might have experienced and what meanings such journeys and places will have had for them, especially when repeated. The relationship of towns to movement through the landscape has been explored by several scholars (Witcher 1998; Laurence 1999; and in the case of 'small towns' Hingley 1989; Millett 1995). The Roman era certainly engendered considerable movement around landscapes and into and out of towns. We should not, however, overlook the fact that much movement was by ship or boat (many towns being on navigable rivers). Often this method of travel, particularly with regard to arrival at towns, would have been more profound for senses and perceptions, and perhaps for some at least, a more regular experience, than terrestrial movement.

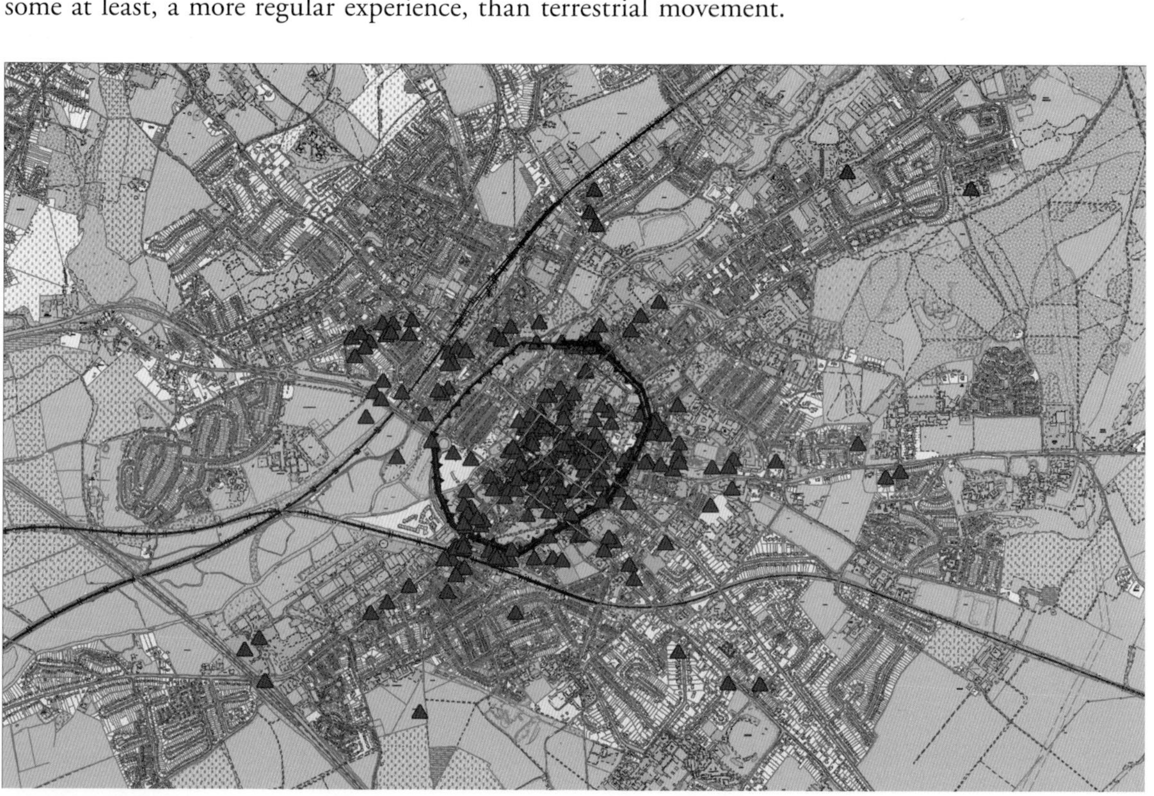

A number of observers have noted that in prehistoric Britain the morphology of man-made monuments and settlements, such as hillforts, often mirrors the character of the 'natural' surrounding topography (*cf.* Willis 1999), but this seems less true for sites dated to the Roman era. While placement of settlements was carefully structured, the settlements themselves no longer appear to represent a microcosm of landscape, and topography is often not reflected in settlement layout, form or material expression. Conversely, there is acknowledgment of 'nature' in other ways, albeit in controlled forms: the formal gardens of elaborate houses; the apparent innovation of 'market gardens'; the decoration of Roman houses with painted wall-plaster with leafy/floral designs. Some rural houses of the period were located with a view to water, across valleys, or to 'owned' land.

FIGURE 60. Canterbury, Kent. A map from the Canterbury Urban Archaeology Database showing Roman Canterbury, its defences and environs, overlaid on a modern Ordnance Survey map. The triangles locate records of finds of Roman date (including buildings, burials, artefacts, etc.). Note the location of the town in relation to the Great Stour river and the absence of findspots recorded from the area of the river floodplain. A few findspots from the hinterland of the Roman town need to be added to this plot, nonetheless the extra-mural areas and suburbs of Roman Canterbury are comparatively under-explored. The author wishes to thank Richard Cross of Canterbury City Council for his assistance. © Crwon copyright. All rights reserved (Canterbury City Council) (100019614) (2007)

The social life of water

A linking pattern exists between culturally significant places and settlement sites through their relationship with water. A cultural association with water is well observed in prehistory (e.g. Richards 1996; Fitzpatrick 1984) and the Roman period sees an intimate linkage. All Roman legionary fortresses in Britain are located by major rivers. Between Dorset and Essex one can point to a dozen or more temple sites that overlook, or are located by, the point where a river joins the sea, where freshwater meets seawater (Willis 2007). Roman London may have been originally established around a shrine situated by the Walbrook stream to its deity (Merrifield 1965). Across Lincolnshire and Leicestershire both small towns and large towns of the Roman era are located either at the heads of rivers, at a ford or at other crossing points or confluences (May 1984; Willis 1997a); appropriately, the new reading of the name for the tribal occupants of this region (i.e. Lincolnshire and Leicestershire), the Corieltauvi, is 'the people of the land of many rivers' (*cf.* Tomlin 1983).

A key aspect in the location of towns in the Roman era is their close proximity to rivers. This often reflects their pre-Roman origins, following through a choice exercised by Iron Age people. However, the association is more readily apparent in the Roman era. Recent papers have suggested that the oppida of late Iron Age temperate Europe grew at points in the landscape that were traditional meeting places on routes across the country, perhaps politically neutral locations. River crossings or areas besides ponds/marshes may have been such locations. Verlamion (Verulamium) has been discussed in such terms (Bryant and Niblett 1997; Haselgrove and Millett 1997), while Amiens, on the Somme, may have had such a character. Roman Lincoln (with its apparent Iron Age precursor) lies at a key transit point where the Witham cuts through the Lincolnshire Edge, with the Brayford pool upstream of the gap (Darling and Jones 1988); Roman Arlon (again with Iron Age origins) is located by the source of the Semois, a major tributary of the Meuse, with a shrine to Apollo constructed at the source (*cf.* inscription, muse luxembourgeois, accession no. GR/S 01); York is located at a river confluence (Wacher 1995); London lies at the lowest bridging point on the Thames where a freshwater stream joins the tidal river (*cf.* above); while Leicester and Canterbury (like Amiens) lie at points of river braiding and probable crossing (Clay and Mellor 1985; Wacher 1995). There were clear practical reasons for locating next to rivers and wet locations: for watering animals, or transport of bulk and heavy goods, for public health, and so on; all central to the creation and re-creation of towns. However, the evidence suggests that there was more to town placement than pragmatics. At Caistor St Edmund, the *civitas* capital of the Iceni, the town is located on the flood-plain of the river Tas; indeed, the river often floods to the town walls (e.g. *Current Archaeology* 141, 349). Similarly, the town wall of Cirencester, Roman Britain's second largest town, encloses what was in Roman times a marsh (Richard Reece, pers. comm.).

Given, therefore, the cultural and ideological significance of rivers, it is likely that the symbolic and religious importance of water was an enduring determinant of settlement and town location. Indeed, of the string of temples located besides the Colne, outside the walled area at Colchester (Table 7), some at least may overlie Iron Age shrines, a sequence attested elsewhere in Essex (e.g. Atkinson and Preston 1998). Today the Colne is the river that one associates with Colchester, flowing through the modern town to the North Sea. However, as Crummy and others have observed, the widespread foci and elements that formed late Iron Age and Roman Colchester (*cf.* Table 7) lay essentially between two rivers: the Colne and the now aptly named Roman River which likewise runs east, approximately 5 km south of the Colne (*cf.* Crummy 1999, fig. 1). The pair evidently had a key role in defining the location and identity of the site in the late Iron Age and Roman eras. The Roman River joins the Colne estuary by Fingringhoe Wick, which seems to

FIGURE 61. Caistor St Edmund, Norfolk. The walls of *Venta Icenorum*, in a playing card shape, are clear in the centre of the picture. The River Tas, in flood, occupies the left-hand side of the picture. This photo, which was taken by Derek Edwards, is the copyright of Norfolk Museums and Archaeology Service, and is reproduced by permission.

be the site of a Conquest-period military installation (Willis 1990; Crummy 1999), and may too have been the site of a shrine and temple (Willis 2007). This is but one way we can conceive of towns – not as urban islands but as expansive entities embedded in the physical and ideological topography of their setting.

While the veneration of water sources in the Roman era follows directly from evident later prehistoric practices (as at the sanctuary of Sequana at St Germain-source-Seine and at Bath (Isserlin 2007)), and a close cultural relationship with wet places has a later prehistoric pedigree (e.g. Bradley 1990; 2002), we can also note contrasts to earlier times. The Roman period saw the channelling of water over long distances on a truly remarkable scale; for instance, the great, enigmatic monument known as the Car Dyke (Simmons 1979; *cf.* Hoskins 1975, 33, 39–40), the aqueducts at Dorchester, Metz and Tongeren, and the well-known long Eifel vaulted aqueduct channel serving Cologne. Archaeology reveals reservoirs, tanks, piped water and fountains, plus waste control; wood, lead and ceramic pipes are found at villas and towns. People in the Roman world seemed to like to cover water as it flowed through the land: covered rills, aqueducts and drains proliferate in and around towns. In addition to the obvious practical reasons, one must now wonder if there was a symbolic aspect to flowing water and its subterranean (albeit artificial) presence, just as there may have been to the *crossing* of flowing water. Water flowing to towns may have held special significance as it was collected from the hinterland landscape of the *civitas* and flowed to the central place – a metaphor perhaps for cultural relations between town and country.

Roman towns in temperate Europe: dynamics of change

Although some towns may have owed much to Iron Age origins, this heritage became blurred. So many new cultural reconfigurations came with absorption into the empire that within a generation or two ideas and understandings that existed in the late Iron Age were likely to have been dramatically changed. Perhaps that is why we see marked changes occurring in Gaul and Britain *c.*20–40 years after their initial incorporation into the empire.

Towns were, in a variety of ways, different from nucleated settlements of later prehistory. Towns in the north-west provinces were often large, sprawling, poly-focal, functionally varied, and 'never very far away'. They were different in that their most culturally impressive components (public buildings, town walls, arches, elite houses, roads, urban monuments, columns, fountains, statuary) were constructed out of selected materials that were essentially unprecedented for building: stone (local and exotic), brick, tile, gravel, sand, lime and mortar. These new hard building materials and their uses would have been culturally charged. Thus came into being buildings and structures that signalled power, wealth, endurance, permanence and order, a 3-D materialisation, as others have observed, for the empire's projected image of itself.

The circumstances of extracting such raw materials, which was novel and large-scale, of changing them into a state in which they were ready to use 'on site', and of conveying them to the towns will have impacted on particular landscapes and engendered new relationships with the land (as the source of materials), and between people, as they were affected by changed circumstances and relations. Wood and clay certainly remained very important and an increase in consumption of these basics must have occurred. However, the architecture and most of the materials of construction chosen carried a political message. Towns proliferated the message of empire like lighthouses across the new Roman landscape. They were like nothing witnessed previously; they brought into being a new reality for people. Some colossal buildings, a novel housing culture (in spatial terms), and the political economy of these new towns with regard to social relations and consumption underscored the differences from what had passed before in the late Iron Age, even in comparison to sites such as Manching and Condé-sur-Suippe (*cf.* Haselgrove 1996).

The Roman towns and cities will have been places where on a daily basis one encountered 'sisters and strangers': that is, local people, people of the *civitas* and people of different backgrounds. With this will have come a complex mix of familiarity, difference and possibility. While the oppida of late Iron Age Europe will undoubtedly have been places of human 'coming and going', of visitors and traders, the degree of human flux and mix in the Roman towns will have been on a new scale. There will have been a daily inflow of people from the *civitas* to markets, for retail, to festivals, to pay taxes, and to undertake civic, judicial, political and religious affairs (*cf.* MacMahon 2006; Evans 2001; Creighton 2006). There will have been visitors with diverse agendas. Doubtless there was a periodic turnover of persons residing in towns before moving on. The epigraphic and now scientific (DNA and isotope analysis) evidence underscores this geographic mobility (see, for instance, RIB nos 9, 110, 149, 163, 202, 251; Birley 1979; 1981; Laurence 1999; *cf.* Adams and Laurence 2001). Roman towns created new social configurations and new experiences in north-west Europe. Herein lies a fascinating sociology of human life that is yet to be explored.

A new underworld of social life

Symmetrical edifices, vibrant markets and orthogonal street plans might be psychologically 'reassuring' yet, as the ancient authors so often remind us, threats to urban harmony, the poor and disorder may never have been far away in the ancient town. The imagined sun-lit orderly classical town was subject to rain-streaking, litter and graffiti, added to which were the fleas, fevers, faeces and felons that often proliferate in habitats where humans are gathered; wherever 'over-worlds' are established by the powerful, cultural underworlds also flourish (Goffman 1991). Roman towns had locales of pollution and environmental corruption, due to, among other practices, industries employing heat and generating dust, smoke, noxious fumes and unpleasant waste. Industries which processed animal bone were, for example, set within the heart of Roman Tongeren and Lincoln (Vanderhoeven and Ervynck 2007; Dobney *et al.* 1999), not in the suburbs. In the later Roman period urban waste management systems may have failed (*cf.* Reece 1980; 1999). Disease might flourish in urban places and be communicated to the surrounding landscape by the flow of people to and from the countryside; Roman towns bred threats to the people of their hinterlands.

People were doubtless attracted to the urban milieu for complex reasons. For some, presumably, motivations will have included the comparative freedoms, anonymity and chances urban environments offered. Towns will have been places of potential excitement, for the indulgence of illicit and peculiar tastes and opportunity. Those with lessened ties to roots will have gravitated to such places.

The archaeological record lies in drifts across the past, thick in some places, thin elsewhere (*cf.* Dyer 1994). The thickness of the record determines our ability to engage with that past, and the nature of the record will have been dependent upon who was making it. Not surprisingly, perhaps, we know quite a lot about the elites in Roman towns through their archaeological footprint: their institutional buildings, their urban houses (e.g. at Rheims (Balmelle and Neiss 2003)) and their material culture. We know less about the 'ordinary folk', such as those who resided in the areas that are now occupied by the Boulevard Joffre and the Rue Gambetta in Rheims, with their dense Roman housing (*cf.* Balmelle *et al.* 1988; Berthelot *et al.* 1994; *cf.* Perring 1987; 1992) and even less about the less than ordinary folk, urban and rural. Archaeologists will continue to explore the town house and the basilica but we need to know more, too, in sociological parlance, of the context of the 'underclass'. We need to think about the places 'the others' inhabited or used: decaying buildings, the 'backwaters' of towns, 'twilight' places likely to be in and besides towns: rubbish heaps, overgrown cemeteries, the gaps between the places of the elites, shanty developments that will have had their own norms and vibrancy. Such places, frequented by people both 'passing through' and long resident, are likely to have left slight archaeological trace (for they were not built in stone) that we have not looked for, nor, evidently, been astute in identifying. This face of 'the wrong side' of town needs to be recognised in the framing of research agendas. These places and lives warrant attention in the same way that villas and named citizens do, although the discrepancy in the archaeological visibility of these different consumers means that the sheer quantity and qualitative extent of the remains of the established and prosperous are likely to continue to receive more attention.

The darkness of the edge of town

The legal status of suburbs in Roman law is likely to have been ambiguous. It may well be the case that suburbs attracted different types of people to those who lived within the walled areas (just as the *canabae* of forts did). In our contemporary world urban suburbs combine dormitory housing, shopping precincts and multiplexes and have been traditionally cast as safe, planned and orderly (though this stereotype ignores the 'sink estates', while in France, just now, the suburbs are alight with social problems and tensions). Comparison with the suburbs of some Roman towns may reveal contrasts: the unmaintained cemetery may be a sinister place (John Pearce, pers. comm.); the extra-mural settlements may have been places of 'licence and liberty' and legally dubious, catering for human appetites, including drinking, gambling and sexual pursuits. At Colchester the finds assemblage from the area of the extra-mural settlement outside the Balkerne Gate has a stronger representation of glass drinking vessels and of decorated samian bowls (potentially used for drinking) than do assemblages from within the walled area; and this pattern endures from the time when the settlement was a *canabae* outside the Claudian fortress through phases of the *colonia* (Cool and Price 1995; Eckardt 2007; Willis 2005; Willis and Hingley 2007). Punishment, too, is likely to have been exercised in such environments, something which may well explain the human skulls and skull fragments from the town ditches at Canterbury and Colchester (Isserlin 1997).

The imprint of the late Iron Age on Roman towns in north-west Europe?

While oppida were not like Roman towns in many respects, certain characteristics can now be seen to be shared (Millett 1990; Woolf 2000; Creighton 2006; Mattingly 2006). New evidence from Roman towns that suggests much low-density occupation, zoning and a spread of foci and functional elements across a wide area seems to parallel characteristics seen at many Iron Age oppida (*cf.* Woolf 1993b). Landscape and its making are key constructs in the ways in which societies articulate, remember, and understand the world (Schama 1995; Connerton 1989; Yegül 2000). With this in mind, Creighton's contention that towns could emerge because they largely respected elements and manifestations of indigenous Iron Age ideology and power systems becomes more understandable and persuasive (Creighton 2006). Their integration with the existing cultural landscape may have given them a claim to legitimacy while plugging them into 'the power of the place'. This is not to suggest, however, that their development was uncomplicatedly harmonious.

Roads to the future

Human actions and social processes often result in unanticipated consequences. The Roman roads that linked towns and landscapes were to bring into being important settlements that complemented the large towns. Roman roads soon developed a centripetal effect, accruing cemeteries, tumuli, mausolea, quarries, watering holes, and, from the turn of the first century (*c.* AD 90–120) we see the wide development of 'small towns' and roadside settlements. This is a strong pattern, seemingly demonstrating an acceptance of the roads as a 'commercial main chance'. These settlements are conventionally associated with the local populations, evidently moving to be sited on roads. In this way farms, crafts and services moved to the roads, in Britain as in Gaul, with these settlements displaying a markedly rural character (lacking baths, mosaics and associated with low levels of fine pottery). They represent a reconfiguration of indigenous settlement and a counter-weight (in degree) to the power of the large towns. This movement to the roads changed the layout and appearance of the countryside, and people's relationships with places. In the early years of Roman Britain roads were built over existing roundhouses, but then, in turn even roundhouses came to be built by roads, as along Ermin Street in Gloucestershire (*cf.* Mudd *et al.* 1999). Some might say that this reconfiguration of rural settlement patterns a generation or two after the conquest, that seems to 'accept' the fact of Roman roads, is a function of a system of Roman hegemony, not a matter of 'native choice'.

Conclusion

The accumulated evidence, old and new, shows that we have *under-imagined* Roman urbanism. The suburbs of towns hold great potential for understanding the phenomenon of towns and their integration into their wider landscape environments. These places should not be seen as marginal but, rather, had a central role in 'the everyday'. There is now a great prospect of learning more about such components of towns given the pattern of current development. Evidence now emerging from routine investigations of the suburbs of modern towns with a Roman past means that there is new data to absorb, and new thinking is necessary as the archaeological picture changes.

While there were differences in town origins and identities in the north-west provinces, they evidently shared a pivotal political role, mediating between empire and territory (the *civitas*), in terms of policy, law, taxes and so on, and were about local power and administration. They included religious centres for, for instance, imperial worship and, later, churches. They were places of high consumption of local and mundane staples, as well as exotic goods. They were ringed by extensive burial places. Yet while they had recognisable hubs, they had, too, a broader spread that was tied into functional specialisation around the core, diffusing the town physically and psychologically into the landscape (through everyday practice and human experience).

By far the majority of the population lived in the countryside at this time, yet cultural life would have been expressed via social relationships that connected with both the rural and the urban. Economic, political and cultural ties were linked via towns with hinterlands, the *civitates* and the provinces. In comprehending the movement of people, material culture and other resources between the countryside and the towns, and the role of towns as central places in regional religious life, as places to come to for festivals, and in order to be buried, we can construct something of the network of locales that people inhabited. Landscapes exist as a process constructed out of such connections, made via dispersed acts that were embedded in people's everyday lives. The archaeology of the era contains a strong record of this town–country symbiosis and our appreciation of this potential has moved forward from the paradigm of the preceding fifty years.

Abbreviations

RIB   The Roman Inscriptions of Britain corpus

Acknowledgements

I am grateful to Andrew Fleming, Richard Hingley, Adam Rogers and Chris Dyer for comments upon an earlier version of this paper.

Contributors

Mike Allen runs Allen Environmental Archaeology.

Richard Bradley is Professor of Archaeology, University of Reading.

Nick Card is Projects Manager for the Orkney Archaeological Trust.

Patrick Clay is Director of University of Leicester Archaeological Services.

Toby Driver is Project Manager, Aerial Survey, Royal Commission on the Ancient and Historical Monuments of Wales.

Andrew Fleming is Emeritus Professor of Archaeology, University of Wales Lampeter.

Chris Gaffney is Consultant at Remote Vision Research.

John Gater is a Director of GSB Prospection Ltd.

Richard Hingley is Reader in Archaeology at Durham University.

Adam Rogers is a research student in the Department of Archaeology, Durham University.

Rob Scaife is Visiting Honorary Reader, University of Southampton, and also a freelance consultant.

Irene Schrüfer-Kolb is Research Associate in the Department of Classical Studies, at The Open University

Steve Willis is Head of Classical and Archaeological Studies, University of Kent.

Emma Wood is Geophysicist at GSB Prospection Ltd.

David Yates is Research Fellow in the Department of Archaeology at the University of Reading.

Bibliography

Abbott, F. F. and Johnson, A. C. (1926) *Municipal Administration in the Roman Empire*, Princeton University Press, Princeton.

Abrams, P. (1982) *Historical Sociology*, Open Books, near Shepton Mallet.

Abrams, P. and Wrigley, E. A. eds (1978) *Towns in Societies. Essays in Economic History and Historical Sociology*, Cambridge University Press, Cambridge.

Adams, C. and Laurence, R. eds (2001) *Travel and Geography in the Roman Empire*, Routledge, London.

Aitken, M. (1958) 'Magnetic Prospecting 1. The Water Newton Survey', *Archaeometry* **1** (1), 24–9.

Albone, J. (2000) 'Elmsthorpe Rise (SK 564 035)', *Transactions of the Leicestershire Archaeological and Historical Society* **74**, 224.

Alcock, L. (1962) 'Settlement patterns in Celtic Britain', *Antiquity* **36**, 51–4.

Alcock, S. E. ed. (1997) *The Early Roman Empire in the East*, Oxbow Monograph 95, Oxbow Books, Oxford.

Alcock, S. E. (2002) *Archaeologies of the Greek Past: Landscape, Monuments and Memories*, Cambridge University Press, Cambridge.

Aldhouse-Green, M. (2002) 'Any old iron! Symbolism and ironworking in Iron Age Europe' in eds M. Aldhouse-Green and P. Webster, *Artefacts and Archaeology: Aspects of the Celtic and Roman World*, University of Wales Press, Cardiff, 8–19.

Alföldi, A. (1949) 'The bronze mace from Willingham Fen, Cambridgeshire', *Journal of Roman Studies* **39**, 19–22.

Allen, G. W. G. (1938) 'Marks seen from the air in the crops near Dorchester', *Oxoniensia* **3**, 169–71.

Allen, G. W. G. (1940) 'Crop marks seen from the air, Northfield Farm, Long Wittenham', *Oxoniensia* **5**, 164–5.

Allen, M. J. (1988) 'Archaeological and environmental aspects of colluviation in South-East England' in eds W. Groenmann-van Waateringe and M. Robinson, *Man-Made Soils*, British Archaeological Reports International Series 410, Oxford, 69–92.

Allen, M. J. (1991) 'Analysing the landscape: a geographical approach to archaeological problems' in ed. J. Schofield, *Interpreting Artefact Scatters: Contributions to Ploughzone Archaeology*, Oxbow Monograph 4, Oxbow Books, Oxford, 39–57.

Allen, M. J. (1992) 'Products of erosion and the prehistoric land-use of the Wessex chalk' in eds M. G. Bell and J. Boardman, *Past and Present Soil Erosion: Archaeological and Geographical Perspectives*, Oxbow Books, Oxford, 37–52.

Allen, M. J. (1995a) 'The prehistoric land-use and human ecology of the Malling-Caburn Downs; two late Neolithic/Early Bronze Age sites beneath colluvium', *Sussex Archaeological Collections* **133**, 19–43.

Allen, M. J. (1995b) 'Before Stonehenge' in R. M. J. Cleal, K. E. Walker and R. Montague, *Stonehenge in its Landscape: Twentieth-Century Excavations*, English Heritage Archaeological Report 10, 41–63.

Allen, M. J. (1997a) 'Landscape, land-use and farming' in R. J. C. Smith, F. Healy, M. J. Allen, E. L. Morris, I. Barnes and P. J. Woodward, *Excavations Along the Route of the Dorchester By-pass, Dorset, 1986–8*, Wessex Archaeology Report 11, Salisbury, 277–83.

Allen, M. J. (1997b) 'Environment and land-use; the economic development of the communities who built Stonehenge; an economy to support the stones' in eds B. Cunliffe and C. Renfrew, *Science and Stonehenge*, Proceedings of the British Academy, Oxford, 115–44.

Allen, M. J. (2000a) 'High resolution mapping of Neolithic and Bronze Age landscapes and land-use; the combination of multiple palaeo-environmental analysis and topographic modelling' in ed. A. S. Fairbairn, *Plants in Neolithic Britain and Beyond*, Neolithic Studies Group Seminar Papers 5, Oxbow Books, 9–26.

Allen, M. J. (2000b) 'Soils, pollen and lots of snails' in M. G. Green, *A Landscape Revealed: 10,000 Years on a Chalkland Farm*, Tempus, Stroud, 36–49.

Allen, M. J. (2002) 'The chalkland landscape of Cranborne Chase: a prehistoric human ecology', *Landscapes* **3**, 55–69.

Allen, M. J. (2005a) 'Beaker occupation and development of the downland landscape at Ashcombe Bottom, near Lewes, East Sussex', *Sussex Archaeological Collections* **143**, 7–33.

Allen, M. J. (2005b) 'Beaker settlement and environment on the chalk downs of southern England', *Proceedings of the Prehistoric Society* **71**, 219–45.

Allen, M.J. (2005c) 'Considering prehistoric environmental changes on the Marlborough Downs' in eds G. Brown, D. Field and D. McOmish, *The Avebury Landscape: Aspects of Field Archaeology of the Marlborough Downs*, Oxbow Books, Oxford, 77–86.

Allen, M.J. (2006) 'Professor John Gwynne Evans, aka 'snails' Evans', *Journal of Conchology* **39**, 111–17.

Allen, M.J. (forthcoming) 'If you go down the woods today you're in for a big surprise' in M.J. Allen, T.P. O'Connor and N. Sharples, *Land and People*, Prehistoric Society Research Papers 1.

Allen, M.J. and Gardiner, J. (2002) 'A sense of time – cultural markers in the Mesolithic of southern England' in eds B. David and M.Wilson, *Inscribed Landscapes: Marking and Making Place*, University of Hawaii Press, Honolulu, 139–53.

Allen, M.J., Entwistle, R. and Richards, J. (1990) 'Molluscan studies' in J.C. Richards, *The Stonehenge Environs Project*, English Heritage Archaeological Reports 16, 253–8.

Allerston, P. (1970) 'English village development: findings from the Pickering district of North Yorkshire', *Transactions of the Institute of British Geographers* **51**, 95–109.

Ammerman, A.J. (1990) 'On the Origins of the Forum Romanum', *American Journal of Archaeology* **94**, 627–45.

Arnold, J., Green, M., Lewis, B. and Bradley, R. (1988) 'The Mesolithic of Cranborne Chase', *Proceedings of the Dorset Natural History and Archaeological Society* **110**, 117–25.

Arnold, M. (1976; first published 1867) *On the Study of Celtic Literature and Other Essays*, J.M. Dent, London.

Aston, M. (1992) 'The Shapwick Project, Somerset: A study in need of remote sensing' in ed. P. Spoerry, *Geoprospection and the Archaeological Landscape*, Oxbow Monograph 18, Oxbow Books, Oxford, 141–54.

Aston, M. (1993) *Monasteries*, Batsford, London.

Atkinson, M. and Preston, S.J. (1998) 'The late Iron Age and Roman settlement at Elms Farm, Heybridge, Essex, excavations 1993–5: an interim report', *Britannia* **29**, 85–110.

Atkinson, R.J.C. (1952) 'The date of Stonehenge', *Proceedings of the Prehistoric Society* **18**, 236–7.

Babington, C.C. (1883) *Ancient Cambridgeshire*, Cambridge Antiquarian Society, Cambridge.

Ballin Smith, B. (2003) *A New Late Neolithic House at Brodgar Farm, Stenness, Orkney*, unpublished report for GUARD Project 1506, Glasgow.

Balmelle, A. and Neiss, R. (2003) *Les maisons de l'élite à Durocortorvm*, Archéologie urbaine à Reims 5, Société archéologique champenoise, Reims.

Balmelle, A., Berthelot, F. and Podgorny, A. (1988) *La fouille du 28, bd Joffre, n d'inventaire de site: 51 454 34*, DFS, SRA, Champagne-Ardenne.

Barber, B. and Bowsher, D. (2000) *The Eastern Cemetery of Roman London, Excavations 1983–90*, MoLAS Monograph 4, Museum of London Archaeology Service, London.

Barclay, A. and Bayliss, A. (1999) 'Cursus monuments and the radiocarbon problem' in eds A. Barclay and J. Harding, *Pathways and Ceremonies: The Cursus Monuments of Britain and Ireland*, Oxbow Books, Oxford, 11–29

Barclay, A. and Harding, J. eds (1999) *Pathways and Ceremonies: The Cursus Monuments of Britain and Ireland*, Oxbow Books, Oxford.

Barclay, G.J. (2001) ''Metropolitan' and 'parochial' / 'core' and 'periphery': a historiography of the Neolithic of Scotland', *Proceedings of the Prehistoric Society* **67**, 1–18.

Barclay, G. and Maxwell, G. (1998) *The Cleaven Dyke and Littleour: Monuments in the Neolithic of Tayside*, Society of Antiquaries of Scotland, Edinburgh.

Barclay, G., Brophy, K., and MacGregor, G. (2002) 'Claish, Stirling: an early Neolithic structure and its context', *Proceedings of the Society of Antiquaries of Scotland* **132**, 65–137.

Barrett, J.C. (1994) *Fragments from Antiquity: The Archaeology of Social Life in Britain, 2900–1200BC*, Blackwell, Oxford.

Barrett, J., Bradley, R. and Green, M. (1991) *Landscape, Monuments and Society: The Prehistory of Cranborne Chase*, Cambridge University Press, Cambridge.

Barrett, J.C., Lewis, J.S.C. and Welsh, K. (2001) 'Perry Oaks – a history of inhabitation, part 2', *London Archaeologist* **9**, no. 8, 221–7.

Bartlett, A.D.H. and Clark, A.J. (1973)*Ring of Brodgar, Orkney: Magnetometer Survey*, Ancient Monuments Laboratory (Old Series) 1616, unpublished survey.

Beddoe, J. (1971; first published 1885) *The Races of Britain: A Contribution to the Anthropology of Western Europe*, Hutchinson, London.

Beinart, W. and Coates, P. (1995) *Environment and History: The Taming of Nature in the USA and South Africa*, Routledge, London.

Bell, M.G. (1981) 'Valley sediments and environmental change' in eds M. Jones and G. Dimbleby, *The Environment of Man: The Iron Age to Anglo-Saxon Period*, British Archaeological Reports, British Series 87, Oxford, 75–91.

Bell, M.G. (1983) 'Valley sediments as evidence of prehistoric land-use on the South Downs', *Proceedings of the Prehistoric Society* **49**, 119–50.

Bell, M.G. (1992) 'The prehistory of soil erosion' in eds M.G. Bell and J. Boardman, *Past and Present Soil Erosion*, Oxbow Books, Oxford, 21–35.

Bender, B. (1993) 'Landscape – Meaning and Action' in ed. B. Bender, *Landscape: Politics and Perspectives*, Berg Publishers, Providence and Oxford, 1–17.

Bennett, P., Frere, S.S. and Stow, S. (1982) *Excavations at Canterbury Castle*, Canterbury Archaeological Trust and the Kent Archaeological Society, Maidstone.

Benson, D. and Miles, D. (1974) *The Upper Thames Valley: An Archaeological Survey of the River Gravels*, Oxford Archaeological Unit, Oxford.

Berger, J. (1972) *Ways of Seeing*, Penguin, Harmondsworth.

Bersu, G. (1940) 'Excavations at Little Woodbury, Wiltshire', *Proceedings of the Prehistoric Society* **6**, 30–111.

Berthelot, F., Balmelle, A. and Rollet, P. (1994) *Reims Fouilles Archéologiques: Site du Conservatoire National de Région de Musique et de Danse, rue Gambetta, Reims (Marne)*, Archéologie urbaine à Reims 3, Société archéologique champenoise, Reims.

Bevan, B. ed. (1999) *Northern Exposure: Interpretative Devolution and the Iron Ages in Britain*, Leicester Archaeology Monographs 4, Leicester.

Birley, A.R. (1979) *The People of Roman Britain*, Batsford, London.

Birley, A.R. (1981) *The Fasti of Roman Britain*, Clarendon Press, London.

Blockley, K., Blockley, M., Blockley, P., Frere, S.S. and Stow, S. (1995) *Excavations in the Marlowe Car Park and Surrounding Areas*, Canterbury Archaeological Trust, Canterbury.

Boardman, J. (1992) 'Current erosion on the South Downs: implications for the past' in eds M.G. Bell and J. Boardman, *Past and Present Soil Erosion*, Oxbow Books, Oxford, 9–19.

Bogucki, P. (1988) *Forest Farmers and Foragers*, Cambridge University Press, Cambridge.

Bond, J. (2000) 'Landscapes of Monasticism' in ed. D. Hooke, *Landscape: The Richest Historical Record*, The Society for Landscape Studies, Amesbury, 63–74.

Booth, P. and Lawrence, S. (2000) 'Ashford, Westhawk Farm', *Current Archaeology* **168**, 478–81.

Bowden, M. and McOmish, D. (1987) 'The Required Barrier', *Scottish Archaeological Review* **4**, 76–84.

Bowen, E.G. (1957) 'Race and culture' in ed. E.G. Bowen, *Wales: A Physical, Historical and Regional Geography*, Methuen, London, 131–40.

Bowen, H.C. (1961) *Ancient Fields. A Tentative Analysis of Vanishing Earthworks and Landscapes*, British Association for the Advancement of Science, London.

Bowen, H.C. and Fowler, P. (1966) 'Romano-British Rural settlements in Dorset and Wiltshire' in ed. C. Thomas, *Rural Settlement in Roman Britain*, Council for British Archaeology, London, 43–67.

Bowen, H.C. and Fowler, P. eds (1978) *Early Land Allotment in the British Isles*, British Archaeological Reports 48, Oxford.

Bradley, R. (1978) 'Prehistoric field systems in Britain and north-west Europe – a review of some recent work', *World Archaeology* **9**, 265–80.

Bradley, R. (1984) *The Social Foundations of British Prehistory: Themes and Variations in the Archaeology of Power*, Longman Group Ltd, London.

Bradley, R. (1989) 'Herbert Toms – a pioneer of analytical field survey' in eds M. Bowden, D. Mackay and P. Topping, *From Cornwall to Caithness. Some aspects of British Field Archaeology. Papers presented to Norman V. Quinnell*, British Archaeological Reports British Series 209, Oxford, 29–47.

Bradley, R. (1990) *The Passage of Arms: An Archaeological Analysis of Prehistoric Hoards and Votive Deposits*, Cambridge University Press, Cambridge.

Bradley, R. (2000) *An Archaeology of Natural Places*, Routledge, London.

Bradley, R. (2002 reprint) *An Archaeology of Natural Places*, Routledge, London.

Bradley, R. (2003) 'A life less ordinary: the ritualization of the domestic sphere in later prehistoric Europe', *Cambridge Archaeological Journal* **13** no. 1, 5–23.

Bradley, R. and Chambers, R. (1988) 'A new study of the cursus complex at Dorchester on Thames', *Oxford Journal of Archaeology* **7**, 271–89.

Bradley, R. and Yates, D. (in press) 'After 'Celtic' fields: the social organisation of Iron Age agriculture' in eds C. Haselgrove and R. Pope, *The Earlier Iron Age in Britain and the Near Continent*.

Bradley, R., Entwistle, R. and Raymond, F. (1994) *Prehistoric Land Divisions on Salisbury Plain. The Work of the Wessex Linear Ditches Project*, English Heritage, London.

Branigan, K. (1977) *Gatcombe Roman Villa*, British Archaeological Reports British Series 44, Oxford.

Braund, D. (1996) *Ruling Roman Britain: Kings, Queens, Governors and Emperors from Julius Caesar to Agricola*, Routledge, London.

Britnell, W. (1989) 'The Collfryn Hillslope Enclosure, Llansantffraid Deuddwr, Powys: excavations 1980–2', *Proceedings of the Prehistoric Society* **55**, 89–134.

Bromwich, J. (1970) 'Freshwater flooding along the Fen margins south of the Isle of Ely during the Roman period' in ed. C.W. Phillips, *The Fenland in Roman Times: Studies of a Major Area of Peasant Colonisation with a Gazetteer Covering all Known Sites and Finds*, The Royal Geographical Society, London, 114–25.

Brooks, H. (2002) 'A Bronze Age and Saxon occupation site at Frog Hall Farm, Fingringhoe', *Essex Archaeology and History* **33**, 54–62.

Brophy, K. (2000) 'Water coincidence: cursus monuments and rivers' in ed. A. Ritchie, *Neolithic Orkney in its European Context*, McDonald Institute for Archaeological Research, University of Cambridge, 59–70.

Brown, A. G. (2000) 'Floodplain vegetation history: clearings as potential ritual spaces?' in ed. A. S. Fairbairn, *Plants in Neolithic Britain and Beyond*, Neolithic Studies Group Seminar Papers 5, Oxbow Books, Oxford, 49–62.

Browne, D. M. (1976) 'Excavations at Burwell, Cambridgeshire', *Proceedings of the Cambridge Antiquarian Society* **66**, 81–91.

Browne, D. and Driver, T. (2001) *Bryngaer Pen Dinas Hillfort, A Prehistoric Fortress at Aberystwyth*, RCAHMW, Aberystwyth.

Brück, J. and Goodman, M. (1999) 'Introduction: themes for a critical archaeology of prehistoric settlement' in eds J. Brück and M. Goodman, *Making Places in the Prehistoric World: Themes in Settlement Archaeology*, UCL Press, London, 1–19.

Brulet, R. (1987) *Liberchies I. Vicus Gallo-Romain*, Publications d'histoire de l'art et d'archéologie de l'Université Catholique de Louvain-la-Neuve LIV, Louvain-la-Neuve.

Bryant, S. R. and Niblett, R. (1997) 'The late Iron Age in Hertfordshire and the north Chilterns' in eds A. Gwilt and C. C. Haselgrove, *Reconstructing Iron Age Societies*, Oxbow Monograph 71, Oxbow Books, Oxford, 270–81.

Burl, A. (1987) *The Stonehenge People*, Dent, London.

Burl, A. (1993) *From Carnac to Callanish*, Yale University Press, New Haven.

Burnham, B.C. (1986) 'The origins of Romano-British small towns', *Oxford Journal of Archaeology* **5/2**, 185–203.

Burnham, B. (1993) 'The "small towns" of Roman Britain – the last fifty years' in ed. S. J. Greep, *Roman Towns: The Wheeler Inheritance*, Council for British Archaeology Research Report 93, London, 99–110.

Burnham, B. and Wacher, J. (1990) *The Small Towns of Roman Britain*, Batsford, London.

Burnham, B., Collis, J., Dobinson, C., Haselgrove, C. and Jones, M. (2001) 'Themes for urban research: *c.*100 BC to AD 200' in eds. S. James and M. Millett, *Britons and Romans: Advancing an Archaeological Agenda*, Council for British Archaeology Research Report 125, York, 67–76.

Burnham, H. (1995) *A Guide to Ancient and Historic Wales: Clwyd and Powys*, Cadw, HMSO, London.

Bush, M. B. (1988) 'Early Mesolithic disturbance: a force on the landscape', *Journal of Archaeological Science* **15**, 453–62.

Bush, M. B. (1989) 'On the antiquity of British grasslands: a response to Thomas', *Journal of Archaeological Science* **16**, 555–60.

Bush, M. B. and Flenley, J. R. (1986) 'The age of the British chalk grasslands', *Nature* **395**, 484–5.

Campbell, C. (1995) 'Conspicuous confusion? A critique of Veblen's theory of Conspicuous Consumption', *Sociological Theory* **13**, 37–47.

Card, N. (2004) *Ness of Brodgar Excavations 2004, Data Structure Report*, unpublished report for Orkney Archaeological Trust.

Card, N. and Cluett, J. (2005) *Ness of Brodgar Excavations 2005, Data Structure Report*, unpublished report for Historic Scotland.

Carroll, M. (2001) *Romans, Celts and Germans: the German provinces of Rome*, Tempus, Stroud.

Casey, P. J. (1989) 'A votive deposit from the River Tees at Piercebridge, County Durham', *Durham Archaeological Journal* **5**, 37–42.

Cato trans. A. Dalby (1998) *De Agricultura*, Prospect Books, Totnes.

Catt, J. A. (1978) 'The contribution of loess to soils in lowland Britain' in eds S. Limbrey and J. G. Evans, *The Effect of Man on the Landscape: The Lowland Zone*, CBA Research Report **21**, London, 12–20.

Champion, T. and Collis, J. eds (1996) *The Iron Age in Britain and Ireland: Recent Trends*, University of Sheffield.

Chapman, A., Carlyle, S. and Leigh, D. (2005) 'Neolithic and Beaker pits, and a Bronze Age landscape at Fenstanton, Cambridgeshire', *Proceedings of the Cambridge Antiquarian Society* **94**, 5–20.

Chapman, H. (2005) 'Rethinking the 'cursus problem': investigating the Neolithic landscape archaeology of Rudston, East Yorkshire, UK, using GIS', *Proceedings of the Prehistoric Society* **71**, 159–70.

Chapman, J. (1997a) 'Landscapes in flux and the colonisation of time' in eds J. Chapman and P. Dolukhanov, *Landscapes in Flux: Central and Eastern Europe in Antiquity*, Oxbow Books, Oxford, 1–21.

Chapman, J. (1997b) 'Places as timemarks – the social construction of prehistoric landscapes in eastern Hungary' in eds J. Chapman and P. Dolukhanov, *Landscapes in Flux: Central and Eastern Europe in Antiquity*, Oxbow Books, Oxford, 137–161.

Childe, V. G. (1925) *The Dawn of European Civilisation*, Routledge and Kegan Paul Ltd, London.

Childe, V. G. (1940) *Prehistoric Communities of the British Isles*, W. and R. Chambers, London.

Childe, V. G. (1956) *Piecing Together the Past*, Routledge and Kegan Paul, London.

Clark, A. J. (1973) *Stones of Stenness, Orkney: Magnetometer Survey*, Ancient Monuments Laboratory (Old Series) 1613, unpublished survey.

Clark, A.J. (1996) *Seeing Beneath the Soil*, Batsford, London.

Clark, G. (1940) *Prehistoric England*, Batsford, London.

Clark, J.G.D. (1945) 'Farmers and forests in Neolithic Europe', *Antiquity* **19**, 57–71.

Clark, P. (2004) *The Dover Bronze Age Boat in Context: Society and Water Transport in Prehistoric Europe*, Oxbow Books, Oxford.

Clark, R.H. and Schofield, A.J. (1991) 'By experiment and calibration: an integrated approach to archaeology of the ploughsoil' in ed. A.J. Schofield, *Interpreting Artefact Scatters: Contributions to Ploughzone Archaeology*, Oxbow Books, Oxford, 93–106.

Clarke, L.C.G. (1931) 'Roman pewter bowl from the Isle of Ely', *Proceedings of the Cambridge Antiquarian Society* **31**, 66–75.

Clarke, S. (1997) 'Abandonment, rubbish disposal and 'special' deposits at Newstead' in eds K. Meadows, C. Lemke and J. Heron, *TRAC 96: Proceedings of the Sixth Annual Theoretical Roman Archaeology Conference*, Oxbow Books, Oxford, 38–54.

Clay, P. (1989) 'Out of the unknown. Approaches to prehistoric archaeology in Leicestershire' in ed. A. Gibson, *Midlands Prehistory*, British Archaeological Reports British Series 204, Oxford, 111–21.

Clay, P. (1996) *The Exploitation of the East Midlands Claylands in Later Prehistory. Aspects of Settlement and Land-Use from the Mesolithic to the Iron Age*, unpublished PhD thesis, University of Leicester.

Clay, P. (1998) 'Neolithic–Earlier Bronze Age pit circles and their environs at Burley Road, Oakham, Rutland', *Proceedings of the Prehistoric Society* **64**, 293–330.

Clay, P. (2002) *The Prehistory of the East Midlands Claylands. Aspects of Settlement and Land-Use from the Mesolithic to the Iron Age in Central England*, Leicester Archaeology Monograph 9, University of Leicester.

Clay, P. (2006) 'The Neolithic and Early to Middle Bronze Age' in ed. N. Cooper, *The Archaeology of the East Midlands. An Archaeological Resource Assessment and Research Agenda*, Leicester Archaeology Monograph 13, Leicester, 69–88.

Clay, P. and Mellor, J.E. (1985) *Excavations in Bath Lane, Leicester*, Leicestershire Museums, Art Galleries and Records Service, Leicester.

Cleere, H.F. (1972) 'The classification of early iron-smelting furnaces', *Antiquaries Journal* **52**, 8–23.

Cleere, H.F. and Crossley, D. (1995) *The Iron Industry of the Weald*, Merton Priory Press, Cardiff.

Coates, R. and Breeze, A. (2000) *Celtic Voices English places*, Shaun Tyas, Stamford.

Coles, J. (1998) *Changing Landscapes: The Ancient Fenlands*, Wetland Archaeology Research Project, Cambridge.

Collens, J. (1988) *Iron Age and Romano-British Settlement in the Upper Severn Valley*, unpublished PhD thesis, 2 vols, Department of Ancient History and Archaeology, Faculty of Arts, University of Birmingham.

Collingwood, R.G. and Myres, J.N.L. (1936) *Roman Britain and the English Settlement*, Clarendon Press, Oxford.

Collis, J. (1979) 'City and state in pre-Roman Britain' in eds B.C. Burnham and H.B. Johnson, *Invasion and Response*, British Archaeological Reports British Series 73, Oxford, 231–40.

Collis, J. (1994) 'The Iron Age' in ed. B. Vyner, *Building on the Past, Papers Celebrating 150 Years of the Royal Archaeological Institute*, The Royal Archaeological Institute, 123–48.

Collis, J. (2003) *The Celts: Origins, Myths and Inventions*, Tempus, Stroud.

Connerton, P. (1989) *How Societies Remember*, Cambridge University Press, Cambridge.

Cool, H.E.M. and Baxter, M.J. (1999) 'Peeling an onion: an approach to comparing vessel glass assemblages', *Journal of Roman Archaeology* **12**, 72–100.

Cool, H.E.M. and Price, J. (1995) *Roman Vessel Glass from Excavations in Colchester, 1971–85*, Colchester Archaeological Trust, Colchester.

Coombs, D. (1992) 'Flag Fen platform and Fengate Power Station post alignment – the metalwork', Antiquity **66**, 504–17.

Cooney, G. (1997) 'Images of settlement and landscape in the Neolithic' in ed. P. Topping, *Neolithic Landscapes*, Neolithic Studies Group Seminar Papers 2, Oxbow Monograph 86, Oxbow Books, Oxford, 23–32.

Cooper, L. and Hunt, L. (2005) 'An engraved Neolithic plaque with Grooved Ware associations', *Past* **50** (July), 14–15.

Cooper, N.J. (1996) 'Searching for the blank generation: consumer choice in Roman and post-Roman Britain' in eds J. Webster and N.J. Cooper, *Roman Imperialism: Post-Colonial Perspectives*, University of Leicester, Leicester, 85–98.

Cooper, N. and Clay, P. (2006) 'The national and regional context of the regional framework' in ed. N. Cooper, *The Archaeology of the East Midlands. An Archaeological Resource Assessment and Research Agenda*, Leicester Archaeology Monograph 13, Leicester, 1–10.

Corrigan, P. (1997) *The Sociology of Consumption*, SAGE Publications, London.

Cosgrove, D.E. (1984) *Social Formation and Symbolic Landscape*, Croom Helm, London.

Crawford, O.G.S. (1921) *Man and his Past*, Oxford University Press, London.

Crawford, O.G.S. (1923) 'Air survey and archaeology', *Geographical Journal* **61**, 342–66.

Crawford, O.G.S. (1928) *Air survey and archaeology*, HMSO, Southampton.

Crawford, O.G.S. (1953) *Archaeology in the Field*, J.M. Dent, London.

Crawford, O.G.S. (1955) *Said and Done*, Phoenix House, London.

Crawford, O.G.S. and Keiller, A. (1928) *Wessex from the Air*, Clarendon Press, Oxford.

Creighton, J.D. (2006) *Britannia: The Creation of a Roman Province*, Routledge, London.

Cromarty, A.M., Barclay, A., Lambrick, G. and Robinson, M. (2006) *The Archaeology of the Wallingford Bypass. Late Bronze Age Ritual and Habitation on a Thames Eyot at Whitecross Farm, Wallingford*, Thames Valley Landscapes Monograph 22, Oxford Archaeology.

Crummy, P. (1980) 'The temples of Roman Colchester' in ed. W. Rodwell, *Temples, Churches and Religion: Recent Research in Roman Britain*, British Archaeological Reports British Series 77, Oxford, 243–8.

Crummy, P. (1984) *Excavations at Lion Walk, Balkerne Lane, and Middleborough, Colchester, Essex*, Colchester Archaeological Trust, Colchester.

Crummy, P. (1992) *Excavations at Culver Street, the Gilberd School and other Sites in Colchester 1971–85*, Colchester Archaeological Trust, Colchester.

Crummy, P. (1997) *City of Victory*, Colchester Archaeological Trust, Colchester.

Crummy, P. (1999) 'Colchester: making towns out of fortresses and the first urban fortifications in Britain' in ed. H. Hurst, *The Coloniae of Roman Britain, Journal of Roman Archaeology* Supplementary Series 36, Portsmouth, Rhode Island, 88–100.

Crummy, P. (2005) 'The circus at Colchester (*Colonia Victricensis*)', *Journal of Roman Archaeology* **18**, 267–77.

Crummy, N., Crummy, P. and Crossan, C. (1993) *Excavations of Roman and Later Cemeteries, Churches, and Monastic Sites in Colchester, 1971–86*, Colchester Archaeological Trust, Colchester.

Cunliffe, B.W. (1974) *Iron Age Communities in Britain*, Routledge, London.

Cunliffe, B. (1993; 2nd edn) *English Heritage Book of Danebury*, Batsford/English Heritage, London.

Cunliffe, B. (1997) *The Ancient Celts*, Penguin Books, London.

Cunliffe, B. (2001) *Facing the Ocean*, Oxford University Press, Oxford.

Curtis, L.F., Courtney, F.M. and Trudgill, S. (1976) *Soils in the British Isles*, Longman, London.

Curwen, E.C. (1937) *The Archaeology of Sussex*, Metheun and Co., London.

Curwen, E.C. (1954; 2nd edn) *The Archaeology of Sussex*, Metheun and Co., London.

Curwen, E. and Curwen E.C. (1923) 'Sussex lynchets and their associated field-ways', *Sussex Archaeological Collections* **64**, 1–65. Cunliffe, B. (1991) *Iron Age Communities of Britain*, Routledge, London.

Daniel, G. (1943) *The Three Ages: An Essay on Archaeological Method*, Cambridge University Press, Cambridge.

Daniel, G. (1950) *The Prehistoric Chamber Tombs of England and Wales*, Cambridge University Press, Cambridge.

Daniels, S. and Cosgrove, D. (1988) 'Introduction: iconography of landscape' in eds D. Cosgrove and S. Daniels, *The Iconography of Landscape*, Cambridge University Press, Cambridge, 1–10.

Darby, H.C. (1973) 'The age of the improver: 1600–1800' in ed. H.C. Darby, *A New Historical Geography of England*, Cambridge University Press, Cambridge, 302–88.

Darby, H.C. (1983) *The Changing Fenland*, Cambridge University Press, Cambridge.

Dark, K. (1993) 'Roman-period activity at prehistoric ritual monuments in Britain and in the Armorican Peninsula' in ed. E. Scott, *Theoretical Roman Archaeology First Conference Proceedings*, Avebury, Aldershot, 133–46.

Dark, P. (1999) 'Pollen evidence for the environment of Roman Britain', *Britannia* **30**, 247–72.

Dark, K. and Dark, P. (1997) *The Landscape of Roman Britain*, Sutton Publishing, Stroud.

Darling, M.J. and Jones, M.J. (1988) 'Early settlement at Lincoln', *Britannia* **19**, 1–57.

David, A. and Payne, A. (1997) 'Geophysical surveys within the Stonehenge landscape: a review of past endeavour and future potential' *Proceedings of the British Academy* **92**, 73–113.

Davies, J.L. and Hogg, A.H.A. (1994) 'The Iron Age' in eds J.L. Davies and D.P. Kirby, *Cardiganshire County History. Volume 1, From the Earliest Times to the Coming of the Normans*, University of Wales Press, Cardiff.

Davies, J.L. and Lynch, F. (2000) 'The Late Bronze and Iron Age' in F. Lynch, S. Aldhouse-Green and J.L. Davies, *Prehistoric Wales*, Sutton Publishing, Stroud, 139–219.

Davis, J.B. and Thurnam, J. (1865) *Crania Britannica*, privately printed for subscribers, London.

Dawkins, B. (1912) 'Certain fixed points in the pre-history of Wales', *Archaeologia Cambrensis* 6th series **12**, 61–108.

Denham, T., Evans, C., Malim, T. and Reynolds, T. (1995) 'Field-Work in Cambridgeshire: September 1994 – May 1996', *Proceedings of the Cambridge Antiquarian Society* **84**, 167–86.

Dennis, M. and Faulkner, N. (2005) *The Sedgeford Hoard*, Tempus, Stroud.

Department of the Environment (1990) *Planning and Archaeology. Planning Policy Guidance Note No. 16*, HMSO, London.

Dimbleby, G.W. (1957) 'Pollen analysis of terrestrial soils', *New Phytologist* **56**, 12–28.

Dimbleby, G.W. (1961) 'Soil pollen analysis', *Journal of Soil Science* **12**, 1–11.

Dimbleby, G.W. (1976) 'Climate, soils and man', *Philosophical Transaction of the Royal Society, London* **B 275**, 197–208.

Dimbleby, G.W. (1984) 'Anthropogenic changes from Neolithic through medieval times', *New Phytologist* **98**, 57–72.

Dimbleby, G.W. (1985) *The Palynology of Archaeological Sites*, Academic Press, London.

Dimbleby, G.W. and Evans, J.G. (1979) 'Pollen analysis and land snail analysis of calcareous soils', *Journal of Archaeological Science* **1**, 117–33.

Dinnin, M. and Van de Noort, R. (1999) 'Wetland habitats, their resource potential and exploitation. A case study from the Humber wetlands' in eds B.Coles, J.Coles and M.Schou Jørgensen, *Bog Bodies, Sacred Sites and Wetland Archaeology*, Wetland Archaeology Research Project Occasional Paper 12, University of Exeter, Exeter, 69–78.

Diodorus Siculus trans. C.H.Oldfather (1939) Heinemann, London.

Dobney, K. (2001) 'A place at the table: the role of vertebrate zooarchaeology within a Roman research agenda for Britain' in eds S.James and M.Millett, *Britons and Romans: Advancing an Archaeological Agenda*, Council for British Archaeology Research Report 125, York, 36–45.

Dobney, K., Hall, A. and Kenward, H. (1999) 'It's all garbage ... A review of bioarchaeology in the four English *colonia* towns' in ed. H.Hurst, *The Coloniae of Roman Britain, Journal of Roman Archaeology* Supplementary Series, 36, Portsmouth, Rhode Island, 15–35.

Dodgshon, R.A. (1998) *From Chiefs to Landlords: Social and Economic Change in the Western Highlands and Islands, c. 1493–1820*, Edinburgh University Press, Edinburgh.

Downes, J., Foster, S.M. and Wickham-Jones, C.R., with Callister, J. (2005) *The Heart of Neolithic Orkney World Heritage Site Research Agenda*, Edinburgh.

Drinkwater, J.F. (1985) 'Urbanization in the three Gauls: some observations' in eds F.Grew and B.Hobley, *Roman Urban Topography and the Western Empire*, Council for British Archaeology Research Report 59, London, 49–55.

Driver, T. (1996) 'Darren Hillfort, Trefeurig (SN 678 830), Ceredigion', *Archaeology in Wales* **36**, 61.

Driver, T. (2005) *The Hillforts of North Ceredigion: Architecture, Landscape Setting and Cultural Contexts*, unpublished PhD thesis, University of Wales, Lampeter.

Driver, T. (2006) 'New surveys of two Iron Age hillforts in north Ceredigion', *Archaeology in Wales* **45**, 94–8.

Dungworth, D. (1998) 'Mystifying Roman nails: clavus annulis, defixiones and mintisi' in eds C.Forcey, J.Hawthorne and R.Witcher, *TRAC 97: Proceedings of the Seventh Annual Theoretical Roman Archaeology Conference*, Oxbow Books, Oxford, 148–59.

Dunkin, D.J. (2001) 'Metalwork, burnt mounds and settlement on the West Sussex Coastal Plain: a contextual study', *Antiquity* **75**, no. 288, 261–2.

Dunnett, B.R.K. (1971) 'The excavation of the Roman theatre at Gosbecks', *Britannia* **2**, 27–47.

Durden, T. (1995) 'The production of specialised flintwork in the later Neolithic: a case study from the Yorkshire Wolds', *Proceedings of the Prehistoric Society* **61**, 409–32.

Dury, G.H. (1963) *The East Midlands and the Peak*, Thomas Nelson and Sons, London.

Dyer, C. (1994) *The Missing of the Somme*, Phoenix, London.

Earle, T.K. (1991) 'The evolution of chiefdoms' in ed. T.K.Earle, *Chiefdoms: Power, Economy and Ideology*, Cambridge University Press, Cambridge, 1–15.

Eckardt, H. (2002) *Illuminating Roman Britain*, Monographies instrumentum 23, Éditions Monique Mergoil, Montagnac.

Eckardt, H. (2007) 'Contexts in Colchester' in eds R.Hingley and S.Willis, *Roman Finds: Context and Theory*, Oxbow Books, Oxford.

Edmonds, M. (1999) *Ancestral Geographies of the Neolithic. Landscapes, Monuments and Memory*, Routledge, London.

Ellis, C. (2004) *A Prehistoric Ritual Complex at Eynesbury, Cambridgeshire*, East Anglian Archaeology Occasional Paper 17.

English Heritage (2003) *Ripping up History. Archaeology under Plough*, English Heritage, London.

Entwistle, R. and Bowden, M. (1991) 'Cranborne Chase: the Molluscan evidence' in eds J.Barrett, R.Bradley and M.Hall, *Papers on the Prehistoric Archaeology of Cranborne Chase*, Oxbow Monograph 11, Oxbow Books, Oxford, 20–48.

Esmonde Cleary, A.S. (1987) *Extra-Mural Areas of Romano-British Towns*, British Archaeological Reports British Series 169, Oxford.

Evans, C. (1984) 'A shrine provenance from the Willingham Fen hoard', *Antiquity* **58**, 212–14.

Evans, C. (1989) 'Archaeology and Modern Times: Bersu's Woodbury 1939 and 1940', *Antiquity* **63**, 436–50.

Evans, C. (1997) 'Sentimental prehistories: the construction of the Fenland past', *Journal of European Archaeology* **5**, 105–36.

Evans, C. and Hodder, I. (2006) *Marshland Communities and Cultural Landscapes from the Bronze Age to Present Day*, McDonald Institute for Archaeological Research, Cambridge.

Evans, E. (1957) *Irish Folk Ways*, Routledge and Kegan Paul, London.

Evans, J. (2001) 'Material approaches to the identification of different Romano-British site types' in eds S.T. James and M.J. Millett, *Britons and Romans: Advancing an Archaeological Agenda*, Council for British Archaeology Research Report 125, York, 26–35.

Evans, J.G. (1971) 'Habitat changes on the calcareous soils of Britain; the impact of Neolithic man' in ed. D.D.A. Simpson, *Economy and Settlement in Neolithic and Early Bronze Age Britain and Europe*, Leicester University Press, Leicester, 27–73.

Evans, J.G. (1972) *Land Snails in Archaeology*, Seminar Press, London.

Evans, J.G. (1975) *The Environment of Early Man in the British Isles*, Paul Elek, London.

Evans, J.G. (2006) 'Discussion (the environmental setting)' in eds D. Benson and A. Whittle, *Building Memories: The Neolithic Cotswold Long Barrow at Ascott-under-Wychwood, Oxfordshire*, Oxbow Books, Oxford, 75–7.

Evans, J.G. and Jones, H. (1979) 'Mount Pleasant and Woodhenge: the land Mollusca' in G.J. Wainwright, *Mount Pleasant, Dorset: Excavations 1970–1971*, Research Report of the Society of Antiquaries 37, London, 190–213.

Evans, J.G. and Rouse, A. (1991) 'The land Mollusca' in N. Sharples, *Maiden Castle; excavations and field survey 1985–6*, English Heritage Archaeological Report 19, London, 118–25.

Evans, J.G., Limbrey, S. and Macphail, R.I. (2006) 'The environmental setting' in ed. D. Benson and A. Whittle, *Building Memories; the Neolithic Cotswold Long Barrow at Ascott-under-Wychwood, Oxfordshire*, Oxbow Books, Oxford, 55–77.

Faudet, I. (1993) *Les Temples de Tradition Celtique en Gaule Romaine*, Editions Errance, Paris.

Faudet, I. and Bertin, D. (1993) *Atlas des Sanctuaries Romano-Celtiques de Gaule*, Epona, Paris.

Favis-Mortlock, D., Boardman, J. and Bell, M. (1997) 'Modelling long-term anthropogenic erosion of a loess cover: South Downs, UK', *The Holocene* **7.1**, 79–89.

Field, N. and Parker Pearson, M. (2003) *Fiskerton: An Iron Age Timber Causeway with Iron Age and Roman Votive Offerings*, Oxbow Books, Oxford.

Fincham, G. (2000) 'Romanisation, Status and the landscape: extracting a discrepant perspective from survey data' in eds G. Fincham, G. Harrison, R.R. Holland and L. Revell, *TRAC 99: Proceedings of the Ninth Annual Theoretical Roman Archaeology Conference Durham 1999*, Oxbow Books, Oxford, 30–6.

Fincham, G. (2002) *Landscapes of Imperialism: Roman and Native Interaction in the East Anglian Fenland*, British Archaeological Reports British Series 738, Oxford.

Fishpool, M. (1999) 'Land Mollusca' in A. Whittle, J. Pollard and C. Grigson, *The Harmony of Symbols; The Windmill Hill Causewayed Enclosure*, Oxbow Books, Oxford, 127–38.

Fitzpatrick, A.P. (1984) 'The deposition of La Tène Iron Age metalwork in watery contexts in southern England' in eds B.W. Cunliffe and D. Miles, *Aspects of the Iron Age in Central Southern Britain*, Oxford University, Oxford, 178–90.

Fleming, A. (1987) 'Coaxial field systems: some questions of time and space', *Antiquity* **61**, 188–202.

Fleming, A. (1988) *The Dartmoor Reaves. Investigating Prehistoric Land Divisions*, Batsford, London.

Fleure, H.J. (1917) 'Ancient Wales – anthropological evidences', *Transactions of the Honourable Society of the Cymmrodorion* 1915–16, 75–151.

Fleure, H.J. (1923) 'Problems of Welsh archaeology', *Archaeologia Cambrensis* **78**, 225–42.

Fleure, H.J. (1951) *A Natural History of Man in Britain*, Collins, London.

Fleure, H.J. and Davies, E. (1958) 'Physical character among Welshmen', *Journal of the Royal Anthropological Institute* **88**, 45–95.

Fleure, H.J. and James, T.C. (1916) 'Geographical distribution of anthropological types in Wales', *Journal of the Royal Anthropological Institute of Great Britain and Ireland* **46**, 35–153.

Fleure, H.J. and Whitehouse, W.E. (1916) 'Early distribution and valley-ward movement of population in South Britain', *Archaeologia Cambrensis* 6th series **16**, 101–40.

Floyd, R. (2004) '449 and All That: nineteenth- and twentieth-century interpretations of the 'Anglo-Saxon Invasion' of Britain' in eds H. Brocklehurst and R. Phillips, *History, Nationhood and the Question of Britain*, Palgrave, London, 184–96.

Floyd-Wilson, M. (2002) 'Delving to the roots: *Cymbeline*, Scotland, and the English race' in eds D.J. Baker and W. Maley, *British Identities and English Renaissance Literatures*, Cambridge University Press, Cambridge, 101–17.

Fokkens, H. (1999) 'Cattle and martiality: changing relations between man and landscape in the Late Neolithic and the Bronze Age' in eds C. Fabech and J. Ringtved, *Settlement and Landscape. Proceedings of a Conference in Århus, Denmark, May 4–7 1998*, Jutland Archaeological Society, Højbjerg, 35–43.

Ford, S. (1987) *East Berkshire Archaeological Survey*, Department of Highways and Planning, Berkshire County Council Occasional Paper 1, Reading.

Forde, C.D., Griffiths, W.E., Hogg, A.H.A. and Houlder, C.H. (1963) 'Excavations at Pen Dinas, Aberystwyth', *Archaeologia Cambrensis* **112**, 125–53.

Fowler, P. (1975) 'Continuity in the landscape: a summary of some local archaeology in Wiltshire, Somerset and Gloucestershire' in ed. P. Fowler, *Recent Work in Rural Archaeology*, Butler and Tanner, London, 121–35.

Fowler, P. (1978) 'Preface' in eds H.C. Bowen and P.J. Fowler, *Early Land Allotment in the British Isles. A Survey of Recent Work*, British Archaeological Reports 48, Oxford, i–v.

Fowler, P. (1983) *The Farming of Prehistoric Britain*, Cambridge University Press, Cambridge.

Fowler, P. (2000) *Landscape Plotted and Pieced. Landscape History and Local Archaeology in Fyfield and Overton, Wiltshire*, The Society of Antiquaries, London.

Fowler, P.J. and Thomas, C. (1962) 'Arable fields of the pre-Norman period at Gwithian', *Cornish Archaeology* **1**, 61–84.

Fox, A. (1954) 'Excavations at Kestor, an early Iron Age settlement near Chagford, Devon', *Report and Transactions of the Devonshire Association for the Advancement of Science, Literature and Art* **86**, 21–62.

Fox, A. (2000) *Aileen: A Pioneering Archaeologist*, Gracewing, Leominster.

Fox, C. (1923) *The Archaeology of the Cambridge Region*, Cambridge University Press, Cambridge.

Fox, C. (1932) *The Personality of Britain: Its Influence on Inhabitant and Invader in Prehistoric and Early Historic Times*, National Museum of Wales, Cardiff.

Fox, C. and Raglan, Lord (1951–4) *Monmouthshire Houses*, 3 vols, National Museum of Wales, Cardiff.

French, C.A.I. (2003) *Geoarchaeology in Action. Studies in Soil Micromorphology and Landscape Evolution*, Routledge, London.

French, C., Lewis, H., Allen, M.J., Scaife, R.G. and Green, M. (2003) 'Archaeological and palaeo-environmental investigations of the Upper Allen Valley, Cranborne Chase, Dorset (1998–2000): a new model of earlier Holocene landscape development', *Proceedings of the Prehistoric Society* **69**, 201–34.

French, C., Lewis, H., Scaife, R. and Allen, M.J. (2005) 'New perspectives on Holocene landscape development in the southern English chalklands; the upper Allen valley, Cranborne Chase, Dorset', *Geoarchaeology* **20**, 109–34.

French, C., Lewis, H., Allen, M.J., Green, M., Scaife, R. and Gardiner, J. (2007) *Prehistoric Landscape Development and the Human Impact in the Upper Allen Valley, Cranborne Chase Dorset*, Macdonald Institute Monograph, Cambridge.

Frere, S.S. (1972) *Verulamium Excavations. Vol. 1*, The Society of Antiquaries, London.

Fulford, M. (2001) 'Links with the past: pervasive 'ritual' behaviour in Roman Britain', *Britannia* **32**, 199–218.

Fulford, M. (2004) 'Economic structures' in ed. M.Todd, *A Companion to Roman Britain*, Blackwell, London, 309–26.

Fulford, M.G. and Allen, J.R.L. (1992) 'Iron-making at the Chesters Villa, Woolaston, Gloucestershire: Survey and Excavation 1987–91', *Britannia* **23**, 159–215.

Fulford, M.G. and Timby, J. (2000) *Late Iron Age and Roman Silchester: Excavations on the Site of the Forum-Basilica, 1977, 1980–86*, *Britannia* Monograph Series 15, Society for the Promotion of Roman Studies, London.

Gaffney, C.F. and Gaffney, V.L. (1986) 'From Boeotia to Berkshire: an integrated approach to geophysics and rural field survey', *Prospezioni Archaeologiche* **10**, 65–70.

Gaffney, C.F. and Gater, J.A. (2003) *Revealing the Buried Past: Geophysics for Archaeologists*, Tempus, Stroud.

Gaffney, C.F. and Shiel, D. (in press) 'Geophysical survey at Shapwick' in eds M.A. Aston and C.M. Gerrard, *The Shapwick Project. A Rural Landscape Explored*, Society for Medieval Archaeology monograph, Leeds.

Gaffney, V. and Tingle, M. (1989) *The Maddle Farm Project – An Integrated Survey of Prehistoric and Rural Landscapes on the Berkshire Downs*, British Archaeological Reports British Series 200, Oxford.

Gardiner, J. (1985) 'Intra-site patterning in the flint assemblage from the Dorset cursus', *Proceedings of the Dorset Natural History and Archaeological Society* **105**, 87–9.

Giblett, R. (1996) *Postmodern Wetlands: Culture, History, Ecology*, Edinburgh University Press, Edinburgh.

Giddens, A. (1986) *The Constitution of Society: Outline of the Theory of Structuration*, Polity Press, Cambridge.

Gingell, C. (1992) *The Marlborough Downs: A Later Bronze Age Landscape and its Origins*, Wiltshire Archaeological and Natural History Society Monograph 1.

Godwin, H. (1940) 'Pollen analysis and forest history of England and Wales', *New Phytologist* **39**, 370–400.

Godwin, H. (1962) 'Vegetational history of the Kentish chalk downs as seen at Wingham and Frogholt', *Veröffentlichungen des Geobotanischen Institutes Rubel, Zurich* **37**, 83–99.

Godwin, H. (1975) *The History of the British Flora*, Cambridge University Press, Cambridge.

Godwin, H. and Tansely, A.G. (1941) 'Prehistoric charcoals as evidence of former vegetation, soil and climate', *Journal of Ecology* **29**, 117–26.

Goffman, E. (1991) *Asylums: Essays on the Social Situation of Mental Patients and other Inmates*, Penguin, London.

Gosden, C. and Lock, G. (2003) 'Frilford: A Romano-British ritual pool in Oxfordshire?' *Current Archaeology* **184**, **16/4**, 156–9.

Grant, A. (2004) 'Domestic animals and their uses' in ed. M.Todd, *A Companion to Roman Britain*, Blackwell, London, 371–92.

Green, M.J. (1986) *The Gods of the Celts*, Alan Sutton, Gloucester.

Green, M.J. (1995) *Celtic Goddesses: Warriors, Virgins and Mothers*, British Museum Press, London.

Greene, K. (1986) *The Archaeology of the Roman Economy*, University of California Press, Berkeley.

Greep, S. ed. (1993) *Roman Towns: the Wheeler Inheritance. A review of 50 years research*, Council for British Archaeology Research Report 93, York.

Gregory, T. (1976) 'A hoard of Roman bronze bowls from Burwell, Cambridgeshire', *Proceedings of the Cambridge Antiquarian Society* **66**, 63–79.

Gregson, N. (1985) 'The multiple estate model: some critical questions', *Journal of Historical Geography* **11**, 339–51.

Grimes, P. (1946) 'Prehistoric period' in ed. V. Nash-Williams, *A Hundred Years of Welsh Archaeology (Centenary Volume of the Cambrian Archaeological Association)*, John Bellows, Gloucester, 24–79.

Grinsell, L.V. (1936) *The Ancient Burial Mounds of England*, Methuen, London.

GSB Prospection (1999) *Report on the Geophysical Survey at Stones of Stenness*, GSB Prospection, Report 99/55, unpublished.

Guilbert, G. and Morris, E. (1979) 'Montgomeryshire, Cefn Carnedd', *Archaeology in Wales* **19**, 19.

Gurney, D. (1986) *Settlement, Religion and Industry on the Fen-edge: Three Romano-British Sites in Norfolk*, East Anglia Archaeology 31, Dereham.

Guttmann, E.B.A. (2005) 'Midden cultivation in prehistoric Britain: arable crops in gardens', *World Archaeology* **37(2)**, 224–39.

Guttmann, E.B.A. and Last, J. (2000) 'A late Bronze Age landscape at South Hornchurch, Essex', *Proceedings of the Prehistoric Society* **66**, 319–59.

Guy, C.J. (1978) 'A Roman lead tank from Burwell, Cambridgeshire', *Proceedings of the Cambridge Antiquarian Society* **68**, 1–4.

Gwilt, A. (2003) 'Understanding the Iron Age: towards agenda for Wales' in ed. C.S. Briggs, *Towards a Research Agenda for Welsh Archaeology: Proceedings of the IFA Wales/Cymru Conference, Aberystwyth 2001*, British Archaeological Reports British Series 343, 105–22.

Gwilt, A. and Haselgrove, C. eds (1997) *Reconstructing Iron Age Societies, New Approaches to the British Iron Age*, Oxbow Monograph 71, Oxbow Books, Oxford.

Hall, D. (1985) 'Survey work in eastern England' in eds S. Macready and F.H. Thompson, *Archaeological Field Survey in Britain and Abroad*, Society of Antiquities Occasional Paper 6, London, 25–44.

Hall, D. (1987) *The Fenland Project, Number 2: Cambridgeshire Survey, Peterborough to March*, East Anglia Archaeology 35, Cambridge.

Hall, D. (1992) *The Fenland Project, Number 6: The Southwest Cambridgeshire Fenland*, East Anglia Archaeology 56, Cambridge.

Hall, D. (1996) *The Fenland Project, Number 10, Cambridgeshire Survey, The Isle of Ely and Wisbech*, East Anglia Archaeology 79, Cambridge.

Hall, D. and Coles, J. (1994) *Fenland Survey: An Essay in Landscape and Persistence*, English Heritage, London.

Hall, D., Evans, C., Hodder, I. and Pryor, F. (1987) 'The Fenlands of East Anglia, England: Survey and excavation' in eds J.M. Coles and A.J. Lawson, *European Wetlands in Prehistory*, Clarendon Press, Oxford, 169–201.

Hamilton, S. and Manley, J. (1997) 'Points of View, Prominent Enclosures in 1st Millennium BC Sussex', *Sussex Archaeological Collections* **135**, 93–122.

Hamilton, S. and Manley, J. (2001) 'Hillforts, monumentality and place: a chronological and topographic review of first millennium BC hillforts of south-east England', *European Journal of Archaeology* **4 (1)**, 7–42.

Harding, A.F. (2000) *European Societies in the Bronze Age*, Cambridge University Press, Cambridge.

Harding, J. (2000) 'Later Neolithic ceremonial centres, ritual and pilgrimage: the monument complex at Thornborough, North Yorkshire' in ed. A. Ritchie, *Neolithic Orkney in its European Context*, McDonald Institute for Archaeological Research, University of Cambridge, 31–46.

Haselgrove, C. (1987) *Iron Age Coinage in South-East England: The Archaeological Context*, British Archaeological Reports British Series 174, Oxford.

Haselgrove, C.C. (1996) 'Roman impact on rural settlement and society in southern Picardy' in ed. N. Roymans, *From the Sword to the Plough: Three Studies on the Earliest Romanisation of Northern Gaul*, Amsterdam University Press, Amsterdam, 127–87.

Haselgrove, C.C. and Millett, M.J. (1997) 'Verlamion reconsidered' in eds A. Gwilt and C.C. Haselgrove, *Reconstructing Iron Age Societies*, Oxbow Monograph 71, Oxbow Books, Oxford, 282–96.

Haselgrove, C., Armit, I., Champion, T., Creighton, J., Gwilt, A., Hill, J.D., Hunter, F. and Woodward, A. (2001) *Understanding the British Iron Age: An Agenda for Action*, Iron Age Research Seminar and the Council of the Prehistoric Society, Salisbury.

Hawkes, C. (1931) 'Hill-forts', *Antiquity* **5**, 60–97.

Hawkes, C. (1959) 'The ABC of the British Iron Age', *Antiquity* **33**, 170–82.

Hawkes, J. (1951) *A Land*, Cresset Press, London.

Hawkes, J. (1982) *Mortimer Wheeler: Adventurer in Archaeology*, Weidenfeld and Nicolson, London.

Hawkes, J. and Hawkes, C. (1943) *Prehistoric Britain*, Penguin Books, Harmondsworth.

Hawkes, J. and Hawkes, C. (1947; hardback edn) *Prehistoric Britain*, Chatto and Windus, London.

Hayes, P.P. and Lane, T.W. (1992) *The Fenland Project Number 5: Lincolnshire Survey, The Southwest Fens*, East Anglia Archaeology 55, Sleaford.

Heaney, S. (1984) *Station Island*, Faber and Faber, London.

Heichelheim, F.M. (1937) 'On some unpublished Roman bronze statuettes in the museum of archaeology and ethnology, Cambridge', *Proceedings of the Cambridge Antiquarian Society* **37**, 52–67.

Herring, P. (forthcoming) 'Commons, fields and communities in prehistoric Cornwall'.

Herring, P. and Thomas, N. (1990) *The Archaeology of Kit Hill. Kit Hill Archaeological Survey Project Final Report*, Cornwall County Council, Truro.

Hill, J.D. (1989) 'Rethinking the Iron Age', *Scottish Archaeological Review* **6**, 16–24.

Hill, J.D. (1995a) 'How should we understand Iron Age societies and hillforts? A contextual study from southern Britain' in eds J.D.Hill and C.G.Cumberpatch, *Different Iron Ages: Studies on the Iron Age in Temperate Europe*, British Archaeological Reports International Series 602, Oxford, 45–66.

Hill, J.D. (1995b) *Ritual and Rubbish in the Iron Age of Wessex: A Study on the Formation of a Specific Archaeological Record*, British Archaeological Reports British Series 242, Oxford.

Hill, J.D. (2001) 'Romanisation, gender and class: recent approaches to identity in Britain and their possible consequences' in eds S.James and M.Millett, *Britons and Romans: Advancing an Archaeological Agenda*, Council for British Archaeology Research Report 125, York, 12–8.

Hill, J.D. (2002) 'Just about the potter's wheel? Using, making and depositing middle and later Iron Age pots in East Anglia' in eds A.Woodward and J.D.Hill, *Prehistoric Britain: The Ceramic Basis*, Oxbow Books, Oxford, 143–60.

Hill, J.D. (2006) 'Are we any closer to understanding how later Iron Age societies worked (or did not work)?' in ed. V.Guichard, *Celtes et Gaulois. Les mutations de la fin de 'age du fer'*, Bibracte.

Hill, J.D. and Cumberpatch, C.G. eds (1995) *Different Iron Ages: Studies on the Iron Age in Temperate Europe*, British Archaeological Reports International Series 602, Oxford.

Hingley, R. (1985) 'Location, function and status: a Romano-British 'religious complex' at the Noah's Ark Inn, Frilford (Oxfordshire)', *Oxford Journal of Archaeology* **4/2**, 201–14.

Hingley, R. (1989) *Rural Settlement in Roman Britain*, Seaby, London.

Hingley, R. (1990a) 'Iron Age 'currency bars': the archaeological and social context', *The Archaeological Journal* **147**, 91–117.

Hingley, R. (1990b) 'Boundaries surrounding Iron Age and Romano-British settlements', *Scottish Archaeological Review* 7, 96–103.

Hingley, R. (1991) 'The Romano-British Countryside: the significance of rural settlement forms' in ed. R.F.J.Jones, *Britain in the Roman Period: Recent Trends*, J.R.Collis Publications, Sheffield, 75–80.

Hingley, R. (1996) 'Ancestors and identity in the later prehistory of Atlantic Scotland: the reuse and reinvention of Neolithic monuments and material culture', *World Archaeology* **28**, 231–43.

Hingley, R. (1997a) 'Resistance and domination: social change in Roman Britain' in ed. D.J.Mattingly, *Dialogues in Roman Imperialism: Power, Discourse, and Discrepant Experiences in the Roman Empire, Journal of Roman Archaeology* Supplementary Series 23, Portsmouth, Rhode Island, 81–100.

Hingley, R. (1997b) 'Iron, ironworking and regeneration: a study of the symbolic meaning of metalworking in Iron Age Britain' in eds A.Gwilt and C.Haselgrove, *Reconstructing Iron Age Societies: New Approaches to the British Iron Age*, Oxbow Books, Oxford.

Hingley, R. (1999) 'The creation of later prehistoric landscapes and the context of the reuse of Neolithic and earlier Bronze Age monuments in Britain and Ireland' in ed. B.Bevan, *Northern Exposure: Interpretative Devolution and the Iron Ages in Britain*, Leicester Archaeology Monographs 4, Leicester, 233–51.

Hingley, R. (2000) *Roman Officers and English Gentlemen: The Imperial Origins of Roman Archaeology*, Routledge, London.

Hingley, R. (2005a) *Globalizing Roman Culture: Unity, Diversity and Empire*, Routledge, London.

Hingley, R. (2005b) 'Settlement in *Britannia*' in eds C.F.Ochoa and P.Garcia Diaz, *Unidad y diversidad en el Arco Atlantico en época romana*, British Archaeological Reports International Series 1371, Oxford, 267–77.

Hingley, R. and Ingram, H.A.P. (2002) 'History as an aid to understanding peat bogs' in ed. T.C.Smout, *Understanding the Historical Landscape in its Environmental Setting*, Scottish Cultural Press, Dalkeith, 60–86.

Hingley, R. and Miles, D. (2002) 'The human impact on the landscape: agriculture, settlement, industry, infrastructure' in ed. P.Salway, *Short Oxford History of the British Isles: The Roman Era. The British Isles: 55 BC–AD 410*, Oxford University Press, Oxford, 141–71.

Hirsch, E. (1995) 'Landscape: Between Place and Space' in eds E.Hirsch and M.O'Hanlon, *The Anthropology of Landscape: Perspectives on Place and Space*, Clarendon Press, Oxford, 1–30.

Hoare, R.C. (1810) *The History of Ancient Wiltshire. Part 1*, William Miller, London.

Hoare, R.C. (1821) *The Ancient History of Wiltshire: Volume II*, Lackington, Hughes, Harding, Mavor and Lepard, London.

Hodder, I.R. (1972) 'Locational models and the study of Romano-British settlements' in ed. D.L.Clarke, *Models in Archaeology*, London, 887–907.

Hodder, I.R. (1979) 'Pre-Roman and Romano-British tribal economies' in eds B.C.Burnham and H.B.Johnson, *Invasion and Response: The Case of Roman Britain*, British Archaeological Reports British Series 73, Oxford, 189–96.

Hodder, I.R. and Millett, M. (1980) 'Romano-British villas and towns: a systematic analysis', *World Archaeology* **12**, 69–76.

Hodder, M.A. and Barfield, L.H. (1987) 'Burnt mounds as saunas, and the prehistory of bathing', *Antiquity* **61**, 370–9.

Hodgson, J.M. (1967) *Soils of the West Sussex Coastal Plain*, Bulletin of the Soil Survey of Great Britain 3, Harpenden.

Hogg, A.H.A. (1975) *Hill-forts of Britain*, Hart-Davis, MacGibbon, London.

Hogg, A.H.A. (1994) 'The hillforts and later prehistoric settlements' in eds J.L.Davies and D.P.Kirby, *Cardiganshire County History. Volume 1, From the Earliest Times to the Coming of the Normans*, University of Wales Press, Cardiff, 234–8.

Holbrook, N. ed. (1998) *Cirencester. The Roman Town Defences, Public Buildings and Shops*, Cotswold Archaeological Trust, Cirencester.

Holleyman, G.A. (1935) 'The Celtic field-system in south Britain: a survey of the Brighton district', *Antiquity* **9**, no. 36, 443–54.

Hoskins, W.G. (1949) *Midland England*, Batsford, London.

Hoskins, W.G. (1952) 'The making of the agrarian landscape' in eds W.G.Hoskins and H.P.R.Finberg, *Devonshire Studies*, Jonathan Cape, London, 289–333.

Hoskins, W.G. (1954) *Devon*, Collins, London.

Hoskins, W.G. (1955) *The Making of the English Landscape*, Hodder and Stoughton, London.

Hoskins, W.G. (1957a) *The Midland Peasant*, Macmillan, London.

Hoskins, W.G. (1957b) *Leicestershire: An Illustrated Essay on the History of the Landscape*, Hodder and Stoughton, London.

Hoskins, W.G. (1973a) *English Landscapes*, British Broadcasting Corporation, London.

Hoskins, W.G. (1973b; revised edn) *The Making of the English Landscape*, Penguin, London.

Hoskins, W.G. (1975) *The Making of the English Landscape*, Penguin, Harmondsworth.

Hoskins, W.G. (1985; reprint) *The Making of the English Landscape*, Penguin Books, Harmondsworth.

Hoskins, W.G. (1988) *The Making of the English Landscape*, Hodder and Stoughton, London.

Hülka, K. (2006) 'Bronze Age occupation of Newbury Park: further evidence of prehistoric Redbridge', *London Archaeologist* **11**, no. 4, 101–8.

Hull, M.R. (1958) *Roman Colchester*, The Society of Antiquaries, Oxford.

Hurst, H. (2005) 'Roman Cirencester and Gloucester compared', *Oxford Journal of Archaeology* **24/3**, 293–305.

Hurst, H. ed. (1999) *The Coloniae of Roman Britain: New Studies and a Review*, *Journal of Roman Archaeology* Supplementary Series, 36, Portsmouth, Rhode Island.

Hutcheson, N. (2004) *Later Iron Age Norfolk: Metalwork, Landscape and Society*, British Archaeological Reports British Series 361, Oxford.

Ingold, T. (1997) 'The picture is not the terrain: maps, paintings and the dwelt-in word', *Archaeological Dialogues* **4**, 29–31.

Ingold, T. (2000) *The Perception of the Environment. Essays on Livelihood, Dwelling and Skill*, Routledge, London.

Isserlin, R.M.J. (1997) 'Thinking the unthinkable: human sacrifice in Roman Britain' in eds K.Meadows, C.Lemke and J.Heron, *TRAC 96: Proceedings of the Sixth Theoretical Roman Archaeology Conference, Sheffield 1996*, Oxbow Books, Oxford, 91–100.

Isserlin, R.M.J. (2007) 'Deposit or withdrawal?' in eds R.Hingley and S.Willis, *Roman Finds: Context and Theory*, Oxbow Books, Oxford.

Jacks, G.V. (1954) *Soil*, Thomas Nelson, London.

Jackson, D. (1999) 'Variation in the size distribution of hillforts in the Welsh Marches and its implication for social organisation' in ed. B.Bevan, *Northern Exposure: Interpretative Devolution and the Iron Ages in Britain*, Leicester Archaeology Monographs 4, Leicester, 197–216.

Jackson, D.A. and Ambrose, T.M. (1978) 'Excavations at Wakerley, Northants, 1972–75', *Britannia* **9**, 115–242.

Jackson, D.A. and Tylecote, R.F. (1988) 'Two new Romano-British iron-working sites in Northamptonshire – a new type of furnace?', *Britannia* **19**, 275–98.

Jackson, R.P.J. and Potter, P.W. (1996) *Excavations at Stonea Cambridgeshire 1980–1985*, British Museum Press, London.

Jacobs, J. (1970) *The Economy of Cities*, Cape, London.

Jacobs, J. (1984) *Cities and the Wealth of Nations*, Penguin, Harmondsworth.

James, S. (2001) 'Soldiers and civilians: identity and interaction in Roman Britain' in eds S. James and M. Millett, *Britons and Romans: Advancing an Archaeological Agenda*, Council for British Archaeology Research Report 125, York, 77–89.

James, S. and Millett, M. eds (2001) *Britons and Romans: Advancing an Archaeological Agenda*, Council for British Archaeology Research Report 125, York.

Jobey, G. (1966) 'Homesteads and settlements of the frontier area' in ed. C. Thomas, *Rural Settlement in Roman Britain*, Council for British Archaeology, London, 1–14.

Johns, C. (1986) 'The Roman silver cups from Hockwold, Norfolk', *Archaeologia* **108**, 1–13.

Johns, C. (1994) 'Romano-British precious-metal hoards: some comments on Martin Millett's paper' in eds S. Cottam, D. Dungworth, S. Scott and J. Taylor, *TRAC 94 Proceedings of the Forth Annual Theoretical Roman Archaeology Conference*, Oxbow Books, Oxford, 107–17.

Johns, C. (1996) 'The classification and interpretation of Romano-British treasures', *Britannia* **27**, 1–16.

Johns, C. and Herring, P. (1996) *St. Keverne Historic Landscape Assessment*, Cornwall Archaeological Unit, unpublished client report.

Johnson, N. and Rose, P. (1994) *Bodmin Moor. An Archaeological Survey. Vol. 1: The Human Landscape to c.1800*, English Heritage and Royal Commission on the Historical Monuments of England, London.

Johnston, P. A. (1980) *Vergil's Agricultural Golden Age: A Study of the Georgics*, E. J. Brill, Leiden.

Jones, G. D. B. (1984) *Past Imperfect: The story of Rescue Archaeology*, Heinmann, London.

Jones, G. D. B. and Mattingly, D. J. (1990) *An Atlas of Roman Britain*, Basil Blackwell, Oxford.

Jones, G. R. J. (1961) 'Settlement patterns in Anglo-Saxon England', *Antiquity* **35**, 221–32.

Jones, G. R. J. (1971) 'The multiple estate as a model for tracing early stages in the evolution of rural settlement' in ed. F. Dussart, *L'habitat et les paysages ruraux d'Europe*, University of Liège, Liège, 251–63.

Jones, G. R. J. (1976) 'Multiple estates and early settlement' in ed. P. H. Sawyer, *Medieval settlement: continuity and change*, Edward Arnold, London, 15–40.

Jones, M. (1984) *England before Domesday*, Batsford, London.

Kehoe, D. P. (1988) *The Economics of Agriculture on Roman Imperial Estates in North Africa*, Vandenhoeck and Ruprecht, Göttingen.

Kendrick, J. (1995) 'Excavation of a Neolithic enclosure and Iron Age settlement at Douglasmuir, Angus', *Proceedings of the Society of Antiquaries of Scotland* **125**, 29–67.

Kennard, A. S (1933) 'Report on the marine Mollusca' in J. F. S. Stone, 'Excavations at Easton Down, Winterslow, 1931–32', *Wiltshire Archaeological Magazine* **46**, 235–41.

Kennard, A. S. (1935) 'Report on the non-marine Mollusca from the Stonehenge excavations of 1920–6', *Antiquaries Journal* **15**, 432–4.

Kennard, A. S. (1936) 'Report on the non-marine Mollusca' in C. D. Drew and S. Piggott, 'The excavation of long barrow 163a on Thickthorn Down, Dorset', *Proceedings of the Prehistoric Society* **2**, 94–5.

Kennard, A. S. (1943) 'Report on the Mollusca' in R. E. M. Wheeler, *Maiden Castle, Dorset*, Reports of the Research Committee of the Society of Antiquaries of London 12, London, 372–4.

Kent, J. P. C. (1974) 'Interpreting coin-finds' in eds J. Casey and R. Reece, *Coins and the Archaeologist*, Seaby, London, 184–200.

Kerney, M. P., Brown E. H. and Chandler, T. J. (1964) 'The Late-Glacial and Post-Glacial history of the chalk escarpment near Brook, Kent', *Philosophical Transactions of the Royal Society, London* **B 248**, 135–204.

Kerney, M. P., Preece, R. C. and Turner, C. (1980) 'Molluscan and plant biostratigraphy of some Late Devensian and Flandrian deposits in Kent', *Philosophical Transactions of the Royal Society, London* **B 291**, 1–43.

King, A. (2004) 'Rural settlement in southern Britain: a regional survey' in ed. M. Todd, *A Companion to Roman Britain*, Blackwell, London, 349–70.

Kinnes, I. A. (1988) 'The Cattleship Potemkin: the first Neolithic in Britain' in eds J. Barrett and I. A. Kinnes, *The Archaeology of Context in the Neolithic and Bronze Age: Recent Trends*, Department of Archaeology and Prehistory, University of Sheffield, Sheffield, 2–8.

Knapp, A. B. and Ashmore, W. (1999) 'Archaeological Landscapes: Constructed, Conceptualised, Ideational' in eds W. Ashmore and A. B. Knapp, *Archaeologies of Landscape: Contemporary Perspectives*, Blackwell Publishers, Oxford, 1–30.

Knight, D. and Howard, A. (2004) *Trent Valley Landscapes: The Archaeology of 500,000 Years of Change*, Heritage Marketing and Publications, King's Lynn.

Knight, M. (2002) *New Prison at Former Rockwell and APV works Westfield Road, Peterborough. Peterborough's Upland Prehistory*, Cambridge Archaeological Unit, unpublished client report.

Kristiansen, K. (1991) 'Chiefdoms, states, and systems of social evolution' in ed. T. K. Earle, *Chiefdoms: Power, Economy and Ideology*, Cambridge University Press, Cambridge, 16–43.

Kristiansen, K. and Larsson, T. B. (2005) *The Rise of Bronze Age Society: Travels, Transmissions and Transformations*, Cambridge University Press, Cambridge.

Kvamme, K.L. and Jochim, M.A. (1988) 'The environmental basis of Mesolithic settlement' in ed. C.Bonsall, *The Mesolithic in Europe*, J.Donald, Edinburgh, 1–12.

Lane, T. and Morris, E.L. (2001) *A Millennium of Saltmaking: Prehistoric and Romano-British Salt Production in the Fenland*, Lincolnshire Archaeology and Heritage Reports Series 4, Heritage Trust of Lincolnshire, Sleaford.

Langouët, L. and Jumel, G. (1991) 'Les campagnes gallo-romaines de la civitas des Coriosolites' in ed. L.Langouët, *Terriors, Territoires et Campagnes Antiques. La Prospection Archéologique en Haute Bretagne. Traitment et Synthèse des Donnees*, RAO supplement 4, Rennes, 127–34.

Laurence, R. (1994) *Roman Pompeii: Space and Society*, Routledge, London.

Laurence, R. (1999) *The Roads of Roman Italy: Mobility and Cultural Change*, Routledge, London.

Lawson, A.J. (2000) *Potterne 1982–5: Animal Husbandry in Later Prehistoric Wiltshire*, Wessex Archaeology, Salisbury.

Lethbridge, T.C. (1934) 'Pottery of the Roman period from Isleham Fen', *Proceedings of the Cambridge Antiquarian Society* **34**, 93.

Lethbridge, T.C. (1951) 'Roman pottery from the 'Old Croft' River at Welney', *Proceedings of the Cambridge Antiquarian Society* **4**, 18–21.

Lethbridge, T.C. and O'Reilly, M.M. (1933) 'Archaeological Notes', *Proceedings of the Cambridge Antiquarian Society* **33**, 164–7.

Liddle, P. (1982) *Leicestershire Archaeology: The Present State of Knowledge; Vol.1 to the end of the Roman period*, Leicestershire Museums, Art Galleries and Records Service, Leicester.

Liddle, P. (1985) *Community Archaeology: A fieldworkers handbook of Organisation and Techniques*, Leicestershire Museums, Art Galleries and Records Service, Leicester.

Liddle, P. (1994) 'The Medbourne Area Survey' in eds M.Parker Pearson and R.T.Schadla-Hall, *Looking at the Land. Archaeological Landscapes in Eastern England. Recent Work and Future Directions*, Leicestershire Museums, Art Galleries and Records Service, Leicester, 34–6.

Limbrey, S. (1975) *Soil Science in Archaeology*, Academic Press, London.

van der Linden, E. (forthcoming) *Terra Sigillata at Nijmegen*, doctoral study, Katholieke Universiteit, Nijmegen, The Netherlands.

Liversidge, J. (1956) 'A hoard of Romano-British ironwork from Worlington', *Proceedings of the Cambridge Antiquarian Society* **59**, 89.

Liversidge, J. (1959) 'A new hoard of Romano-British pewter from Icklingham', *Proceedings of the Cambridge Antiquarian Society* **52**, 6–10.

Lowe, J.J. and Walker, M.J.C. (1984; 1st edn) *Reconstructing Quaternary Environments*, Longman, London.

Lubbock, J. (1865) *Pre-Historic Times as Illustrated by Ancient Remains, and the Manners and Customs of Modern Savages*, Williams and Norgate, London.

McCullagh, P. (1969) *The East Midlands. A Regional Study*, Oxford University Press, Oxford.

McFadyen, L. (2000) *Archaeological Excavations at Eye Quarry, Peterborough (Phase 2)*', Cambridge Archaeological Unit, unpublished client report.

MacMahon, A. (2006) 'Fixed-point retail location in the major towns of Roman Britain', *Oxford Journal of Archaeology* **25/3**, 289–309.

McOmish, D. (2005) 'Bronze Age land allotment on the Marlborough Downs' in G.Brown, D.Field and D.McOmish, *The Avebury Landscape. Aspects of the Field Archaeology of the Marlborough Downs*, Oxbow Books, Oxford, 133–6.

McOmish, D., Field, D. and Brown, G. (2002) *The Field Archaeology of the Salisbury Plain Training Area*, English Heritage, Swindon.

Malim, T. (1999) 'Cursuses and related monuments of the Cambridgeshire Ouse' in eds A.Barclay and J.Harding, *Pathways and Ceremonies: The Cursus Monuments of Britain and Ireland*, Oxbow Books, Oxford, 77–85.

Marcigny, C. and Ghesquière, E. (2003) *L'île de Tatihou (Manche) à l'âge du Bronze. Habitats et Occupation du Sol*, Éditions de la Maison des sciences de l'Homme, Paris.

Martins, C. (2003) 'Becoming consumers: looking beyond wealth as an explanation for villa variability' in ed. G.Carr, E.Swift and J.Weekes, *TRAC 2002: Proceedings of the Twelfth Annual Theoretical Roman Archaeology Conference, Canterbury 2002*, Oxbow Books, Oxford, 84–100.

Martins, C. (2005) *Becoming Consumers: Looking beyond Wealth as an Explanation of Villa Variability*, British Archaeological Reports British Series 403, Oxford.

Masefield, R., Branch, N., Couldrey, P., Goodburn, D. and Tyers, I. (2003) 'A later Bronze Age well complex at Swalecliffe, Kent', *Antiquaries Journal* **83**, 47–121.

Mason, R.S. (1981) *Conspicuous Consumption: A Study of Exceptional Consumer Behaviour*, Gower, Farnborough.

Mattingly, D. (2004) 'Being Roman: expressing identity in a provincial setting', *Journal of Roman Archaeology* **17**, 5–25.

Mattingly, D.J. (2006) *An Imperial Possession: Britain in the Roman Empire 54 BC–AD 409*, Penguin, Harmondsworth.

Mattingly, D.J. and Schrüfer-Kolb, I.E. (2003) 'Les mines romaines en Grande Bretagne' in eds A.Orejas and J.Sanchez-Palencia, *Atlas Historique des Zones Minieres d'Europe II*, Office des publications officielles des Communautés européennes, Luxemburg, Dossiers IX–XII.

Mattingly, D. and Witcher, R. (2004) 'Mapping the Roman world: the contribution of field survey data' in eds S.E.Alcock and J.F.Cherry, *Side-by-Side Survey: Comparative Regional Studies in the Mediterranean World*, Oxbow Books, Oxford, 173–86.

Mattingly, H. (1932) 'Hoards of Roman coins found in Britain and a coin survey of the Roman province', *Journal of Roman Studies* **22**, 88–95.

Mauss, M. (2002 (1925)) *The Gift: The Form and Reason for Exchange in Archaic Societies*, Routledge, London.

May, J. (1984) 'The major settlements of the later Iron Age in Lincolnshire' in eds N.Field and A.White, *A Prospect of Lincolnshire*, County Hall, Lincoln, 18–22.

Meredith, J. (2006) *The Iron Industry of the Forest of Dean*, Tempus, Stroud.

Merrifield, R. (1965) *The Roman City of London*, Ernest Benn, London.

Merrifield, R. (1987) *The Archaeology of Ritual and Magic*, B.T.Batsford, London.

Middleton, R., Wells, C.E. and Huckerby, E. (1995) *The Wetlands of North Lancashire*, North West Wetlands Survey 3, Lancaster University Archaeology Unit, Lancaster.

Miles, D. ed. (1982) *The Romano-British Countryside: Studies in Rural Settlement and Economy*, British Archaeological Reports British Series 103, Oxford.

Millett, M.J. (1990) *The Romanization of Britain*, Cambridge University Press, Cambridge.

Millett, M.J. (1992) 'Roman towns and their territories: an archaeological perspective' in eds J.Rich and A.Wallace-Hadrill, *City and Country in the Ancient World*, Routledge, London, 169–89.

Millett, M. (1994) 'Treasure: interpreting Roman hoards' in eds S.Cottam, D.Dungworth, S.Scott and J.Taylor, *TRAC 94 Proceedings of the Forth Annual Theoretical Roman Archaeology Conference*, Oxbow Books, Oxford, 99–106.

Millett, M.J. (1995) 'Strategies for Roman small towns' in ed. A.E.Brown, *Roman Small Towns in the East of England and Beyond*, Oxbow Monograph 52, Oxbow Books, Oxford, 29–38.

Millett, M.J. (2001) 'Approaches to urban societies' in eds S.T.James and M.J.Millett, *Britons and Romans: Advancing an Archaeological Agenda*, Council for British Archaeology Research Report 125, York, 60–6.

Mills, N.W.T. (1985) 'Sample bias, regional analysis and fieldwalking in British Archaeology' in eds C. Haselgrove, M.Millett and I.Smith, *Archaeology from the Ploughsoil. Studies in the Collection and Interpretation of Field Survey Sata*, Department of Archaeology and Prehistory, University of Sheffield, Sheffield, 39–47.

Milne, G. and Wardle, A. (1993) 'Early Roman development at Leadenhall Court, London and related research', *Transactions of the London and Middlesex Archaeological Society* **44**, 23–169.

Mithen, S.J. (1990) *Thoughtful Foragers: A Study of Prehistoric Decision Making*, Cambridge University Press, Cambridge.

Morris, E.L. (1985) 'Prehistoric salt distributions: two case studies from western Britain', *Bulletin of the Board of Celtic Studies* **32**, 336–79.

Morris, E.L. (1994) 'Production and distribution of pottery and salt in Iron Age Britain: a review', *Proceedings of the Prehistoric Society* **60**, 371–93.

Morris, E.L. (2007) 'Making magic: later prehistoric and early Roman salt production in the Lincolnshire Fenland' in eds C.Haselgrove and T.Moore, *The Later Iron Age in Britain and Beyond*, Oxbow Books, Oxford, 430–43.

Morse, M.A. (2005) *How the Celts Came to Britain: Druids, Ancient Skulls and the Birth of Archaeology*, Tempus, Stroud.

Mortimer, J.R. (1905) *Forty Years' Researches in British and Saxon Burial Mounds of East Yorkshire*, A Brown and Sons, London.

Mudd, A., Williams, R.J. and Lupton, A. (1999) *Excavations alongside Roman Ermin Street, Gloucestershire and Wiltshire: The Archaeology of the A419/A417 Swindon to Gloucester Road Scheme*, Oxford Archaeological Unit, Oxford.

Mullin, D. (2003) *The Bronze Age Landscape of the Northern English Midlands*, British Archaeological Reports British Series 351, Oxford.

Murphy, K. (1989) 'Odyn-Fach Enclosure, Ceulanymaesmawr (SN 648 877) DAT PRN 7463', *Archaeology in Wales* **29**, 43–4.

Murphy, K. (1992) 'Plas Gogerddan, Dyfed: a multi-period burial and ritual site', *The Archaeological Journal* **149**, 1–38.

Murphy, P.L. (1992) 'Environmental studies: Culver Street' in P.Crummy, *Excavations at Culver Street, the Gilberd School and other Sites in Colchester 1971–85*, Colchester Archaeological Trust, Colchester, 273–87.

Musson, C. (1991) *The Breiddin Hillfort: A Later Prehistoric Settlement in the Welsh Marches*, Council for British Archaeology Research Report 76, London.

Naas, P. (1991) 'Les campagnes gallo-romaines de la civitas de Venetes' in ed. L.Langouët, *Terriors, Territoires et Campagnes Antiques. La Prospection Archéologique en Haute Bretagne. Traitment et Synthèse des Donnees*, RAO supplement 4, Rennes, 143–56.

Needham, S. (2000) *The Passage of the Thames. Holocene Environment and Settlement at Runnymede. Runnymede Bridge Research Excavation, Volume 1*, British Museum Press, London.

Niblett, B. R. K. (1985) *Sheepen: An Early Roman Industrial Site at Camulodunum*, Council for British Archaeology Research Report 57, London.

Niblett, R. (2000) 'Funerary rites in Verulamium during the early Roman period' in ed. J. Pearce, M. Millett and M. Struck, *Burial, Society and Context in the Roman World*, Oxbow Books, Oxford, 97–104.

Oppenheimer, S. (2006) *The Origins of the British*, Constable and Robinson, London.

Oswald, A., Dyer, C. and Barber, M. (2001) *The Creation of Monuments. Neolithic Causewayed Enclosures in the British Isles*, English Heritage, Swindon.

Parry, S.J. (1994) 'The Raunds Area Project Survey' in eds M. Parker Pearson and R.T. Schadla-Hall, *Looking at the Land. Archaeological Landscapes in Eastern England. Recent Work and Future Directions*, Leicestershire Museums, Art Galleries and Records Service, Leicester, 36–42.

Parry, S.J. (2006) *The Raunds Area Survey. An Archaeological Study of the Landscape of Raunds, Northamptonshire 1985–94*, Oxbow Books, Oxford.

Peacock, D.P.S. (1968) 'A petrological study of certain Iron Age pottery from western England', *Proceedings of the Prehistoric Society, New Series* **34**, February 1969, 414–26.

Peal, C.A. (1967) 'Romano-British pewter plate and dishes', *Proceedings of the Cambridge Antiquarian Society* **60**, 19–37.

Peate, I. (1926) 'Early Bronze Age finds in the Dyfi basin', *Archaeologia Cambrensis* **81**, 350–62.

Peate, I. (1940) *The Welsh House: A Study in Folk Culture*, Hugh Evans and Sons Ltd: The Brython Press, Liverpool.

Perring, D. (1987) 'Domestic buildings in Romano-British towns' in eds J. Schofield and R. Leech, *Urban Archaeology in Britain*, Council for British Archaeology Research Report 61, York, 147–55.

Perring, D. (1989) 'Cellars and cults in Roman Britain', *The Archaeological Journal* **146**, 279–301.

Perring, D. (1991) *Roman London*, Seaby, London.

Perring, D. (1992) 'Spatial organization and social change in Roman towns' in eds J. Rich and A. Wallace-Hadrill, *City and Country in the Ancient World*, Routledge, London, 273–93.

Perring, D. (2002) *Town and Country in England: Frameworks for Archaeological Research*, Council for British Archaeology, London.

Perring, D. and Roskams, S., with Allen, P. (1991) *Early Development of Roman London west of the Walbrook*, The Archaeology of Roman London, Vol. 2, Council for British Archaeology Research Report 70, London.

Petts, D. (2003) 'Votive deposits and Christian practice in late Roman Britain' in ed. M. Carver, *The Cross Goes North: Processes of Conversion in Northern Europe AD 300–1300*, York Medieval Press, York, 109–18.

Phillips, C.W. ed. (1970) *The Fenland in Roman Times: Studies of a Major Area of Peasant Colonisation with a Gazetteer Covering all Known Sites and Finds*, The Royal Geographical Society, London.

Pierpoint, S. (1980) *Social Patterns in Yorkshire Prehistory 3500–750 BC*, British Archaeological Reports, Oxford.

Piggott, C.M. (1944) 'The Grim's Ditch complex in Cranborne Chase', *Antiquity* **18**, 65–71.

Piggott, S. (1954) *The Neolithic Cultures of the British Isles: A Study of the Stone-Using Agricultural Communities of Britain in the Second Millennium BC*, Cambridge University Press, Cambridge.

Piggott, S. (1958) 'Native economies and the Roman occupation of North Britain' in ed. I. A. Richmond, *Roman and Native in North Britain*, Nelson, Edinburgh, 1–27.

Pilgrim, T. (1987) *Predicting Archaeological Sites from Environmental Variables. A Mathematical Model for the Sierra Nevada Foothills, California*, British Archaeological Reports International Series 320, Oxford.

Pittock, M. (1999) *Celtic Identity and the British Image*, Manchester University Press, Manchester.

Pitts, L.F. (1979) *Roman Bronze Figurines of the Catuvellauni and Trinovantes*, British Archaeological Reports British Series 60, Oxford.

Polanyi, K. (1957) 'The Economy as Institutional Process' in eds K. Polanyi, C. M. Arensberg and H.W. Pearson, *Trade and Market in the Early Empires*, The Free Press, Glencoe, Illinois, 243–270.

Poole, E.G., Williams, B.J. and Hains, B.A. (1968) *Geology of the Country around Market Harborough*, Natural Environmental Research Council, Institute of Geological Sciences, Memoirs of the Geological Survey of Great Britain, HMSO, London.

Porter, R. (1988) *Gibbon, making history*, Phoenix, London.

Porter, R. (2000) *Enlightenment: Britain and the Creation of the Modern World*, Penguin, London.

Porter, R. (2001) *The Enlightenment*, Palgrave, Basingstoke.

Potter, T.W. (1981) 'The Roman occupation of the central Fenland', *Britannia* **12**, 79–133.

Poulton, R. and Scott, E. (1993) 'The hoarding, deposition and use of pewter in Roman Britain' in ed. E. Scott, *Theoretical Roman Archaeology: First Conference Proceedings*, Aldershot, Avebury, 115–32.

Powell, T.G.E. (1958) *The Celts*, Thames and Hudson, London.

Pryor, F. (1998) *Farmers in Prehistoric Britain*, Tempus, Stroud.

Pryor, F. (2001) *The Flag Fen Basin: Archaeology and Environment of a Fenland Landscape*, English Heritage, Swindon.

Purcell, N. (1991) 'The creation of provincial landscape: the Roman impact on Cisalpine Gaul' in eds T.Blagg and M.Millett, *The Early Roman Empire in the West*, Oxbow Books, Oxford, 7–29.

Purcell, N. (1996) 'Rome and the management of water: environment, culture and power' in eds G.Shipley and J.Salmon, *Human Landscapes in Classical Antiquity: Environment and Culture*, Routledge, London, 180–212.

Purseglove, J. (1988) *Taming the Flood: A History and Natural History of Rivers and Wetlands*, Oxford University Press, Oxford.

Pye, N. ed. (1972) *Leicester and its Region*, Leicester University Press for the local committee of the British Association, Leicester.

Rackham, O. (1976) *Trees and Woodland in the British Landscape*, J.M.Dent & Sons, London.

Radford, C.A.R. (1952) 'Prehistoric settlement on Dartmoor and the Cornish moors', *Proceedings of the Prehistoric Society* **18**, 55–84.

Ralston, I. (2006) *Celtic Fortifications*, Tempus, Stroud.

RCAHMW (Royal Commission on the Ancient and Historical Monuments of Wales) (1986) *An Inventory of the Ancient Monuments in Brecknock (Brycheiniog): The Prehistoric and Roman Monuments, Part ii: Hill-forts and Roman Remains*, HMSO, London.

RCHME (Royal Commission on the Historical Monuments of England) (1960) *A Matter of Time: An Archaeological Survey of the River Gravels of England*, HMSO, London.

RCHME (Royal Commission on the Historical Monuments of England) (1975) *County of Dorset, Volume 5. East Dorset*, HMSO, London.

Reece, R. (1980) 'Town and country: the end of Roman Britain', *World Archaeology* **12/1**, 77–92.

Reece, R. (1988) 'Interpreting Roman Hoards', *World Archaeology* **20**, 261–9.

Reece, R. (1999) *The Later Roman Empire: An Archaeology, AD 150–600*, Tempus, Stroud.

Renfrew, C. (1987) *Archaeology and Language*, Jonathan Cape, London.

Revell, L. (1999) 'Constructing Romanitas: Roman public architecture and the archaeology of practice' in eds P.Baker, C.Forcey, S.Jundi and R.Witcher, *TRAC 98: Proceedings of the Eight Theoretical Roman Archaeology Conference, Leicester 1998*, Oxbow Books, Oxford, 52–8.

Revell, L. (2000) 'The creation of multiple identities in Roman Italica' in eds G.Fincham, G.Harrison, R.Holland and L.Revell, *TRAC 99: Proceedings of the Ninth Theoretical Roman Archaeology Conference, Durham 1999*, Oxbow Books, Oxford, 1–7.

Richards, C. (1992) *Survey and Excavation of Barnhouse, Stenness, Orkney 1991*, University of Glasgow.

Richards, C.C. (1996) 'Henges and water: towards an elemental understanding of monumentality and landscape in late Neolithic Britain', *Journal of Material Culture* **1**, 313–36.

Richards, C. ed. (2005) *Dwelling Among the Monuments*, McDonald Institute for Archaeological Research, University of Cambridge.

Richards, J. (1990) *The Stonehenge Environs Project*, Historic Buildings and Monuments Commission, London.

Richmond, I. (1955) *Roman Britain*, Penguin, London.

Riley, H. and Wilson-North, R. (2001) *The Field Archaeology of Exmoor*, English Heritage, Swindon.

Rippon, S. (1997) *The Severn Estuary: Landscape Evolution and Wetland Reclamation*, Leicester University Press, London.

Rippon, S. (2000) *The Transformation of Coastal Wetlands: Exploitation and Management of Marshland Landscapes in North West Europe during the Roman and Medieval Periods*, The British Academy, Oxford University Press, Oxford.

Ritchie, A. (1976) *Neolithic Orkney in its European Context*, McDonald Institute for Archaeological Research, University of Cambridge.

Rivet, A.L.F. (1964) *Town and Country in Roman Britain*, Hutchinson, London.

Roberts, C. and Cox, M. (2004) 'The human population: health and disease' in ed. M.Todd, *A Companion to Roman Britain*, Blackwell, London, 242–72.

Robertson, A.S. (1988) 'Romano-British coin hoards: their numismatic, archaeological and historical significance' in eds J.Casey and R.Reece, *Coins and the Archaeologist*, Seaby, London, 13–38.

Robertson, A.S. (2000) *An Inventory of Romano-British Coin Hoards*, Royal Numismatic Society Special Publication 20, London.

Robinson, M. (2006) 'Macroscopic plant and invertebrate remains' in A.M.Cromarty, A.Barclay, G.Lambrick and M.Robinson, *The Archaeology of the Wallingford Bypass. Late Bronze Age Ritual and Habitation on a Thames Eyot at Whitecross Farm, Wallingford*, Thames Valley Landscapes Monograph 22, Oxford Archaeology, 110–41.

Rodwell, W. and T.Rowley eds (1975) *The 'Small Towns' of Roman Britain*, British Archaeological Reports 15, Oxford.

Romm, J.S. (1992) *The Edges of the Earth in Ancient Thought: Exploration and Fiction*, Princeton University Press, Princeton.

Roskams, S. (1999) 'The hinterlands of Roman York: present patterns and future strategies' in ed. H. Hurst, *The Coloniae of Roman Britain: New Studies and a Review, Journal of Roman Archaeology* Supplementary Series 36, Portsmouth, Rhode Island, 45–72.

Rowlands, M.J. (1980) 'Kinship, Alliance and Exchange in the European Bronze Age' in eds J. Barrett and R. Bradley, *Settlement and Society in the British Later Bronze Age Part i*, British Archaeological Reports British Series 83(i), Oxford, 15–55.

Rowsome, P. (1998) 'The development of the town plan of early Roman London' in ed. B. Watson, *Roman London: Recent Archaeological Work, Journal of Roman Archaeology* Supplementary Series, 24, Portsmouth, Rhode Island, 35–46.

Roymans, N. (1990) *Tribal Societies in Northern Gaul. An Anthropological Perspective*, Universiteit van Amsterdam Cingula 12.

Salisbury, E.J. and Jane, F.W. (1940) 'Charcoals from Maiden Castle and their significance in relation to the vegetation and climatic conditions in prehistoric times', *Journal of Ecology* **28**, 310–25.

Salway, P. (1970) 'The Roman Fenland' in ed. C.W. Phillips, *The Fenland in Roman Times: Studies of a Major Area of Peasant Colonisation with a Gazetteer Covering all Known Sites and Finds*, The Royal Geographical Society, London, 1–21.

Salway, P. (1993) *The Oxford Illustrated History of Roman Britain*, Oxford University Press, Oxford.

Salway, P. ed. (2002) *Short Oxford History of the British Isles: the Roman Era*, Oxford University Press, Oxford.

Sarris, A. and Jones, R.E. (2000) 'Geophysical and related techniques applied to archaeological survey in the Mediterranean: a review', *Journal of Mediterranean Archaeology* **13 (1)**, 3–75.

Savory, H.N. (1976) 'Welsh hillforts: A reappraisal of recent research' in ed. D.W. Harding, *Hillforts: Later Prehistoric Earthworks in Britain and Ireland*, Academic Press, London, 237–92.

Scaife, R.G. (1980) *Late-Devensian and Flandrian Palaeoecological Studies in the Isle of Wight*, unpublished PhD thesis, King's College, University of London.

Scaife, R.G. (1982) 'Late-Devensian and early Flandrian vegetational changes in southern England' in eds M.G. Bell and S. Limbrey, *Archaeological Aspects of Woodland Ecology*, British Archaeological Reports, International Series 146, Oxford, 57–74.

Scaife, R.G. (1984) *Gallibury Down, Isle of Wight: Pollen Analysis of a Bronze Age Downland Palaeosol*, Ancient Monuments Laboratory Report 4240.

Scaife, R.G. (1987a) 'A review of later quaternary plant microfossil and macrofossil research in southern England; with special reference to environmental archaeological evidence' in ed. H.C.M. Keeley, *Environmental Archaeology: a regional review, volume II*, Historic Buildings and Monuments Commission for England, Occasional Paper 1, London, 125–203.

Scaife, R.G. (1987b) 'The Late-Devensian and Flandrian vegetation of the Isle of Wight' in ed. K.E. Barber, *Wessex and the Isle of Wight: Field Guide*, Quaternary Research Association, Cambridge, 156–80.

Scaife, R.G. (1995) 'Boreal and sub-Boreal chalk landscape; pollen evidence' in R.M.J. Cleal, K.E. Walker and R. Montague, *Stonehenge in its Landscape: Twentieth-Century Excavations*, English Heritage Archaeological Report 10, London, 51–5.

Scaife, R.G. (2004) 'Avon valley floodplain sediments: the pre-Roman vegetational history, in R.M.J. Cleal, M.J. Allen and C. Newman, 'An archaeological and environmental study of the Neolithic and later prehistoric landscape of the Avon Valley and Durrington Walls environs', *Wiltshire Archaeological and Natural History Magazine* **97**, 228–34.

Scaife, R.G. (in prep.) *Pollen Analysis and the Vegetational History of Southern England*, English Heritage.

Scaife, R., Allen, M.J. and Dix, J.K. (2000) 'Palaeoenvironmental background' in M.J. Allen and J. Gardiner, *Changing Coast: A Survey of the Intertidal Archaeology of Langstone Harbour, Hampshire*, CBA Research Report 124, 32–4.

Schama, S. (1995) *Landscape and Memory*, Harper Collins, London.

Scheid, J. (2003) *An Introduction to Roman Religion*, Edinburgh University Press, Edinburgh.

Schofield, A.J. (1991) 'Artefact distributions as activity areas: examples from south-east Hampshire' in ed. A.J. Schofield, *Interpreting Artefact Scatters: Contributions to Ploughzone Archaeology*, Oxbow Books, Oxford, 117–28.

Schrüfer-Kolb, I.E. (1999) 'Environmental use and landscape – Roman iron production in the East Midlands in its context' in eds C. Fabech and J. Ringtved, *Settlement and Landscape*, Jutland Archaeological Society and Århus University Press, Højbjerg, 268–9.

Schrüfer-Kolb, I.E. (2004) *Roman iron production in Britain. Technological and socio-economic landscape development along the Jurassic Ridge*, British Archaeological Reports British Series 380, Oxford.

Scott-Fox, C. (2002) *Cyril Fox: Archaeologist Extraordinary*, Oxbow Books, Oxford.

Seebohm, F. (1883) *The English Village Community Examined in its Relations to the Manorial and Tribal Systems and to the Common or Open Field System of Husbandry*, Longmans, Green and Co, London.

Sharples, N. (1991) *Maiden Castle: Excavation and Field Survey 1985–6*, English Heritage, London.

Sheppard, J. (1966) 'Pre-enclosure field and settlement patterns in an English township', *Geografisker Annaler* **48**, 59–77.

Shotton, F.W. (1953) 'The Pleistocene deposits of the area between Coventry, Rugby and Leamington and their bearing upon the topographic development of the Midlands', *Transactions of the Royal Society* (Series B) **237**, 209–60.

Silvester, R.J. (1991) *The Fenland Project, Number 4: The Wissey Embayment and the Fen Causeway, Norfolk*, East Anglia Archaeology 52, Dereham.

Simmons, B.B. (1979) 'The Lincolnshire Car Dyke: navigation or drainage?', *Britannia* **10**, 183–96.

Skertchly, S.B.J. (1877) *The Geology of the Fenland*, HMSO, London.

Smith, G. (1996) 'Archaeology and environment of a Bronze Age cairn and prehistoric and Romano-British field system at Chysauster, Gulval, near Penzance, Cornwall', *Proceedings of the Prehistoric Society* **62**, 167–219.

Smith, R.W. (1984) 'The ecology of Neolithic farming systems as exemplified by the Avebury region of Wiltshire', *Proceedings of the Prehistoric Society* **50**, 99–120.

Spoerry, P. ed. (1992) *Geoprospection and the Archaeological Landscape*, Oxbow Monograph 18, Oxbow Books, Oxford.

Spurgeon, C.J. (1972) 'Enclosures of Iron Age type in the Upper Severn Basin' in eds F.Lynch and C.Burgess, *Prehistoric Man in Wales and the West, Essays in Honour of Lily F. Chitty*, Adams and Dart, Bath, 321–44.

Stocker, D. and Everson, P. (2003) 'The straight and narrow way: Fenland causeways and the conversion of the landscapes in the Witham valley, Lincolnshire' in ed. M.Carver, *The Cross Goes North: Processes of Conversion in Northern Europe AD 300–1300*, York Medieval Press, The University of York, 271–88.

Stoertz, C. (1997) *Ancient Landscapes of the Yorkshire Wolds*, Royal Commission on the Historical Monuments of England, Swindon.

Strabo trans. H.L.Jones (1923) *Geography*, Heinemann, London.

Summerson, J.N. (2000) *Inigo Jones*, Yale University Press, New Haven.

Sumption, K.J. and Flowerdew, J.R. (1985) 'The ecological effects of the decline in rabbits *Oryctolagus coniculus* L.due to mxyomatosis', *Mammal Review* **15**, 151–86.

Sykes, B. (2006) *Blood of the Isles*, Bantam, London.

Tabor, R. ed. (2002) *South Cadbury Environs Project: Interim Fieldwork Report, 1998, 2001*, University of Bristol.

Tansley, A.G. (1939) *The British Islands and their Vegetation*, Cambridge University Press, Cambridge.

Tansley, A.G. (1949) *Britain's Green Mantle: Past, Present and Future*, Allen and Unwin, London.

Taylor, A. (1985) 'Prehistoric, Roman, Saxon and medieval artefacts from the southern Fen edge, Cambridgeshire', *Proceedings of the Cambridge Antiquarian Society* **74**, 1–52.

Taylor, A., Hall, D. and Pryor, F. (1980) 'Field officers' reports, 1978–9', *Proceedings of the Cambridgeshire Archaeological Society* **69**, xi–xiii.

Taylor, C. (1975) 'Roman settlement in the Nene Valley: the impact of recent archaeology' in ed. P.Fowler, *Recent Work in Rural Archaeology*, Butler and Tanner, London, 107–19.

Taylor, C. (1983) *The Archaeology of Gardens*, Shire Archaeology, Aylesbury.

Taylor, C. (1988) 'General Introduction' in W.G.Hoskins, *The Making of the English Landscape*, revised edition, Hodder and Stoughton, London.

Taylor, J. (2000) 'Stonea in its Fenland context: moving beyond an imperial estate', *Journal of Roman Archaeology* **13**, 647–58.

Taylor, J. (2001) 'Rural society in Roman Britain' in eds S.James and M.Millett, *Britons and Romans: Advancing an Archaeological Agenda*, Council for British Archaeology Research Report 125, York, 46–59.

Temin, P. (2001) 'A market economy in the early Roman Empire', *Journal of Roman Studies* **91**, 169–81.

Thirsk, J. (1964) 'The common fields', *Past and Present* **29**, 3–25.

Thomas, A.S. (1960) 'Changes in vegetation since the advent of myxomatosis', *Journal of Ecology* **48**, 287–305.

Thomas, A.S. (1963) 'Further changes in vegetation since the advent of myxomatosis', *Journal of Ecology* **51**, 151–83.

Thomas, C. ed. (1966) *Rural Settlement in Roman Britain*, Council for British Archaeology, London.

Thomas, F.W.L. (1852) 'An account of some of the Celtic antiquities of Orkney, including the Stones of Stenness, tumuli, Picts houses etc. with plans', *Archaeologia* **34**, 88–136.

Thomas, J. (1991) *Rethinking the Neolithic*, Cambridge University Press, Cambridge.

Thomas, J. (1993) 'The Politics of Vision and the Archaeologies of Landscape' in ed. B.Bender, *Landscape: Politics and Perspectives*, Berg Publishers, Providence and Oxford, 19–48.

Thomas, K. D. (1982) 'Neolithic enclosures and woodland habitats on the South Downs in Sussex, England' in eds M.G. Bell and S. Limbrey, *Archaeological Aspects of Woodland Ecology*, British Archaeological Reports International Series 146, Oxford, 147–70.

Thomas, K. D. (1989) 'Vegetation of the British chalklands in the Flandrian period: a response to Bush', *Journal of Archaeological Science* **16**, 549–53.

Thompson, D.J. (1987) 'Imperial Estates' in ed. J. Wacher, *The Roman World*, Routledge, London, 555–67.

Thorley, A. (1971) 'Vegetational history of the Vale of Brooks', *Institute of British Geographers' Conference Proceedings* Part 5, 47–50.

Thorley, A. (1981) 'Pollen analytical evidence relating to the vegetational history of the Chalk', *Journal of Biogeography* **8**, 93–106.

Tilley, C. (1994) *A Phenomenology of Landscape, Places, Paths and Monuments*, Berg, Oxford.

Timberlake, T. and Driver, T. (2006) 'Excavations at Darren Camp and Darren Mine (opencuts), Banc-y-darren, Trefeurig, Ceredigion' in *Archaeology in Wales* **45**, 98–102.

Tingle, C. (1991) *The Vale of the White Horse Survey. A Study of a Changing Landscape in the Clay Lowlands of Southern Britain from Prehistory to the Present Day*, British Archaeological Report British Series 218, Oxford.

Tinsley, H. M. (1981) 'The Bronze Age' in eds I. G. Simmons and M. Tooley, *The Environment in British Prehistory*, G. Duckworth and Co. Ltd, London, 210–249.

Todd, M. (1970) 'The Small Towns of Roman Britain', *Britannia* **1**, 114–30.

Todd, M. ed. (2004a) *A Companion to Roman Britain*, Blackwell, London.

Todd, M. (2004b) 'The Rediscovery of Roman Britain' in ed. M. Todd, *A Companion to Roman Britain*, Blackwell Publishing, Oxford, 443–59.

Tomalin, D.J. and Scaife, R.G. (1979) 'A Neolithic flint assemblage and associated palynological sequence at Gatcombe, Isle of Wight', *Proceedings of the Hampshire Field Club and Archaeological Society* **36**, 25–33.

Tomlin, R.S.O. (1983) 'Non Coritani sed Corieltauvi', *Antiquaries Journal* **63**, 353–5.

Toms, H.S. (1925) 'Bronze Age, or earlier, lynchets', *Proceedings of the Dorset Natural History and Antiquarian Field Club* **46**, 89–100.

Toynbee, J.M.C. (1962) *Art in Roman Britain*, Phaidon Press, London.

Toynbee, J.M.C. (1964) *Art in Britain Under the Romans*, Clarendon Press, Oxford.

Turner, J. (1970) 'Post-Neolithic disturbance of British vegetation' in eds D. Walker and R.G. West, *Studies in the Vegetational History of the British Isles*, Cambridge University Press, Cambridge, 97–116.

Turner, J. (1981) 'The Iron Age' in eds I.G. Simmons and M. Tooley, *The Environment in British Prehistory*, G. Duckworth and Co. Ltd, London, 250–81.

Turner, R. (1999) *Capability Brown and the Eighteenth-Century British Landscape*, Phillimore, Chichester.

Tylecote, R.F. (1986) *The Prehistory of Metallurgy in the British Isles*, The Institute of Metals, London.

Upex, S.G. (2001) 'The Roman villa at Cotterstock, Northamptonshire', *Britannia* **32**, 57–91.

Van de Noort, R. and Ellis, S. (1995) *Wetland Heritage of Holderness: An Archaeological Survey*, Humber Wetlands Project, Hull.

Van de Noort, R. and Ellis, S. (1998) *Wetland Heritage of the Ancholme and Lower Trent Valleys: An Archaeological Survey*, Humber Wetlands Project, Hull.

Vanderhoeven, A. (1996) 'The earliest urbanisation in Northern Gaul: some implications of recent research in Tongres' in ed. N. Roymans, *From the Sword to the Plough: Three Studies on the Earliest Romanisation of Northern Gaul*, Amsterdam University Press, Amsterdam, 189–260.

Vanderhoeven, A. and Ervynck, A. (2007) 'Not in my backyard!? The industry of secondary animal products within the Roman *civitas* capital of Tongeren (Belgium)' in eds R. Hingley and S. Willis, *Roman Finds: Context and Theory*, Oxbow Books, Oxford.

Vanderhoeven, A., Martens, M. and Vynckier, G. (2001) 'Romanization and settlement in the central part of the *Civitas* Tungrorum' in eds S. Altekamp and A. Schäfer, *The Impact of Rome on Settlement in the Northwestern and Danube Provinces*, British Archaeological Report International Series 921, Oxford, 57–90.

Veblen, T. (1925) *The Theory of the Leisure Class*, Allen and Unwin, London.

Vera, F.W.M. (2000) *Grazing Ecology and Forest History*, CABI, Wallingford.

Verhulst, A. (1999) *The Rise of Cities in North-West Europe*, Cambridge University Press, Cambridge.

Vermeulen, F. (1995) 'The role of local centres in the Romanization of northern Belgica' in eds J. Metzler, M. Millett, N. Roymans and J. Slofstra, *Integration in the Early Roman West: The Role of Culture and Ideology*, Dossiers d'Archéologie du Musée National d'Historie et d'Art IV, Luxembourg, 183–98.

Wacher, J.S. (1974) *The Towns of Roman Britain*, Batsford, London.

Wacher, J.S. (1995; 2nd edn) *The Towns of Roman Britain*, Batsford, London.

Wait, G.A. (1985) *Ritual and Religion in Iron Age Britain*, British Archaeological Reports British Series 149, Oxford.

Waller, M. and Hamilton, S.D. (2000) 'Vegetation history of the English chalklands: a mid-Holocene pollen sequence from the Caburn, East Sussex', *Journal of Quaternary Science* **15**, 253–72.

Walters, B. (1992) *The Forest of Dean Iron Industry: 1st to 4th Centuries AD*, unpublished MPhil thesis, The Open University, Milton Keynes.

Waton, P.V. (1982) 'Man's impact on the chalklands: some new pollen evidence' in *Archaeological Aspects of Woodland Ecology*, eds M.G. Bell and S. Limbrey, British Archaeological Reports International Series, 146, Oxford, 75–91.

Waton, P.V. (1986) 'Palynological evidence for early and permanent woodland on the chalk of Central Hampshire' in eds G. de G. Sieveking and M.B. Hart, *The Scientific Study of Flint Artefacts*, Cambridge University Press, Cambridge, 169–74.

Watson, B. ed. (1998) *Roman London: Recent Archaeological Work, Journal of Roman Archaeology* Supplementary Series, 24, Portsmouth, Rhode Island.

Webster, G. and Hobley, B. (1964) 'Aerial reconnaissance over the Warwickshire Avon', *The Archaeological Journal* **121**, 1–22.

Webster, J. (2001) 'Creolizing the Roman provinces', *American Journal of Archaeology* **105**, 209–25.

Wedlake, W.J. (1958) *Excavations at Camerton, Somerset: A Record of Excavation Covering the Period from Neolithic to Saxon Times: 1926–56*, Camerton Excavation Club, Camerton.

Weiss, A.S. (1995) *Mirrors of Infinity: The French Formal Garden and 17th-Century Metaphysics*, Princeton Architectural Press, New York.

Wessex Archaeology (2000) *Tilly's Lane, Staines, Surrey. Interim Assessment Report. Excavations at Tilly's Lane East and West*, Wessex Archaeology Ltd, unpublished client report.

Wheeler, R.E.M. (1925) *Prehistoric and Roman Wales*, Clarendon Press, Oxford.

Wheeler, R.E.M. (1943) *Maiden Castle, Dorset*, Oxford University Press, Oxford.

Wheeler, R.E.M. and Wheeler, T.V. (1932) *Report on the Excavation of the Prehistoric, Roman, and Post-Roman Site in Lydney Park, Gloucestershire*, Oxford University Press for the Society of Antiquaries, Oxford.

Whelan, K. (1994) 'Settlement patterns in the west of Ireland in the pre-Famine period' in ed. T. Collins, *Decoding the Landscape*, University College, Galway, 60–78.

White, R. (in press) *The Wroxeter Hinterland Survey*, English Heritage.

White, R. and Barker, P. (1998) *Wroxeter: Life and Death of a Roman City*, Tempus, Stroud.

Whittle, A.W.R. (1978) 'Resources and population in the British Neolithic', *Antiquity* **52**, 34–42.

Whittle, A.W.R. (1996) *Europe in the Neolithic: The Creation of New Worlds*, Cambridge University Press, Cambridge.

Whittle, A., Atkinson, R., Chambers, R. and Thomas, N. (1992) 'Excavations in the Neolithic and Bronze Age complex at Dorchester-on-Thames, Oxfordshire, 1947–52 and 1981', *Proceedings of the Prehistoric Society* **58**, 143–201.

Whittle, A., Pollard, J. and Grigson, C. (1999) *The Harmony of Symbols; the Windmill Hill Causeway Enclosure*, Oxbow Books, Oxford.

Wightman, E.M. (1970) *Roman Trier and the Treveri*, Hart-Davis, London.

Wightman, E.M. (1985) *Gallia Belgica*, Batsford, London.

Wilkinson, T.J. and Murphy, P.L. (1995) *The Archaeology of the Essex Coast, Volume 1: The Hullbridge Survey*, East Anglian Archaeology **71**, Chelmsford.

Williams, H.M.R. (1998) 'The Ancient Monument in Romano-British Ritual Practices' in eds C. Forcey, J. Hawthorne and R. Witcher, *TRAC 97: Proceedings of the Seventh Annual Theoretical Roman Archaeology Conference*, Oxbow Books, Oxford, 71–86.

Williams, J.H. (2003) 'New light on Roman Kent', *Journal of Roman Archaeology* **16**, 219–36.

Williams, M. (2003) 'Growing metaphors. The agricultural cycle as metaphor in the later prehistoric period of Britain and North-Western Europe', *Journal of Social Archaeology* **3** (**2**), 223–55.

Williams, R. (1973) *The Country and the City*, Paladin, London.

Williamson, T. and Bellamy, L. (1983) *Ley Lines in Question*, World's Work, Tadworth.

Willis, S.H. (1990) 'Mould-decorated South Gaulish colour-coated cups from Fingringhoe Wick, Essex', *Journal of Roman Pottery Studies* **3**, 30–4.

Willis, S.H. (1997a) 'Settlement, materiality and landscape in the Iron Age of the East Midlands: evidence, interpretation and wider resonance' in eds A. Gwilt and C.C. Haselgrove, *Reconstructing Iron Age Societies*, Oxbow Monograph 71, Oxbow Books, Oxford, 205–15.

Willis, S.H. (1997b) 'Samian: beyond dating' in eds K. Meadows, C. Lemke and J. Heron, *TRAC 96: Proceedings of the Sixth Annual Theoretical Roman Archaeology Conference*, Oxbow Books, Oxford, 38–54.

Willis, S.H. (1999) 'Without and within: aspects of culture and community in the Iron Age of north-eastern England' in ed. B. Bevan, *Northern Exposure: Interpretative Devolution and the Iron Ages in Britain*, Leicester University Press, Leicester, 81–110.

Willis, S.H. (2004) 'Samian pottery, a resource for the study of Roman Britain and beyond: the results of the English Heritage funded Samian Project. An e-monograph', *Internet Archaeology* **17** (http://intarch.ac.uk/journal/issue17/).

Willis, S.H. (2007) 'Sea, coast, estuary, land, and culture in Iron Age Britain', in eds C. Haselgrove and T. Moore, *The Later Iron Age in Britain and Beyond*, Oxbow Books, Oxford, 107–29.

Willis, S.H. and Hingley, R. (2007) 'Roman finds: context and theory' in eds R. Hingley and S. Willis, *Roman Finds: Context and Theory*, Oxbow Books, Oxford.

Wilmott, A.R. and Rahtz, S.P.Q. (1985) 'An Iron Age and Roman settlement outside Kenchester (*Magnis*), Herefordshire: excavations 1977–79', *Transactions of the Woolhope Naturalists' Field Club* **45/1**, 36–185.

Wilson, P.R. (2002) *Cataractonium: Roman Catterick and its Hinterland. Excavations and Research 1958–1997*, Council for British Archaeology Research Reports 128 and 129, with English Heritage, York.

Witcher, R. (1998) 'Roman roads: phenomenological perspectives on roads in the landscape' in eds C. Forcey, J. Hawthorne and J. Witcher, *TRAC 97: Proceedings of the Seventh Annual Theoretical Roman Archaeological Conference, Nottingham, 1997*, Oxbow Books, Oxford, 60–70.

Witcher, R. (2005) 'The extended metropolis: *Urbs, suburbium* and population', *Journal of Roman Archaeology* **18**, 120–38.

Wood, D. (2002) *Medieval Economic Thought*, Cambridge University Press, Cambridge.

Wood, R.F. and Nimmo, N. (1962) *Chalk Downland Afforestation*, Forestry Commission Bulletin 34, HSMO, London.

Woodward, P.J. (1991) *The South Dorset Ridgeway. Survey and Excavations 1977–84*, Dorset Natural History and Archaeological Society Monograph Series 8, Bridport.

Woodward, P. and Woodward, A. (2004) 'Dedicating the town: urban foundation deposits in Roman Britain', World Archaeology **36**, 68–86.

Wooldridge, S.W. and Linton, D.H. (1933) 'The Loam-Terrains of Southeast England and their relation to its early history', *Antiquity* **7.27**, 297–310.

Woolf, G. (1993a) 'The social significance of trade in late Iron Age Europe' in eds C. Scarre and E. Healy, *Trade and Exchange in Prehistoric Europe*, Oxbow Monograph 33, Oxbow Books /The Prehistoric Society and the Société Préhistorique Francaise, 211–18.

Woolf, G. (1993b) 'Rethinking the oppida', *Oxford Journal of Archaeology* **12**, 223–34.

Woolf, G. (1997) 'Urbanization' in ed. S. Alcock, *The Early Roman Empire in the East*, Oxbow Monograph 95, Oxbow Books, Oxford.

Woolf, G. (1998) *Becoming Roman: The Origins of Provincial Civilization in Gaul*, Cambridge University Press, Cambridge.

Woolf, G. (2000) 'Urbanization and its discontents in early Roman Gaul' in ed. E. Fentress, *Romanization and the City: Creations, Transformations and Failures, Journal of Roman Archaeology* Supplementary Series, 38, Portsmouth, Rhode Island, 115–31.

Yates, D.T. (forthcoming) *Land, Power and Prestige. Bronze Age Field Systems in Southern England*, Oxbow Books, Oxford.

Yegül, F. (2000) 'Memory, metaphor and meaning in the cities of Asia Minor' in ed. E. Fentress, *Romanization and the City: Creations, Transformations and Failures, Journal of Roman Archaeology* Supplementary Series, 38, Portsmouth, Rhode Island, 133–53.

York, J. (2002) 'The life cycle of Bronze Age metalwork from the Thames', *Oxford Journal of Archaeology* **21(1)**, 77–92.

Yorston, R.M., Gaffney, V.L. and Reynolds, P.J. (1990) 'Simulation of Artefact Movement due to cultivation', *Journal of Archaeological Science* **17**, 67–83.

Index

aerial photography 36, 38, 40, 59, 60, 83, 103, 154
agriculture *see* farming
Aitken, Martin 43
Alcock, Leslie 8
alluvium 21, 67, 71
Amiens, France 149, 155, 157, 158
Ancholme Valley, the 119, 125
Ancient Monuments Laboratory, English Heritage 46, 47
Anglesey 97
Anglo-Saxon period, the 10, 15, 45, 101, 102, 104, 105, 106, 109, 139, 142
Anglo-Saxons, the 1, 3, 4, 7–8, 11, 14–15, 70, 102, 106, 132
  origin myth 104–5
animals 25, 27, 57, 61, 66, 68, 69, 110, 158
  management of 67, 77, 80, 81
anthropologists xvi
anthropology 5, 8, 112, 119
archaeologists xiii, xv, 2, 4, 14, 17, 18, 23, 33, 58, 101, 102, 105, 106, 107, 131, 144, 146, 161
  environmental archaeologists 16, 17
archaeology 1, 2, 4, 7, 9, 17, 59–60, 64, 71, 72, 80, 82, 83, 106, 107–8, 111, 113, 127, 141, 146, 148, 149, 150, 151, 159, 164
  commercial 21, 44–5, 46, 47, 59–60, 65, 67, 71, 150
  evidence 10, 14, 17, 43, 105, 110, 113, 115, 129, 132, 136, 140, 142, 145, 161
  methodology 4, 9, 14, 43, 74, 107–8, 145
  rescue 69, 106, 107–8
  theory of xvi, 126, 129, 145, 151
Ariconium 140, 141
Arlon, Belgium 149, 157
artefacts 2, 5, 17, 37, 39, 41, 44, 57, 67, 68, 71, 74, 86, 119, 120, 128
Ashcombe, E. Sussex 21, 29, **31**, **32**
Aspinall, Arnold 46
Avebury, Wilts. 22, 38

Babington, C. 113
Barleycroft, Cambs. 64
barrows 51, 121
  bank 35, 38, 40
  disc 50
  long 3, 6, 21, 23, 35, 36, 37, 40
  round 6, 28, 41
Bath, Somerset 150, 159
Bavay, France 150, 155
Beaker period, the 28, 29
beakers 3
Bedfordshire 71
Berkshire 44
Bodmin Moor, Cornwall 59
bone
  animal 102, 125, 129, 161
  human 37, 38, 41
brochs 52
Bronze Age, the 4, 6, 7, 8, 12, 14, 15, 20, 21, 22, 23, 28, 29, 32, 41, 42, 49, 57–69, 70, 71, 74, 77, 78, 79, 80, 81, 82, 83, 121, 125, 126, 127, 129
Brook, Kent 27
buildings 49, 54, 144, 146, 148, 153, 155–6, 159, 160, 161
Bullock's Haste, Cambs. 117
burial 66, 78, 81, 148, 154, 155, 163
burial mounds 3, 34, 37, 38, 40, 41
buried soils 19
burnt mounds 50, 51, 55, 60, 81
burnt remains 49, 50, 52
Burwell, Cambs. 117
Bwlch-y-ddwyallt 89

Cadbury Castle, Somerset 45
Caerleon, Wales 154
Caerwent, Wales 153
cairns 50, 52
Caistor St Edmund, Norfolk 158
Cambridgeshire 103
Canterbury, Kent 149, 153, **155**, 156, 158, 162
Cardiganshire 84
Car Dyke, the 126, 159
Carlisle, Cumbria 151, 154
Catterick, Yorks. 151, 154
causewayed camps 3, 27
'Celts', Celtic 3–4, 6–7, 8–9, 10, 11, 12, 13, 14, 15, 83, 105, 116
'Celtic fields' 59
cemeteries 42, 145, 148, 151, 152, 154, 161, 162

central places 14, 146, 154, 159, 163
ceremonial activity 143, 151
monuments xv, 3, 17, 19, 24, 25, 27, 33, 34–8, 39, 40, 41, 42, 43, 44, 45, 46, 49, 50, 53, 55, 71, 72, 80, 81, 84, 86, 88, 91, 98, 99, 103, 107, 116, 120, 121, 127, 146, 157, 159
destruction of 34
chalklands 16–32, 57, 59, 61, 67, 68, 69, 70, 74, 103, 107
development of 16–17, 18, 19
charcoal 18, 21, 22–3, 27, 134
Cheshire 96, 97
Chichester, W. Sussex 151
Childe, Gordon 1, 10, 18
Chysauster, Cornwall 3, 10, 59, 62
circles 107
stone
timber 41
Cirencester, Glos. 149, 155, 158
cist burials 52
Clark, Grahame 1, 102, 113
Clark, Tony 46, 47
classical texts 7, 104, 119, 124, 125, 130
climate 20, 72, 78, 81
climatic phases 17, 18, 19
Atlantic 19, 22
Boreal 22, 27
Pre-Boreal 22
Sub-Atlantic 19
Sub-Boreal 19, 23
coastal landscapes 11, 60, 61–2, 64, 66, 68, 69, 84, 95, 99, 112
coins 115, 125, 150
Colchester, Essex 148, 149, 151, 152, 153, 154, 156, 158, 162
Gosbecks 154, 152
Coldham, Cambs. 118
Collingwood, R.G. 101, 102, 104, 105, 108
colluvium 27, 28, 29, 71
Cologne, Germany 159
Colt Hoare, Richard 35, 102
continuity 2, 3–4, 5, 12, 13, 15, 105, 107, 109, 146, 153
Corieltauvi, the 157
Cornwall 3, 6, 14, 59, 62
Cottenham, Cambs. 129
Cranbourne Chase, Dorset 17, 21, 24, 25, 28, 102
craniology 4, 5–6
Crawford, O.G.S. 2, 59
cremations 41
cropmarks 54, 71, 103, 107
cultivation 22, 23, 28, 29, 32, 33, 42, 59, 69, 71, 79, 80, 81, 123, 131, 153
cultural landscapes 60, 69, 120, 121, 127, 157, 162
cultural processes 128, 145, 159
cultural succession 2, 13
cultural traditions 9, 97
Cunliffe, Barry 7, 14
cursuses 34–42, 107
alignment of 37, 38, 39, 40
Auchenlaich 35
Balneaves 38, **39**
Brampton 38, **39**
Claish 35
Cleaven Dyke 35, 36
disuse of 41–2
Dorchester on Thames, Oxon. 37, 38, **39**, 41, 42
Dorset Cursus, the 35, 36–7, 38, 39, 41, 42
Douglasmuir 35, 38
Etton 40
Eynesbury 37
Fornham All Saints 40
influence of 39–41
interpretation of 35
purposes of 38
relationship with topography 36, 38
Rudston complex, the 35–6, 38, 39, 41, 42
Stonehenge 37, 41, 42
Thornborough 41
Curwen, Cecil 18, 59

Danebury, Hants 14, 24
Daniel, Glyn 4, 8
Dartmoor, Devon 3, 10, 11, 59, 62, 68
Deeping St James, Lincs. 121
Defoe, Daniel 6
deposition 41, 68, 82, 114, 115, 116, 117, 118–19, 120, 121, 125, 128
as an expression of status 119, 128
contexts of 115, 119–23
Devon 3, 7, 8, 11, 12, 14, 59, 62
disorder 160–1
distribution maps 9–10
ditches 4, 35, 40, 41, 42, 52, 54, 57, 59, 60, 62, 64, 67, 151, 162
Dorchester, Dorset 21, 24, 25, 159
Dorset 22, 23, 27, 58, 62, 108, 157
Dover, Kent 156
drainage 68, 72, 79, 119, 120, 123, 125, 126
droveways 57, 59, 63, 67
Durobrivae 141
Durrington Walls, Wilts. 21, 27

Earith, Cambs. 129
earthworks 2, 35, 38, 39, 40, 41, 42, 49, 55, 59, 60, 64, 71, 107
degradation of 41, 51
linear 4, 40, 42, 59, 64, 67
survey of 103, 107, 108
East Anglia 60, 62–4, 109

economies, economics 57, 62, 64, 65–6, 69, 79, 110, 111–12, 113, 114, 115, 116, 119, 123–4, 125, 126, 127, 128, 129, 139, 140, 141, 142, 143, 146, 147, 148, 153, 154, 163
elites 14, 15, 60, 66, 97, 119, 124, 146, 147, 161
enclosure xv, 54, 61, 62, 68
enclosures 14, 35, 38, 39, 40, 41, 42, 54, 59, 61, 63, 67, 83, 86, 99, 107
England
  north 108
  south 2, 14, 16, 17, 20, 23, 57, 60, 64, 83, 102, 103, 107, 110
  south-east 14, 62, 64, 66
  south-west 3, 4, 11, 14, 62
English Channel 64, 66
  coast 60, 61–2, 66
entertainment *see* recreation
Essex 62, 157
  Marshes 119
estuaries 60, 61, 64, 84, 126, 133, 141, 158
ethnicity 5, 6, 7, 9, 10, 15
ethnography 9, 127
ethnology 1, 4, 5, 6, 13, 15
Europe 4, 6, 14, 17, 19, 57, 64–6, 77, 79, 83, 125, 143, 147, 150, 157, 159, 160
Evans, Estyn 9
excavation 3, 10, 29, 44, 51, 52, 55, 56, 59, 60, 64, 68, 69, 84, 86, 97, 101, 102, 103, 106, 107, 108, 109, 111, 115, 121, 129, 153, 154
exchange/contact networks 57, 61, 62, 64, 65–6, 94, 95, 99, 124
Exmoor, Devon and Somerset 59

farming xv, 6, 12, 15, 17, 28, 42, 61, 66, 67, 68, 69, 70, 71, 72, 74, 77–9, 80, 81, 82, 109, 124, 131, 132, 140, 141, 151, 153, 155
  arable 14, 71, 77, 78–9, 104, 131
  pastoral 14, 78–9, 104
farms 14, 33, 59, 60, 83, 103, 108, 124, 153, 163
fences 58, 60, 67
fen-edge, the 115, 117, 120–1, 128
Fengate, Cambs. 59
Fenland, the 60, 63–4, 66, 68, 69, 79, 103, 109, 113–30
  silt fens 120
Fenland Project, the 113
Fenland Research Committee, the 113
fields 3–4, 6, 7, 10, 16, 28, 33, 42, 110, 131
field systems xv, 10, 15, 42, 52, 53, 57–9, 61, 63, 64, 67, 69, 83
  aggregate 57, 58
  coaxial 10, 57–8, 59, 60, 62, 64, 65, 66, 67, 69
    alignment of 69
    chronology of 67
fieldwalking 68, 70, 71, 72, 82, 126
fieldwork xv, 5, 44, 45–56, 58, 70, 71, 73, 106, 145, 150
Fiskerton, Lincs. 120, 125
Flag Fen, Cambs. 64, 125
Fleure, H.J. 2, 5–6, 7, 11, 13
flint scatters *see* lithics
flooding 68
Forde, Daryll 2, 86
Forest of Dean 132–42
fortifications xv
Fowler, Peter 109
Fox, Sir Cyril 2, 4, 9, 10, 12, 15, 113
France 64, 65, 150, 162
Frogholt, Kent 19
funerary rituals 117
funerary sites *see* mortuary sites
Fyfield Down, Wilts. 2

Gallibury Down, Isle of Wight 21
Gatcombe Withy Beds, Isle of Wight 21, 22
Gaul 143, 147, 149, 153, 155, 159, 163
geographers xiii, 17, 18
geography 2
geology 74, 133
geophysics 43–56, 82
  advantages of 44, 45
Germany 14, 143, 147
Gibbon, Edward 104
Gloucester 141, 153
Gloucestershire 109, 132, 163
grassland 16, 18, 22, 25, 32, 58, 68, 71, 81, 104
Grey Pit, E. Sussex 21
ground-penetrating radar 55
Gwithian, Cornwall 10

Haddenham, Cambs. 117, 121
Hambledon Hill, Dorset 21
Hawkes, Jacquetta 1, 6, 11, 13, 83
hearths 52
hedges 57, 58, 60, 74
henges 41, 50
Herefordshire 96
Heslerton, North Yorks. 45
hillforts 2, 3, 8, 14, 45, 71, 72, 83–100, 146, 157
  approaches to 86, 88, 90, 92, 99
  architecture of 85, 86–8, 90–1, 92, 94, 95, 96, 97, 98, 99
  Caer Lletty Llwyd 88, 89, 95
  Castell Grogwynion 91–2, **93**, 95
  Castell Tregaron 95
  Cefncarnedd 95, 97
  chronology of 83–4, 86, 88, 99
  classification of 84–5, 86

construction of 84, 87, 88, 89, 95, 99
Cors Caron façade scheme 94, 95
development of 83–4, 86
distribution of 85
Gaer Fawr **93**, 94, 95
landscape setting of 84, 86, 87–8, 89, 92, 94, 95, 97
Pen Dinas, Aberystwyth 2, 86, 94, 95–6, 97
Pen Dinas, Elerch 88, 89, 90
Pen Dinas façade scheme 88, 94–5
Pen y Bannau 95
Penyffrwdllwyd 95
symbolism of 87, 91, 97–8, 99
Tan y Ffordd 94
Trecoll 95
visibility of 87, 89, 91–2, 97
hillwash 21, 29
historians xiii, xvi, xvii
historical geography 2
hoards 114, 115, 117, 118, 119, 120, 123, 125, 128, 129
as wealth storage 115, 116, 119, 128
of coins 115, 116, 119, 125
of vessels 117
Hockwold-cum-Wilton, Norfolk 116, 117, 120, 121, 123
Holderness 119, 125
Holocene, the 17
Holywell Coombe, Kent 27
Hoskins, W.G. xiii–xiv, xv, xvi, 1, 2–4, 5, 6, 7, 8, 10–13, 15, 16, 17, 33, 34, 43, 44, 56, 70, 82, 83, 101–6, 107, 108, 109, 110, 111, 112, 131, 134, 142, 143, 149
Humberside 132
hunter-gatherers xv, 17, 77

Industrial Revolution, the 132
industry, industrialisation xv, 123, 132, 139, 140, 141, 142, 150, 160–1
Ireland 9, 14, 62, 77
Iron Age, the xv, 3, 4, 6, 7, 8, 14, 20, 22, 29, 42, 45, 52, 59, 60, 70, 71, 72, 83–100, 102, 110, 120, 121, 124, 125, 126, 129, 139, 142, 146, 147, 149, 152, 153, 154, 157, 158, 159, 160, 162
iron ore deposits 132, 133, 134
iron production 131–42
chronology of 141
forging 139, 140
furnaces 136, 138, 140, 141, 142
ore benefication 138–9
slag 136, 139, 140, 142
smelting 133, 134, 136, 139, 140
smithing 139, 140
hearths 139
islands 61
Isleham Fen, Cambs. 118, 129
Isle of Ely, Cambs. 129
Italy 153
Itford Bottom, E. Sussex 21

James, T.C. 5
Jones, Glanville 8, 10, 15
Jurassic Ridge, the 132, 134, 142

Kent 27, 62, 64, 68
kilns 43

lamps 117
land boundaries xv, 4, 33, 42, 45, 57, 60, 62, 64, 68, 83, 110
land division 10, 42, 45, 52, 57, 59, 60, 61, 62, 66, 67
land management 10, 105
landscape historians 8, 13, 105, 107
land snails 18, 19, 21, 24, 27, 29
Leicester 141, 153, 158
Leicestershire 12, 70, 157
Lewes, E. Sussex 22
ley lines 42
liminality 120
Lincoln 141, 154, 156, 157, 161
Lincolnshire 103, 134, 157
lithics 52, 72, 74, 79, 82
Little Woodbury, Wilts. 3, 102
livestock *see* animals
Lode, Cambs. 122
London 143, 148, 149, 150, 152, 154, 155, 156, 157, 158
longhouses 64
lowlands 8, 38, 39, 59, 60, 61, 64, 67, 68, 69, 70, 74, 88, 89, 91, 97, 104, 111
lynchets 59, 68

magnetic survey 47–55
Maiden Castle, Dorset 3, 18, 24, 40
Malling, Sussex 8
Malvern Hills 96
manors 105
manuring 68, 72
March Island, Cambs. 118
markets xv, 141, 154, 160
Marlborough Downs 59
material culture 15, 17
Medbourne, Leics. 74, 78, 79
medieval period, the 8, 12, 22, 52, 53, 70, 71, 83, 103, 106, 107, 134, 139, 142, 145, 152
Mediterranean, the 44, 124, 149
megalithic tombs 3, 14, 35
Merionethshire 97
Mesolithic, the 6, 17, 20, 21, 22, 23, 24, 25, 74, 77, 78, 80, 81

metalwork 57, 60, 61, 62, 63, 66, 68, 115, 116, 118, 120, 123
bronze 116, 121, 125, 129
copper alloy 118
gold/silver 116, 119, 121, 123, 125
iron 117
pewter 116, 117, 118, 119, 123, 129
metalworking 132
Metz, France 159
middens 49, 51, 52, 68, 161
Middle Ages, the *see* medieval period, the
Midlands, the 11, 12, 64, 70–82, 131–42
Mildenhall, Suffolk 118, 129
Mildenhall Treasure, the 116
mining 132, 134, 135, 141, 142
modern period, the 6, 17, 29, 54, 72, 86, 87, 106, 113, 115, 118, 121, 124, 125, 128, 129, 132, 139, 142, 145, 146, 147, 150, 152, 158, 162, 163
monasteries 123
Montgomeryshire 95
moorland 62, 70
mortuary sites 38, 39, 50, 154, 162
movement 83, 89, 91, 96, 121, 156, 163
Mucking, Essex 61
multiple estates 8, 10, 14, 15
Myers, J. N. L. 101, 105
myxomatosis 19

National Monuments Record Scotland 50
Neolithic, the 5, 6, 11, 12, 13, 14, 15, 17, 18, 20, 21, 22, 23, 25, 27, 34, 35, 39, 41, 42, 51, 52, 67, 68, 71, 74, 77, 78, 79, 80, 81, 82, 124, 126
Netherlands, The 150
Nijmegen, The Netherlands 154
Norfolk 120, 125
Normandy 62, 64
Northamptonshire 71, 134, 142
North Ceredigion 84–100
North Sea coast 62

Oakham, Rutland 74, 78
occupation 55, 56, 81, 82, 112, 113, 127, 152, 154, 155, 162
open fields 4, 7, 10
Oppenheimer, Stephen 14
oppida 112, 149, 154, 157, 160, 162
Ordnance Survey xiii, 50, 73, 104
Orkney 43–56, 72
Barnhouse settlement 46, 52
Barnhouse Stone 46, 53, **54**
Big Howe 52, **53**
Comet Stone 50
Loch of Harray 49, 52, 54
Loch of Stenness 50, 51
Maes Howe 46, 48, 52, 54, **55**
Ness of Brodgar 51
Ring of Brodgar 46, 50–1, 52, 55
Skara Brae 46
Stones of Stenness 46, 47, 51, 52, 53, 55
Wasbister 49, 55
Watch Stone 46
Oudenburg, Belgium 154
Oxfordshire 102, 132, 133

palaeoecologists 19
palaeoenvironmentalists xv
palaeogeographers 16, 23
pasture *see* grassland
peat 17, 18, 19, 24, 27, 120
Peate, Iorwerth 2, 9
pedology *see* soils
Penwith, Cornwall 10
phenomonology 112, 126, 128, 151, 155
Phillips, C.W. 113
Piggott, Stuart 8, 13, 14, 18
pit alignments 64, 107, 134
pits 50, 67, 102, 117, 125
Pitt-Rivers, General 58
place-names 3, 13
plant species 32, 110
alder 20
ash 20
beech 20
birch 20, 22
elm 20
hazel 20, 22, 24, 27
juniper 20, 22, 27
lime 20
oak 20, 22, 27
pine 20, 22, 23, 24, 27
ploughing 22, 42, 51, 52, 53, 54, 59, 68, 71, 72, 74
Plymouth, Devon 62
pollen analysis xv, 3, 7, 17–18, 19, 20, 21, 22, 24, 27, 29, 107, 110
preservation of 17
Poole, Dorset 62
population 102, 104, 105, 109, 110, 147, 150, 153, 163
post-glacial, the 17, 19, 20, 22, 23, 28
post-holes 60, 82
post-medieval period, the 71, 123–4, 128, 130
post-Roman dislocation 102, 104–5
pottery 29, 62, 66, 68, 82, 86, 95, 97, 102, 111, 115, 117, 118, 129, 140, 141, 162, 163
Powell, Terence 6
PPG16 71, 108, 150
prehistorians xv, xvi, xvii, 1, 2, 7, 10, 11, 12, 13, 14, 15, 18, 33, 72

prehistory, 1, 3, 4, 5, 6, 9, 10, 13, 28, 29, 32, 33, 34, 38, 41, 42, 58, 59, 62, 70, 71, 72, 79, 80, 81, 82, 83, 86, 89, 99, 102, 103, 106, 107, 108, 109, 112, 113, 116, 118, 120, 125, 127, 134, 136, 146, 157, 159
  cacial narratives of 4–6, 10–12
  study of xv–xvii, 1–2, 3, 4–7

Rackham, Oliver 107
Radford, Ralegh 3
radiocarbon dating 2, 107
Raunds Area Survey, the 73, 74, 78, 79
reaves 10, 59, 62
religion xv, 116, 120, 121–2, 123, 125, 126, 128, 129, 143, 146, 147, 152, 154, 160, 163
  religious material 114, 115, 117, 121
resistance survey 46, 55
Reynolds, Fiona xiv
Rheims, France 148, 149, 161
Richborough, Kent 156
ring-ditches 78
ringworks 60–1, 62, 63–4
Rio, Elizabeth Zadora xiv
ritual activity 68–9, 78, 81, 112, 116, 117, 118, 121, 124, 126, 128
river gravels 60, 68, 74, 107
rivers *see* watercourses
roads 33, 42, 45, 47, 61, 89, 99, 112, 156 *and see* Roman roads
Romanisation 11, 145
Roman period, the xv, 1, 5, 8, 17, 20, 22, 59, 60, 70, 83, 84, 99, 101–12, 113–30, 131–42, 143–64
  administrative organisation 101, 108, 109, 132, 141, 148, 163
  canabae 147, 153, 154, 161, 162
  canals 102, 109
  centuriation 149
  churches 155, 163
  circuses 150, 152, 154, 155
  civitates 108, 143, 148, 150, 152, 155, 159, 160, 163
  estates 105, 110, 124, 125, 140
  forts 110, 111, 112, 139, 147, 153, 154, 157, 161, 162
  impact on landscape 101–2, 104, 105, 131, 146, 149, 150
  military organisation 101, 108, 109, 110, 139, 141, 149, 153, 154, 159
  roads 102, 109, 111, 132, 141, 146, 149, 151, 153, 154, 159, 162–3
  roadside settlements 147, 151, 162–3
  rural landscape 101, 104, 106, 108, 110, 111, 112, 127, 132, 140, 143, 144, 145, 147, 149, 150, 153, 159, 163
  'small towns' 108, 109, 110, 111, 112, 140, 141, 145, 147, 151, 156, 162
  study of xv–xvii, 1, 101
  suburbs 140, 144, 145, 151, 152, 153, 154, 155, 161, 162, 163
  theatres 147, 151, 154, 155
  towns 101, 104, 108, 110, 111, 112, 141, 143–64
    boundaries of 151, 154
    construction of 149, 159, 160
    cores of 145, 146, 150, 151, 152, 153, 154, 163
    decline of 148, 161
    definitions of 146
    development of 147–8
    elements of 143, 144–5, 146, 150–1, 152, 153, 154, 162
    legal status of 146, 151, 153, 161
    plans of 144–5, 155, 160
    roles of 147, 151, 154, 159
  villas 101, 102, 105, 110, 111, 112, 125, 130, 136, 138, 140, 141, 147, 153, 161
roundhouses 3, 60, 102, 108, 163
routeways *see* roads
Royal Commission on the Historical Monuments of England 107, 108, 112
recreation 143, 147, 151

sacred landscapes 114, 123, 127
Salisbury Plain, Wilts. 27, 28
  Training Area 59
salt production 97, 113, 127
Scandinavia 14
Scotland 8, 35, 38, 108
Sedgeford, Norfolk 125
Seebohm, F. 105
settlement xv, 3, 4, 5, 7, 8, 10, 11, 12, 14, 15, 33, 37, 39, 42, 46, 49, 52, 54, 55, 56, 60, 61, 62, 66, 67, 69, 70, 71, 72, 77, 79, 81, 83, 84, 89, 91, 99, 101, 102, 103–4, 105, 106, 108–9, 110, 111, 112, 113, 131, 132, 140, 146, 149, 150, 151, 152, 153, 154, 155, 157, 162, 163
Shapwick Project, the 44
shrines 116, 117, 121–3, 128, 154, 157, 158, 159
Shropshire 96
Silchester, Hants 149, 150, 155
Sites and Monuments Records 73, 74
Society for Landscape Studies xiii
social relations 143–4, 145, 149, 150, 152, 160, 163
socio-economic/socio-political structures 14, 60, 61, 62, 63, 64, 65–6, 67, 97, 99, 132, 140, 145, 146, 147, 148, 149, 151, 152, 160
soilmarks 60
soils xv, 17, 23, 28, 47, 61, 64, 66, 67–8, 70–1, 72, 74, 78–80, 81, 82, 106, 131, 134
  erosion of 28–9, 32, 68
  improvement of 67–8
Soissons, France 147, 149
Somerset 109

South Cadbury Environs Project, the 45
South Dorset Ridgeway 59
South Hornchurch, Essex 58, 67
Southwark, London 152, 154, 155
standing stones 36, 46
statuettes 116, 117, 121, 129
Steeple Barton, Oxon. 12
St Germain-source-Seine, France 159
Stonea, Cambs. 117, 120, 121, 125
Stonehenge, Wilts. 3, 21, 24, 25, 38, 41, 44–5, 46, 47
stonework 117
  querns 117–18
Strawberry Hill, Wilts. 21, 27, 29, **30**
Stukeley, William 35
Stuntney Island, Cambs. 117, 129
Suffolk 116
Sussex 18, 23, 27, 28, 58, 59, 61, 68, 99
Sutton, Cambs. 129
Swift valley, Leics. 74, 78

Taylor, Christopher xiv, 107, 109
temples 116, 121, 122, 130, 147, 150, 152, 154, 155, 157, 158, 159, *and see* shrines
Tendring, Essex 62
territories 8, 14, 35, 80, 81, 99
Thames valley 60–1, 64, 66, 69
The Making of the English Landscape xiii, xv, 1, 3, 4, 6, 10, 12, 13, 14, 15, 16, 34, 101, 106, 131
Thickthorn Down, Dorset 21
Thiessen polygons 14
Thomas, Charles 106, 108, 112
Three Age system, the 4, 5, 13
Toadeshole, E. Sussex 21
Tongeron, Belgium 148, 149, 154, 155, 159, 161
topography 23, 33, 38, 39, 41, 57, 74, 80, 85, 86, 87, 88, 91, 92, 95, 97, 99, 157
trackways 83, 89
trade 95, 96, 97, 132, 141, 160
Trier, Germany 150, 155

UNESCO 46
uplands 3, 23, 59, 60, 64, 66, 68, 69, 70, 88, 89, 91
Upper Palaeolithic, the 22
urbanisation xv, 71, 111, 132, 145, 146, 150

Vale of York, the 119
valleys 19, 22, 24, 27, 29, 35, 38, 39, 62, 66, 74, 79, 84, 92, 97, 103, 156, 157
vegetation 16, 17–18, 23, 25, 32, 41
  history of 17, 21
vernacular architecture 9
Verulamium 148, 149, 157
villages *see* settlement

Wales 5, 6, 8, 9, 13, 14, 83–100
  borderlands 83, 94, 95, 97, 98
walls 44, 50, 57, 60, 87, 95, 144, 145, 146, 150, 151, 152, 153, 159
Wash, the 64, 120, 141
water 38, 80, 81, 115, 119, 120, 121, 125, 126, 127, 128, 154, 157, 158, 159
  cultural significance of 38, 125–6, 157, 158, 159
  management of 159
watercourses 14, 36, 38, 39, 40, 54, 60, 63, 64, 69, 80, 96, 112, 118, 120, 141, 156, 157, 158
  Arun 61
  Avon 74
  Blackwater 62
  Cam 63, 118
  Chelmer 62
  Colne 60, 62, 152, 154, 158
  crossings of 157, 158, 159
  Exe 62
  extinct courses of 118, 119
  Frome 62
  Granta 63
  Great Ouse 63
  Humber 133
  Lark 63
  Lea 60
  Little Ouse 63, 116
  Lower Kennet 60
  Meuse 157
  Nene 63, 74, 109, 117, 118
  Old Croft River 118
  Otter 62
  Ouse 22, 74, 117, 119
  Rhee 63
  Semois 157
  Severn 95, 96, 97, 99, 126, 141
  Soar 74
  Somme 157
  Stour 62, 63
  Swift 74
  Tas 158
  Test 62
  Thames 60–1, 158
  Tiber 125–6
  Trent 74
  Usk 96
  Walbrook 157
  Wandle 60
  Welland 63, 74, 118
  Witham 123, 157
  Wye 96, 141
  Ystwyth 91

watersources 54, 67, 68, 80, 125, 154, 157, 162
Weald, the 132, 134
Welland Bank, Lincs. 64,
Wessex 4, 14, 18, 27, 35, 69, 72, 83, 98
Wessex culture, the 3
wetlands 17, 19, 20, 21, 22, 63, 67, 110, 113–14, 119, 125, 126, 128, 158
Wheeler, Mortimer 7, 102
Whittlesey, Cambs. 117, 119
Wigston Magna, Leics. 1, 12
Wilburton, Cambs. 129
Willingham Fen, Cambs. 117, 121, 129
Wiltshire 22, 27, 28, 108, 109
Wimborne St Giles, Dorset 24
Windmill Hill, Wilts. 3
Wingham, Kent 19
Winnal Moor, Hants 22
Wisbech, Cambs. 129
Woodhenge, Wilts. 22
woodland 16, 17, 18, 19, 20, 22, 23, 24, 25, 27, 70, 71, 72, 110, 134, 142
  clearance of 4, 11, 16, 19, 23, 27, 28, 32, 33, 70, 80, 102, 106–7, 109, 110, 131
  including pine 17, 22, 23, 28
  management of 110, 136
  mixed oak 16, 20, 22
  nature of 17, 18, 19, 23, 24, 25, 27, 28, 32
  regeneration 19, 20, 22
Worcester 141
World Heritage Sites 43, 44–5, 46, 47, **48**, 52, 55, 56
Worlington, Suffolk 117
Wroxeter 145, 154, 155

Xanten, Germany 154

York 125, 145, 154, 158
Yorkshire 151
  Wolds 4, 20, 25, 35